Forensic Nursing
a concise manual

Forensic Nursing
a concise manual

Donna M. Garbacz Bader
Sue Gabriel

With contributions by

Theresa G. Di Maio
Vincent J. M. Di Maio
Erin H. Kimmerle
Stacey A. Mitchell
Gary Plank
Matthias I. Okoye

CRC Press
Taylor & Francis Group
Boca Raton   London   New York

CRC Press is an imprint of the
Taylor & Francis Group, an **informa** business

BP45

CRC Press
Taylor & Francis Group
6000 Broken Sound Parkway NW, Suite 300
Boca Raton, FL 33487-2742

© 2010 by Taylor & Francis Group, LLC
CRC Press is an imprint of Taylor & Francis Group, an Informa business

No claim to original U.S. Government works
Printed in the United States of America on acid-free paper
10 9 8 7 6 5 4 3 2 1

International Standard Book Number-13: 978-1-4200-6730-9 (Softcover)

Library of Congress Cataloging-in-Publication Data

Garbacz Bader, Donna M.
    Forensic nursing : a concise manual / Donna M. Garbacz Bader, Sue Gabriel.
        p. ; cm.
    "A CRC title."
    Includes bibliographical references and index.
    ISBN-13: 978-1-4200-6730-9 (alk. paper)
    ISBN-10: 1-4200-6730-3 (alk. paper)
    1. Forensic nursing--Handbooks, manuals, etc. I. Gabriel, Sue, 1948- II. Title.
    [DNLM: 1. Forensic Nursing--methods--United States--Handbooks. 2.
Crime Victims--rehabilitation--United States--Handbooks. 3. Forensic
Medicine--methods--United States--Handbooks. 4. Mandatory Reporting--United
States--Handbooks. 5. Nurse-Patient Relations--United States--Handbooks. WY 49
G213f 2010]

    RA1155.G37 2010
    614'.1--dc22   2009009051

Visit the Taylor & Francis Web site at
http://www.taylorandfrancis.com

and the CRC Press Web site at
http://www.crcpress.com

2/17/10

Dedication

To Jan and Katarzyna Garbacz

To D. Michelle, who knows me best, and Lavern

To Stanley G. and Janina L.

Finally to Dr. M. I. O., Jan H., and Phylis H.
This is where the forensic nursing process began.

Donna Garbacz Bader

***

This book is dedicated to those who are near and dear
and who encouraged and supported this endeavor:

My children and their families: Jonathan, Jennifer, Owen,
the Boston Bean, Benjamin, Mitchell, Nathan and
Sing Wei, Joel, Kathrine, Ella, Nicole, Steve, Matthea,
Michaela, Christopher, and Nicholas

My husband, Duane, who was ever so supportive and patient

My parents, Carol and Marvin

Brother Randy and family

Peers and dear friends Tonya and Kim, who unknowingly
ignited my interest in the field of forensic nursing many years ago

Friends, relatives, and colleagues

Sue Gabriel

Table of Contents

Foreword

Television has brought forensic science to the forefront, and we are now seeing an explosion in young people who want to work in this arena. The public is more informed, sometimes misinformed, about how the pieces of the puzzle fit together. Real life is more than what you see on television.

Scientists, law enforcement, and health care professionals are part of the team seeking to end violence in the world. Each has its own specific role in the investigation.

The specialty of forensic nursing is much needed in health care today. The forensic nurse plays an important role in injury identification, documentation, and prevention. When injured patients access health care, they are not immediately thinking about any legal outcomes. They just want to be treated. It is later, when there is a legal case, that the documentation of injuries becomes important. This is one way the impact of forensic nursing may be felt. The forensic nurse documents the injury, not only charting that there was one, but describing in detail the color, depth, degree, location, and size of the wound and also photographing and diagramming it. They are also key in documenting the history of the event. Does the mechanism match the history? What if it does not? Forensic nurses are able to address these questions.

Forensic nurses are practicing in hospitals and out in the community, making a difference in people's lives. They identify issues that will have a legal impact on society. They document injuries and pull communities together to address issues such as domestic violence, sexual assault, and child abuse. They work with grieving family members when death comes unexpectedly. They care for inmates and those in the psychiatric facilities who are unable to understand the consequences of their actions. Forensic nurses contribute to disaster planning and response. They are also entrepreneurs and consult on legal cases, assisting attorneys to understand the intricate medical terminology and how care is provided to the community. Anywhere there is an injury or potential for injury, there is a role for the forensic nurse.

Forensic Nursing: A Concise Manual will provide nurses and student nurses with the tools to better identify patients who are at risk for injury and how to plan their care appropriately. The forensic nursing process is utilized as a valuable organizational tool in assessing the physical and psychological data; identifying needs for the victim, the family, the community, and the perpetrator; planning and establishing goals and outcomes; implementing nursing interventions; and making evaluations. Identification of injuries, collection of evidence, documentation, and communication with members of the multidisciplinary investigation team are essential parts of all nursing practice.

An introduction to the fields of forensic nursing death investigation, clinical forensic nursing, forensic anthropology, forensic profiling, excited delirium syndrome, forensic gerontology, and legal issues in forensic nursing identifies the role of the forensic nurse as an invaluable member of a multidisciplinary investigation team. The forensic science principles included in this text may be integrated into nursing practice at any level. It is especially important for undergraduate nursing students to become familiar with concepts associated with forensic nursing. As members of the medical team, nurses many times are the initial contact for victims of violence as well as the perpetrators. They are on the front lines and the first ones to interact with this population. By understanding principles of wound identification, documentation, and injury and violence, the nurse will be able to better care for the individuals in the community. It is a very necessary part of nursing practice as forensic patients may be encountered in any health care setting. Therefore, it is imperative that the nurse know what to do and how to refer the patient to the most suitable specialist, whether it is a forensic nurse or other community agency.

Forensic nursing is not a fad. It is the missing piece in health care that allows us to provide holistic care not only to individual patients but also to entire communities. If you are able to incorporate one concept from this text into your practice, then you have already made a difference.

Stacey A. Mitchell, DNP, RN, SANE-A, D-ABMDI

Director, Forensic Nursing Program
Harris County Hospital District
Houston, Texas
Former Deputy Chief Forensic Nurse Investigator
Harris County Medical Examiner's Office
2008 President, International Association of Forensic Nurses

Preface

As nurses working in many areas of practice, it is inevitable that we come into contact with not only victims and families of violent crimes, injuries and fatalities, but also perpetrators, law enforcement, legal advocates, medical examiners, and many other community partners. Nurses have the unique ability to network with these partners in ways often overlooked by our profession and our partners. Nurses are at the forefront of evidence collection, preservation, and maintaining a chain of custody for law enforcement, testifying in a court of law, in injury cases and medicolegal cases. Administering care to victims of illness, accident, and injury is the commonly thought of and self-imposed role of nurses and the community. Imagine what kind of care could be given when assessment skills of the nurse are taken to a higher level. When a nurse becomes aware of what causes blunt force injuries, sharp force injuries, injuries related to child abuse, domestic violence, elder abuse and a host of others, she/he has taken their assessment skills to the next level, and is able to anticipate additional injuries. Lacerations are noted and documented with a new fervor; measurements taken, color noted, along with the location of the injury. The nurse begins to ask: "Does this injury fit the story?" Questions of why and how begin to emerge. What obvious evidence is there to collect and what potential evidence should be collected? Learning how to preserve the evidence, how to maintain proper chain of custody all take nursing assessment skills to a higher level. Have nurses ever considered how much valuable evidence is lost in hospitals that could be crucial to the legal system? Ask any law enforcement officer.

What alerts the nurse to strange markings on a pregnant woman admitted to deliver her baby? An area that is generally filled with the jubilance of birth can also contain victims of intimate partner violence. Returning a newborn and mother in a weakened condition to a violent situation can put an already fragile new mother and baby at an even greater risk.

Children who are seen in clinics as well as acute care settings with multiple bruises in uncommon areas and injuries or stories that do not necessarily match the injury are often victims of abuse. Most of these cases are missed by healthcare providers if they do not have some basic information available. This text was purposefully designed to be an introduction into the world of forensics; it can be both a useful, as well as an enlightening tool for nurses and others working in any area of the healthcare profession.

Sue Gabriel

We offer our heartfelt gratitude to the contributing authors: Vincent J. M. Di Maio, MD and Teresa Di Maio, BSN, RN; Matthias I. Okoye, MD, JD; Erin Kimmerle, PhD; and Gary Plank.

And we extend special thanks to Lisa V. for her gracious nature and all her help with the computer aspects of this project. Sincere appreciation also goes to Becky McEldowney Masterman, senior acquisitions editor; Jill J. Jurgensen, senior project coordinator; Marsha Hecht, project editor; and Shayna Murry, graphic designer, Taylor & Francis/CRC Press, for all your support and guidance and a kind and gentle manner.

Donna and Sue

About the Editors

Donna Garbacz Bader, M.A., M.S.N., R.N., D-ABMDI, is an associate professor at BryanLGH College of Health Sciences, School of Nursing, and codeveloper of one of the first senior forensic nursing electives in an undergraduate baccalaureate nursing program with a clinical hands-on component of 90 hours. At the February 2008 meeting of the American Academy of Forensic Science, Donna was a corecipient of the 2008 General Section Achievement Award for work in the field of forensic nursing education.

Donna has taught clinical and theory critical care, psychiatric, and other nursing courses at Bryan School of Nursing for more than 30 years. She continues to work as a staff nurse on an as needed basis. Donna is a guest lecturer at the University of Nebraska–Lincoln in the undergraduate forensic science program and has also lectured on forensic nursing and forensic science in the undergraduate program at the College of Saint Mary in Omaha, Nebraska and as adjunct faculty in the certificate forensic science program at Nebraska Wesleyan University in Lincoln. Donna was one of three who developed the first certificate program in forensic science in Nebraska in 1997 and in 1998 the first master's in forensic science program at Nebraska Wesleyan University. In 2005, Donna developed the curriculum for a master's in forensic science degree program with three specialty tracks, including forensic nursing, for Lagos State University College of Medicine in Lagos, Nigeria, and was appointed as a senior lecturer in the program in 2007.

Donna is a member of the International Association of Forensic Nurses, American Academy of Forensic Sciences, Disaster Mortuary Response Team Region VII, American College of Forensic Examiners, American Association of Critical Care Nursing, National League for Nurses, and the Nebraska Medical Reserve Corp. A diploma graduate of St. Elizabeth Hospital School of Nursing in Lincoln, Donna earned a bachelor of science in biology from Nebraska Wesleyan University, a bachelor of science in nursing from the University of Nebraska Medical Center College of Nursing, a master of arts degree in adult education from the University of Nebraska, and a master of science in nursing with a specialty track in critical care nursing and nursing education from Clarkson College in Omaha, Nebraska. Donna is also board certified in medical surgical nursing through the American Nurses Credentialing Center, is a certified forensic nurse and a diplomate of the

American Board of Medicolegal Death Investigators. She has written several articles on forensic nursing and forensic nursing education and is a reviewer for several critical care nursing texts.

Sue Gabriel M.S.N., M.F.S., Ed.D., R.N., SANE-A, C.F.N., is an associate professor at BryanLGH College of Health Sciences, School of Nursing, and codeveloper of one of the first senior forensic nursing electives with a 90-hour clinical component in an undergraduate program, receiving the General Section's Achievement Award from the American Academy of Forensic Sciences for this endeavor. She is a national and international speaker and workshop presenter on forensic nursing, child abuse, sexual assault, human trafficking, and intimate partner violence. Sue is guest lecturer at the University of Nebraska in the undergraduate forensic program, College of Saint Mary, and has lectured at Nebraska Wesleyan University in the master's programs in forensic science. Sue is a member of the International Association of Forensic Nurses, American Academy of Forensic Sciences, Disaster Mortuary Response Team Region VII, American College of Forensic Examiners International, and Commission on Forensic Education. She is on the editorial board for the *Journal of Forensic Nursing* and sits of the board of directors for forensic nursing with the American College of Forensic Examiners International. A graduate of the University of Nebraska Medical Center College of Nursing with a bachelor of science in nursing, and of Nebraska Wesleyan University with a master's degree in forensic science and a master's degree in nursing, Sue also has a doctorate in health care education from the College of Saint Mary's in Omaha, Nebraska. She is a certified sexual assault nurse examiner and member of a citywide SART team, certified forensic nurse reviewer of numerous nursing texts, contributor to the *Forensic Investigation and Management of Mass Disasters* text by Cyril Wecht and Matthias Okoye (*Lawyers and Judges*, 2007), in addition to being coauthor of this entry-level forensic nursing text.

Contributors

Theresa G. Di Maio, R.N., B.S.N.
Forensic nurse and author
San Antonio, Texas

Vincent J. M. Di Maio, M.D.
Forensic pathologist
San Antonio, Texas

Erin H. Kimmerle, Ph.D.
Department of Anthropology
University of South Florida
Tampa, Florida

Stacey A. Mitchell, R.N.
Forensic Nursing Program
Harris County Hospital District
Houston, Texas

Gary Plank, M.G.
Plank Forensic Services
Lincoln, Nebraska

Matthias I. Okoye, M.D., J.D.
Nebraska Institute of Forensic Sciences
Lincoln, Nebraska

Introduction

This text is intended to be an introduction into the specialty of forensic nursing. Nurses in all arenas of practice have or will come in contact with victims, families, and perpetrators of violent crime. Collaboration with various law enforcement agencies, those within the criminal justice system, medical examiners, coroners, and a variety of social service advocates enables working together, providing support, care, and justice for the victims and all those affected by violent crime and trauma. Nursing education provides the nurse with concepts and principles necessary to provide holistic nursing care and social support to members of the community. Nurses continue to be in the forefront when identifying, collecting, and preserving evidence and maintaining the chain of custody when providing care and treatment for those victims suffering from injuries identified as medicolegally significant. Combining the concepts and theories of nursing with those of forensic science identifies the forensic nurse as an expert with the knowledge and ability to utilize developed assessment skills to assist the victim, the family, and the perpetrator.

This text can also be a useful reference for other health care professionals, in addition to those in the criminal justice system, the law enforcement system, and the advocates, to gain a better understanding of the role of the forensic nurse as a member of the multidisciplinary investigative team.

Donna and Sue

Forensic Nursing

1

DONNA GARBACZ BADER

I. Forensic Nursing
  A. A specialty of nursing
    1. The application of nursing science to public or legal proceedings
    2. A registered nurse with additional education and training in medical-legal investigation
    3. Essential when addressing the health needs of the perpetrators and victims of violence, wrongful death, and associated medicolegal issues associated with the aftermath of these events
    4. Incorporates a specific body of knowledge, enhanced critical thinking skills, and professional forensic science skills to practice in diverse settings from acute care, to the courtroom, the community, and the medical examiner/coroner's office
    5. Combines the theory and concepts of forensic science with the biological, psychological, and social theories and concepts of nursing
    6. Is a career field in which the professional nurse can combine career training and education and work with those in the legal profession
    7. Applies specific approaches to the assessment and planning of care based on conditions defined within the criminal justice system
      a. What constitutes a crime?
      b. Intent versus no intent relating to the commission of a crime
      c. Effect of the crime on the victim, perpetrator, family, support system, and community members
      d. Mental illness as it relates to the victims of crime and the perpetrators of crime
      e. Types of rehabilitation services provided for victims
      f. Rehabilitation services for perpetrators

8. Ability to conduct a scientific investigation and provide treatment to perpetrators and victims of trauma that has resulted in severe injury or death
   a. Physical and psychological abuse
   b. Violence
   c. Criminal activity
   d. Accidents
9. Ability to identify, collect, and preserve evidence that may be used in a court of law
10. Ability to manage numerous details outside nursing and medical intervention

B. Background
   1. The theoretical framework for forensic nursing was developed by Virginia A. Lynch as a result of original research conducted at the University of Texas in Arlington in 1990.
   2. Basic concept of forensic nursing grew from the practice field of clinical forensic medicine and was developed
      a. To address the needs of a special population
         (1) Victims of crime
         (2) Perpetrators of crime
         (3) Victims and perpetrators of crime presenting with mental disorders
         (4) Victim and perpetrator families and support systems
      b. Because of awareness of the increase in violence and concepts associated with violence
      c. Due to increased demand for law enforcement and the judicial system to respond to the human outcome of violence: victimization, which involves
         (1) Fear of individual or community injury or death
         (2) Powerlessness of individual/groups/communities
         (3) Anger toward and distrust of agencies responsible for maintaining a safe environment
            (a) Legal
            (b) Judicial
            (c) Medical
            (d) Local, state, and national government
      d. To provide patient advocacy for victims of criminal violence, living and deceased
         (1) Assess and provide care for the victims
         (2) Detect neglect or abuse
         (3) Provide team approach regarding victims' immediate and long-term needs

    (4) Support victims' legal and human rights
    (5) Recognize the need for outside intervention
   e. To provide a forensic nursing framework
    (1) With a structure for understanding abnormal human responses in relation to the medical and legal systems and provide an awareness of suitable nursing responses
    (2) To account for the changing nature of society complementing cultural trends with universal care needs
    (3) To provide knowledge of the criminal justice and social system that may direct the forensic nurses' care of the clients
    (4) To identify and label content as forensic nursing specialty
    (5) To identify and incorporate forensic nursing concepts into basic nursing curriculum
 C. Relevance to nursing practice
  1. Nursing care and treatment have long been provided to forensic patients, both victims of violence and perpetrators of violence.
  2. The majority of forensic nursing care is delivered within primary health care settings.
  3. Forensic nurses function as a patient advocate.
  4. Primary care nurses are in a position to suspect or to identify victims and perpetrators of violence by assessing
   a. Physical injuries
   b. Verbal and nonverbal behaviors
  5. Documentation of patients' care and treatment, the patients' response to treatment, evaluation of patients' daily assessment data, and provision of patient education is a nursing responsibility.
  6. The nurse works with the patients' family, support systems, additional health care providers, social services, and law enforcement.
  7. A forensic nurse provides education to the patient, family, and support system at the time of the patient's admission, throughout the patient's stay, and at the time of discharge.
  8. Forensic nurses develop and provide education related to aspects of
   a. Health prevention
   b. Community safety measures
   c. Current health concerns

       d. Criminal violence
       e. Victimization
   9. Forensic nursing addresses the medical care and legal issues for victims of violence.
 10. Forensic nurses are part of a multidisciplinary investigative team.
 11. Forensic nursing expands the concept of holistic nursing.
- Body
- Mind
- Spirit

Forensic Nursing is:

- The application of nursing sciences to public and legal proceedings
- The application of a scientific investigation to the forensic aspects of health care
- The provision of treatment for trauma or death to victims and the perpetrators of abuse, violence, criminal offenses, traumatic accidents, and events of nature

---

II. Forensic Nursing Practice: A Diverse Role for the Registered Nurse
   A. Subspecialties in forensic nursing

• Forensic nursing sexual assault examiner	• Correctional nurse
• Forensic nurse educators/consultants	• Forensic gerontology nurse
• Nurse coroners	• Forensic psychiatric nurse
• Death investigators	• Clinical nurse specialist, such as
• Legal nurse consultants	Trauma nurse
• Nurse attorney	Critical care nurse
• Forensic pediatric nurse	Transplant nurse
	Emergency room nurse

   B. The forensic nurse practice deals with
      1. Interpersonal violence
         a. Domestic violence or sexual assault
         b. Child and elder abuse or neglect
         c. Physiological or psychological abuse
         d. Religion
         e. Human trafficking
      2. Patient care facilities
         a. Accidents or injury
         b. Neglect

      c. Unacceptable treatments and medication

      d. Management

  3. Death investigation

      a. Homicides or suicides

      b. Suspicious or accidental deaths

      c. Mass disasters

  4. Emergency or trauma services/department

      a. Automobile or pedestrian accidents

      b. Traumatic injuries

      c. Suicide attempts

      d. Disasters

      e. Work-related injuries

  5. Forensic mental health

  6. Correctional nursing

  7. Legal nurse consulting

  8. Public health and safety

      a. Environmental hazards

      b. Drug or alcohol abuse

      c. Food/drug tampering

      d. Illegal abortion practices

      e. Epidemiological issues

      f. Tissue or organ donation

III. Forensic Nursing Roles and Responsibilities

  A. The safety of the living victim and the deceased victim's body remains *the first priority.*

  B. Collecting and preserving evidence from the victim should *never compromise the safety or integrity of the body.*

  C. The forensic nurse performs a forensic examination.

    1. The purpose is to identify and collect evidence that has transferred from the perpetrator to the victim.

    2. Law enforcement personnel may collect evidence from the crime scene; however, forensic nurses and other health care providers collect evidence from the *victim.*

  D. Evidence must be collected in an organized and comprehensive manner.

    1. Without bias and without inducing any physical or psychological harm to the victim

    2. Without bias and without producing any physical injury or damage to the deceased victim

    3. Examination and evidence identification and collection require a careful search of the entire body.

      4. Meticulous documentation requires identification of all evidence, preservation method, and retention (chain of custody).
- E. The forensic nurse must develop interviewing techniques.
  1. To interview the victim
  2. To interview the suspected perpetrator
  3. To interview the convicted perpetrator
  4. To interview family, friends, and all those who may add to the investigation
- F. Evidence includes the following:
  1. All clothing
  2. All jewelry
  3. Any items in pockets
  4. Any items removed from the body
     - a. Dirt (physical evidence)
     - b. Saliva (biological evidence)
     - c. Paint chips (physical evidence)
     - d. Semen (biological evidence)
     - e. Insects (biological evidence)
     - f. Plant material (biological evidence)
     - g. Dried or fresh blood (biological evidence)
     - h. Fabric (physical material)
     - i. Additional physical and biological material
- G. Preservation of evidence is dependent on the type of material, whether physical or biological.

IV. Documentation
- A. Documentation should be objective, legible, clear, timely, and descriptive.
- B. *Documentation does not provide a diagnosis* (e.g., blunt force, sharp force, entry wound, exit wound, cause of death).
- C. State boards of nursing scope and standards of nursing practice outline and define nursing practice based on the individual nurse's status as an advanced practice practitioner; advanced practice status is defined in the individual state nurse practice act.

V. Forensic Nurses

- Work independently
- Are nonjudgmental
- Provide education to self and others
- Provide referrals
- Provide treatment based on medical protocol
- Maintain chain of custody
- Are active members of an investigative team
- Are victim advocates
- Are liaisons for law enforcement and facility staff
- Provide crisis interventions
- Facilitate the reporting of a death to the medical examiner/coroner

Continued

- Assess injuries
- Provide complete and accurate documentation
- Provide identification, collection, and preservation of evidence
- Provide expert witness testimony in court
- Implement community safety programs

VI. Additional Roles of the Forensic Nurse:
 A. May assist in the development of evidence-based policies and procedures related to evidence identification, collection, and preservation and photographic documentation
 B. Is able to develop and implement orientation and continuing education programs for the staff related to forensic nursing and forensic science techniques
 C. May also act as a consultant with risk management administration
 D. May review medical records as a consultant for the facility legal counsel
 E. In a school setting is able to identify children at risk for abuse or neglect
 F. In a law enforcement setting is able to provide direct evaluation and care for the victims of violence and at the same time is able to collect evidence and provide referrals
 G. In the home care setting is able to assess the living conditions for safety; assess the patient for evidence of exploitation, abuse, or neglect; provides referral for community service agency assistance
 H. Professional Nurse Education + Forensic Science Education + Forensic Nursing Education = A professional nurse trained to provide care and treatment to the victims, both the living and the dead, of violent crime or traumatic events

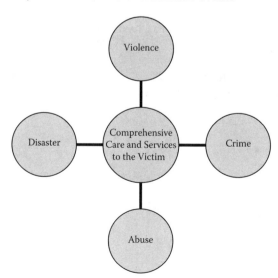

VII. Forensic Nursing Practice
  A. Scope and standards of forensic nursing practice
    1. The American Nurses Association (ANA) is the professional organization representing registered nurses throughout the United States.
    2. In 1995, forensic nursing was granted specialty status on approval of the *Scope and Standards of Forensic Nursing Practice* by the ANA's Congress of Nursing Practice.
    3. The *Scope and Standards of Forensic Nursing Practice* was published by the ANA in conjunction with the International Association of Forensic Nurses (IAFN) in 1997.
    4. The IAFN has completed new revisions to the current *Scope and Standards of Forensic Nursing Practice*; the ANA is in the process of reviewing this revised version at this writing.
    5. The IAFN has submitted to the ANA the newly developed *Scope and Standards of Practice for the Forensic Nurse Death Investigator*; the ANA is currently in the process of reviewing this document.
  B. Scope and standards of forensic nursing practice as defined by the IAFN

Scope of Practice	Standards of Practice

• Specialty of forensic nursing
• Core of practice
• Dimensions of practice
• Boundaries of practice
• Intersections with professional and governmental groups
	• Role of standards
	• Development of standards
	• Organizing principles of the standards of practice for forensic nurses
	  Standards of care
	  Standards of professional performance
	• Criteria
	• Assumptions
	• Purpose

  C. Standards for forensic nursing care practices as identified by the IAFN correlated with the nursing process

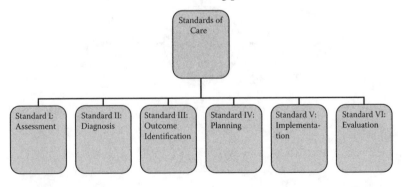

Bibliography

American Nurses Association. (2001). *Code of ethics for nurses with interpretive statements*. Silver Spring, MO: Nursesbooks.org.

American Nurses Association. (2004). *Nursing scope and standards of nursing practice*. Silver Spring, MO: Nursesbooks.org.

American Nurses Association, Congress for Nursing Practice. (1980). *Nursing: A social policy statement*. Kansas City, MO: American Nurses Association.

American Nurses Association & International Association of Forensic Nurses. (1997). *Scope and standards of forensic nursing practice*. Washington, DC: American Nurses.

Benak, L. D. (2001). Forensics and the critical role of the ER nurse. *On the Edge, 7*(3), 1, 20–22.

Boersma, R. R. (2008, May). Forensic nursing. *Nursing Management*, pp. 31–34.

Burgess, A. W. (2002). *Violence through a forensic lens* (2nd ed.). King of Prussia, PA: Nursing Spectrum, pp. 372–382.

Hammer, R. M., Moynihan, B., & Pagliaro, E. M. (Eds.). (2006). *Forensic nursing: A handbook for practice*. Sudbury, MA: Jones and Bartlett, pp. 8–11.

Lynch, V. (with Duval, J. B.) (2006). The specialty of forensic nursing. *Forensic nursing*. St. Louis, MO: Mosby, pp. 3–12.

Lynch, V. (2006). Concepts and theory of forensic nursing. *Forensic Nursing*. St. Louis, MO: Mosby, pp. 19–27.

North American Nursing Diagnosis Association International (NANDA-I). (2007–2008). *Nursing diagnosis: Definitions and classification*. Philadelphia: Author.

Smock, W. S. (2006). Genesis and development. *Forensic Nursing*. St. Louis, MO: Mosby, pp. 13–18.

Forensic Nursing Today

DONNA GARBACZ BADER

2

I. Practice Organization

  A. The American Academy of Forensic Sciences was the first professional organization to recognize forensic nursing as a scientific discipline and provided credibility to this new specialty in 1991. Established in 1948, it is the oldest and most prestigious professional organization for forensic science specialists worldwide.

  B. Virginia A. Lynch (1990), provided well-defined evidence of the need to utilize well-trained professional nurses in the scientific investigation, care, and treatment of victims of violent crime or trauma or who have died.

  C. The International Association of Forensic Nursing (IAFN) was established in 1992 to promote the education of forensic nurses and to implement the forensic nursing roles on an international scope.

   1. South Africa was the first country to identify forensic nursing as a national program priority.

   2. The IAFN currently has a membership of over 2,500 in 11 different countries and territories; membership continues to increase each year.

   3. Institutions of higher learning currently offer formal and informal curriculum in forensic nursing; these include institutions in the United States, Australia, Canada, England, Scotland, Turkey, Zimbabwe, North America, Italy, Sweden, and South Africa.

   4. IAFN developed the Forensic Nursing Code of Ethics and the Scope and Standards of Forensic Nursing Practice (1997).

  D. The IAFN, in conjunction with the American Nurses Association, published the *Scope and Standards of Forensic Nursing Practice* in 1997.

  E. The Joint Commission on the Accreditation of Healthcare Organizations (JCAHO) has set standards related to the medicolegal care, medicolegal research, and the investigation of death that can be met by the forensic nurse.

II. Forensic Nursing on a Local or International Level
   A. Federal Health and Human Services disaster response teams
      1. The Disaster Mortuary Operational Response Team (DMORT) is a team of experts activated in response to any large-scale disaster in the United States to assist in the search and identification of deceased individuals and the storage of bodies until the bodies are released as outlined in the state or local statutes.
      2. The National Disaster Medical System (NDMS) is a team of specialized medical personnel activated in response to any large-scale disaster in the United States. The primary focus is on public health and medical capabilities.
      3. DMORT and NDMS work under local jurisdictional authorities such as coroners or medical examiners, law enforcement, and emergency managers.
      4. International governments may request assistance with the investigation of mass graves.
      5. The team members may provide testimony before the International Court of Justice.
   B. At the request of a government, the forensic nurse may assist in the development of a forensic nursing program.
   C. The forensic nurse may also be actively involved in the educational process, providing both didactic and clinical assistance, on request of university or governmental officials.

III. Forensic Nursing Organizations
   A. International Association of Forensic Nurses (IAFN)
   B. American Association of Legal Nurse Consultants (AALNC)
   C. American Academy of Forensic Science (AAFS), includes the designation of Fellow of the American Academy of Forensic Sciences (FAAFS)
   D. American College of Forensic Examiners Institute (ACFEI)

IV. Forensic Nursing Certification and Credentialing
  A. International Association of Forensic Nurses (IAFN)
    1. The IAFN developed the first certification examination for the sexual assault nurse examiner (SANE) on requirements approved by the Council of Sexual Assault Nurse Examiners.
    2. The *Scope and Standards of Forensic Nursing Practice* defines forensic nursing and identifies components of forensic nursing practice.
    3. Additional forensic nursing specialty certification examinations will become available as they are developed.
  B. American Association of Legal Nurse Consultants (AALNC)
    1. Legal nurse consultant certification (LNCC) is available.
    2. Certification is provided by the AALNC Certification Board in compliance with the standards and requirements of the American Board of Nursing Specialties.
    3. The FAAFS is a credential achieved by forensic nurses dedicated to advancing forensic science in nursing practice.
  C. American College of Forensic Examiners Institute (ACFEI)
    1. ACFEI is a multidisciplinary, independent, scientific, and professional association representing forensic examiners worldwide.
    2. It serves as the national center for the purpose of disseminating forensic information and the advancement of forensic examinations and consultation across the various fields of membership specialties through
      a. An official journal
      b. Lectures
      c. Seminars
      d. Continuing education and home study courses
      e. Conferences and workshops
    3. Certifications

ACFEI Certification Examinations

- Certified forensic nurse (CFN)
- Certified forensic accountant (Cr. FA)
- Certified forensic consultant (CFC)
- Certified medical investigator (CMI)
- Certified in homeland security (CHS)
- Sensitive security information (SSI, Certified)

  D. American Board of Medicolegal Death Investigators (ABMDI)
    1. The ABMDI is a national independent professional certification board established to promote the highest standards of practice for medicolegal death investigators.

2. The ABMDI provides certification to those individuals who have proven knowledge and skills necessary to perform a medicolegal death investigation as established by the National Institutes of Justice.
3. Certification designation is that of Diplomate of the American Board of Medicolegal Death Investigators (D-ABMDI).

Bibliography

American Academy of Forensic Science. "About us." Retrieved Jan. 10, 2008 from http://www.aafs.org

American Association of Legal Nurse Consultants. Mission Statement. Retrieved Jan. 10, 2008 from http://www.aalnc.org

American Board of Medicolegal Death Investigations. "About us." Retrieved Jan. 10, 2008 from http://www.slu.edu/organizations/abmdi/

American College of Forensic Examiners. "Certification-Forensic Nursing." Retrieved Jan. 10, 2008 from http://www.acfei.com/index.php

American Nurses Association, Congress for Nursing Practice. (1980). *Nursing: A social policy statement.* Kansas City, MO: American Nurses Association.

American Nurses Association & International Association of Forensic Nurses. (1997). *Scope and standards of forensic nursing practice.* Washington, DC: American Nurses.

Brenner, J. (2002). *Forensic science: An illustrated dictionary.* Boca Raton, FL: CRC Press.

Burgess, A. W. (2002). *Violence through a forensic lens.* King of Prussia, PA: Nursing Spectrum.

Cabelus, N. B., & Sheridan, G. T. (2007). Forensic investigation of sex crimes in Colombia. *Journal of Forensic Nursing, 3*(3&4), 111–116.

Carney, A. Y. (2007). Poverty and crime in southern California. *Journal of Forensic Nursing, 3*(3&4), 132–136.

Cashin, A., & Potter, E. (2006). Research and evaluation of clinical nurse mentoring: Implications for the forensic context. *Journal of Forensic Nursing, 2*(4), 189–193.

Dole, P. (2004). Medicolegal investigation in South Africa. *On the Edge, 10*(3), 10–13.

Early, S. (2003). International news: British Columbia. *On the Edge, 10*(3), 18–19.

Gilson, J. A. (2002). The Virginia Supreme Court case: Forensic nursing comes of age. *On the Edge, 8*(2), 1, 7–13.

Gorea, R. K. (2004). Bringing hope to India. *On the Edge, 10*(3), 3–5, 16.

Hammer, R. M., Moynihan, B., & Pagliaro, E. M. (Eds.). (2006). *Forensic nursing: A handbook for practice.* Sudbury, MA: Jones and Bartlett, pp. 200–202.

Holmes, D., Perron, A., Michaud, G. (2007). Nursing in corrections: Lessons from France. *Journal of Forensic Nursing, 3*(3&4), 126–131.

International Association of Forensic Nursing. "About us." Retrieved Jan. 10, 2008 from http://www.iafn.org

International Association of Forensic Nursing Ethics Committee (2008). The vision of ethical practice. Retrieved June 1, 2009 from http://www.iafn.org/displaycommon.cfm?an=18subarticlenbr=56

Johnson, M. (2003). Bioterrorism response: Should an event occur, the forensic nurse would be an essential part of the multidisciplinary team. *On the Edge, 9*(3), 1, 24–26.

Lambe, A., & Gage-Lindner, N. (2007). Pushing the limit: Forensic nursing in Germany. *Journal of Forensic Nursing, 3*(3&4), 117–125.

Lowry, P. (2002). Merging roles: Legal nurse consultants and forensic nurses are in demand as new opportunities emerge in fight violent crime. *On the Edge, 10*(3), 1, 7–9.

Lynch, V. (1990). Clinical Forensic Nursing (master's thesis, University of Texas at Arlington).

Lynch, V. (2006). *Forensic nursing.* St. Louis, MO: Mosby.

Lynch, V. (2007). Forensic nursing science and the global agenda. *Journal of Forensic Nursing, 3*(3&4), 101–111.

NANDA International. (2007). *NANDA-1 nursing diagnoses: Definitions and classifications, 2007–2008.* Philadelphia: Author.

Turner, E. J. (2004). Rebuilding a war-torn region. *On the Edge, 10*(3), 6–9.

http://www.hhs.gov/news/press/2001pres/20010911c.html

http://www.hhs.gov/aspr/opeo/ndms/index.html

Forensic Nursing Education Guidelines and Qualifications

3

DONNA GARBACZ BADER

I. Forensic Nursing Education Guidelines
   A. Standards of nursing practice define the profession of nursing, identifying both responsibility and accountability.
   B. The International Association of Forensic Nurses in October 2001 proposed a resolution for the development and implementation of forensic nursing content at all levels of nursing education.
   C. Graduate forensic nursing curricula have been developed and taught throughout the United States as well as on an international level.
   D. Undergraduate forensic nursing courses have been developed as a senior nursing elective or in accordance with the nursing program mission and curriculum.
   E. The *Scope and Standards of Forensic Nursing Practice* (American Nurses Association [ANA] and International Association of Forensic Nurses [IAFN], 1997) encourages the forensic nurse to continue forensic nursing education and maintain professional forensic nursing skills.
   F. The *Scope and Standards of Forensic Nursing Practice* also encourages the forensic nurse to become an active participant in forensic nursing educational programs, activities, professional meetings, conferences, workshops, and research.
   G. As a result of the various forensic nursing subspecialties, it is necessary for the forensic nurse to become knowledgeable regarding culturally diverse groups.
   H. Cultural awareness and sensitivity to diverse groups are required components in all nursing curricula in North America.
   I. Education encourages development of research based on identified needs for forensic nursing services with private organizations (American Academy of Pediatrics, entertainment organizations,

nursing organizations, forensic science organizations, law/legal medicine organizations, medical associations), social service agencies, law enforcement, and the criminal justice system.

II. Educational Qualification
   A. Didactic and clinical
      1. Baccalaureate degree in nursing (BSN, bachelor of science in nursing)
      2. Licensed registered nurse
      3. Five to 10 years of nursing practice in such areas as
         a. Medical-surgical nursing
         b. Psychiatric nursing
         c. Maternal/child nursing
         d. Critical care nursing
         e. Emergency/trauma nursing
   B. Forensic nursing curriculum combines instruction in
      1. Nursing science
      2. Forensic science
      3. Law
      4. Health care and associated legal issues regarding patient care
   C. Graduate preparation programs include didactic and clinical experiences in forensic nursing subspecialty and forensic science procedures
      1. Didactic studies to include
         a. Judicial and legal system
         b. Federal rules of evidence
         c. Advanced concepts of forensic science theory
         d. Advanced concepts of human behavior
         e. Advanced human anatomy and pathophysiology
         f. Writing skills
         g. Adaptation of forensic nursing to the nursing process
         h. Research development
      2. Clinical experience in forensic nursing subspecialty; the total number of required clinical hours dependent on the specialty
         a. Death investigation: 120 hours with a board-certified forensic pathologist
         b. Domestic violence: clinical hours required depend on the course requirements and accredited clinical sites
         c. Sexual assault: clinical hours required depend on the course requirements; accredited clinical sites may include, but are not limited to, emergency departments, free-standing clinics, child advocacy centers, or any site licensed to perform sexual assault examinations; didactic

portion of the sexual assault nurse examiner (SANE) course composed of 40 hours of content

d. Fingerprint analysis: clinical hours determined by the graduate college in conjunction with the accredited clinical site and are based on suggested clinical hours of the professional specialty organization

e. Ballistics: hours determined by the graduate college in conjunction with the accredited clinical site and are based on the suggested clinical hours of professional specialty organization

f. Evidence identification, collection, and preservation: total number of clinical hours may vary depending on the forensic nursing subspecialty (e.g., death investigation incorporates this activity within the 120 hours of required clinical experience)

g. Sexual assault nurse examiner: clinical hours, according to the IAFN, determined on the total number of examinations, individual competence, and examiner's comfort; clinical competency hours may depend on individual training, the preceptor, or the internship facility/employer requirements

h. Law enforcement: clinical hours determined by established departmental and educational guidelines within the law enforcement field and the agency involved (e.g., state police, local police, sheriff's department divisions such as cold case investigation, legal division, crime laboratory, criminal investigation, and additional agency divisions)

3. Additional internship experiences may be developed if the clinical activity is appropriate for fulfillment of subspecialty or agency requirements

a. Gerontology-specific services (e.g., long-term care/ retirement facility, department of aging within a department of health and human services)

b. Incarceration facility: state penitentiary, jail, detention centers, mental health facilities that focus on the care of criminal offenders such as the forensic unit, which treats those who have committed felony offenses such as murder, severe injury to another, rape, and additional offenses; some offenders require mental evaluations to determine individual competency at the time the offense was committed (e.g., exacerbated psychiatric conditions resulting from possible lack of treatment or misuse of prescription medication or those with a known diagnosed mental or physical handicap)

    c. Social service agencies, including welfare programs; crisis intervention specific for domestic violence, sexual assault, physical abuse, psychological abuse; social service interventions with perpetrators who are incarcerated, on parole; child welfare; elder abuse are only a few of the divisions within this system

    d. A Department of Health and Human Services (DHHS) provides additional clinical experiences within the divisions of public health and state board of nursing

    e. Prosecution and defense legal agencies: provide additional clinical experience relating to before or after court trials; review of current and past case files; attend both criminal and civil trials; become familiar with the roles and responsibilities of the county, local, state, and national judicial systems and the various law enforcement agencies, social service agencies, and medical facilities and health care facilities; become a learning member of the multidiscipline investigative team

    f. Additional agencies, facilities, and forensic nursing/forensic science specialty areas should be considered potential clinical sites

---

NOTE

Advanced practice as a forensic nurse is defined within the rules and regulations of the individual state board of nursing and is within the ANA and IAFN *Scope and Standards of Forensic Nursing Practice*.

  D. Graduate degrees

    1. Graduate degree in nursing (master of science in nursing, MSN) with a clinical specialty in forensic nursing: additional courses include forensic photography, human rights, sexual assault, physical and psychological abuse, domestic violence (both didactic and clinical and law), legal issues, the judicial system, and death investigation; evidence-based forensic nursing research a major aspect of these programs

    2. Graduate degree in forensic science (master in forensic science, MFS): provides additional coursework in forensic photography; domestic violence; psychology and behavior as they relate to both victim and perpetrator; death investigation; and toxicology

    3. Doctor of nursing practice (DNP) with a specialty in forensic nursing

4. Online education programs: provide academic credits and continuing nursing education contact hours required by some states to maintain licensure

5. Certification of specialty short courses: provide both didactic and clinical experience (e.g., medicolegal death investigation and sexual assault nurse examiner)

6. Internships: require 120 contact hours of clinical training under supervision of a trained forensic nurse, law enforcement personnel, prosecutor or defense (plaintiff) attorney

E. Membership and participation in professional nursing or specialty nursing organizations

1. American Nurses Association (ANA).

2. American Association of Critical Care Nurses (AACN).

3. National League for Nursing (NLN).

4. Additional established professional organizations: including those for nursing specialties in emergency/trauma, maternal/child, surgery, palliative care, gerontology, postanesthesia recovery room, transplant nursing, and rehabilitation nursing (to mention only a few). As new specialty nursing fields develop, professional nursing organizations will arise to provide education, support, updates in the field; present research opportunities; and offer a variety of scholarship opportunities to develop the specialty. These various nursing organizations may offer certifications within the specialty field and provide study material, test administration, and certification.

5. It is essential for each nurse to learn as much as possible about an organization prior to becoming a member.

   a. Some questions to ask are as follows:

   Is the organization recognized by other professional nursing organizations as a valid professional group?

   Will certification, if offered, be accepted as a valid proof of specialty competency by employers, peers, and other professional organizations within the nursing and health care field?

   What are the advantages of becoming a member of this organization?

   What types of educational support and continuing education and research opportunities will this organization provide?

   Will membership allow me to become a more knowledgeable nurse and improve my nursing practice in providing the care and services to my patients or clients?

F. Membership in professional organizations allow the forensic nurse to
   1. Become actively involved in the promotion of forensic nursing
   2. Take advantage of the numerous continuing education offerings
   3. Meet with other forensic science professionals and specialists
   4. Become active within the organization as a member of one or more of the various committees

---

 International Association of Forensic Nurses

Beyond Tradition. Advancing Humanity.

Graduate & Certificate Programs

The Education section of the IAFN's website is specifically geared toward providing members with information about graduate and certificate programs in forensic nursing and its related subspecialties.

The educational forensic programs listed on this page are a service to our members. IAFN does not endorse or promote any particular educational program, nor are we able to give advice as to which program would be most suitable for any particular individual. Each person looking to enter into an educational program should conduct their own personal research and evaluation.

*Denotes Online Program

Local Programs

Know of a local education program? Submit an education program, and we'll post it today.

Program	Program Type	Location
Medicolegal Death Investigation		Bossier Parish Community College Bossier City, LA, USA
Advanced Specialty Certificate in Forensic Health Sciences	Certificate	British Columbia Institute of Technology Burnaby, BC, Canada
Forensic Nursing		BryanLGH College of Health Sciences Lincoln, NE, USA
Clinical Forensic Nursing	Certificate	Cabarrus College of Health Sciences Concord, NC, USA
Diploma in Forensic Science	Graduate	Calcutta University Calcutta, West Bengal, India
Clinical Forensics	Certificate	Charlotte Mecklenburg Forensic Medicine Program Charlotte, NC, USA

Continued

Program	Program Type	Location
Master of Science in Nursing– Forensic Tract	Graduate	Cleveland State University Cleveland, OH, USA
Master of Science in Nursing	Graduate*	Duquesne University Pittsburgh, PA, USA
Post-Master of Science Program	Certificate*	Duquesne University Pittsburgh, PA, USA
Pathways to Health: A Holistic Approach	Certificate	EdComp, Inc Wilmington, NC, USA
MSN	Graduate	Fairleigh Dickinson University Teaneck, NJ, USA
Fitchburg State College Master of Science in Forensic Nursing	Graduate*	Fitchburg State College Fitchburg, MA, USA
Fitchburg State Post Master's Certificate in Forensic Nursing Completely On Line Program	Certificate*	Fitchburg State College Fitchburg, MA, USA
Master of Science in Nursing Certificate in Forensic Nursing	Certificate	George Mason University Fairfax, VA, USA
Clinical Nurse Specialist: Forensic Nursing Focus	Graduate	Johns Hopkins University Baltimore, MD, USA
Forensic Nursing Certificate Program	Certificate*	Kaplan University Boca Raton, FL, USA
Online Forensic Nursing Certificate	Certificate*	Kaplan University
Forensic Nursing Certificate Program	Certificate	La Roche College Pittsburgh, PA, USA
MSN: Forensic Nursing	Graduate*	Monmouth University West Long Branch, NJ, USA
Forensic Nursing Certificate	Certificate*	Monmouth University West Long Branch, NJ, USA
Forensic Studies: Advanced Specialty Health Studies	Certificate*	Mount Royal College Calgary, AB, Canada
Credit-Bearing Forensic Coursework		National Forensic Nursing Institute at the University of Rochester Rochester, NY, USA
Master's or Certificate in Forensic Medicine	Graduate/ Certificate	Philadelphia College of Osteopathic Medicine Philadelphia, PA, USA
Forensic Nurse Clinical Specialist	Graduate	Quinnipiac University Hamden, CT, USA
Forensic Health Studies	Certificate	Seneca College King City, ON, Canada
Acute Care Nurse Practitioner Program	Graduate*	Seton Hall University South Orange, NJ, USA
Forensic Nursing		Texas Christian University Fort Worth, TX, USA
Forensic Nursing Certificate Program	Certificate*	University of California Riverside Extension Riverside, CA, USA

Continued

Program	Program Type	Location
MSN: Clinical Nurse Specialist with Forensic Nursing Subspecialty	Graduate	University of Colorado—Bethel College of Nursing Colorado Springs, CO, USA
Forensic Nursing Certificate Program	Certificate	University of Colorado–Bethel College of Nursing Colorado Springs, CO, USA
Advanced Practice Forensic Nursing Certificate Program	Graduate*	University of Illinois at Chicago, College of Nursing Chicago, IL, USA
Forensic Science Minor	Graduate	University of Pennsylvania Philadelphia, PA, USA
Certificate in Forensic Nursing and Legal Nurse Consulting	Certificate	University of Pittsburgh School of Nursing Pittsburgh, PA, USA
Adult Health Nursing Specialist with Concentration in Forensic Nursing	Graduate	University of Scranton Scranton, PA, USA
Doctor of Nursing Practice (DNP) in Forensic Nursing	Graduate*	The University of Tennessee Health Science Center Memphis, TN, USA
Advanced Practice Forensic Nurse Specialist	Graduate*	University of Washington Seattle, WA, USA
MSN: Forensic Nursing	Graduate*	Vanderbilt University School of Nursing Nashville, TN, USA
Master of Science in Forensic Nursing	Graduate	Xavier University Cincinnati, OH, USA

References

American Nurses Association, Congress for Nursing Practice. (1980). *Nursing: A social policy statement.* Kansas City, MO. American Nurses Association.

American Nurses Association. (1997–2000). *Ethics and human rights position statements: Cultural diversity in nursing practice.* Washington, DC. Retrieved June 5, 2008, from http://www.Nursingworld.org/readroom/position/ethics/etcldv.htm

American Nurses Association and International Association of Forensic Nurses. (1997). *Scope and standards of forensic nursing practice.* Washington, DC: American Nurses.

Butts, J. B., & Rich, K. L. (2008). *Nursing ethics across the curriculum and into practice* (2nd ed.). Sudbury, MA. Jones and Bartlett.

Cashin, A., & Potter, E. (2006). Research and evaluation of clinical nurse mentoring: Implications for the forensic context. *Journal of Forensic Nursing, 2*(4), 189–193.

Charleston County's Nursing Internship Program. *Introduction to medicolegal death investigation: A nursing internship.* Retrieved from http://www.charlestoncounty.org

Hammer, R. M., Moynihan, B., & Pagliaro, E. M. (Eds.). (2006). *Forensic nursing: A handbook for practice.* Sudbury, MA: Jones and Bartlett, pp. 787–789.

International Association of Forensic Nursing. *Education and events: Graduate and certificate programs.* Retrieved from http://www.forensicnurse.org/displaycommon.cfm?an=1&subarticlenbr=5. Retrieved and updated June 4, 2009.

Lynch, V. (2006). *Forensic nursing.* St. Louis, MO: Mosby, pp. 593–598.

McLaughlin, C., and Marrone, D. (2002). The death investigation interns. *On the Edge, 8*(3), 3–6.

Troy, A., and Clements, P. T. (2007). Changing the lens for youth "gone wild": The call for primary prevention research by forensic nurses. *Journal of Forensic Nursing, 3*(3&4), 137–140.

Educational Foundation for Forensic Nursing Practice

4

DONNA GARBACZ BADER

I. The Profession of Nursing
   A. Nursing is an art and science.
      - "Nurses help people, sick or well, to do those things needed for health or a peaceful death that people would do on their own if they had the strength, will, or knowledge" (Henderson, 1961).
      - "Nursing is the protection, promotion and optimization of health and abilities, prevention of illness and injury, alleviation of suffering through the diagnosis and treatment of human response, and advocacy in the care of individuals, families, communities, and populations" (American Nurses Association, 2003).
   B. The nursing curriculum is designed to provide knowledge in physical science and human behavior to provide holistic care for those individuals in physical or psychological distress and to address issues of the family, support system, and community members in education and in the maintenance of health and personal safety.
      - Curriculum concepts are based on four basic skills:

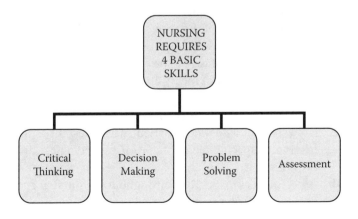

II. Critical Thinking Skills
   A. The art of critical thinking allows the forensic nurse to:
      1. Analyze data
      2. Apply standards
      3. Recognize differences and similarities among things or situations
      4. Seek information by identifying relevant sources and collecting objective, subjective, historical, and current data
      5. Utilize logical reasoning
      6. Plan and predict consequences
      7. Transform knowledge to performance
   B. Critical thinking is incorporated into each aspect of the nursing curriculum:
      1. Didactic content to clinical skills
      2. Clinical skills to research
      3. Patient/victim care to forensic nursing concepts
      4. Forensic nursing concepts to research development of forensic nursing skills to provide the victim, family, friends, perpetrator, and community member with safety, justice, rehabilitation
   C. Assessment begins the critical thinking process:
      1. Assess the situation
      2. Identify the task (evidence collection, dressing change)
      3. Predict potential problems (rain may destroy the evidence, patient's restlessness may cause wounds to become contaminated)
      4. Evaluate the results

III. Decision Making Skills
   A. Developed at every level throughout the nursing curriculum
   B. The primary thread in decision making is the nursing process
   C. Correlates of theoretical concepts to clinical assessment data in a variety of environments
   D. Decision making on practice is established in curriculum design and challenges the nursing student and the professional nurse in defining priority of care to provide the most positive outcome for the patient/victim of injury and/or illness.

IV. Problem Solving and Assessment
   A. Collection of assessment patient data is essential to the identification of specific physical and/or psychological disruptions in the holistic health of the patient.
   B. Assessment skills mature throughout the nursing curriculum
   C. Become the primary nursing tool in the critical thinking, decision making, and problem solving skills of the professional nurse

V. Nursing Integrates a Specific Body of Knowledge to Include:
  A. Pathophysiology
  B. Psychology and behavior
  C. The art of caring
  D. The holistic human response:

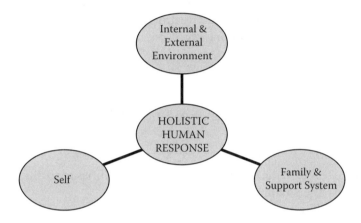

VI. Care and Treatment Based on the Nursing Process

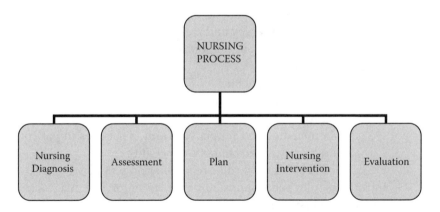

VII. Nursing Education
  A. Incorporates nursing skills related to physical care, psychological support, and education for the patient, family, or caregiver; during hospitalization, long-term care/rehabilitation facility stay, or home care
  B. Identifies the nursing role and responsibilities with various community and social service agencies
  C. Identifies the impact of nursing care in relation to legal responsibilities related to the care of the patient, client, or victim

D. Correlates individual nursing actions to those related to legal responsibilities to the employer and the institution (e.g., hospital, clinic, long-term care and rehabilitation facilities, and any other facility in which the professional nurse is practicing)

E. Understands the legal issues related to individual nursing practice as identified in the state board of nursing rules and regulations:
- provision of care and treatment for the patient/client/victim
- maintenance of one's professional continuing education and competencies

> **NOTE**
> State board of nursing rules and regulations differ according to the individual state.

F. Correlates the nursing role and responsibilities regarding various partners in providing health care:
1. Physicians
2. Ancillary departments
   a. Physical therapy
   b. Radiology
   c. Pulmonary diagnostic and treatment departments: respiratory therapy and treatment, pulmonary diagnostic procedures, pulmonary rehabilitation and education
   d. Laboratory
   e. Nutrition and dietary
   f. Housekeeping in patient care areas and throughout the facility
   g. Maintenance and proper function of services in patient care areas and throughout the facility
   h. Social services, cardiac rehabilitation services

G. Introduces roles and responsibilities of law enforcement agencies and judicial system personnel:
1. State law enforcement
2. Police
3. Sheriff
4. Lawyers
5. Court system
6. Detectives and investigators

H. Identifies the need to collaborate with local, state, national, and international individuals and agencies
1. Health care professionals and agencies
2. Legal professionals and agencies

   3. Law enforcement professionals and agencies
   4. Social welfare professionals and agencies

VIII. Nursing Curriculum Framework
   A. Is integrated

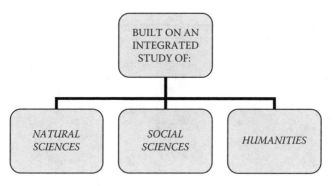

**NURSING CURRICULUM PROVIDES A
FRAMEWORK FOR FORENSIC NURSING.**

---

   1. Human anatomy and physiology
   2. Chemistry and physical principles
   3. Microbiology and biochemistry
   4. Pharmacology
   5. Human psychology and behavior
   6. Human response to internal and external stressors
   7. Family systems
   8. Community resources
   9. Medical professional ethics
  10. Legal issues:
       a. Documentation
       b. Confidentiality
       c. Chain of custody

Scientific-based nursing education and critical thinking skills provide the forensic nurse with the ability to identify, collect, and preserve physical and biological evidence with precision and accuracy (Lynch, 2006).

   B. Basic nursing curriculum plus additional specialized education in forensic science and forensic nursing allow the forensic nurse to

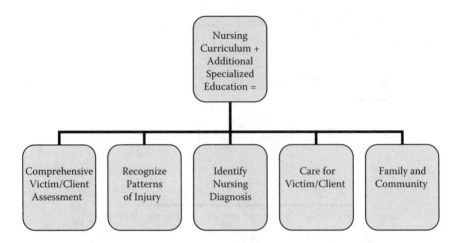

Bibliography

American Nurses Association (2003). *Nursing: A social policy statement* (2nd ed.). Washington, DC: American Nurses Association, p. 6.

American Nurses Association and International Association of Forensic Nurses. (1997). *Scope and standards of forensic nursing practice.* Washington, DC: American Nurses.

Burgess, A. W. (2002). *Violence through a forensic lens.* King of Prussia, PA: Nursing Spectrum, pp. 371–381.

Butts, J. B., & Rich, K. L. (2008). *Nursing ethics across the curriculum and into practice* (2nd ed.). Sudbury, MA: Jones and Bartlett.

Cashin, A., & Potter, E. (2006). Research and evaluation of clinical nurse mentoring: Implications for the forensic context. *Journal of Forensic Nursing, 2*(4), 189–193.

Cochran, M. (1999). The real meaning of patient-nurse confidentiality. *Critical Care Quarterly: Confronting Forensic Issues, 22*(1), 41–50.

Goll-McGee, B. (1999). The role of the clinical forensic nurse in critical care. *Critical Care Quarterly, 22*(1), 8–17.

Hammer, R. M., Moynihan, B., & Pagliaro, E. M. (Eds.). (2006). *Forensic nursing: A handbook for practice.* Sudbury, MA: Jones and Bartlett, pp. 200–202.

Hoyt, C. A. (1999). Evidence recognition and collection in the clinical setting. *Critical Care Quarterly, 22*(1), 19–22.

James, S. H., & Nordby, J. J. (Eds.). (2005). *Forensic science: An introduction to scientific and investigative techniques.* Boca Raton, FL: CRC Press.

Lynch, V. (2006). *Forensic nursing.* St. Louis, MO: Mosby.

Mosby's surefire documentation: How, what, and when nurses need to document (2nd ed.). (2006). St. Louis, MO: Mosby Elsevier.

NANDA International. (2007). *NANDA-1 nursing diagnoses: Definitions and classifications, 2007–2008.* Philadelphia: Author.

Porth, C. M. (2002). *Pathophysiology: Concepts of altered health states* (6th ed.). Hagerstown, MD: Lippincott Williams & Wilkins.

Quinn, C. (2005), *The medical record as a forensic resource.* Sudbury, MA: Jones and Bartlett.

Rubenfeld, M. G., & Scheffer, B. K. (2006). *Critical thinking tactics for nurses.* Sudbury, MA: Jones and Bartlett, pp. 13–30.

Souryal, S. S. (2007). *Ethics in criminal justice: In search of the truth* (4th ed.). Newark, NJ: LexisNexis Group; Bender.

Tomey, A. M., & Alligood, M. R. (1998). *Nursing theorists and their work.* St. Louis, MO: Mosby, p. 102.

U.S. Department of Justice Office for Victims of Crime. (2007, April 19). *Victim needs from a faith-based perspective; Vicarious trauma.* Washington, DC: U.S. Department of Justice, pp. 1–2.

Winfrey, M. E., & Smith, A. R. (1999). The suspiciousness factor: Critical care nursing and forensics. *Critical Care Quarterly, 22*(1), 1–6.

Forensic Science

DONNA GARBACZ BADER

5

I. Forensic Science Background
   A. The word *forensic* originates from the Latin word *forum,* which refers to the law, and *science,* which is the application of the various disciplines of science to the law.
   B. The American Academy of Forensic Science, established in 1948, is the oldest and most influential professional organization of forensic scientists throughout the world, with a current membership of 5,000.
   C. The field involves the application of scientific theory, concepts, and principles to civil and criminal laws.
   D. Proof of guilt or innocence is often determined by the results of the forensic evidence.
   E. Forensic science is a combination of knowledge:
      1. Weapons identification
      2. Fingerprinting
      3. Questioned document analysis
      4. Chemical identification
      5. Trace analysis of hair, fiber, or soil
      6. Deoxyribonucleic acid (DNA) analysis
      7. Investigation of explosives
      8. Criminal justice system
      9. Crime scene photography
      10. Terrorism
      11. Disaster response
         a. Caused by humans
         b. Natural
         c. Nuclear
      12. Cybercrime
      13. Human rights violations: international and regional
         a. Genocide
         b. Torture: sexual and psychological
         c. Human trafficking
         d. Mass executions

    e. Child labor

    f. Slavery

  14. Human response to stress

II. History of Forensic Science

 A. Forensic science history can be traced to the ancient Egyptians, who developed a system of law and a judicial system that was adapted into later Greek and Roman laws.

 B. Egyptian law was based on a sense of right and wrong and that everyone should be viewed as equal under the law; the one exception to this was the slave.

  1. Criminal offenses were investigated prior to rendering a final judgment.

  2. Religious beliefs would not allow an autopsy to be performed for the purpose of establishing cause and manner of death.

  3. Written records of the trial proceedings and judgment were used as a precedent when similar legal issues arose.

 C. The ancient Greeks relied on the principle of reason, taught by Aristotle, to resolve issues of self, politics, developing strategies of war, understanding religion, and the individual's relationship to the gods.

  1. The Greeks created a court system.

  2. A council was appointed to administer both the government and the court system.

  3. There were appointed officials whose only job was to write laws.

  4. The Greeks developed procedural laws that were the guidelines for judges on how to use the laws.

  5. The Greeks created laws that dictated how public services were to be provided and family laws that regulated the behavior of men and women.

  6. The Greeks identified homicide as a tort law.

 D. The Roman Empire developed a sophisticated process of criminal investigation and punishment.

  1. The first people to make law into a science

  2. Wrote the first legal code for Roman law, *The Law of the Twelve Tables*, which provided the foundation for all Western civil and criminal law

 E. China provided the first recorded text, *The Washing Away of Wrongs* by Sung Tz'u, written in 1186–1249 (McKnight, 1981), as a guidebook for death investigation.

  1. The text identifies many of the specific forensic science principles and concepts that are currently part of forensic science criminal investigation.

2. During the 12th and 13th centuries in China, most homicides were the result of sudden violence, robberies, or disagreements among families, coworkers, and others.

3. The focus of the text is an attempt to resolve the cause of death as homicide, suicide, natural causes, or accident.

4. Investigation of a death followed a well-organized system of
   a. Reporting a death
   b. An inquest, or a judicial inquiry, into the death in the presence of a jury
   c. Trial by jury
   d. Sentencing of the guilty suspect

5. Focus was placed on the position of the body, condition of the body, and the instrument used that resulted in the death.

6. People who may have information regarding the death were questioned (interrogated).

7. Instruments were identified that may produce a specific type of injury or death.

III. Technology and Forensic Science Techniques
A. After the late 17th century, technology, the development of instruments such as the microscope and photography, the use of x-ray, and the introduction of new laboratory equipment and tests such as blood typing and application of the principles of physics to ballistic trajectories all made the science of criminal investigation more accurate.

B. Locard's exchange principle became the cornerstone of forensic science: Human contact with any person, place or thing, will result in an exchange of physical materials or evidence.
   1. Fibers from a sofa you sat on will become part of you, your clothing, or any object placed on the sofa; in addition, physical material (trace material from your skin, hair, fingernails, clothes) will remain on the sofa. If collected and preserved properly, the materials left by you on the sofa will provide information regarding your activities that day, several days prior to the time you sat on the sofa, and if another individual wore your clothes. Stains left on the sofa can be identified by type of stain, who was responsible for producing the stain, and the approximate time the stain occurred.
   2. Dirt on shoes can identify the location of crime; microscopic materials in the dirt may provide information to a specific location and may also assist in determining the weather conditions at the time the shoes stepped in the dirt.

3. The shoe will also contain the individual's skin cells from either the feet or the fingers that tied the shoelaces, including any additional material left from the hands such as dirt, food, hair, sweat, and any materials that the hand and fingers may have been in contact with prior to tying the shoelaces.

LOCARD'S EXCHANGE PRINCIPLE

"You touch it, it's yours."

C. In 1932, the U.S. Federal Bureau of Investigation (FBI), under Director J. Edgar Hoover, designated the organization of a national laboratory with the main purpose to offer forensic science services to all law enforcement agencies throughout the country. Currently, the FBI Laboratory is the largest forensic laboratory in the world.

IV. Basics of Forensic Science

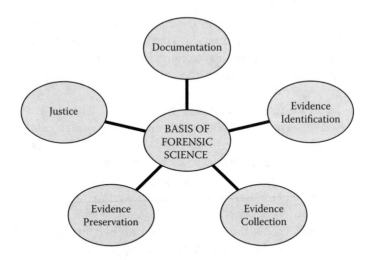

V. Functions of a Forensic Scientist
   A. Identification, collection, and preservation of physical and biological evidence
   B. Analysis of physical evidence
   C. Provide expert witness testimony
   D. Prove the existence of a crime or identify connection to the crime
   E. Provide skilled documentation related to chain of custody and precise record maintenance

F. Work as a member within an investigative team, including
   1. Police officers
   2. Sheriff deputies
   3. Both prosecuting and defense attorneys
   4. Federal agencies such as the FBI, Central Intelligence Agency (CIA)
   5. Immigration officials
   6. Other professionals involved in the investigation (e.g., forensic psychiatrist/psychologist, forensic pathologist, forensic nurse, or other scientific or legal specialists assisting with the investigation process)
G. Provide death notification
H. Determine the who, what, where, when, and why of a crime

VI. Forensic Science Specialty Areas
   A. As classified by the American Academy of Forensic Science (AAFS) in 2008, specialty areas involve the following:

Criminalistics: Application of the physical sciences to criminal investigation

Engineering science: Application of physical science failure of structures resulting from accidents, fires, or human causes

Jurisprudence: Application of the science or philosophy of law

Digital and multimedia sciences: Application of the science of computer data processes and media recording to the legal investigation of possible criminal activity

Odontology: Dentistry; application of the science of dentistry to the legal system

Questioned documents: Use of forensic science methods to determine the authenticity or origin of a document

Toxicology: Study of drugs and poisons that may have legal implications

Pathology/Biology:

Pathology/forensic medicine: Specialty of medicine and subspecialty of pathology that deals with investigating the cause, manner, and mechanism of death

Forensic medicine: Subspecialty of medicine with application to the investigation, diagnosis, care, and treatment of the living and the dead

Forensic pathology (in the practice of forensic medicine): Subspecialty of medicine with application to the investigation of the deceased

Biology: Application of the biological sciences to the field of criminal investigation

Archaeology

Taphonomy: Study of the postmortem process and its relationship to the environment

Physical anthropology: Application of the methods and theories of human skeletal biology to solve medicolegal questions

Psychiatry and behavioral science: Application of the principles of human psychology to the law and the legal process; includes criminal profiling

General section

B. General section forensic science specialist as identified by the AAFS (2008) is a scientist with forensic specialties in

  1. Laboratory investigation
  2. Field investigation
  3. Education
  4. Research
  5. Clinical work
  6. Communications

- Accountant
- Archaeologist
- Facial reconstructionist
- Artist/sculptor
- Aviation accident investigator
- Ballistics analyst
- Computer crime investigator
- Computer specialist
- Forensic consultant
- Coroner (nonpathologist)
- Crime scene investigator
- Medicolegal investigator
- Educator for all areas of forensic science
- Image enhancer
- Marine biologist
- Nurse examiner
- Photographer
- Polygraph examiner
- Radiologist
- Researcher
- Rehabilitation specialist
- Social worker with forensic science application
- Speech specialist

C. Developing specialty areas in forensic science identified by the AAFS (2008):

- Computer imaging of crime scenes
- Suspect composites
- Victim characteristics for potential identification
- Tape recordings and digital voice identification
- Acoustic and speech analysis
- Accurate detailed identification of financial schemes, money laundering
- Internet fraud
- Forestry and wildlife science
- Veterinary medicine
- Botany
- Ecological awareness

D. National and international system of information
  1. United States system of information banks that provide statistical and epidemiological data:
      a. Classification of diseases, injuries, and causes of death
      b. Standard format for death certificates
  2. Automated Fingerprint Identification System (AFIS): National and international computer-based identification systems for the storage and retrieval of fingerprint files; also allows for the comparison of latent fingerprints with print records in these files
  3. Combined DNA Index System (CODIS)
      a. A national database that contains the DNA of any individual convicted of committing a sexual or a violent crime

       b. Originated as part of the DNA Identification Act passed by Congress in 1994

    4. Integrated Ballistics Information System (IBIS): Database used for obtaining, storing, and analyzing images of cartridge casings and bullets

E. Future forensic science: Specialties in both the physical and biological sciences will appear as technology and research provide more sophisticated and accurate tools for

    1. Investigation of crime

    2. Developing a more efficient criminal judicial system

    3. Working with victims to provide services for long-term physical and psychological recovery

    4. Continued demand for DNA analysis of evidence obtained from past crime scenes to verify or overturn guilty verdicts

    5. Improved laboratory technology to increase the speed of DNA analysis and additional evidence analysis laboratory testing

    6. Portable devices capable of DNA analysis

    7. The use of digital radiology

    8. Ultraviolet and infrared injury photography to detect biological and biochemical changes after an injury has occurred

    9. Fingerprint rejuvenation to assist in the identification of deteriorated remains

   10. Scene investigation following natural and human–human disasters

   11. Ultimate goals: care of the victim, victim justice, community safety; punishment or rehabilitation for the perpetrator

   12. Improvements in computer technology

Bibliography

American Academy of Forensic Science (2009). "Choosing a Career." Retrieved June 8, 2008 from http://www.aafs.org/?section_id=resources&page_id=choosing_a_career.

Brenner, J. (2002). *Forensic science: An illustrated dictionary.* Boca Raton, FL: CRC Press.

Burdick W. L. (2004). *The principles of Roman law and their relation to modern law.* Rochester, NY: The Lawyers Co-operative Publishing Company, pp. 84–112.

Clark, S. C., Ernst, M. F., Haglund, W. D., & Jentzen, J. M. (1996). *Medicolegal death investigator: A systematic training program for the professional death investigator, training text.* Big Springs, MI: Occupational Research and Assessment.

Durose, M. R. (2008, July). *Census of publicly funded forensic crime laboratories, 2005* (Bureau of Justice Statistics Bulletin, NCJ 222181). Washington, DC: US Department of Justice, Office of Justice Programs.

Federal Bureau of Investigation. (2008). *What we investigate.* Retrieved July 7, 2008, from http://www.fbi.gov/hq.htm

Garrison, D. (2008). Identified after 59 years: Recovering prints from a badly dete-
    riorated hand defied the odds…but they managed to do it. *Evidence Technology
    Magazine, 6*(5), 30–37.
Girard, J. E. (2008). *Criminalistics: Forensic science and crime.* Sudbury, MA: Jones
    and Bartlett, pp. 6, 376.
Hammer, R. M., Moynihan, B., & Pagliaro, E. M. (Eds.). (2006). *Forensic nursing: A
    handbook for practice.* Sudbury, MA: Jones and Bartlett, pp. 4–5.
Harris, R. J. (Ed.). (1971). The Legacy of Egypt, Theodorides, Aristide. *The concept of
    law in ancient Egypt.* Oxford, UK: Oxford University Press, pp. 14–16.
Hoyt, C. A. (1999). Evidence recognition and collection in the clinical setting. *Critical
    Care Quarterly, 22*(1), 19–22.
James, S. H., & Nordby, J. J. (Eds.). (2005). *Forensic science: An introduction to scientific
    and investigative techniques.* Boca Raton, FL: CRC Press, pp. 4–9, 636, 638, 643.
Klingle, C., & Reiter, K. (2008). Ultraviolet and infrared injury photography. *Evidence
    Technology Magazine, 6*(5), 26–29.
Lanni, A. (2006). *Law and justice in the courts of classical Athens.* Cambridge:
    Cambridge University Press.
Lynch, V. (2006). *Forensic nursing.* St. Louis, MO: Mosby, pp. 28, 33–41.
National Institute of Justice. (2003). DNA evidence: What law enforcement officers
    should know. *National Institute of Justice Journal,* 249, 10–22.
Souryal, S. S. (2007). *Ethics in criminal justice: In search of the truth* (4th ed.). Newark,
    NJ: LexisNexis Group; Bender.
Spitz, W. U., Spitz, D., & Clark, R. (Eds.). (2006). *Spitz and Fisher's medicolegal investi-
    gation of death: Guidelines for the application of pathology to crime investigation*
    (4th ed.). Springfield, IL: Charles C. Thomas, pp. 3–6.
Sung Tz'u. *The washing away of wrongs: Science, medicine, and technology in East
    Asia 1.* McKnight, B. E. (Trans.). (1981). Ann Arbor, MI: Center for Chinese
    Studies, University of Michigan.

Coroners, Medical Examiners, and Forensic Pathologists

6

DONNA GARBACZ BADER

I. Differences between the Medical Examiner and Coroner Systems
   A. State statutes identify the type of system used and outline the duties and responsibilities of the medical examiner or coroner.
   B. Coroners or medical examiners are responsible for determining the cause and manner of death, overseeing the analysis of evidence, and presenting the findings in a court of law.

II. Coroner System
   A. History
      1. The word *coroner* originated in England around 1194 and means "crowner."
      2. Originally, the coroner was appointed by the king and assigned various responsibilities, such as appraiser, and was to safeguard the king's lands and possessions.
      3. The coroner was responsible for investigating the scene of a death; the coroner collected materials and belongings left at the scene, which became the property of the king.
      4. In conducting death investigations, the coroner would assess injuries, document the crime scene, and investigate any accusations that were made by witnesses or suspects.
      5. The coroner could arrest both witnesses and suspects.
   B. Coroner system in the United States
      1. The English coroner system was adopted in the American colonies and then become the law in each state.
      2. Death investigation was considered a local county function.
      3. The U.S. Constitution makes no provision for a coroner.
      4. Each state enacts its own coroner laws.
      5. The coroner is often an elected position held for four years; some states may vary in the length of time the position is held, and in some states the coroner is delegated by a county official such as the county attorney, sheriff, or other elected official.

    6. The coroner is an employee of the county and may or may not be a physician.

    7. Qualifications of the coroner are determined by each district within the state, and each district has its own statutes regarding roles and responsibilities. These statutes need to comply with the state statutes and regulations required for any death investigation and treatment of the body.

    8. When a request for an autopsy is made, the coroner must contact a pathologist within the area; if a forensic autopsy is necessary, the coroner must contact a forensic pathologist or a pathologist with experience in conducting a forensic autopsy.

    9. In most coroner states, it is not necessary for the coroner to have any medical knowledge; some states do not require the coroner to possess a high school education.

    10. The coroner will determine the cause and manner of death and has the authority to sign the death certificate.

III. Medical Examiner System

    A. The first formal medical examiner system was established in January 1991 with the creation of the Armed Services Medical Examiner System. This document defined the purpose and responsibilities of the M. E. Office. It outlined the organizational structure and functions of the office.

    B. The Massachusetts legislature, in 1877, was the first state to pass a statute that replaced the coroner with the medical examiner; the statute also required the medical examiner to be licensed to practice medicine.

    C. With industrialization, the coroner was the most difficult to replace with a licensed physician, especially in rural areas of the United States.

    D. At the time of World War II, the National Conference of Commissioners on Uniform State Laws was created to develop laws that could easily be adopted by all states to maintain consistency between states.

    E. The Model Post-Mortem Examination Act was one such Uniform State Law that was passed by many states for the establishment of M. E. death investigations.

    F. Those states that chose to retain the coroner system are now requiring additional training and continuing education for individuals to be elected or designated as the local coroner.

    G. A few states maintain both coroner and medical examiner systems.

    H. Funding is the responsibility of the state and requires a self-contained, independent facility with all necessary equipment and staff (e.g., forensic pathologist, forensic death investigators, laboratory facilities, qualified autopsy personnel, coolers, autopsy tables, and associated equipment, materials, and supplies).

IV. Forensic Pathologist
  A. Overview
    1. A forensic pathologist is a physician licensed to practice medicine as a medical doctor (MD) or doctor of osteopathic medicine (DO) and is trained in pathology with additional training and certification in forensic pathology.
    2. In the middle of the 20th century, law enforcement and coroners recognized the need for a pathologist to perform autopsies to determine the cause of death in those individuals who died suddenly and unexpectedly.
    3. After World War II, the American Board of Pathologists recognized the formal specialty of forensic pathology.
    4. Today, large cities require that the medical examiner be a forensic pathologist.
    5. Forensic pathologists are also sought by coroners to perform autopsies in rural areas.
  B. Educational and training requirements for the forensic pathologist
    1. The forensic pathologist must graduate from an accredited medical program followed by a residency in pathology (anatomical and clinical pathology).
    2. Additional training for the forensic pathologist may be at a large coroner's or medical examiner's office.
    3. Forensic pathologists deal with the law and criminal justice system.
    4. Some forensic pathologists choose to have additional education and training and go to law school to obtain a jurist doctorate; they may be licensed to practice as an attorneys-at-law.
    5. The National Association of Medical Examiners in May 2008 identified a total of 14 certified forensic pathologists who also hold a jurist doctorate degree in the United States.
  C. Duties of a forensic pathologist
    1. The forensic pathologist is responsible for determining all aspects of death and criminal injury.
    2. A medical history review most often initiates the death investigation.
    3. Sudden and unexpected deaths are those reviewed by a forensic pathologist; in addition, the jurisdiction in which the death or injury occurred plays a vital role in determination

of factors such as time (e.g., a person who suffers a gunshot wound is admitted to the hospital for surgery and treatment, develops pneumonia, sepsis, or other complications, and dies).

   a. In reviewing the medical record and victim's history, the forensic pathologist needs to determine the cause and manner of death: Was the death due to a preexisting condition and not the gunshot wound, or was death the result of the gunshot wound?

4. Knowledge of legal investigation allows the forensic pathologist to review witness statements and advise law enforcement regarding potentially valuable information to assist in the investigation.

5. The forensic pathologist is also able to provide medical consultation regarding the cause of the injury and the approximate time of death and to correlate injuries and wounds to possible tools used that resulted in the injury and possibly death.

6. The ideal situation is for the forensic pathologist to examine the scene of the death or the location where the death occurred; however, this is not practical from a financial viewpoint, so the cost to the county in compensating the pathologist may prohibit the pathologist from investigating the crime scene.

7. Photographs, videos, crime scene diagrams, and crime scene reports are reviewed by the forensic pathologist as part of the death investigation.

8. Autopsy

   a. Conducts autopsy examinations to determine the cause of death

   b. Dissects the human body to determine the cause of death

D. Forensic pathologist as an expert witness

   1. The primary duty of the medical examiner as an expert witness is to present the facts in court and to offer an unbiased opinion based on facts obtained during the medical examiner's investigation of the victim and associated circumstances surrounding the victim's death.

   2. The medical examiner as an expert witness becomes an educator as well as a scientist.

   3. It is the responsibility of the medical examiner to explain the complex scientific information to the jury in an understandable manner.

Bibliography

American Association of Osteopathic Examiners. *Member list.* Retrieved Jan. 10, 2008 from http://www.aaoe-net.org/memlist.html

Brenner, J. (2002). *Forensic science: An illustrated dictionary.* Boca Raton, FL: CRC Press.

Clark, S. C., Ernst, M. F., Haglund, W. D., & Jentzen, J. M. (1996). *Medicolegal death investigator: A systematic training program for the professional death investigator, training text.* Big Springs, MI: Occupational Research and Assessment.

Department of the Army. Department of the Air Force (1991). *Medical Services: Armed Forces Medical Examiner System.* Washington, DC: Department of the Army, chapter 1.

Eckert, W. G. (Ed.). (1997). *Introduction to forensic sciences* (2nd ed.). Boca Raton, FL: CRC Press.

Girard, J. E. (2008). *Criminalistics: Forensic science and crime.* Sudbury, MA: Jones and Bartlett, pp. 9–12.

James, S. H., & Nordby, J. J. (Eds.). (2005). *Forensic science: An introduction to scientific and investigative techniques.* Boca Raton, FL: CRC Press.

Knight, B. (1991). *Forensic pathology.* New York: Oxford University Press.

Lynch, V. (2006). *Forensic nursing.* St. Louis, MO: Mosby.

National Association of Medical Examiners Web site. Retrieved Jan. 10, 2008 from http://thename.org

National Conference of Commissioners on Uniform State Law (1954/Rev. 2005). Model Post-Mortem Examination Act. Chicago, IL: Commissioners on Uniform State Laws, p. 1.

Porth, C. M. (2002). *Pathophysiology: Concepts of altered health states* (6th ed.). Hagerstown, MD: Lippincott Williams & Wilkins.

Spitz, W. U., Spitz, D., & Clark, R. (Eds.). (2006). *Spitz and Fisher's medicolegal investigation of death: Guidelines for the application of pathology to crime investigation* (4th ed.). Springfield, IL: Charles C. Thomas.

Sung Tz'u. *The washing away of wrongs: Science, medicine, and technology in East Asia 1.* McKnight, B. E. (Trans.). (1981). Ann Arbor, MI: Center for Chinese Studies, University of Michigan.

Voltaire. Author and Philosopher. Retrieved Dec. 29, 2007 from http://www.lucidcafe.com/library/95nov/voltaire.html

Cause, Manner, and Mechanism of Death

7

DONNA GARBACZ BADER

I. Definition: death occurs when an individual has sustained irreversible cessation of all functions of the entire brain
   A. A forensic death is classified as one of six categories:
      1. Violent deaths, such as those by
         - Accident
         - Suicide
         - Homicide
      2. Suspicious deaths
      3. Sudden or unexpected deaths
      4. Deaths without a physician in attendance
      5. Deaths occurring in custody, such as those in
         - Jail
         - Penitentiary
         - Detention center
         - During arrest or interrogation
         - Medical health care facility
         - Mental health care facility
      6. Occupational
   B. Death certificate: A legal document that
      - Certifies the identification of the decedent
      - Provides date and time of death
      - Provides cause of death
      - Provides manner of death
      - Does not include mechanism of death: medical treatment may modify or alter the mechanism rather than cause the illness (e.g., furosemide with potassium supplements are appropriate medications for the treatment of congestive heart failure but have no effect on a damaged mitral valve)
      - Includes "other significant conditions" in Part II; these conditions contribute to the death and are unrelated to the cause

C. Legal issues related to death
   1. Insurance companies require proof of death and the cause of death to validate that another individual is not responsible for payment of any treatment or liability expenses
   2. Wills, which are based on inheritance, require proof of date and time of death.
   3. When numerous individuals die as a result, the victims' actions, and the times of death of all victims may be essential to establish charges.
   4. Additional issues include identification and notification of next of kin and worker's compensation claims and benefits.
   5. Priority in any death investigation is to determine the cause and manner of death; criminal and civil legal action may depend on this information.
   6. Manner of death is vital information for relatives when an insurance policy will pay "double indemnity" when the manner of death is accidental and may not pay for suicide.
D. Cause of death
   1. The cause of death is the *initial event* that resulted in the death, such as
      – Gunshot wound (GSW)
      – Blunt force trauma: a blunt object (baseball bat, rock) strikes or impacts (thrown against a wall with extreme force) the body
      – Sharp force trauma: a sharp object (knife, arrow) strikes or impacts (impales) the body with force
   2. Summary of injuries

Blunt Force Trauma Injuries	Sharp Force Injuries
• Abrasions	• Incised wounds
• Contusions	• Penetrating wounds
• Lacerations	
• Fractures	

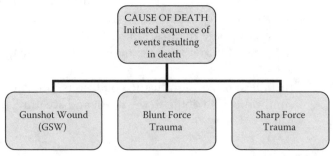

E. Manner of death
1. *Root cause* of the sequence of events that leads to death
    - Natural: death results from natural causes (e.g., congestive heart failure)
    - Homicide: death occurs by the hand of someone other than the deceased
    - Suicide: deliberate termination of one's life; two elements required to identify suicide as manner of death

      Intent to commit suicide

      A particular action that leads to the intent

    - Accident: death results from an unplanned and unforeseen sequence of events
    - Undetermined: the pathologist cannot determine the appropriate category
2. Classification of death

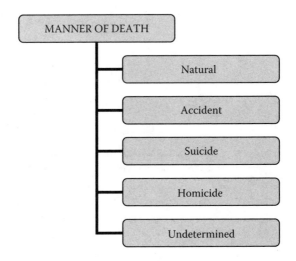

F. Mechanism of death: The *physiological derangement* produced by the cause of death that resulted in the death, such as

- Cardiac arrhythmia
- Septicemia
- Myocardial infarction
- Renal failure
- Arteriosclerosis
- Ruptured aneurysm
- Congestive heart failure

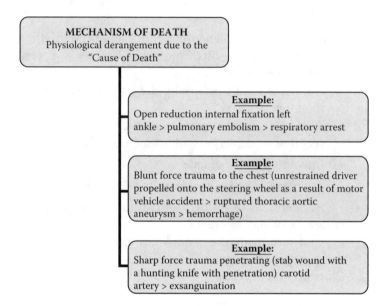

MECHANISM OF DEATH
Physiological derangement due to the
"Cause of Death"

Example:
Open reduction internal fixation left
ankle > pulmonary embolism > respiratory arrest

Example:
Blunt force trauma to the chest (unrestrained driver
propelled onto the steering wheel as a result of motor
vehicle accident > ruptured thoracic aortic
aneurysm > hemorrhage)

Example:
Sharp force trauma penetrating (stab wound with
a hunting knife with penetration) carotid
artery > exsanguination

II. Summary

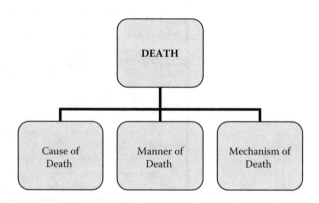

DEATH

Cause of Death | Manner of Death | Mechanism of Death

Bibliography

Brenner, J. (2002). *Forensic science: An illustrated dictionary.* Boca Raton, FL: CRC Press.

Clark, S. C., Ernst, M. F., Haglund, W. D., & Jentzen, J. M. (1996). *Medicolegal death investigator: A systematic training program for the professional death investigator, training text.* Big Springs, MI: Occupational Research and Assessment.

Cochran, M. (1999). The real meaning of patient-nurse confidentiality. *Critical Care Quarterly: Confronting Forensic Issues, 22*(1), 41–50.

Death investigation: A guide for scene investigators. (1996). Big Springs, MI: Occupational Research and Assessment.

Di Maio, V. J. M., & Dana, S. E. (2007). *Handbook of forensic pathology* (2nd ed.). Boca Raton, FL: CRC Press.

Dudley, M. H. (2003). *Forensic medical investigation: Certification exam questions.* Wichita, KS: Dudley.

Geberth, V. J. (1996). *Practical homicide investigation: Tactics, procedures, and forensic techniques* (3rd ed.). Boca, Raton, FL: CRC Press.

Girard, J. E. (2008). *Criminalistics: Forensic science and crime.* Sudbury, MA: Jones and Bartlett, pp. 9–12.

Goll-McGee, B. (1999). The role of the clinical forensic nurse in critical care. *Critical Care Quarterly: 22*(1), 8–17.

Hammer, R. M., Moynihan, B., & Pagliaro, E. M. (Eds.). (2006). *Forensic nursing: A Handbook for Practice.* Sudbury, MA: Jones and Bartlett, pp. 200–202.

Hoyt, C. A. (1999). Evidence recognition and collection in the clinical setting. *Critical Care Quarterly: 22*(1), 19–22.

James, S. H., & Nordby, J. J. (Eds.). (2005). *Forensic science: An introduction to scientific and investigative techniques.* Boca Raton, FL: CRC Press.

Lynch, V. (2006). *Forensic nursing.* St. Louis, MO: Mosby.

Nurses' legal handbook (5th ed.). (2004). Sudbury, MA: Jones and Bartlett.

Porth, C. M. (2002). *Pathophysiology: Concepts of altered health states* (6th ed.). Hagerstown, MD: Lippincott Williams & Wilkins.

Spitz, W. U., Spitz, D., & Clark, R. (Eds.). (2006). *Spitz and Fisher's medicolegal investigation of death: Guidelines for the application of pathology to crime investigation* (4th ed.). Springfield, IL: Thomas.

Sung Tz'u. *The washing away of wrongs: Science, medicine, and technology in East Asia 1.* McKnight, B. E. (Trans.). (1981). Ann Arbor, MI: Center for Chinese Studies, University of Michigan.

Winfrey, M.E., & Smith, A. R. (1999). The suspiciousness factor: Critical care nursing and forensics. *Critical Care Quarterly 22*(1), 1–6.

Crime Scene Investigation

8

MATTHIAS I. OKOYE

Contents

Introduction

Crime scene investigation is usually the beginning point for successful use of physical evidence by forensic scientists, forensic experts, and forensic laboratory and criminal investigators in evaluating crime scenes. It is important to properly manage and investigate the scene of a crime in the best possible manner. Successful and high-quality crime scene investigation is a simple and methodical process. It follows a set of principles, procedures that are reasonable and ensure that all physical evidence is discovered and investigated, with the result that justice is served.

Forensic science has a mark that is a significant element in efforts to solve crime while maintaining a high quality of justice. The value of physical evidence has been demonstrated in all aspects of criminal investigation, and law enforcement offices are becoming increasingly dependent on laboratory results for evidence not obtainable by other avenues or means of investigation. As science and technology continue to advance, the importance and the value of physical evidence in criminal investigation will also continue to expand. Usually, the decisions about the extent of physical evidence involvement in criminal investigation are not made by forensic scientists. In the crime scene search and the initial investigation stages, they are usually made by police officers, criminal investigators, or evidence technicians. In the adjudicative stages, the utilization of physical evidence obtained at crime scenes is usually by prosecutors and defense attorneys. There is no guarantee that either of these groups will sufficiently understand the potential or physical evidence and make proper decisions. As more police officers and attorneys acquire updated information and receive special training in forensic sciences, this situation will improve, enabling better use to be made of physical evidence.

The basic crime scene procedures include physical evidence recognition, documentation, proper collection, packaging, preservation, and finally scene reconstruction. Every crime scene is unique, and with experience, a crime scene investigator will be able to use this logical and systematic approach to investigate even the most challenging crime scenes to a useful conclusion.

Forensic nursing is now a well-developed specialty in forensic sciences. A well-trained forensic nurse should be able to understand the principles and procedures of crime scene investigation. This is because a forensic nurse should interact with other specialists and other experts in the field of forensic sciences and should be able to interact with police officers, prosecutors, defense lawyers, crime scene technicians, crime scene investigators, and other experts in the fields of forensic sciences during the process of investigating crimes and adjudicating criminal cases.

Definition of a Crime Scene

The only thing consistent about crime scenes is their inconsistency. Because of their diversity, crime scenes can be classified in many ways. Crime scenes can be classified according to the location of the original criminal activity. This classification of the crime scene labels the site of the original or first criminal activity as the primary crime scene, and any subsequent crime scenes are secondary. This classification does not infer any priority or importance to the scene but is simply a designation of sequence of locations. Another classification of crime scenes is based on size. Under this classification, a single microscopic crime scene is composed of many crime scenes. For example, a gunshot wound victim's body found in a field represents the following crime scenes within the overall crime scene of the field: the body's wounds and the ground around the body. The microscopic classification of the scene is more focused on the specific types of physical evidence found at microscopic crime scenes. Therefore, the microscopic crime scenes are the trace evidence on the body, gunshot residue around the wound, and the tire tread marks in the ground next to the body. Crime scenes can also be classified based on the type of crime committed, such as homicide, robbery, sexual assault, and so on; the crime scene condition could be used as a method of classification, such as organized or disorganized crime scenes; the physical location of the crime scene (indoors, outdoors, vehicle, etc.) can be used to classify crime scenes. The type of criminal behavior associated with the scene, including passive or active crime scenes, for example, can be used as another method of classification. Even with these classifications, no single definition adequately works for every crime scene. Ultimately, the scene is a combination of adaptation of the classifications that is determined by the investigator. The crime scene investigator must constantly evaluate and frequently change the defined area called the crime scene.

Utilization of and Information from Physical Evidence in Crime Scene Investigation and Reconstruction

The objectives of any crime scene investigation are usually to recognize, preserve, collect, interpret, and reconstruct all relevant physical evidence obtained at the crime scene. A forensic lab has the duty to examine the physical evidence to provide an investigator with information about the evidence in an effort to solve cases. The integration of the crime scene investigation with the forensic examination of the scene's physical evidence forms the basis of scientific crime scene investigation. The following are examples of types of information obtained from the examination of physical evidence in a criminal investigation:

1. Information on the corpus delicti of the crime. This is the determination of the essential facts of an investigation: the physical evidence, the patterns of the evidence, and the laboratory examination of the evidence. For example, the red-brown stains in a kitchen may be significant to an investigation but may be more relevant if their DNA matches that of a victim.
2. Information on the modus operandi. Criminals repeat their behavior, and a certain behavior becomes a criminal's "signature" or preferred

method of operation; for instance, burglars frequently gain entry into scenes using the same techniques, and burglars will use the same type of ignition devices repeatedly.

3. Linkage of persons, scenes, and objects.
4. Proving or disproving witness statements. Crime scene patterns or patterned physical evidence (bloodstain patterns, fingerprints, gunshot residue, etc.) are especially well suited for determination of credibility of witnesses and suspects.
5. Identification of suspects. Forensic examination is usually a process of steps that includes recognition, identification, individualization, and reconstruction utilizing specific materials and comparing the materials to known physical evidence, such as DNA and fingerprints.
6. Identification of unknown substances. Good examples are the identification of drugs, poisons, and even bacteria, such as anthrax.
7. Reconstruction of a crime. This is usually the final step in the forensic examination process; the crime scene investigator is frequently more interested in how a crime occurred than identifying or individualizing the evidence at the scene.
8. Provision of investigative leads. Physical evidence can usually provide direct information for an investigator, such as a footware impression that shows the manufacturer, size, or type of shoe worn by a suspect.

Forensic Nursing and Crime Scene Investigations

Crime scene investigation is not a mechanical process relegated to technicians who go through a series of steps and procedures to process a crime scene. It is usually a dynamic process that requires an active approach by the scene investigator, who must be aware of the linkage, principle of the evidence, use scene analysis and definition techniques, and be able to offer an opinion on the reconstruction of the scene. Scientific crime scene investigation is based on the scientific method, and it is usually methodical and systematic. It is logical and scientific and utilizes forensic techniques applied in physical evidence examinations to develop investigative leads that will ultimately solve a crime. The steps utilized in scientific crime scene investigations include (1) recognition of the physical evidence obtained, which includes scene survey, documentation at the scene, and collection and preservation of physical evidence; (2) identification of the physical evidence, which involves comparison testing; (3) individualization, which includes evaluation and interpretation of the physical evidence collected; (4) crime scene recognition, which includes reporting and presentation of the crime scene.

General Crime Scene

Crime Scene Procedures

The general crime scene procedures can be subdivided into the following areas: (1) scene management; (2) the duties of first respondent law enforcement officers; (3) securing the crime scene; (4) crime scene survey; (5) crime scene documentation; and (6) crime scene searches.

Scene Management

The management of the crime scene is usually teamwork performed by investigators and crime scene personnel and by the combined use of techniques and procedures recognizing the power of crime scenes, physical evidence, records, and witnesses. The four major distinctive components of crime scene management, which are interrelated, are information management, manpower management, technology management, and logistics management. It is important to note that deficiencies, negligence, and overemphasis of any of these components will imperil or disadvantage the overall crime scene investigation.

Duties of First Respondent Law Enforcement

The first respondents at the crime scene are usually police officers, fire department personnel, or emergency medical personnel. They are the only people who view the crime scene in its original condition. Their actions at the crime scene provide the basis for the successful or unsuccessful resolution of the investigation. They must perform their duties and remember that they begin the process that links victims to suspects to crime scenes and must never destroy the links. The first responders must therefore always have open and objective minds when approaching a crime scene. On arrival, safety is a primary concern, and when the scene and the victim are safe, the first responders must begin to thoroughly document their observations and actions at the scene. As soon as possible, they should initiate crime scene security measures. Their duties are to assist the victim; search for and arrest the suspect if the suspect is still on the scene; detain all witnesses because they possess valuable information about the crime scene; protect the crime scene; and note and communicate to crime scene investigators all movements and alterations made to the crime scene.

Securing the Crime Scene

To secure the crime scene, a Locard exchange principle (LEP) is the basis for linking physical evidence from or to the victim, suspect, and crime scene. Anyone entering a crime scene can alter or change the scene and its evidence, so access to a crime scene must be restricted and, if possible, prevented except for essential crime scene personnel. Any physical barriers like vehicles or tapes that help protect the crime scene must be established as soon as possible by the first responders. After scene barriers have been established, an officer should be designated as the scene security officer, and the officer should be responsible for preventing entrance into the crime scene by curious onlookers. A contamination log or security log should be kept to record all entries to and exits from acute areas of the crime scene. Use of a multilevel security approach can successfully prevent untoward entries, and it is important to establish a multilevel crime scene security: Level 1, overall scene security for restriction of general public; Level 2, restriction to official business; Level 3, target area, has the highest security and command center as well as a public relations area for dealing with the media.

Surveying the Crime Scene

Crime scene survey is a major part of the crime scene investigator's duty. When the crime scene investigator has arrived at the crime scene and scene security has been evaluated, the preliminary scene survey should be done. This is usually called a "work-through." A crime scene investigator and the first responder will usually perform the survey together. The lead investigator or detective, if available, can also benefit from participation. Use of instant photography for preliminary documentation can be helpful. Video is usually encouraged. The survey is the first examination or orientation by the crime scene investigator, and these guidelines should be followed:

1. Use the work-through to mentally prepare a reconstruction theory that can and should be changed as the scene investigation progresses.
2. Note any transient (temporary) or conditional (the result of an action) evidence that requires immediate protection or processing.
3. Be aware of weather conditions and take precautions if anticipated.
4. Note all points of entry or exit or paths of travel within the crime scene that may require additional protection; be aware of alteration or contamination of these areas by first responder personnel.
5. Record initial observations of who, what, where, when, and how.
6. Assess the scene for personnel, precautions, or equipment that will be needed and notify superior officers or other agencies as required.

Crime Scene Documentation

After a crime scene has been evaluated by the preliminary scene survey, the crime scene's condition must be documented. Documentation is the most important step in the processing of the crime scene. The purpose of documentation is to record the condition of the crime scene and its physical evidence permanently. It is the most time-consuming activity at the scene and requires the investigator to remain organized and systematic throughout the process. Innovation and originality are also needed. The four major tasks of documentation are note taking, videography, photography, and sketching. All four are necessary, and none is an adequate substitute for the other. Documentation, in all its various forms, begins with initial involvement of the investigator. The documentation never stops; it may slow, but the need for documentation remains constant.

Note Taking Effective notes as part of an investigation provide a written record of all the crime scene activities. The notes are taken as the activities are completed to prevent possible memory loss if notes are made at a later time. Accurate crime scene note taking is crucial at the initial crime scene investigation and also essential for subsequent investigations. A general guideline for note taking is to consider who, what, when, why, and how and specifically include notification information (date and time, method of notification, and information received); arrival information; scene description; victim description, and crime scene team.

Videography Videotaping of the crime scene is highly recommended. It is now a routine documentation procedure, and its acceptance is widespread due to the three-dimensional portrayal of the scene and increased availability of the newest equipment with user-friendly features like zoom lens and compact size. Jurors accept and expect crime scenes to be videotaped and videographed. Videography of the crime scene should follow the scene survey. The videotaping of the crime scene is an orientation format. The operator should remain objective in recording the crime scene. The videotape should not show members of the crime scene team or their equipment. It should not be narrated or include audio discussion of subjective information at the scene. Videotaping of crime scenes is a valuable tool that allows clear perception that is often not possible with the other documentation tags.

Photography Photography of the crime scene is useful and provides a true and accurate pictorial record of the crime scene and physical evidence present. Still photography records the initial condition of the scene. It provides investigators and others with a record that can be analyzed or examined subsequent to the scene investigation and serves as a permanent record for legal concerns. Photography of the crime scene is normally done immediately following videography of the scene or after preliminary scene survey. A systematic, organized method for recording the crime scene, victim, and physical evidence is best achieved by proceeding from the general to specific guidelines. Adherence to these guidelines is important. Every photograph taken at the crime scene must be recorded in a photo log. The log should show the time and date the photograph was taken, the roll number, exposure number, camera settings (F-stop, shutter speed, etc.); an indication of distance to the subject; type of photograph taken; and a brief description. The following is a list of basic equipment needed for photographic documentation of crime scenes: camera (35-mm is the most common type); normal lens (50–60 mm); wide-angle lens (28–35 mm); close-up lens with accessories; electronic flash with cord; tripod, film (color and black and white); label materials (cards, pens, markers); scales or rulers; flashlight; extra batteries; and photo log sheets. Digital cameras also are helpful, and they have all the above features.

Sketching the Crime Scene   The final task in documentation of a crime scene is sketching. All the previous tags for documentation record the crime scene without regard to size or measurement of the scene and its physical evidence. Sketching the crime scene is the assignment of units of measurement or correct perspective to the overall scene and the relevant physical evidence identified within the scene. The two basic types of sketches made during crime scene investigation are rough sketches and final and finished sketches. The sketches should include the overhead or bird's-eye view sketch and the elevation or side view sketch. Occasionally, a combination perspective sketch called a cross-projection sketch is used to integrate an overhead sketch with an elevation sketch. Three-dimensional sketches and scale models are not common, but they can be used as forms of crime scene documentation.

Digital image technology provides a crime scene investigator with powerful new tools for capturing, analyzing, and storing records of the crime scene and its physical evidence. These digital imaging tools compliment the traditional video and still photography used in crime scene documentation. The advantages of digital imaging include instant access to the images, integration into existing electronic technologies, and no need for expensive film-processing equipment and darkrooms. Among the disadvantages is the inadmissibility in court because of image manipulation. However, it is important to remember that the investigator testifies to production and the availability of these images. Written and implemented policies and procedures for using digital images can eliminate the disadvantage listed. The law enforcement community agrees that digital imaging in crime scene documentation can best be used as a supplemental technique and not to replace completely the traditional techniques.

Crime Scene Searches

The preliminary crime scene search is an initial quasi search for physical evidence present at the crime scene. It is usually an attempt to note obvious items of evidence, and it is done for orientation purposes before the documentation begins After scene documentation as described is completed, a more efficient and effective search for less-obvious or overlooked items of evidence must be done. This intensive search is done before the evidence is collected and packaged. If any new items of evidence are found, then they must be subjected to the same documentation task already completed.

Crime scene search patterns may vary, but they share a common goal of providing organization and a systematic structure to ensure that no items of physical evidence are missed or lost. No single method applies to specific types of scenes. An experienced crime scene investigator will be able to recognize and adapt the site method that best suits the situation or the crime scene. It is important to use an established method. Most investigators commonly employ site methods and geometric patterns. The six patterns are link, line or straight, grid, zone, wheel or ray, and spiral. Each has advantages and disadvantages, and some are better suited for outdoor or indoor crime scenes. The link method is based on linkage theory, and it is the most common and productive method. One type of evidence leads to another, and it is experiential, logical, and systematic and works with large and small indoor and outdoor scenes. The line or strip method works best on large outdoor scenes and requires a search coordinator. Searchers are usually volunteers who require preliminary instructions. The grid method is a modified double-line search and is effective but time consuming. The zoom method is best used on scenes with defined zooms or areas and is effective in houses or buildings; the teams are assigned small zones for searching. Combined with other methods, it is good for warrant searches. The wheel or ray method is used for special situations and has limited application; it is best used in small, circular crime scenes. The spiral method applies inward or outward spirals, is best used on crime scenes with no physical barriers (open water, etc.), and requires the ability to trace a regular pattern with fixed diameters; it has limited applications.

Types of Physical Evidence at Crime Scenes

Virtually any type of material can become physical evidence. It may be as small as a dust particle or as large as an airplane. It can be in the form of gas or liquid. In general, a crime scene investigator may encounter the following four categories of physical evidence: transient, patterned, conditional, and transfer.

Transient Evidence

Transient evidence is the type of physical evidence that is temporary in nature. This form of physical evidence can be easily changed or lost. The most commonly encountered transient evidence includes the following: odor, temperature, imprints and indentations, and markings. Odor includes odors of feet, perfume, carbon monoxide, cyanide, body, urine, and cigarettes. Temperature includes that in a room, in a car, of coffee or tea, of a cadaver, or of a fire. Imprints and indentations include tooth marks on meltable material or tire marks on wet beach sand.

Patterned Evidence

Patterned evidence is generally produced by a physical pattern between persons or objects. There are a variety of physical patterns that can be found at crime scenes. Most of these physical patterns are in the forms of imprints, indentations, striations, markings, fractures, or depositions. Patterned evidence has not attracted as much attention, and its potential has not been fully realized. Patterned evidence at crime scenes, however, is extremely valuable in the reconstruction of events. It can often be used to prove or disprove a suspect's alibi or a witness version of what took place, to associate or disassociate the involvement of persons or objects in particular events, or to provide investigators with new leads. The following is a list of patterns commonly found at different crime scenes: blood spatter; glass fracture; fire burns; furniture position; projectile trajectory; track trail; tire or skid marks; clothing or articles; modus operandi; and powder residue. The reconstruction from blood stain patterns has long been a neglected area but has received more attention recently. Blood stain patterns are often at least as valuable as serological analysis in solving cases. Much can be learned from a careful examination and study of blood stain patterns; some examples include the approximate speed of blood droplets; the approximate direction of travel of blood droplets; the approximate distance between the blood source and the target surface; approximate angle of incidence of blood droplets; positions of persons involved from radial spatter patterns; arc from swinging weapons; interpretation of patterns from artery spurts; determination of blood trails and their direction; interpretation of blood flow patterns and pools; interpretation of contact transfer, swipe, and wiping patterns; reconstruction of shootings from blood patterns; estimation of elapsed time after blood has been deposited; fallen, projected, or impact pattern determination; reconstruction of sequence of events; and determination of geometric and special relationships.

Similarly, glass fracture patterns involve broken glass at crime scenes, which can sometimes aid in reconstruction, providing information about the events that took place, and assist in proving or disproving an alibi or a witness story. The most common types of information that can be obtained by studying glass fracture patterns are the direction of application of impact force; the approximate force of impact; the approximate angle of impact; whether a window was broken inward or not; the time of glass fracture; sequence of shots from bullet holes in glass; direction of shots from bullet holes in glass; angle of shots from bullet holes in glass; type of projectile used from holes in glass; fire temperature from the degree of melting of glass fragments; fire travel from melted glass; types of breaks from examination of glass fractures. The use of fracture patterns in crime scene reconstruction relies on careful observation, documentation, and study of radial and concentric fractures of glass. Other information is obtained by analysis of rib marks, special relationships, crack marks, and the condition of melted glass.

Fire burn patterns often provide information on the various factors that led to or caused the fire. Detailed study of the burn patterns generally helps determine the point of origin, direction of fire travel, degree of damage by a fire, and possible presence of acid. The following is a partial list of common patterns found at fire scenes: inverted cone or "V" pattern; multiple origin burn patterns; low burn pattern configuration; depth of charring patterns; direction of charring pattern positions; trailer patterns; smoke stain patterns; material melting patterns; concrete spalling patterns; and alligator ring patterns. Every fire forms a certain pattern that is determined chiefly by the configuration of the environment and the availability of combustible material. From a study of a fire pattern and the determination of any deviations from normal or expected patterns, an experienced investigator can reconstruct the fire scene.

Projectile trajectory patterns are useful in crime scene investigations. Studies of bullet trajectories combined with knowledge of scene geometry, witness statements, and other physical evidence can assist in reconstruction of a shooting case. Correct interpretation of projectile trajectory patterns can help in establishing the following information: direction of the projectile; position of the shooter and the target; possible estimation of range; number of shots fired; possible sequence of multiple shots; possible angle of shots; entry and exit holes made by shots; primary and secondary projectiles; possible projectile deflections; and position of intermediate or intermediary targets. Studies of projectile trajectory patterns can assist in locating and recovering bullets or cartridge cases for analysis as well.

Tire and skid mark patterns are often seen at outdoor crime scenes and can provide important reconstruction information. The value of skid mark patterns in traffic accident reconstructions is well known and documented. However, the use of these patterns in crime scene investigation and reconstruction is often neglected. These markings can yield information about the number and type of vehicles involved, the possible speed of travel, the direction of travel, whether brakes were applied, and whether any turns were made.

Powder residue patterns help in investigations of shooting cases and sometimes play an important role in deciding the answers to questions about such things as whether the case represents a homicide, suicide, or accidental death; the muzzle-to-target distance; the trajectory of the fired bullet; whether a suspect recently discharged or handled a weapon; maximum distance from victim to perpetrator; and the relative locations and relationships between multiple targets. Pattern evidence found at crime scenes should be carefully recorded, measured, documented, and interpreted. Some pattern evidence can also be collected for further analysis.

Conditional Evidence

Conditional physical evidence commonly encountered at the crime scene is generally produced by an event or action. Such evidence, if not documented correctly, may result in changes or loss. Conditional evidence such as light, smoke, fire, location, and vehicle is extremely important for reconstruction of events.

Transfer Evidence

Transfer evidence is generally produced by physical contact of persons, objects, or between persons or objects. Transfer evidence can be classified from several different perspectives. Some of the resulting classifications are more practical than others. However, no single one is completely satisfactory because none can take all the different perspectives into account.

Crime Scene Reconstruction

Crime scene reconstruction is the process of determining or eliminating the events that occurred at the crime scene by analysis of the crime scene appearance, the locations and positions of the physical evidence, and forensic laboratory examination of physical evidence. It involves scientific crime scene investigation, interpretation of pattern evidence at the scene, laboratory testing of the physical evidence, systematic study of related case information, and the logical formation of a theory.

Crime scene reconstruction is based on scientific experimentation and experience of the investigator. Its steps and stages follow scientific basic principles, theory formulation, and logical methodology. It usually incorporates all investigative information with physical evidence analysis and interpretation molded into a reasonable explanation of the criminal activity and related events. Logic, careful observation, and considerable experience, both in crime scene investigation and in forensic testing of physical evidence, are necessary for proper interpretation, analysis, and crime scene investigation.

Stages in Crime Scene Reconstruction

Crime scene reconstruction is a scientific fact-gathering process that involves a set of actions or stages:

1. Data collection. All information or documentation obtained at the crime scene from the victim or witnesses is critical
2. All data concerning the data from physical evidence, patterns, and impressions, condition of the victim, and so on will be reviewed, organized, and studied.
3. Conjecture. Before edited analysis of the evidence is accomplished, a possible explanation or conjecture of the actions involved in the

crime scene may be formulated. It is not a fixed explanation or even the only possible explanation at this point.

4. Hypothesis formulation. Additional accumulation of data is based on examination of physical evidence and continuing investigation; scene examination and inspection of the evidence; interpretation of blood stain and impression patterns, gunshot residue patterns, fingerprint evidence; and analysis of trace evidence will lead to the formulation of the reconstruction hypothesis.

5. Testing. After a hypothesis has been developed, additional testing or experimentation must be done to confirm or disprove the overall interpretation or specific aspects of the hypothesis; this stage includes comparison of samples collected at the scene with nonstandards, microscopic examinations, chemical analysis, and other testing. Controlled experiments of possible scenarios of physical activities must be done to corroborate the hypothesis.

6. Theory formulation. Additional information may be acquired in the investigation about the condition of the victim or the suspect, the activities of the individual involved, accuracy of witness accounts, and other information about the circumstances of the event. When the hypothesis has been thoroughly tested and verified by analysis, the reconstruction theory can be formulated.

A reconstruction can only be as good as the information provided. Information may come from the crime scene, physical evidence, records, statements, witness accounts, and known data. The information-gathering process described and its use in crime scene reconstruction show the scientific nature of scene reconstruction and, as a result, allow its successful use by investigators.

Bibliography

Bevel, T., & Gardner, R. (2002) *Bloodstain pattern analysis with an introduction to crime scene reconstruction* (2nd ed.). Boca Raton, FL: CRC Press.

Deforest, P., Gaensslen, R., & Lee, H. (1983). *Forensic science: An introduction to criminalistics*. New York: McGraw-Hill.

Di Maio, V. (1999). *Gunshot wounds: Practical aspects of firearms, ballistics, and forensic techniques* (2nd ed.). Boca Raton, FL: CRC Press.

Dix, J. (1999). *Handbook for death scene investigations*. Boca Raton, FL: CRC Press.

Fisher, B. (2000). *Techniques of crime scene investigation* (6th ed.). Boca Raton, FL: CRC Press.

Lee, H., et al. (1994). *Crime scene investigation*. Taoyuan, Taiwan: Central Police University Press.

Lee, H., & Harris H. (2000). *Physical evidence in forensic sciences*. Tucson, AZ: Lawyers and Judges.

Technical Working Group on Crime Scene Investigation. (2000, January). *Crime scene investigation: A guide for law enforcement.* Washington, DC: National Institute of Justice and U.S. Department of Justice.

Technical Working Group on Fire/Arson Scene Investigation. (2000, June). *Fire and arson scene evidence: A guide for public safety personnel.* Washington, DC: National Institute of Justice and U.S. Department of Justice.

Forensic Nursing Crime Scene Investigation

9

DONNA GARBACZ BADER

I. The Crime Scene
   A. Crime scene classifications
      1. Crime location
         a. Original criminal activity: Primary crime scene
         b. Subsequent crime scene: Secondary crime scene
      2. Size of crime scene
         a. Macroscopic crime scene: composite of numerous crime scenes, for example:

            A body

            The inflicted wounds

            The area surrounding the body

         b. Microscopic crime scene: the trace evidence on the body, for example:

            Gunshot residue

            Blood

            Clear body fluids

      3. Type of crime
         a. Homicide
         b. Sexual assault
         c. Robbery
         d. Nonfatal physical assault (e.g., beating with a blunt or sharp object)
         e. Organized criminal offender
            (1) Crime is preplanned
            (2) Rehearses crime and all options taken into the planning of the crime
            (3) Familiar with the type of injury to inflict, the location, gender
            (4) Leaves little evidence for perpetrator identification
            (5) Selects victims who cannot be associated with the perpetrator

       f. Disorganized criminal offender
- (1) Impulsive
- (2) Uses readily available tools to commit the offense
- (3) Lacks planning, which results in a scene that is chaotic and messy
- (4) Lacks control of the victim, resulting in evidence that links the crime to the perpetrator

4. Site of the crime
   a. Indoors
   b. Outdoors
   c. Vehicle
   d. Any area within a hospital
      - (1) Victim's or patient's room
      - (2) Emergency room
      - (3) Radiology
      - (4) Cafeteria
      - (5) Surgery
   e. Parking garage
   f. Can occur in any environment

II. Crime Scene Investigation
   A. Concepts
      1. The primary objective of all crime scene investigations is to identify, collect, and preserve all the physical evidence at the scene.
      2. Safety of all crime scene personnel must be maintained.
      3. The integrity of the body must be maintained.
      4. Maintaining the integrity of the crime scene and the identification, collection, and preservation of physical evidence are the basis of crime scene investigation.
      5. Crime scene investigation is a conscientious, meticulous, systematic, and lengthy process.
      6. Use of the nursing process (scientific method) and knowledge of forensic science techniques are involved.
      7. Investigation is based on the Locard exchange principle.
      8. Documentation should be done in an orderly, objective manner to ensure the chain of custody and admissibility in any legal action.
   B. Crime scene procedures for the *living victim*
      1. The *first* priority is to provide any immediate medical care, call for medical assistance, and maintain the victim's health and safety until assistance arrives, for example:

      a. Apply pressure to an artery or large area of bleeding.

      b. Begin and maintain cardiopulmonary resuscitation.

      c. Call for help.

      d. Call a code.

      e. Call 911.

2. Once the victim is assessed and stable, provide basic comfort.

3. Identify the victim.

4. Avoid moving the victim unless medical and environmental conditions warrant moving to a safe location or to a health care facility for medical treatment and care.

5. Secure the crime scene.

6. Establish that the crime scene is secure.

      a. Close the door if in a health care facility such as an emergency room or any area where the crime occurred.

      b. Provide privacy if in a private home, apartment, public building, or outdoor environment.

      c. If possible, interview the victim and request all other individuals to exit the area; this includes family, friends, law enforcement, or any other authorized or unauthorized persons unless the victim specifically requests the person's presence.

      d. For victims who are blind, deaf, physically or mentally challenged, or unable to speak the general language, the forensic nurse should make every effort to contact the appropriate social service agency for assistance.

         (1) When the victim insists that a specific person, such as the victim's sign language coach, the primary caregiver for the physically or mentally challenged victim, or a friend or family member who acts as the victim's interpreter, remain during the interview or if a frightened blind victim refuses to speak with anyone unless a specific individual is contacted, it is essential that the forensic nurse assess each situation on an individual basis and determine the most appropriate course of action.

         (2) The question of allowing a requested individual to stay with the victim requires careful assessment by the forensic nurse based on each individual situation.

         (3) If the forensic nurse suspects possible domestic violence and the victim insists that a specific person

remain during the interview, the nurse should consider all possible avenues and request the individual
to allow for a private interview as the most effective
means of caring for the patient (e.g., possible domestic violence when the spouse or companion remains
with the victim).

7. Prevent alteration or any disruption of the victim's body and
the crime scene to preserve as much evidence as possible.

8. For the forensic nurse working with a victim of trauma or
violent crime who has survived, it is imperative to know the
policies and procedures regarding victim interview and evidence collection, and preservation.

9. Policies and procedures are developed by health care facilities, law enforcement agencies, and judicial system professionals regarding providing physical and psychiatric care,
notification of appropriate agency or agencies, evidence collection, preservation, victim interview, suspected perpetra-
tion interview, and required documentation.

C. Documentation at the crime scene: living forensics
  1. The survivor
     a. Each victim admitted as a forensic case may require dif-
        ferent assessment data; however, the main requirement
        regardless of the injury is accurate documentation.
     b. The victims identified as forensic cases are those victims of

        Adult sexual or physical abuse

        Child sexual or physical abuse

        Assault and battery

        Suspect traumatic injuries such as gunshot wounds, sharp
        force injuries (injuries resulting from a sharp object such
        as a knife), blunt force injuries (injuries resulting from a
        blunt object such as a baseball bat, fist)

        A traumatic "accidental" injury (fall from a ladder; fall
        on a wet surface; injury to a large vessel such as the femo-
        ral artery or vein, carotid artery, radial artery)

        Elder sexual or physical abuse

        Sexual or physical abuse of the mentally challenged or
        physically disabled

        Any identified traumatic injury suspect regarding
        whether the injury was accidental or intentional

     c. Health care facilities and all law enforcement agencies
        have policies and procedures that are established based

on local and state statutes and federal laws regarding documentation and identification, collection, and preservation of evidence in any forensic case or suspect forensic case.

d. Knowledge and adherence to these policies and procedures will provide the victim and those affected by the criminal act with the knowledge that they will receive justice.

e. It is important for the forensic nurse to understand that documentation in written form, photographs, and videos should be concise and focus on the victim and injuries.

f. All photographs should be dated, timed, identify the photographer, and describe the photograph; the degree of description is dependent on the photograph. Maintain a chain of custody for all photographs taken as defined by established policy.

g. Any and all videos should be dated, timed, identify the person taking the video, and have a verbal description at the beginning of the video regarding the purpose for the video, stating the time and date, and identifying the victim (either by name or ID number). Maintain a chain of custody for any and all videos taken as defined by established policy.

2. Documentation Points:

- Utilize your five senses: what do you hear, feel, see, smell, and taste? Odors may stimulate the taste buds, producing a taste reflective of the odor for the forensic nurse; for example, the smell of a very sweet odor on a victim's breath may stimulate the bitter or sweet taste buds on the tongue of the investigator.
- Answer five basic questions: Who? What? When? Where? Why?
- Contact established with victim: time, date, location.
- Mode of arrival.
- Detailed description of initial contact, voice annotation, clothing, verbal and nonverbal behavior, hygiene.
- Develop a nursing process as an organized method of determining victim priorities and immediate interventions.
- Name and relationship of any individual accompanying the victim.
- Detailed description of accompanying individual to include voice annotation, verbal and nonverbal behavior, and any additional information that may relate to the victim and injuries.

Continued

- Obtain written consent for medical treatment and care.
- Obtain written consent for photography, examination, and evidence collection.
- If required, obtain written or verbal consent for agency contact and referral.
- Photographs of victim, injuries, evidence with related written documentation.
- Document victim statement as stated using quotation marks to indicate exact victim verbiage
- Documentation should be complete and legible; storage of documents is the responsibility of the records department; making sure your documentation is complete is your responsibility. If in doubt, "Write it out."
- Do not worry about how much time it takes to produce a report, how much paper will be used, how much space it will take in the computer file; whatever you need to chart, chart it.
- Remember: Make it objective, legible, with correct grammar and spelling.
- If any evidence was removed or moved prior to being photographed, this needs to be documented (e.g., the victim's clothing, cleaning and bandaging the injury, if the injury is scored as minor and would not alter the victim's immediate health).
- *Do not* reintroduce evidence once it has been moved or removed for the purpose of photography; for example, do not request that the victim redress, do not undo a wound that has been cleaned and bandaged or replace any additional item or items that have been collected as evidence.
- Update the nursing process to include follow-up intervention and evaluation regarding the victim's rehabilitation/health maintenance process.

    D. Crime scene procedure for the *deceased victim*:
        1. Secure the crime scene.
            a. Close the door to the entrance of the victim's room.
            b. Pull the curtain and request that any family or visitors leave the room.
            c. Prevent any intrusion into the area of the crime scene by either roping or taping off the area.
            d. If the body is exposed to the environment, it may be necessary to cover the body to prevent any disintegration

or loss of evidence until such time as the investigation may begin.

A plastic cover or some waterproof cover is preferred if the body is located in an environment that is wet (such as from rain, activated fire sprinklers, snow, fog, mist, or any other environments where the body may be exposed to continuous moisture).

A cloth or paper covering may be appropriate if the body is to remain at the scene for a prolonged period of time in an environment where there is no immediate environmental threat, such as an enclosed room, tent, or any enclosed area.

This will prevent or decrease the possibility of introducing unrelated materials (such as insects, rodents, fibers, dust, saliva) to the body or the immediate area surrounding the body.

Covering the body may also decrease any deterioration of material already present on the body and the surrounding area.

e. Do not move the body unless absolutely necessary to maintain the integrity of the body or to maintain the safety of the staff or investigative team (e.g., caused by an unsafe building, an actively burning area, deteriorating environmental conditions, possible airborne or toxic contaminants, possible additional insult to the body and the investigative team by the perpetrator).

f. Remove all nonessential individuals from immediate area.

g. Notify the official agency/supervisory personnel.

(1) Charge nurse.

(2) House supervisor.

(3) Physician.

(4) Local law enforcement (e.g., police, state police, sheriff).

(5) Family, if known.

(6) Next of kin, if known.

(7) If the identity of the victim is in question or unknown, one member of the team should be assigned to investigate the identity of the victim (e.g., examine a wallet, check for any identifying markings, review the medical record, interview the individual who accompanied the victim to the hospital, locate and interviewing the taxi driver who transported the victim to the hospital).

        (8) If the unidentified victim is found in an area where identification is not required (e.g., public building, theater, store, public park), the investigator may need to conduct interviews within the surrounding area where the body was located.

   h. On arrival of appropriate law enforcement personnel, the first responder should

       (1) Provide identification by name, agency, time of arrival

       (2) Brief the agency representative (e.g., lead investigator)

       (3) Provide time of arrival, scene description, condition of deceased, and any activity conducted by the forensic nurse prior to the arrival of agency personnel

2. On notification for assistance, the forensic nurse death investigator must observe all rules and regulations at the crime scene site. On arrival at the scene, the forensic nurses should

   a. Establish contact with official agency representative responsible for managing the crime scene

   b. Establish scene safety prior to entering the investigation scene

   c. Develop a nursing process as an organization tool to prioritize your crime scene investigation process

   d. Assess and establish physical boundaries

   e. Utilize personal protective safety devices, such as cover suit, goggles, shoe covers, protective eyewear, head cover, and any additional protective materials based on established policy

   f. Obtain clearance or authorization to enter the scene from the appropriate individual

   g. Protect the integrity of the scene and the evidence to the extent possible from contamination or loss of evidence

3. Confirm the status of the victim.

4. Follow established policy/procedures regarding deposition of the body and evidence.

5. Conduct an overview of the entire scene.

6. Review with law enforcement to determine the need for a search warrant.

7. Identify valuable or fragile evidence.

8. Every effort should be made to photograph the body and any and all evidence on and around the body and crime scene.

   a. Photography is a recognized and established procedure for all crime scene investigation; without photographs it may be difficult for even the best evidence to stand up in court. Nothing describes the scene and the victim as well as a picture.

   b. The standard in any crime investigation is visual recording of facts; anything else is basically unacceptable.

9. Determine the investigative procedure based on established policy and procedures.

10. Establish a chain of custody.

11. Place decedent's hands and feet in unused clean paper bags and tape the bag opening with a wood fiber tape such as masking tape; adhesive tape should not be used as it is made from a petroleum base and may melt if the environment is hot, may cause skin breakdown or peeling, and may disintegrate evidence left on the skin. Wood-based tape may also cause some postmortem skin injury; however, it does not cause as much skin damage as the petroleum-based tape.

12. Collect all trace evidence before transporting the body; exceptions may include immediate danger to the body and investigative team.

   a. Follow local, jurisdictional, state, and federal statutory laws for the collection of evidence to ensure that it will be admissible in a court of law. Develop a nursing process as an organized method of determining victim priorities and immediate interventions.

13. Update the nursing process to follow up on long-term goals and interventions, including autopsy report; toxicology and other laboratory reports; crisis intervention for investigative team; status of suspected or unsuspected perpetrator, family members, community members; spectator interviews.

  E. Death scene investigation documentation

- Make notification by phone, personal verbal contact, intercom page.
- Provide name of the individual if contact made by phone.
- Arrival at the scene should include time, date, location.
- Identify lead investigator and document related account of incident.
- Utilize your five senses: what do you hear, feel, see, smell, and taste? Taste can be affected by visual, auditory, olfactory, and touch senses.
- Certain odors may stimulate the taste buds, producing a taste reflective of the odor for the forensic nurse (e.g., the smell of a decomposing body may stimulate a bitter taste on the tongue of the investigator or may produce other physical symptoms).

Continued

- Answer five basic questions: Who? What? When? Where? Why?
- Indicate confirmation of death by the forensic nurse or the medical examiner if present at the scene.
- If the scene is outdoors, document weather conditions, any safety issues, and any issues requiring immediate action (e.g., immediate removal of the body prior to any documentation, fire, natural disasters, human-made disasters).
- Describe the scene, location of the body, the body, the injuries.
- If evidence has been moved or removed prior to photography, it needs to be documented.
- *Do not* reintroduce the body or other evidence once it has been moved or removed.
- Document visible physical and fragile evidence.
- All photographs should be dated and time indicated by the camera used, and the name of the photographer should be noted.
- The use of a photo log provides a complete and acceptable form of evidence documentation.
- The use of an evidence log provides a complete and acceptable form of evidence documentation.
- Any and all initials used should be identified (e.g., J.J. would be identified as Jane Jones, RN).
- Document custodians of the evidence, the agency or agencies responsible for collection of specific types of evidence, and evidence collection priority for fragile/fleeting evidence.
- Document the collection of all evidence by recording the evidence location at the scene, time of collection, and time and location of disposition for the chain of custody.
- Document the names of all individuals involved in the investigation or present at the scene.
- Document the deposition of the body (e.g., the facility, such as a funeral home, hospital mortuary, or separate medical examiner facility, where the body will be maintained until an autopsy is performed by the medical examiner, forensic pathologist, or a pathologist with experience performing forensic autopsies).
- Indicate the name of the individual receiving the body, the time and date the body was released, the type of transportation for body transport.
- Document all interviews conducted with family members, friends, community members, spectators, or others.

1. Visual record

PHOTOGRAPH / VIDEO LOG

CASE NUMBER _____

Item-Number	Time	Date: Spell Out	Content	Location	Initials
Initials:	Name/Title:				
Initials:	Name/Title:				
Initials:	Name/Title:				

Log developed by Donna Garbacz Bader.

2. Evidence log

DEATH SCENE INVESTIGATION EVIDENCE LOG
CASE NUMBER _____

Date: Spell Out	Military Time	Evidence/Container	Location	Initials

Initials:	Name/Title:
Initials:	Name/Title:
Initials:	Name/Title:

Log developed by Donna Garbacz Bader.

3. Evidence tag
    a. An individual evidence tag needs to be completed for every piece of evidence collected.
    b. Evidence tag information may be imprinted on evidence collection containers (e.g., paper bags, plastic bags and containers, coolers, or any containers used for the purpose of evidence collection).
    c. Individual evidence tags may also be used and attached to the evidence container after completion.

Evidence

Date:_____Time:_____

Collected by_____

Agency_____

Case Number_____ Log Item Number_____

Description_____

_____

_____

Location_____

_____

_____

Container_____

_____

_____

Comments_____

_____

_____

Chain of Custody

Received From_____

Received by_____

Reason for Transfer_____

_____

Date_____Time_____

Received From_____

Received By_____

Date_____Time_____

Reason for Transfer_____

Received From _____

Received by_____

Date_____Time_____

Reason for Transfer_____

Initials: Name:

Initials: Name:

Initials: Name:

Created by Donna Garbacz Bader.

F. Forensic nurse crime scene investigation responsibilities

- Recognize that all crime scenes are unique.
- Recognize that all victims are individuals.
- Protect the crime scene.
- Preserve physical evidence.
- Draw or diagram an injury, evidence, the scene.
- If drawing is not a skill that the forensic nurse possesses, photography or a written description may be more descriptive.
- Collect and submit the evidence for scientific examination.
- Physical evidence plays a critical role in the investigation and resolution of a suspected criminal act and prosecution of suspected perpetrator.
- Legal significance of evidence is dependent on objective, thorough, and meticulous approach to the investigation.
- The forensic nurse should approach each crime scene investigation as if it will be the only opportunity to recover and preserve evidence. The initial investigation will only occur once.
- Evidence may be physical, verbal, nonverbal, or a direct observation.
- Evidence includes interviews with family, friends, peers, coworkers, spectators, and any additional individuals who may assist in the investigation related to the crime and injuries incurred.
- Recognize your limitations, whether physical or mental.
- Realize that the victim is *always* the first priority.

III. Forensic Nursing: Disasters
   A. One common factor in a disaster is multiple damage that results in multiple injuries and fatalities.
   B. Disaster preparedness is necessary as a result of
       1. International terrorism
       2. Accumulation and storage of worldwide nuclear, biological, and chemical agents
       3. Use of military weapons in world conflicts
   C. Disaster teams are composed of individuals from formal professional disciplines with specialties and subspecialties in the fields of medicine, nursing, psychology, engineering, DNA identification, anthropology, entomology, odontology, and numerous additional forensic disciplines.
   D. Scene investigation: The disaster aftermath
       1. The American Medical Association (AMA), Federal Emergency Management Association (FEMA), and the Centers for

Disease Control and Prevention (CDC) have identified the types of disasters as follows:
   a. Manmade and natural disasters
   b. Traumatic and explosive events
   c. Nuclear and radiological events
   d. Biological events
   e. Chemical events
2. There are psychosocial aspects of terrorism and disasters.
3. The public health system deals with
   a. Pandemic outbreaks
   b. Disaster preparedness, which includes
      (1) The DISASTER paradigm, an organizational tool for preparation and response to disaster management
      (2) A uniform, coordinated approach that is essential to health care preparedness
      (3) Local, regional, state, federal coordination
   c. There are three types of disasters:
      (1) Local
      (2) State
      (3) Federal
   d. Some disaster responses can go beyond a nation's ability to handle them, at which time disaster relief can be requested of other nations.
   e. The role of the forensic nurse and other forensic scientists includes
      (1) Recognition of disaster event
      (2) Response based on the designed disaster preparedness plan
      (3) Determination of designated role and responsibilities
      (4) Identification of victims
      (5) Following established triage method for the care and treatment of the living victims
      (6) Following established procedure for recovery, care, and containment of the body or body parts

---

Forensic nurses and all specialty trained nurses possess a unique set of skills that allows them to be extremely effective when called to assist in a disaster:

Strong scientific and psychological knowledge base
Strong assessment skills
A commitment to provide care and treatment to all victims suffering from physical and psychological injuries

      f. Disaster nursing and disaster preparedness comprise an expanding field within nursing, and understanding the structural organization of a disaster team and its function is basic to the provision of safe care and treatment of victims and the safety of all disaster team members

Bibliography

Adelman, D., & Legg, T. (2009). *Disaster nursing: A handbook of practice.* Sudbury, MA: Jones and Bartlett, pp. 2–8.

American Medical Association. (2007). *Basic disaster life support provider manual version 2.6.* Chapters 1–8.

American Nurses Association, Center for Health Policy. (2008). *Adapting standards of care under extreme conditions: Guidance for professionals during disaster, pandemics, and other extreme emergencies.* Washington, DC: American Nurses.

American Nurses Association, Congress for Nursing Practice. (1980). *Nursing: A social policy statement.* Kansas City, MO. American Nurses Association.

American Nurses Association and International Association of Forensic Nurses. (1997). *Scope and standards of forensic nursing practice.* Washington, DC: American Nurses.

Clark, S. C., Ernst, M. F., Haglund, W. D., & Jentzen, J. M. (1996). *Medicolegal death investigator: A systematic training program for the professional death investigator, training text.* Big Springs, MI: Occupational Research and Assessment, pp. 73–92, 120–121, 127–172.

Cobelus, N. B., & Spangler, K. (2006). Evidence collection and documentation. In Hammer, R. M., Moynihan, B., & Pagliaro, E. M. (Eds.). *Forensic nursing: A handbook for practice* (ch. 16). Sudbury, MA: Jones and Bartlett, pp. 493–494.

Cox, E., & Briggs, S. (2004, June). Disaster nursing: New frontiers for critical care. *Critical Care Nurse; 24*(3), 16–22.

Dudley, M. H. (2003). *Forensic nursing.* Wichita, KS: Dudley, pp. 1-42–1-57.

Lasseter, S. (2003). Harris County, TX, medical examiner's office expands forensic nursing division. *On the Edge, 9*(3), 17.

Levinson, H. J. (2007, Summer). Responding to bioterrorism: Basics for physicians and allied health-care providers. *The Forensic Examiner,* pp. 22–31.

Lynch, V. (2006). *Forensic nursing.* St. Louis, MO: Mosby, pp. 91–99, 370–371.

National Institutes of Justice, United States Department of Justice Programs. (1999) *Crime scene investigation.* Rockville, MD: National Criminal Justice Information Center, pp. 1–7.

Nurses' legal handbook (5th ed.). (2004). Sudbury, MA: Jones and Bartlett.

Okoye, M. I., & Wecht, C. H. (Eds.). (2007). *Forensic investigation and management of mass disasters.* Tucson, AZ: Lawyers and Judges, pp. 3–16, 81–88.

Morgan, O., Tidball-Binz, M., & Van Alphen, D. (2006). *Management of dead bodies after disasters: A field manual for first responders.* Washington, DC: Pan American Health Organization.

Quinn, C. (2005). *The medical record as a forensic resource.* Sudbury, MA: Jones and Bartlett.

Sorg, M. (2003). Forensic anthropology. In James, S. H., & Nordby, J. J. *Forensic science: An introduction to scientific and investigative techniques* (ch. 17). Boca Raton, FL: CRC Press, pp. 115–121.

Spitz, W. (2006). The medicolegal autopsy report. In Spitz, W. U., Spitz, D., & Clark, R. (Eds.). *Spitz and Fisher's medicolegal investigation of death: Guidelines for the application of pathology to crime investigation* (4th ed., ch. 22). Springfield, IL: Charles C. Thomas, p. 798.

Sung Tz'u. *The washing away of wrongs: Science, medicine, and technology in East Asia 1*. McKnight, B. E. (Trans.). (1981). Ann Arbor, MI: Center for Chinese Studies: University of Michigan, pp. 89–92.

Thibodeau, G. A., & Patton, K. T. (2007). *Anatomy and physiology*. St. Louis, MO: Mosby Elsevier, pp. 554–556.

Warrington, D. (2008, August/September). Crime scene observation. *Forensic Magazine*, p. 42.

Establishing Time of Death and Injury

10

Forensic Nursing Practice and Responsibility

DONNA GARBACZ BADER

I. Overview
- Forensic nurse needs to understand the normal physiological changes that occur after death
- Changes have medicolegal significance
- Postmortem changes directly related to a natural sequence of events are often referred to as the *postmortem clock*

II. Forensic Nurse Consideration
- A. Environmental conditions affect the time frame.
- B. Metabolic state of the deceased prior to death is important.
- C. Changes in the chemical composition of body fluids and tissue must be taken into account.
- D. Residual reactivity of the muscles as a result of chemical or electrical stimuli must be realized.
- E. Evaluation of the normal physiological processes can establish a starting time or the rate of progression and cessation at the time of death.
- F. Survival time after injury is also important when considering the time of death; this becomes even more accurate if the time of injury is known or can readily be determined.

NOTE

1. Due to inherent inaccuracies in estimating postmortem changes and the time of death, conservative estimates are based on mathematical calculation and assessment of various accumulated data. It is imperative to understand the numerous variables and data in determining the time of death

---

Continued

as accurately as possible. Plus, specific data obtained from various factors, such as the outdoor environmental conditions present on a specific date, may provide additional data when estimating a date on which the death may have possibly occurred. *No single* factor will determine a cause of death.

2. The forensic nurse needs to assess the various factors surrounding the body and document the information accurately and completely. This information will assist the pathologist in identifying the cause of death with more accuracy. In addition, the pathologist may be able identify changes not consistent with the history obtained from witnesses, family, or others interviewed regarding the death. The assessment may identify the need for additional scene investigation; a reinterview of family, friends, or those previously interviewed; or to search for a person of interest.

3. The forensic nurse must always be cognizant of the state board of nursing rules and regulations regarding the practice of nursing. Scope and standards of practice differ based on education and certification (e.g., whether the nurse is a licensed certified nurse practitioner, licensed certified physician assistant, or any advanced practice specialty). A nurse with a baccalaureate nursing degree or master's degree in nursing understands that providing a medical diagnosis or prescribing medications is not within the nurse's scope of practice.

III. Medicolegal Implications of Death

A. The Uniform Determination of Death Act defined death as follows: "An individual, who has sustained irreversible cessation of all functions of the entire brain, including the brainstem, is dead. A determination of death shall be made in accordance with accepted medical standards" (ABA, 1981; AMA, 1980).

B. The following are the major legal considerations after a death:

- Survivorship
- Life insurance
- Wills based on successive inheritance
- Proper victim identification
- Numerous deaths as a result of one action
- Workers Compensation
- Civil and criminal actions often depend on the results of death investigation findings

IV. Factors in Estimating the Time of Death
   A. Environmental factors are one of the major contributors to the rate of decomposition
      1. Temperature
         - The hotter the temperature in relation to the body temperature, the more rapid the rate of decomposition.
         - The colder the temperature in relation to the body temperature, the slower the rate of decomposition.
      2. Ventilation
         - In an enclosed area (e.g., barrel, trunk, a room or rooms where all doors and windows are closed), the lack of any or improper ventilation may result in an increased environmental temperature, thus increasing the rate of decomposition. This occurs most often in the summer months when the temperature may rise to the upper 90s or higher; to keep the environment, such as a house, cooler, the resident may close all the windows. This in turn actually increases the temperature in the house or room to such a degree that the resident may die from hyperthermia. In a smaller confined space, hyperthermia develops more rapidly, and the rate of decomposition accelerates, which may lead an investigator to interpret the death as having occurred hours or even days earlier.
      3. Humidity
         - The level of humidity indicates the amount of moisture in the air. When the humidity is low (e.g., 35%) and the temperature is 50°F, an individual may require a coat and would be quite comfortable at a normal walking pace. The same would hold true if the temperature was 95°F and the individual wore shorts and a tee shirt. Decomposition would occur at a slower pace, again dependent on other variables.
         - When the humidity is high (e.g., 90%) and the temperature is 90°F, the individual becomes quite uncomfortable, perspiration does not evaporate, and the individual becomes wet; the individual may have difficulty breathing, and activities demand more energy. Decomposition rates accelerate.
         - Therefore, the rate of decomposition is related to both humidity and temperature.
   B. Physiological changes after death
      1. Livor mortis is also known as postmortem lividity.
         a. Evident 30–120 minutes after death; peak 8–12 hours
         b. Begins when blood ceases circulation

  c. Purplish-blue discoloration of the body

  d. Occurs in the dependent parts of the body as a result of gravitational settling of the blood; occurs in those parts closest to the floor *except* in areas exposed to pressure; for example, if a person is lying in a supine position, lividity will be evident on the backs of the trunk, arms, and legs; if a person is in a sitting position in a chair at the time of death, lividity appears in the area of the buttocks, lower legs, and feet, and if the arms were hanging along the side of the chair, lividity is evident in the hands.

  e. Pressure on any part of the body will leave a pale track.

  f. Dark red lividity, instead of the purplish-blue discoloration, is seen in

   carbon monoxide poisoning

   cold exposure (e.g., the body is placed in a cooler or refrigerator)

   cyanide poisoning

2. *Rigor mortis* is the rigidity of the body after death.

  a. Rigor mortis may become apparent within 30–60 minutes after death and progresses to a peak at 12 hours. It remains for 12 hours, then progressively decreases within the next 12 hours.

  b. Rigor mortis is a physiochemical process that produces a state of acidosis.

  c. Adenosine triphosphate (ATP) is hydrolyzed to adenosine diphosphate (ADP) > production of lactic acid > decreasing cellular pH > formation of a chemical chain between actin and myosin > chain connection is fixed > rigor results.

  d. As the decomposition of body proteins continues, the chemical chain between actin and myosin breaks > muscles relax > muscles become flaccid.

  e. The rate at which rigor mortis first appears and begins to disappear is accelerated by

   (1) prior exercise

   (2) convulsions

   (3) electrocution

   (4) hyperpyrexia (hot environmental temperature)

  f. The rate at which rigor mortis occurs is delayed by (chemical reaction is slowed)

   (1) hypothermia

   (2) cold environments

g. Additional factors affecting the rate of rigor mortis are as follows:
    (1) Drugs such as ecstasy; accelerate the rate of rigor mortis due to the increase in muscle activity > increased heart rate > sudden increase in body temperature > progressive and continuous increase in oxygen demand > continuous rise in body temperature > continuous rapid rise in heart rate > oxygenated cardiac output unable to meet the oxygen demand; the individual may die of cardiac arrhythmia
    (2) Strychnine poisoning
h. Conditions that can be mistaken for rigor mortis:
    (1) Cadaveric spasm, also known as "instant rigidity," occurs at the moment of death. This most often occurs during a violent death or exercise. The chemical physiology of cadaveric spasm is related to rapid depletion of ATP.
    (2) Clenching of the hands may resemble long-term arthritis; however, it results from the shortening and cooling of the tendons in the hands.
    (3) Frozen muscles become stiff.
        (a) When a body has been frozen, ruptured blood cells will be evident on microscopic evaluation.
    (4) Excessive heat will coagulate muscles and cause shortening of the muscles, called a *pugilistic attitude.*

3. Stomach contents are useful for death determination.
    a. The absence, presence, appearance, and amount of the stomach contents may be of assistance in determining the time of death. Evaluation of stomach contents includes:
    b. Description of the amount, size, condition, and nature of the contents is needed.
    c. If the contents are difficult to identify, microscopic examination becomes necessary.
    d. An examination of the small intestines for undigested food such as corn kernels or peels from tomatoes and apples may be helpful.
    e. Toxicology analysis should be made of both blood and stomach contents for the presence or absence of drugs and alcohol. Examine prior medical and psychological history

that may relate to medications and drugs. Consideration should also be given to the effect that drugs and alcohol have on the rate of digestion.

4. Vitreous humor should be examined.
   a. Vitreous humor is the most reliable body fluid used in the analysis of electrolytes, glucose, and urea nitrogen postmortem.
   b. When blood is used for postmortem chemical analysis, many of the chemicals are altered as a result of postmortem changes.
   c. Since the eye is generally well protected and the fluid is isolated to a specific area, the vitreous humor is less susceptible to contamination.
   d. Vitreous electrolytes are helpful in establishing a time of death.
   e. Potassium vitreous levels increase linearly, providing a more definitive time of death.

5. There are additional postmortem considerations.
   a. There may be postmortem drying artifacts (e.g., mummification, dried diaper rash).
   b. Insect activity and age of insect larvae on a body may be used to estimate the time of death. Larvae and maggots may contain drugs such as cocaine in the event there is not sufficient tissue from the deceased.
   c. Postmortem injuries are injuries that occur after death.
   d. Postmortem artifacts may be present, such as broken ribs or chest bruising resulting from cardiopulmonary resuscitative efforts.
   e. There may be faulty autopsy techniques.
   f. There may be incorrect interpretation of decomposition changes.
   g. Artifacts resulting from environmental conditions are possible.
   h. Topography may affect postmortem condition.
   i. Vegetative growth could affect postmortem condition.
   j. Body preparation for transport (e.g., bindings used to secure the body during transport) may cause postmortem effects.
   k. Animals can cause postmortem effects (e.g., rats or mice chewing on the exposed body). Cats and dogs may chew on the body if food is not available; wild animals may quickly skeletonize a body.

C. Summary

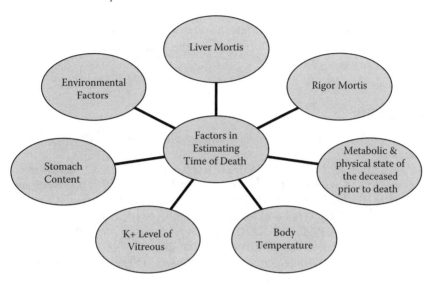

V. Decomposition
   A. Processes
      1. Autolysis (self-digestion)
         – The release of enzymes from cell breakdown
         – Occurs early in organs that are rich in enzymes (liver, pancreas)
         – Gastromalicia gastric acid + rich enzyme content flows up the esophagus = esophageal digestion = autolysis
      2. Putrefaction (tissue autolysis)

PUTREFACTION: PATHOPHYSIOLOGY OF TISSUE AUTOLYSIS

- Greenish discoloration
- Foul odor
- Bloating
- Blistering
- Marbling
- Skin slippage
- Decomposition fluids

---

      3. Adipocere formation
         – White, greasy, waxy substance
         – Forms on the face, extremities, buttocks, female breasts

- Forms over 3–6 months
- Occurs in wet environments in the fatty tissues
- Occurs in bodies left in water, warm and damp areas
4. Mummification: Occurs when the body desiccates in a hot, dry environment

Bibliography

Brenner, J. (2002). *Forensic science: An illustrated dictionary.* Boca Raton, FL: CRC Press.

Clark, S. C., Ernst, M. F., Haglund, W. D., & Jentzen, J. M. (1996). *Medicolegal death investigator: A systematic training program for the professional death investigator, training text.* Big Springs, MI: Occupational Research and Assessment.

Crewe, B. R. B. (2006). Overview of the American justice system. In Hammer, R. M., Moynihan, B., & Pagliaro, E. M. (Eds.). *Forensic nursing: A handbook for practice.* Sudbury, MA: Jones and Bartlett, pp. 200–202.

Death investigation: A guide for scene investigators. (1996). Big Springs, MI: Occupational Research and Assessment.

Eckert, W. G. (Ed.). (1997). *Introduction to forensic sciences* (2nd ed.). Boca Raton, FL: CRC Press.

Geberth, V. J. (1996). *Practical homicide investigation: Tactics, procedures, and forensic techniques* (3rd ed.). Boca Raton, FL: CRC Press.

Girard, J. E. (2008). *Criminalistics: Forensic science and crime.* Sudbury, MA: Jones and Bartlett, pp. 9–12.

Goll-McGee, B. (1999). The role of the clinical forensic nurse in critical care. *Critical Care Quarterly: 22*(1), 8–17.

Hoyt, C. A. (1999). Evidence recognition and collection in the clinical setting. *Critical Care Quarterly: 22*(1), 19–22.

Hoyt, C. A., & Spangler, K. A. (1996). Forensic nursing implications and the forensic autopsy. *Journal of Psychosocial Nursing and Mental Health Services, 34*(10), 24–31.

James, S. H., & Nordby, J. J. (Eds.). (2005). *Forensic science: An introduction to scientific and investigative techniques.* Boca Raton, FL: CRC Press.

Knight, B. (1991). *Forensic pathology.* New York: Oxford University Press.

Lee, H. C. (2000). *Physical evidence in forensic science.* Tucson, AZ: Lawyers and Judges.

Lynch, V. (2006). *Forensic nursing.* St. Louis, MO: Mosby.

Chain of Custody and Identification, Collection, and Preservation of Evidence

Major Concepts of Forensic Nursing

11

DONNA GARBACZ BADER

I. Chain of Custody:
- Chain of custody involves a witnessed, written record of all the individuals who maintained uninterrupted control over the items of evidence.
- Every person who personally handles the evidence must be accounted for and documented as a link in the chain of custody, from the crime scene to the courtroom.
- Any individual who identifies an item of evidence must mark it for identification.
- By maintaining an unbroken chain of custody, each witness can testify in court that each item presented is the exact item that was collected at the scene.

II. Evidence
  A. Definition
   – Anything that you can feel, smell, touch, taste, and hear
   – Any item or information legally submitted and accepted by a court or tribunal for the single purpose of determining the truth of a particular issue in the investigation at hand
   – Either physical or informational; submitted by a witness, documents, or placed on exhibit
  B. Evidence collection: Establishes proof that the items of evidence collected at the (crime, death) scene is the identical evidence that is presented in a court of law
   1. Rules of evidence collection
      a. Rule 1: Provide who, what, when, where, why.
      b. Rule 2: "If you touch it, it belongs to you."

2. Cornerstone of evidence collection: *Locard's exchange principle:* "Whenever two human beings come into contact something from one is exchanged to the other."
3. Legal issues related to evidence collection

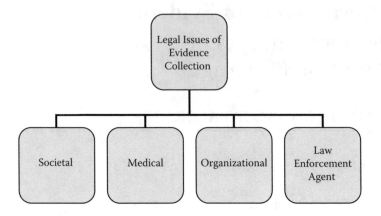

4. Interview as evidence
    a. A living victim may be interviewed with or without the presence of law enforcement personnel
        (1) Obtain the victim's consent.
        (2) It is important to know that the victim's consent to describe the history of the assault and injuries is *different from the consent necessary for obtaining evidence.*
        (3) A written consent from the victim is necessary for an examination of the body and collection of evidence, photography, collection of blood for laboratory testing, administration of medications, or the provision of medical or possible surgical treatment.
        (4) If the victim has been shot or stabbed and is medically stable, this would be identified as a criminal case and must be treated as such.
            (a) Health care policies identify what constitutes a criminal case and define the role and actions of all health care providers regarding evidence collection.
            (b) From a medical standpoint, identification of the type of injury and the need for immediate care and treatment to maintain life take priority

over any policy regarding obtaining consent or evidence collection.

(c) It is imperative that the forensic nurse, nursing staff, and any health care provider working with a victim of crime be familiar with the established policies and procedures regarding consent and evidence collection.

(5) If unable to obtain the victim's consent (e.g., the victim is under the influence of drugs or alcohol, has physical impairment, refuses to answer any questions regarding the possible crime or health history, or is unable to understand the spoken language), documentation should include objective description of the victim's physical and cognitive state.

(6) The need for care and treatment outweigh the need for consent.

(7) Identify physical aspects that require immediate care and treatment.

(8) Document the victim's account of the crime and injuries inflicted.

   (a) If the victim reports being bitten, the perpetrator's saliva may be obtained.

   (b) If the victim reports being hit or beaten, early signs of bruising or patterns of injury may be evident.

   (c) If the victim reports being restrained, signs of restraint use may be evident, with bruising or tape marks, rope marks, or marks from any type of material used as restraints.

   (d) Restraints may have been applied to upper or lower extremities only, to the waist, or to the total body.

(9) Documentation should include victim recall by using direct quotes and placing them in quotation marks.

(10) The victim's words should be exact; *do not* alter or substitute your words for the victim's words.

(11) Documentation of the victim's words is evidence that may be used in court.

(12) The hospitalized victim is allowed the same patient rights as any patient and may refuse any treatment,

medications, surgery, or interview regarding the actions prior to the injury.

(13) If the victim or patient is also the perpetrator of a crime, he or she is to receive the same care, treatment, respect, and courtesy without discrimination or bias.

b. Deceased victim: Interview family, friends, neighbors, or anyone who may have been in recent contact with the victim:

(1) Interviewing identifies aspects of the initial site of injury related to the death of the victim.

(2) Interviewing provides information regarding the victim's behavior and actions prior to the victim's death.

(3) Documentation should include the identification of the person interviewed and relationship to the victim, if any.

(4) Documentation should include the time, date, location, and circumstances of the interview (e.g., whether in the emergency room, in the victim's hospital room, in the victim's private residence, or in the residence where the victim was located).

5. Search warrant

FOURTH AMENDMENT TO THE UNITED STATES CONSITITUTION

PROTECTS CITIZENS "AGAINST UNREASONABLE SEARCH AND SEIZURES": NURSING APPLICATIONS

- All law enforcement and crime scene investigators require a search warrant before they can search for evidence.
- *Note*: This applies in any situation, either a death scene or a crime scene where the victim is alive.
- Forensic nursing/nursing note:

1. This *principle* applies to the sexual assault nurse examiner: Prior to performing the external and internal examinations, permission *must* be obtained from the victim.

Continued

2. This *principle* applies to any patient, victim, or client receiving nursing care: Permission for treatment is obtained on admission for procedures, invasive or noninvasive.
3. Patients, victims, and clients may refuse medications, treatments, or care even if permission was previously obtained.
4. Institutional policies outline procedures to be taken if the individual is not able to provide his or her consent.
5. Exceptions to the principle of unreasonable search and seizure need to be dealt with according to the situation and the *immediate* physical and psychological condition of the individual in question.
6. Search warrants (or consent forms) must state exactly what is being searched for (which procedure or treatment is to be performed).
7. If additional evidence is found other than what is listed on the search warrant, then that evidence can, in most cases, be collected.
8. *General rule*: If a nurse finds a gun or a filled syringe or any *item that may cause harm* or injury to the patient or others when admitting a patient or during the course of the patient's stay, the nurse should *leave the room immediately; if possible, call for immediate assistance as outlined in the policy/procedure, then maintain safety for patients and all others in the immediate area.*

Note: Seizing the items may provoke the patient and expose the nurse or others to immediate harm/danger.

C. Forensic nursing consideration in evidence collection
　　1. Value of credible physical evidence
　　　　a. Proves that a crime has been committed
　　　　b. Establishes major aspects of the crime
　　　　c. Places suspect at the scene
　　　　d. Vindicates the innocent
　　　　e. Substantiates the testimony of the victim
　　　　f. More reliable than an expert witness
　　　　g. Perhaps increased suspect cooperation when confronted with physical evidence
D. Search without a warrant or permission

WARRANTLESS SEARCHES

As with any situation for which written consent is required, there are circumstances when obtaining a warrant or the patient's consent is prohibited, dangerous, or a risk to life and limb.

1. An emergent situation is when the life, health, and safety of a person is in danger.
   a. Removing a victim from an area that is burning and where firearms are identified in the immediate area or on the victim
   b. A victim of a stabbing is admitted to the surgical floor immediately after surgery and a small firearm is recovered when inventorying the patient's belongings.
   c. Nursing implications
      (1) Legal, moral, and professional ethics demand that each situation and each set of circumstances be assessed on its merits.
      (2) It is essential for all members of an investigative team or a health care team to be aware of the policies, procedures, and practices that govern their actions.
      (3) Only by adhering to the guidelines of professional practice can the victim receive justice and the patient receive safe and knowledgeable care.

2. Additional situations for which a search warrant may not be required:
   a. Impending loss of evidence:
      - A patient attempts to swallow a small plastic bag containing white powder-like material
      - An area under suspicion is burning and unless evidence is retrieved, it will be permanently lost or severely damaged
   b. In the event of a lawful arrest, the suspect and any property in his or her immediate control (e.g., home, vehicle) may be searched without a warrant.
   c. Consented search is when a suspected party consents to a search.

E. Major types of evidence

Physical Evidence

Any matter, material, condition, solid, liquid, or gas that may be used in a given situation to determine facts; nonliving inorganic items

Biological Evidence

Living organic matter

- Small (s), microscopic (m), trace (t)
  - s = dental floss, comb, torn paper, drugs, fibers
  - m = sand, water, dirt, liquid left in a glass or cup
  - t = glass fragments, paint chips, wood splinter, gunpowder particles
- Examples of additional physical evidence:
  - Explosives
  - Tool markings
  - Fingerprints
  - Bullet and shell casings
  - Fibers
  - Shoe and tire impressions
  - Creams, lotions, toothpaste
  - Photographs

- Blood and blood stains
- Skeletal remains
- Teeth and bite marks
- Insects
- Plants and plant materials
- Saliva, emesis, urine, feces
- Tissue and organs
- Hair, teeth, bones or bone fragments
- Insects

---

1. Purpose of physical evidence:
   - Indicate location of the crime or injury
   - Identify instruments of injury
   - Confirm or refute an alibi or statement
   - Connect the presence of a suspect in relation to time or date
2. Purpose of biological evidence:
   - Identification of biological markers specific to a particular individual regarding gender, age, physical condition (e.g., DNA, mitochondrial DNA [m-DNA])
   - Identification of ingested substances, such as drugs, poisons, or any other substance that my be ingested (organic and inorganic materials have chemical markers that may identify a specific substance, e.g., arsenic and cyanide have specific chemical compounds that make up the substance, and these can be easily detected by utilizing current laboratory technology)
   - Link a person, place, or item to a crime; chemical compounds in sand, rocks, or water might identify the exact

location of the injury since such materials are easily transferred to clothes, shoes, hair, or vehicles, which can then
be identified by the laboratory

F. General types of evidence

Transient Evidence	Behavioral Evidence
• Temporary • Odors such as gasoline, marijuana, alcohol	• Demeanor • Voice annotation • Mannerisms • Posture

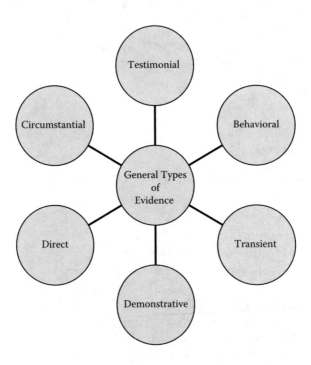

G. The body as evidence
1. Maintain chain of custody.
2. Do not cut or remove any invasive equipment.
3. Do not cut or remove any restraining tools or asphyxiation
material.
4. Enclose hands in a small paper bag and secure with tape.
5. No one is to view the body unless an attendant is present.

H. Forensic nursing and entomology
1. Insects can provide information regarding time of death,
injury, trauma, location, and toxicology.

2. Knowledge of insect activity, types of insects, and proper collection procedure is becoming an essential in forensic nursing/forensic science investigations.
3. In the first written forensic handbook, *The Washing Away of Wrongs*, the author, Sung Tz'u (McKnight, 1981), described the use of insects as valuable evidence in death scene investigations and wrote a time frame for insect development from the larvae stage through the adult stage.
4. Flies and beetles are two of the most important members of the insect family relating to death investigation.
5. Insects may also be transmitted to a living victim who has suffered from repeated incidents of rape.

I. Forensic nursing role and clinical application in the health care environment

- Emphasis on forensic evidence in the courtroom and the revolutions in forensic analysis technology
- Forensic nursing care plans must include policies and procedures for the treatment of the forensic patient
- Policies and procedures for the identification, collection and preservation of forensic evidence
- Basic nursing education teaches the need for providing holistic patient care utilizing critical thinking skills, in addition to skills in providing both physical and psychological care.
- This prepares the forensic nurse to be a credible expert witness and invaluable member of the investigative team
- Identification, collection, and preservation of evidence and documentation of injuries by the clinical forensic nurse are both extremely important and pose various legal issues.
- With the advent of the Health Insurance Portability and Accountability Act of 1996 (HIPAA), permission of the patients, victims, or perpetrators is necessary before medical services can be provided.
- Nursing assessment and cleaning of wounds and injuries should be done in a well-timed manner so trace evidence is not altered or destroyed.
- Institutional policies and procedures outline the responsibility of the forensic nurse regarding evidence collection.
- Nurses providing care and treatment to a victim of crime or trauma are legally responsible for following the policies and procedures

Continued

regarding evidence identification, collection, and preservation even though the nurse is not a forensic nurse specialist.

- Communication between members of the health care team and law enforcement is essential to preserve evidence.
- Once evidence is destroyed or compromised, it may not be used in court.
- Clinical implications regarding the collection of entomological evidence are based on designated procedures.
- When a victim arrives for care and treatment of injuries sustained during a criminal act and dies in the emergency room, during the provision of care documentation should include the chain of events that occurred from admission to the pronouncement of death.
- When a victim arrives for care and treatment of injuries resulting from a criminal act and is treated and admitted for hospitalized care, and death occurs during hospitalization, documentation should consist of all care, treatments, outcomes, activities, and status of the victim or patient prior to death.
- If a crime victim dies during initial emergency treatment or in the hospital room during recovery, that room becomes a crime scene.
- All tubes (e.g., intravenous catheters, urinary catheters, feeding tubes, endotracheal tubes, arterial catheters, drains) or any mechanical devices (e.g., external pacemaker wires, intercrainal pressure catheters) should be left in place to assist the forensic pathologist or pathologist and law enforcement personnel in differentiating injuries created by medical treatment or injuries resulting from the traumatic criminal act.

J. Packaging and preserving evidence

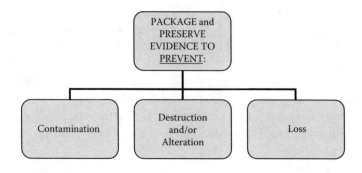

1. Types of packaging and preservation materials and containers

Evidence	Package/Preservation
1. Dry trace evidence such as fiber, hair, dried blood samples, dried fingernail scrapings	1. Clean, dry • envelopes • paper bags • filter paper provides a secure package
2. Nonbiological evidence such as arrow tips, bullet casings, debris, matches, cigarette butts, hats, shoes, clothing	2. Clean, dry • vials • canisters • metal containers • plastic pill bottles • plastic bags
3. Moist or wet biological evidence such as congealed blood, urine, feces, emesis, saliva, fresh DNA swabs, or any materials that are wet or moist with unknown liquid	3. Any piece of evidence such as clothing, from infant to adult, should air dry on clean white sheet if possible; if not possible and depending on the degree of moisture/wetness, place in either a paper bag or a cooler to avoid any bacterial growth that may alter or contaminate the evidence
4. Dry documents	4. Clean, dry • sealed in a plastic cover
5. Photographs	5. Dry picture may be sealed in a plastic cover; however, as a result of photographic paper and the various chemical compounds utilized to produce the image, care must be taken to the time factor if the picture is placed in a plastic cover as moisture may be produced (e.g., heat causes a chemical reaction that may seriously damage the image and paper)
6. Volatile evidence such as charred fire residue that may contain an accelerant such as gasoline or kerosene, which is a hydrocarbon of petroleum	6. Clean, dry • paint can with a secure, tight lid • tightly sealed jar; attention must be paid to secure the glass jar to prevent breakage

K. Photography
  1. The purpose of photography is to record the scene, injuries, and wounds visually
  2. Experience with photographing forensic cases is especially relevant; attention to detail is paramount in establishing credibility and value to the investigation.
  3. A high-quality camera should be used.

4. The quality of the photograph may be altered by over- or underexposure to light.
5. Photographs should be taken prior to disturbing the scene or collection of evidence in any forensic case.
6. Regarding value of photography in forensic cases:

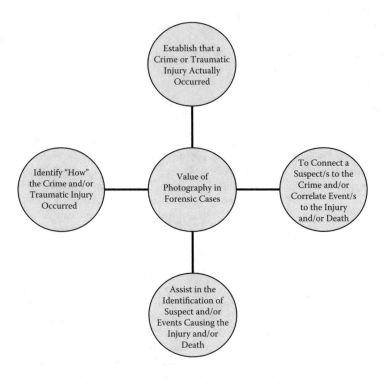

7. Identify every photograph as follows:

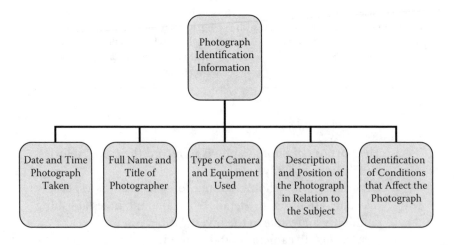

L. Video recording

- Video recording provides visual relationship between the crime scene and various pieces of evidence.
- Combined with photographs, video recording enhances the ability of the jury to understand and correlate events causing injury or death.
- Narration during the video is *not* recommended; descriptions and comments may prove incorrect as the investigation proceeds.
- Documentation should reflect date and time of the recording, full name and title of the recorder, identification of the scene recorded (e.g., living room of the victim's home at 424 East Maple Road; on the southwest street corner of 48th and South Street; Memorial Hospital, emergency room 6; Palm Medical Center, 6th floor radiology waiting room 2).

M. Evidence organization
　1. The forensic nurse or investigator is responsible for establishing a center collection point for all evidence submitted with all identification data completed.
　2. A written log is used to record all evidence as it is collected.
　3. Once all the evidence has been collected and logged, the forensic nurse or investigator should visually survey the area to ensure that all the evidence has been collected and all equipment removed.
　4. The evidence is then transported to the appropriate and secure place, maintaining an unbroken chain of custody.
N. The forensic nurse is a member of a multidisciplinary team.

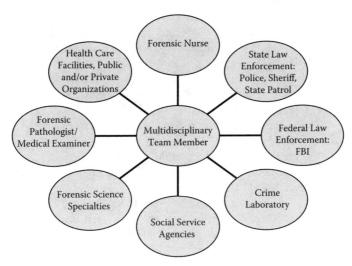

Bibliography

American Nurses Association, Congress for Nursing Practice. (1980). *Nursing: A social policy statement.* Kansas City, MO: American Nurses Association.

American Nurses Association and International Association of Forensic Nurses. (1997). *Scope and standards of forensic nursing practice.* Washington, DC: American Nurses.

Brenner, J. (2002). *Forensic science: An illustrated dictionary.* Boca Raton, FL: CRC Press.

Burgess, A. W. (2002). *Violence through a forensic lens.* King of Prussia, PA: Nursing Spectrum, pp. 371–381.

Butts, J. B., & Rich, K. L. (2008). *Nursing ethics across the curriculum and into practice* (2nd ed.). Sudbury, MA: Jones and Bartlett.

Cashin, A., & Potter, E. (2006). Research and evaluation of clinical nurse mentoring: Implications for the forensic context. *Journal of Forensic Nursing, 2*(4), 189–193.

Cochran, M. (1999). The real meaning of patient-nurse confidentiality. *Critical Care Quarterly: Confronting Forensic Issues, 22*(1), 41–50.

Clark, S. C., Ernst, M. F., Haglund, W. D., & Jentzen, J. M. (1996). *Medicolegal death investigator: A systematic training program for the professional death investigator, training text.* Big Springs, MI: Occupational Research and Assessment.

Eckert, W. G. (Ed.). (1997). *Introduction to forensic sciences* (2nd ed.). Boca Raton, FL: CRC Press.

Ewen, B. M. (2005). Forensic entomology. *On The Edge, 11*(1), 11–15.

Geberth, V. J. (1996). *Practical homicide investigation: Tactics, procedures, and forensic techniques* (3rd ed.). Boca Raton, FL: CRC Press.

Girard, J. E. (2008). *Criminalistics: Forensic science and crime.* Sudbury, MA: Jones and Bartlett, pp. 9–12.

Goll-McGee, B. (1999). The role of the clinical forensic nurse in critical care. *Critical Care Quarterly, 22*(1), 8–17.

Hammer, R. M., Moynihan, B., & Pagliaro, E. M. (Eds.). (2006). *Forensic nursing: A handbook for practice.* Sudbury, MA: Jones and Bartlett, pp. 200–202.

Herdman, H. T., Heath, C., Meyer, G., Seroggins, L., & Vassallo, B. (Editorial Committee). NANDA International. (2007). *NANDA-1 nursing diagnoses: Definitions and classifications, 2007–2008.* Philadelphia: NANDA International.

Hoyt, C. A. (1999). Evidence recognition and collection in the clinical setting. *Critical Care Quarterly, 22*(1), 19–22.

James, S. H., & Nordby, J. J. (Eds.) (2005). *Forensic science: An introduction to scientific and investigative techniques.* Boca Raton, FL: CRC Press.

Knight, B. (1991). *Forensic pathology.* New York: Oxford University Press.

Lee, H. C. (2000). *Physical evidence in forensic science.* Tucson, AZ: Lawyers and Judges.

Lynch, V. (2006). *Forensic nursing.* St. Louis, MO: Mosby.

Mosby's surefire documentation: How, what, and when nurses need to document (2nd ed.). (2006). St. Louis, MO: Mosby Elsevier.

Nurses' legal handbook (5th ed.). (2004). Sudbury, MA: Jones and Bartlett.

Porth, C. M. (2002). *Pathophysiology: Concepts of altered health states* (6th ed.). Hagerstown, MD: Lippincott Williams & Wilkins.

Quinn, C. (2005). *The medical record as a forensic resource.* Sudbury, MA: Jones and Bartlett.

Souryal, S. S. (2007). *Ethics in criminal justice: In search of the truth* (4th ed.). Newark, NJ: LexisNexis Group; Bender.

Sung Tz'u. *The washing away of wrongs: Science, medicine, and technology in East Asia 1.* McKnight, B. E. (Trans.). (1981). Ann Arbor, MI: Center for Chinese Studies, University of Michigan.

Significance of an Autopsy

12

DONNA GARBACZ BADER

I. Autopsy Introduction
   A. Definition
      1. The definition of *autopsy* is "to look at oneself"; this term is most commonly used in the United States.
      2. The accurate definition of *dissection* is "necropsy: looking at the dead."
      3. The earliest written account in which the practice of dissection of the body was mentioned was discussion of the practice in Ancient Egypt; it was used only as a means of decreasing or ceasing postmortem decomposition for mummification.
      4. Under English law, the body was treated for burial, and this was the responsibility and duty of a family member.
      5. English law also stated that dissection of the body was an interference with burial, so permission to perform a dissection was necessary from the surviving family member.
      6. Middle Eastern religions prohibit the dissection of the body of the deceased; the most common of these religions are Judaism and Hinduism.
      7. Laws vary regarding preparation and burial of the body, and this may pose some difficulties, based on the country where the death occurred, in the case of a suspicious, sudden, or unexpected death.
      8. In the United States, an autopsy is mandatory if a death is within proper jurisdiction and the cause of death cannot be determined without an autopsy.
   B. Types of autopsy
      1. Hospital (clinical) autopsy
         a. Purpose
         b. Conducted by a pathologist

111

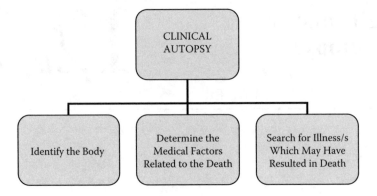

2. Medicolegal (forensic) autopsy
   a. Purpose

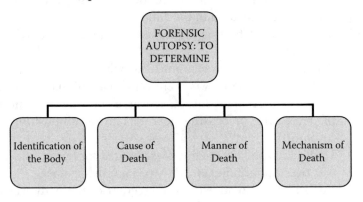

   b. Conducted by a
      (1) Forensic pathologist
      (2) Pathologist with experience in conducting forensic autopsies
   c. Autopsy required when death results from

---

(1) Traumatic event: injury resulting from accident, homicide, or suicide
(2) Unusual event: circumstances appear unnatural or suspicious
(3) Sudden event: occurring shortly after the onset of symptoms
(4) Unexpected: occurring without physical symptomatology

II. Autopsy Examination
    A. External examination: clothing
       1. Provide a detailed description of all clothing with photographs
       2. After the clothing is removed, it should be placed in an appropriate container to maintain integrity for further laboratory

processing, if necessary (e.g., to determine the type of dried material present, such as blood, dirt, vegetation, or any other particles or materials of interest).

    a. If clothing is wet, it may need to be line or air dried before storage; drying at high temperatures will disintegrate or destroy substances or particles that may be used for further investigation (e.g., blood, other body fluids).

    b. If clothing is packaged wet, disintegration of natural materials and fluids occurs, and it also promotes the growth of mildew and other fungi, which will alter the original biological materials.

    c. If dry, clothing is best placed in a clean paper bag.

3. Front and back photographs of the body should be taken.

4. Close-up photographs of all injuries, bruises, and any identifying particulars should be made and should include a measuring tool for accurate dimensions.

B. External examination: body

  1. Front and back photographs of the body should be taken.

  2. Close-up photographs of all bruises, tears, lacerations, and any identifying particulars should be made.

  3. Photographs should also include a tool, such as a ruler, to measure the size of each injury accurately.

  4. Tattoos and skin piercing should be described, measured, and photographed.

  5. Any bindings, ligatures, or gags should be described, photographed, and measured and should be removed with any knots intact.

  6. All equipment used in providing medical care prior to death should be identified and photographed (e.g., endotracheal tube; tracheostomy tube; intravenous catheters; all invasive catheters such as arterial, abdominal, cranial; external pacemakers, chest tubes).

  7. Incisions from previous surgeries or injuries should be identified, described, and photographed.

C. Internal examination: body

  1. Autopsy procedure

---

a. A T-shaped incision across the scapula down the midline to the public bone is made.

b. Incision from behind one ear to behind the other ear is performed.

c. Reflection of the scalp is done, peeling it forward.

Continued

d. The skull is sawed in a circular fashion to remove the skullcap.

e. The internal organs of the chest, abdomen, and head are removed.

f. Organs are weighed and dissected.

g. Small sections of organs, muscle, tissue, bone, and vessels are taken for microscopic evaluation and diagnosis.

h. The brain is dissected immediately or "fixed" (placed in formaldehyde for a week so the tissue may be easier to dissect).

i. Legs and feet are also dissected to check for blood clots or to check for evidence of trauma.

j. Blood or vitreous is obtained for toxicology.

k. Hair may be pulled for DNA analysis.

l. X-rays or digital radiology may be used for additional evaluation and for more accurate visualization of trajectory and degree of injury sustained.

m. Photographs are taken before, during, and sometimes after the autopsy.

n. The skullcap is replaced, and the scalp is drawn back over the skull.

o. Dissection of the cervical spine and the entire spinal cord may be necessary if death resulted from a severe head injury or if some degree of paralysis resulted from the initial injury, which may have caused death.

p. At the conclusion of the autopsy, all organs are returned to the body cavity unless the organ is fixed for later study; the chest is approximated with heavy suture; the body is placed in a body bag and returned to the cooler, where it will be held until the body is released.

q. Any and all personal belongings are kept with the body until the body is released.

r. Any personal belongings may be tagged as evidence and placed in the designated evidence room following chain-of-custody procedure.

D. The virtual autopsy

1. Multidetector computed tomography (MDCT) is an advanced imaging tool that is able to obtain images without destroying forensic objects.

2. It may be used when a standard autopsy cannot be performed or is not feasible, such as at a disaster site or when the family objects to an autopsy for either personal or religious beliefs.

3. MDCT is most frequently used in disasters at a temporary mortuary site.

4. MDCT can be made operational within 20 minutes of arrival.

5. MDCT is capable of examining a single body bag or multiple fragment body bags without the need to open the bag.
6. MDCT can also be utilized to facilitate or reduce the need for a standard autopsy when drowning is the suspected cause of death.
7. Additional aspects of the MDCT are the ability to dissect specific areas of the deep pelvis and neck that may be difficult to reach and the capability to depict and classify fractures in severe skull trauma.
8. This scanner has also been used to detect smuggled and dissolved cocaine.

III. Safety Concerns During an Autopsy
    A. Prevent any injury to the body.
        1. Treat the body with the utmost respect.
        2. Transfer with appropriate assistance.
        3. Clean the body gently with slow running cool water.
        4. Secure the body to the autopsy table if necessary.
        5. Maintain the integrity of any evidence.
        6. Prevent any forceful activity that would result in an unrelated injury or marking on the body.
        7. Cover the body until preparations are complete to begin the autopsy.
    B. Prevent injury to those individuals immediately involved in the autopsy (medical examiner, autopsy assistant, forensic nurse).
        1. Wear protective waterproof gown.
        2. Gloves, in some cases two pairs of gloves, may be necessary (e.g., contagious disease, exhumations, working with toxic chemicals).
        3. Use a hair cover to prevent any material (e.g., insects, dust, body fluids) from entering the hair.
        4. Use eyewear to protect the eyes from materials produced by a saw, irrigation, sudden rupture of a body organ, or accidental spillage of toxic chemical or body fluids.
        5. Wear a mask (a surgical face mask that covers the nose and mouth or a full face mask that covers the entire face, including the eyes).
        6. Immediately report and treat any injury received during the autopsy process (e.g., cuts received from an autopsy instrument or any sharp object retrieved from the body).
    C. Formaldehyde safety
        1. Formaldehyde is the most common chemical used in forensic pathology.

2. The aqueous form is known as formalin.
3. Formaldehyde is a flammable, colorless gas.
4. Formaldehyde is a powerful irritant to mucous membranes (eyes, nose, throat); it produces a tingling and burning sensation and may decrease the sensitivity of the senses.
5. Formaldehyde is a powerful skin irritant.
6. Vapors or solutions may result in pain, white discoloration, roughness, and burns to the body.
7. Limit long-term exposure to formaldehyde.
8. Long-term exposure may result in neuropsychological effects as well as chronic physiological effects.
9. Monitor the autopsy area and maintain the recommended Occupational Safety and Health Administration (OSHA) air exchange.
10. Document maintenance; report and treat any accidental exposure as required.

IV. Medicolegal Autopsy Report
   A. The medicolegal autopsy report is referred to as a "medicolegal opinion as to the cause and manner of death."
   B. The medicolegal opinion is based on the result of the following:

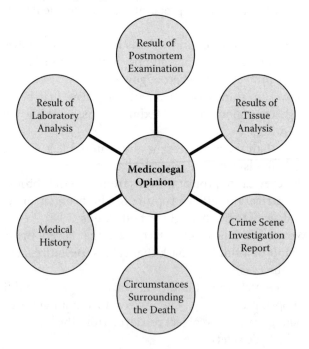

"To be absolutely certain about something, one must know everything or nothing about it." Voltaire (1694–1778)

C. Autopsy report includes the following:

1. Name of the patient/victim
2. Date of birth
3. Date of death
4. Time of autopsy
5. Date of autopsy
6. Medical record and autopsy numbers
7. Name of examining forensic pathologist/pathologist
8. Names of others assisting with the autopsy
9. Names of any additional individuals present during the autopsy (e.g., law enforcement personnel, nursing or medical students)
10. Name of persons who identified the body
11. Any available medical history
12. Complete description of body and external examination
13. Description of all visible injuries
14. Description of any injury or illness to central nervous system
15. Description of internal examination of all organs, skeleton
16. Log of tissues removed for microscopic, toxicological, or additional medical examination (e.g., placing the brain in formaldehyde for more accurate examination at a predetermined future date)
17. Description of microscopic abnormalities
18. Toxicology results or note of pending results
19. Laboratory results or note of pending results
20. Pathologist determination of cause and manner of death

Bibliography

Burgess, A. W. (2002). *Violence through a forensic lens.* King of Prussia, PA: Nursing Spectrum, pp. 381–382.

Cochran, M. (1999). The real meaning of patient-nurse confidentiality. *Critical Care Quarterly: Confronting Forensic Issues, 22*(1), 41–50.

Crewe, B. R. B. (2006). Overview of the American justice system. In Hammer, R. M., Moynihan, B., & Pagliaro, E. M. (Eds.). *Forensic nursing: A handbook for practice.* Sudbury, MA: Jones and Bartlett, pp. 200–202.

Goll-McGee, B. (1999). The role of the clinical forensic nurse in critical care. *Critical Care Quarterly, 22*(1), 8–17.

Hoyt, C. A. (1999). Evidence recognition and collection in the clinical setting. *Critical Care Quarterly, 22*(1), 19–22.

Hoyt, C. A., & Spangler, K. A. (1996). Forensic nursing implications and the forensic autopsy. *Journal of Psychosocial Nursing and Mental Health Services, 34*(10), 24–31.

International Association of Forensic Nurses (IAFN). (2004). *IAFN code of ethics.* Retrieved from www.iafn.org

James, S. H., & Nordby, J. J. (Eds.). (2005). *Forensic science: An introduction to scientific and investigative techniques.* Boca Raton, FL: CRC Press, pp. 19–22.

Lynch, V. (2006). *Forensic nursing.* St. Louis, MO: Mosby, pp. 364–366.

Quinn, C. (2005). *The medical record as a forensic resource.* Sudbury, MA: Jones and Bartlett, pp. 111–112.

Page, D. (2008, August/September). The virtual autopsy: The doctor will scan you now. *Forensic Magazine.*

Silvia, A. J. (1999). Mechanism of injury in gunshot wounds: Myths and reality. *Critical Care Quarterly, 22*(1), 69–70.

Spitz, W. U., Spitz, D., & Clark, R. (Eds.). (2006). *Spitz and Fisher's medicolegal investigation of death: Guidelines for the application of pathology to crime investigation* (4th ed.). Springfield, IL: Thomas.

Sung Tz'i. *The washing away of wrongs: Science, medicine, and technology in East Asia 1.* McKnight, B. E. (Trans.). (1981). Ann Arbor, MI: Center for Chinese Studies, University of Michigan, pp. 25–26.

The Nursing Process

DONNA GARBACZ BADER

13

I. Background

    A. To be accepted as a nursing specialty by the American Nurses Association College of Nursing Practice, forensic nursing was required to relate the practice of forensic nursing in terms of the nursing process.

    B. The forensic nursing process is an organizational tool that is used to care for the individual suffering an illness, injury, or death as a result of an act of violence, abuse, or trauma.

    C. Collaboration with other nurses, physicians, law enforcement, and those within the judicial system is vital in developing an effective nursing process.

II. The Forensic Nursing Process

    A. Based on the concepts of the scientific process

Forensic Nursing Process	Scientific Method
1. Nursing assessment: Identify the problem	1. Data collection
2. Nursing Diagnosis: Summary of facts	2. Develop hypothesis
3. Nursing intervention and planning: Identify scene concerns	3. Test hypothesis
4. Evaluation: Correlate outcomes with interventions	4. Evaluate hypothesis

    B. Development of a Forensic Nursing Process

        1. Nursing diagnosis: The nursing diagnoses listed in this section are not all inclusive for victims of violence, trauma, or death. The North American Nursing Diagnosis Association (NANDA) International is the accepted nursing diagnosis standard and should be used as a reference in identifying a nursing diagnosis.

a. Victim focus

- Anxiety
- Death anxiety
- Disturbed body image
- Risk-prone health behavior
- Defensive coping
- Ineffective coping
- Ineffective denial

b. Family focus

- Complicated grieving
- Interrupted family processes
- Moral distress
- Compromised family coping
- Anxiety
- Ineffective role performance
- Situational low self-esteem

c. Forensic nurse death investigation

- Risk for ineffective role performance
- Risk for trauma syndrome
- Risk for ineffective health maintenance
- Risk for moral distress
- Ineffective denial
- Risk for defensive coping
- Risk for contamination
- Decisional conflict
- Ineffective coping

d. Additional nursing diagnosis related to the
   (1) Forensic nurse death investigator
   (2) Members of the death investigation team
   (3) Forensic nurse examiner
   (4) Members of the health care team

- Risk for ineffective role performance
- Risk for trauma syndrome
- Risk for ineffective health maintenance
- Risk for moral distress

- Ineffective denial
- Risk for defensive coping
- Risk for contamination
- Decisional conflict
- Ineffective coping

  e. Additional forensic nursing diagnosis related to the victim (living or deceased):

- Ineffective protection
- Interrupted respiratory response
- Interrupted breathing pattern
- Interrupted cardiac output
- Dysfunctional cardiac output
- Other-directed violence
- Intentional trauma
- Accidental trauma
- Hypothermia or hyperthermia
- Autonomic dysreflexia
- Interrupted family processes

 2. Assessment
  a. Physical assessment
  b. Psychological assessment
  c. Scene assessment
  d. Assessment of the area surrounding the scene
  e. Identification of evidence
 3. Planning
  a. Make decisions based on each set of assessment data
  b. Determine need for further investigation
  c. Schedule appointments with victim, witnesses, staff
  d. Determine need for family, victim, community member coping resources
 4. Intervention
  a. Photograph
  b. Identify, collect, and preserve evidence
  c. Make death notification if necessary
  d. Discuss support referrals to victim, family, support system, community members
  e. Protect and secure personal property

5. Evaluation: Short-term goals
   a. Identification of victim
   b. Examination of investigation findings
   c. Review laboratory tests
   d. Review medical records
   e. Review postmortem information to identify cause and manner of death
   f. Consider additional review of specific findings and implement interventions
   g. Make investigative peer review and assessment
   h. Debrief team members
6. Evaluation: Long-term goals
   a. Identify perpetrator
   b. Assist in the arrest of the perpetrator
   c. Identify defense team
   d. Identify prosecution team
   e. Testify at the criminal trial
   f. Assess family coping skills
   g. Assess community response/coping
   h. Assess for additional family or community education needs

C. Application of the nursing process to death investigation:
1. The major components of the forensic nurse death investigators nursing process are
   a. The victim
   b. The environment
   c. The concept of health
   d. The role of the forensic nurse
2. The object of nursing care may be
   a. The decedent
   b. The family
   c. The witness
   d. An agency official
   e. Community members
3. The concept of health and health promotion in relation to the decedent is reflected in obtaining the health history prior to death.
   a. The forensic nurse is able to understand and correlate the medical and surgical history of the deceased along with medication prescribed, treatments performed, and physical and mental health.
   b. Nursing knowledge may establish a possible link regarding the client's or victim's death.

4. Patients and clients may include the survivors of the deceased.
    a. Holistic care may be applicable to this population in relation to both physical and mental health needs.
D. Nursing process case study: A deceased 25-year-old male is found in the employee parking lot of the hospital at 18:45 on December 10, 2008.
    1. Assessment: Includes identification of pieces of information that will compose a whole.
        a. Direct observation

            Deceased lying prone with navy blue scrub pants and top

            (1) Questions to consider as part of the assessment data:

                Who is the deceased?

                What happened?

                When did this happen?

                Where did this incident happen?

                Why did this individual die?

                Why is the deceased not wearing a coat or jacket?

                Is the deceased an employee of the hospital?

                Why is the deceased wearing only a white left shoe?

                Was the deceased arriving to begin a shift?

                Was the deceased leaving on completion of a shift?

                In what capacity did the deceased function (professional or nonprofessional)?

        b. Accurate description

            Dried blood along the hairline extending from the temporal region toward the back of the head, from the right nares, on anklefold of the right sock

            Laceration extending from the bend of the right brachial area measuring 3 inches long, 2 inches deep, 1.5 inches wide, along the posterior section of the right arm; serrated edge along right margin of incision, left margin of laceration smooth

            Four-inch rectangular, purplish bruise on both sides of laceration; horizontal, resembling a "t"

            (1) Questions to consider as part of the assessment data:

                Why is there blood only on the right side?

                How long ago did the injury occur?

Did the deceased trip while tying the shoelaces on his right shoe?

Was this a deliberate attempt by another person to cause injury or was this accidental?

Did the deceased suffer from an underlying disease process?

Did the deceased take any prescription or nonprescription drugs?

Where is the object responsible for inflicting the laceration?

What type of object caused the laceration on the right arm?

What type of object has one serrated edge?

Is there an injury under the hairline that created the initial bleeding?

Is there blood under the deceased's head?

Was the deceased pushed backward, resulting in a sudden impact to the back of the head as it hit the concrete floor of the parking garage?

c.   Identification

Environmental factors: ambient temperature, humidity, wind factor, environmental exposure

Location and description of any vehicles within a 15-foot diameter of the deceased

Location and description of any materials on the clothing and any exposed body anatomy (e.g., head, neck, hands, fingers, and fingernails; anterior and posterior sections of left and right extremities) and any exposed areas relating to the torso and lower extremities (the deceased has not yet been moved to examine the anterior section of the body)

Location and description of any materials within a 12-inch radius of the body

(1)   Questions to consider as part of the assessment data:

Did the deceased wear any warm outerwear, and if so, where is it?

Was there a struggle with another individual?

Did the deceased accidentally trip on a sharp object that resulted in the laceration to the right arm?

Do any of the vehicles belong to the deceased?

2. Nursing diagnosis
   a. Develops from the interpretation and analysis of assessment data gathered in the death investigation.
   b. NANDA has identified the domains of a nursing diagnosis as related to
      (1) Physiology
      (2) Behavior
      (3) Family systems
      (4) Health and safety systems
   c. As in the death investigation example, nursing diagnosis may focus on
      (1) The safety and integrity of preserving the body
      (2) Maintaining a safe environment for the deceased and for those involved in the care of the deceased when
         (a) Potential environmental factors may damage or destroy possible evidence.
         (b) The deceased may exhibit signs of a potential communicable disease.
         (c) The deceased has been exposed to toxic chemicals or gases.
         (d) A natural or human-made disaster has occurred or is occurring.
         (e) The deceased is located in a burning building or a building that has been burned.
      (3) There is the presence of family, friends, or support individuals at the scene and evaluation of their verbal and nonverbal behavioral responses is needed.
3. Planning
   a. Develop short- and long-term goals for both simple and complex activities involving the victim, deceased, perpetrator, family, support system
   b. May include other nurses, several professional specialists, agencies, resources
   c. Evaluate plans on regular and frequent basis to assess the response of the victim, family, perpetrator, and details regarding the deceased (evidence collection, exhumation, release of the body)
4. Intervention
   a. The foundation for forensic nursing interventions may include
      (1) Victimization
      (2) Custody
      (3) Human rights
      (4) Coercion

b.   Nursing care is required for the immediate care of the victim, the deceased, the perpetrator, the family, and other support systems.
c.   Direct intervention may be outlined in standing orders, policies, procedures, or directives at the request of law enforcement or a judicial system representative.
d.   Interventions need to be evaluated and changed based on the expected desired outcome.
e.   Examples may include
    (1) Collection and preservation of evidence
    (2) Maintaining chain of custody
    (3) Release of personal belonging
    (4) Release of the body
    (5) Referral to specific agency or agencies
    (6) Referral to forensic specialists (e.g., pathologist, psychologist, psychiatrist, sexual assault nurse examiner, entomologist, toxicologist, anthropologist)
    (7) Establishing and maintaining contact, when necessary, with family, victim, law enforcement, forensic pathologist, social service agencies, judicial system representative, and any additional persons or agency
    (8) Detailed documentation of all care, treatment, evidence collection and chain of custody, response to interventions
5. Evaluation
    a.   Review of all aspects of the nursing process is essential:
        (1) In maintaining continuity of medical care and treatment
        (2) For changing or altering the nursing diagnosis, interventions, short- or long-term goals
        (3) In maintaining evidence viability
        (4) Regarding complete and detailed documentation of events
        (5) In response to any and all interventions
        (6) For determining the need for further follow-up

III. The Nursing Process as a Tool
    A. The nursing process should be utilized at the beginning and throughout the investigation process.
    B. The nursing process provides the nurse with a familiar method of organization, identification of problems, prioritization, and determination of the most appropriate intervention.

C. The nursing process addresses issues and problems related to all individuals affected by the violent act:
   1. Victim: living or deceased
   2. Family, friends, support system
   3. Community members
   4. Forensic nurse investigator
   5. Members of the investigation team
   6. Health care members
   7. Any individuals (professional and nonprofessional) working with the victim
D. The nursing process is incorporated in the scope and standard of nursing practice as defined by the American Nurses Association (ANA) and remains an essential part of the standards of practice for nursing specialty groups and some forensic nursing subspecialty groups (e.g., *Sexual Assault Nurse Examiner Standards of Practice*, International Association of Forensic Nurses, 1996).
E. The nursing process as a standard in providing nursing care may also be used as evidence in a court of law. Nursing documentation of patient care needs to reflect patient assessment, planning, implementation, and evaluation. The nurse's notes in the medical record duplicate a nursing process also including a nursing diagnosis.
F. The nursing process becomes a part of the victim's medical record and should reflect all aspects of the forensic nurse's investigation.
G. The nursing process is recognized as a standard of nursing practice in all the fields of nursing. It is recognized as a forensic nursing organizational tool to identify the care and intervention necessary for the deceased or live victim, the family or support system, the community members, and additional agency personnel during and after the investigation of a crime.

Bibliography

American Nurses Association, Congress for Nursing Practice. (1980). *Nursing: A social policy statement.* Kansas City, MO: American Nurses Association.

American Nurses Association (2004). *Nursing scope and standards of practice.* Silver Spring, MD: American Nurses Association.

American Nurses Association and International Association of Forensic Nurses. (1997). *Scope and standards of forensic nursing practice.* Washington, DC: American Nurses.

Goll-McGee, B. (1999). The role of the clinical forensic nurse in critical care. *Critical Care Quarterly, 22*(1), 8–17.

Hoyt, C. A. (1999). Evidence recognition and collection in the clinical setting. *Critical Care Quarterly, 22*(1), 19–22.

International Association of Forensic Nurses. (1993). *Code of ethics for forensic nursing.* Thorofare, NJ: Author.

International Association of Forensic Nurses. (1996). *Sexual assault nurse examiner standards of practice.* Arnold, MD, pp. 5–12.

Joint Commission on Accreditation of Healthcare Organizations (JCAHO). (2004). *Accreditation manual for hospitals, core standards, and guidelines.* Oak Park, IL: Author.

Lynch, V. (2006). *Forensic nursing.* St. Louis, MO: Mosby, pp. 8–10.

Lynch, V. (2006). Forensic nursing science. In Hammer, R. M., Moynihan, B., & Pagliaro, E. M. (Eds.). *Forensic nursing: A handbook for practice* (ch. 1). Sudbury, MA: Jones and Bartlett.

North American Nursing Diagnosis Association (NANDA). (2007). *NANDA-1 nursing diagnoses: Definitions and classifications, 2007–2008.* Philadelphia: NANDA International.

Quinn, C. (2005). *The medical record as a forensic resource.* Sudbury, MA: Jones and Barlett, p. 116.

Standing Bear, Z. G. (1995). Forensic Nursing and Death Investigation: Will the vision be co-opted? *Journal of Psychosocial Nursing, 33*(9), 59–63.

Wooten, R. (2004, January/February). Applying the nursing process to death investigation: The nursing process and the decedent. *Forensic Nurse,* p. 9.

Forensic Nursing and the Law

14

DONNA GARBACZ BADER

I. Forensic Nursing Practice
   A. Regulated and influenced by
      - State law
      - Federal law
      - International law; applies when a forensic nurse is assisting in investigation of war crimes and human rights violations
   B. Laws passed by state legislatures or U.S. Congress called statutes
   C. Administrative rule development
      - Guidelines for writing federal and legislative rules and regulations
      - Guidelines written to protect the rights of citizens
   D. Rules and regulations often govern details that may be modified/ changes
      - State nurse practice act
      - State and federal courts interpret existing law, create case laws, make decisions in appellate cases
   E. Nurse practice act: First legal responsibility

Every licensed professional registered nurse has a professional, legal, and moral responsibility and obligation to be familiar with his or her state nurse practice act that identifies the scope and standards of practice and the rules and regulations that govern nursing practice in one particular state.

Unfamiliarity with the state nurse practice act exposes the nurse to a multitude of medical, legal, and ethical issues of patient injury and non-compliance with required legal responsibilities.

F. Patient confidentiality
1. Patient confidentiality is the most basic concept in nursing education, practice, and ethics.
2. Failure to follow mandatory policies and laws related to patient confidentiality is considered a misdemeanor criminal offense.
3. According to individual state laws and statutes, patient confidentiality may be breached when reporting abuse, neglect, infectious disease, or when a threat exists that may cause harm, injury, or death to another person.

The forensic nurse/nurse must be familiar with and keep informed of any changes in policies, laws, and statues regarding patient confidentiality.

4. Health Insurance Portability and Accountability Act (HIPAA)
   – Passed by Congress in 1996
   – Mandates the creation of privacy regulations for personal health care information
   – All patients required to receive a written copy of their privacy rights

As a Nurse Providing Health Care	As a Forensic Nurse Providing Health Care as Part of the Forensic Role
HIPAA rules and regulations apply	HIPAA privacy regulations apply to the nurse's forensic practice

INFORMED CONSENT

Informed consent should always be obtained *before* any procedure or treatment is *initiated*.

EXCEPTION TO OBTAINING INFORMED CONSENT

Emergent circumstances that may result in certain death or severe injury and/or harm to self or another (e.g., hemorrhage, fire, motor vehicle accident, sudden violent behavior)

Note: Every situation and circumstance needs to be assessed individually.

G. Consider issues of patient incompetence regarding informed consent
1. The patient's cognitive status needs to be fully assessed and documented.

    2. Obtain appropriate signatures of those persons authorized to provide consent.

    3. Ongoing assessment of the patient's cognitive status is imperative as the patient may regain periods of lucidity or full competency.

H. Temporary or permanent cognitive status alteration as a result of

    1. Medications (e.g., narcotics, intravenous benzodiazepines for immediate relief of disruptive or injurious behavior, medications that result in severe extrapyramidal symptoms, above normal blood alcohol level/s, illegal drugs, anesthesia, benzodiazepines as a sedative agent prior to a medical or interventional procedure, long-term sedation to decrease oxygen demand in those suffering from trauma resulting in severe life-threatening injuries)

    2. Physical disease processes (e.g., dementia, Alzheimer's disease, short- or long-term amnesia, cognitive genetic anomalies)

    3. Mental illness (e.g., *Diagnostic and Statistical Manual of Mental Disorders, Fourth Edition Text Revision* [DSM-IV-TR] diagnosis of psychosis presenting with symptoms such as hallucinations, dystonia not associated with medications, delusions, anhedonia, severe symptoms of depression)

II. American Hospital Association Patient Bill of Rights

  A. According to the American Hospital Association Patient Bill of Rights:

> The patient has the right to the information contained in the medical record.

  B. The patient has a right to know the following:

> - Diagnosis
> - Prognosis
> - Course of treatment
> - Any side effects from medications or treatments

III. Medical Record

> The medical record is the private property of the hospital or health care facility or physician.

IV. Forensic Nursing Documentation
   A. Forensic nursing/nursing rule #1: "If it doubt, write it out."

The responsibilities of the nurse or forensic nurse are to document all treatments and care (physical and psychological) and to account for all patient belongings in either forensic cases or nonforensic situations.

- It is the nurse's responsibility to document with accuracy and completeness.
- Maintenance of patient, victim, and perpetrator records for future reference is the responsibility of the institution/facility.

   B. Documentation
      1. The value of documentation can never be overstated:
         a. Is the principle tool used by health care providers to plan, coordinate, administer, and evaluate delivery of care to the patient
         b. Is a legal and business record
      2. Regarding the purpose of accurate documentation, the medical record is the only legally acceptable document that identifies patient care.
      3. An accurately documented medical record:
         a. Reflects the patient care provided
         b. Identifies the outcome of treatments and medications administered
         c. Allows communication between the various interdisciplinary members of the health care team
         d. Provides evidence of the nurse's legal responsibilities to the patient
         e. Demonstrates the application of standards of practice, scope of practice, and rules and regulations governing practice
         f. Reflects professional and ethical behavior
         g. Provides data for research, quality improvement, analysis of cost benefits or reductions
      4. Federal regulations to some extent determine the form and content of the medical record (e.g., Medicare, Medicaid).
      5. Every state requires all health care facilities to retain medical records in ample detail.

6. Lack of sufficient and accurate documentation may be a deciding factor if the victim is
   a. To receive compensation
   b. To receive justice
7. The license to practice nursing in the issuing state may be
   a. Suspended temporarily or permanently
   b. May face additional professional and legal issues
8. It is essential to be familiar with specific rules and regulations established for documentation based on practice environment (e.g., hospital, clinic, law enforcement).

V. Legal Significance of the Medical Record
   A. The medical record

1. Is legal proof regarding the nature and quality of care provided to the patient
2. Provides a defense against allegations of negligence, improper care, and omissions of care

   B. Regarding accuracy of the medical record:

1. Accuracy is presumed if no evidence of fraud or tampering exists.
2. Evidence of tampering may result in the record being ruled as inadmissible evidence in court.

   C. Accurate and complete documentation is the legal responsibility of every forensic nurse or nurse.

Use the right form
Always write in ink
Record all patient identifiers (e.g., full name, identification numbers)
Document all care given or actions taken in a timely manner
Use quotation marks for any patient or victim statements
Be specific
Document objective data
Write legibly

Use standard abbreviations only
Use medical terms you know
Use patient's or victim's own words
Document behaviors
Write on every line or entry
Leave no empty lines or entries
Sign every entry with your legal name and credentials
Do not use Wite-Out® or similar products
Do not erase
Do not write over
Do not scratch out entry or entries; use a single line to cross out any errors

D. The bottom line

Incomplete charting loses cases.

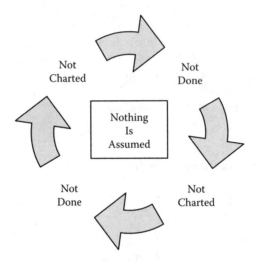

E. The saying "if you didn't chart it, you didn't do it" is as valid today as it was when it was first used and is a difficult thing for a defense to rebut.

VI. Malpractice and Negligence
    A. Negligence:

Continues to be the most common legal charge against nurses in *all* specialty areas

    B. Elements of negligence:

Duty is established when the nurse:

- Provides direct care to an individual
- Identifies an unattended person in need of care
- Observes or is aware of another provider performing care in a manner that may result in harm or injury

1. Breach of duty:

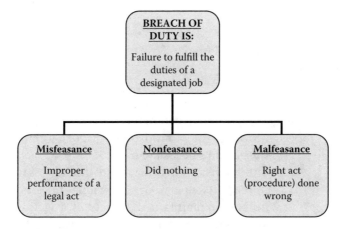

2. Causation:

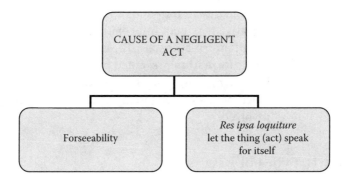

3. Forensic nurse
   a. The most common causes for negligence are

- Improper evidence identification, collection, preservation
- Breaking the chain of custody
- Lack of objective and complete documentation
- Failure to properly identify evidence resulting in damage or loss of evidence

   b. The importance and use of a nursing process cannot be overestimated. According to Sally Austin (2008, p. 35), the five steps of the nursing process recognized as a universal approach to nursing practice are

---

- Nursing diagnosis
- Assessment data
- Plan
- Intervention
- Evaluation

---

  c. Regarding chain of command:
   (1) Move up the administrative ladder to ensure that the patient's needs are met.
   (2) The forensic nurse may find this necessary if the immediate supervisory individual does not act to initiate or maintain the safety of a victim as well as the safety of those providing care for the victim, both living and deceased.
   (3) When the decision is made to report to a higher administrative individual, the nurse needs to have objective pertinent information and be able to present all information clearly.
   (4) The information presented by the nurse should follow the nursing process as an organizational tool.
   (5) Document steps taken and the name of individuals involved.

Appendix 1: Types of Law

Civil law: Statutory law that deals with relations among people (also called private law)

Common law: Law derived from previous decisions, not from statutes (most law in the area of malpractice is court-made law)

Criminal law: Deals with actions against the safety and welfare of the public, such as homicide and robbery

Statutory law: Law passed by a federal or state legislature

Legal Terms

Damages: An amount of money a court orders a defendant to pay the plaintiff

Defamation: An intentional tort in which one person discusses another in terms that diminish that person's reputation

Hearsay: Testimony regarding what others have said other than while testifying under oath; this information is not admissible in court

Libel: Written defamation

Malpractice: A general term referring to a deviation from the standard of care that a reasonable person would use under similar circumstances; may be omission or commission

Objection: A stated opposition to evidence based on law

Slander: Oral defamation

Statute of limitations: Law that specifies the length of time within which a person may file specific types of lawsuits

Tort: A legal wrong committed on a person or property

Respondeat superior: "Let the master answer." A legal doctrine that makes an employer liable for the consequences of his or her employee's wrongful conduct while the employee is acting within the scope of employment; another term used is *vicarious liability*

Assault: An unlawful attempt or threat to injure another physically

Battery: Unlawful touching of another without consent

False imprisonment: Intentional infliction of confinement, unjustifiably

Invasion of/right of privacy: Legal right that includes the freedom to live one's life without having one's name, photograph, or private affairs made public against one's will

Nursing standards of care: The duty the nurse owes to the patient to possess the degree of learning and skill ordinarily possessed by nurses in good standing and to exercise that degree of care ordinarily exercised by other members of the nursing profession acting in similar situations

Liability: Legal responsibility for failure to act and so causing harm to another person or for actions that fail to meet standards of care and so cause another person harm

Informed consent: Permission obtained from a patient to perform a specific test or procedure after the patient has been fully informed about the test or procedure

Patient's bill of rights: A list of patient's rights; the American Hospital Association, health care institution, and various medical, nursing, and consumer organizations have prepared such lists, which in some states have become law

Negligent nondisclosure: The failure to inform a patient completely about his or her treatment

Substitutive consent: Permission obtained from a parent or guardian of a patient who is a minor

Therapeutic privilege: A legal doctrine that permits a doctor, in an emergency situation, to withhold information from the patient if the doctor can prove that disclosing it would adversely affect the patient's health

Vicarious liability: Generally applied to crimes that affect the public welfare but do not require the imposition of a prison term; the

principle is that in such cases, the public interest is more important than private interest, and it is imposed to deter or to create
incentives for employers to impose stricter rules and supervise
more closely

Appendix 2: The Court System

I. Overview of the Judicial Branch
  A. The U.S. Constitution and the state constitutions establish and
    grant power to the courts.
  B. Both federal and state court systems are hierarchical.
    1. Three tiers in this hierarchy:
      a. Trial courts are the lowest level
        (1) The primary function is fact-finding.
        (2) The judge or jury hears evidence and enters a
           judgment.
      b. Second level is the intermediate courts of appeal or appel-
        late court:
        (1) The appellate court does not hold trials.
        (2) These courts hear the majority of appeals, deciding
           (a) Whether the trial court applied the right law
           (b) Whether there is sufficient evidence to support
               the jury's verdict or the trial judge's findings of
               fact and conclusions of law
        (3) The decisions of the appellate courts are based solely
           on the written record and the attorneys' arguments.
      c. The top level is the state supreme courts and the U.S.
        Supreme Court.
        (1) These courts only hear cases that involve issues of
           great public importance.
        (2) These courts hear cases in which different divisions
           of circuits have adopted or applied conflicting rules
           of law.
        (3) These courts do not hear evidence.
        (4) These courts only review the trial court record.

II. State Court System
  A. Individual state constitutions vest the judicial power of the state
    in one of three courts:
    1. Supreme court
    2. Court of appeals

  3. Trial courts:
   a. District courts
   b. County courts
   c. Other such courts as created by law
 B. State supreme court
  1. The Constitution provides original jurisdiction for the supreme court.
  2. The court's basic responsibility is appellate.
   a. Nebraska's court of last resort
  3. State constitution guarantees the right to appeal to the supreme court in capital and life imprisonment cases.
  4. Legislation permits a party to petition for appeal to the court in some other types of cases.
  5. This court regulates the practice of law in Nebraska.
 C. State court of appeals
  1. Created by the legislature in 1991
  2. Is an intermediate state appellate court
  3. Total of six judges on the court who sit in panels of three
  4. Appeals come directly to the court of appeals from
   a. District courts
   b. Separate juvenile courts
   c. Worker's compensation courts
   d. Certain regulatory agencies
  5. Some cases cannot be appealed from the district court to the court of appeals:
   a. Capital cases
   b. Cases for which life imprisonment has been imposed
   c. Cases involving the constitutionality of a statute
  6. Any party to a case appealed to the court of appeals may petition the supreme court for direct review by passing the court of appeals.
  7. Thirty days after the court has issued its decision in a case, any party may petition the supreme court for further review of the decision.
 D. District court
  1. A trial court of general jurisdiction
  2. Also an intermediate appellate court
   a. Decides appeals from the county courts
   b. Various administrative agencies
  3. Tries all felony cases and some misdemeanor ones
  4. Most misdemeanors tried in county court
  5. Tries all civil cases involving more than $10,000
  6. Some cases involving lesser amounts may also be tried

E. County court
    1. Exclusive jurisdiction in all cases regarding
        a. Probate
        b. Guardianship
        c. Conservatorship
        d. Adoption
        e. Eminent domain
    2. Provides all preliminary hearings in felony cases
    3. Sits as a juvenile court unless a separate juvenile court has been established in that county
F. Juvenile court
    1. Focus is to act in the best interest of the child
    2. Handles four types of cases, those involving
        a. Juvenile law violations (delinquents)
        b. Truant or uncontrollable children
        c. Neglect and dependency
        d. Termination of parental rights

III. Federal Court System
A. Article III, Section 1, of the U.S. Constitution vests the judicial power of the United States in one supreme court and in such inferior courts as Congress may establish.
B. U.S. Supreme Court
    1. Highest federal court
    2. Limits on power of the Supreme Court
    3. Can only play one of two roles:
        a. First role is to review decisions of the U.S. Court of Appeals and other federal courts
        b. Second role is
            (1) As the final arbiter of federal constitutional law
            (2) To interpret the U.S. Constitution
            (3) To determine whether the federal government or a state has violated rights granted under the U.S. Constitution
            (4) To mediate disputes between the federal government and the states and various state governments
        c. Can only hear a case if it involves a question of federal constitutional law or a federal statute
        d. Does not have the power to hear cases involving only questions of state law
C. U.S. Court of Appeals
    1. Intermediate court of appeals is the U.S. Court of Appeals

2. Thirteen circuits:
   a. Eleven numbered circuits
   b. District of Columbia circuit
   c. Federal circuit
      (1) Created in 1982; reviews decisions of the U.S. Claims Court and the U.S. Court of International Trade
      (2) Reviews some district courts and administrative decisions
   d. Reviews the written record and exhibits from the trial court

D. Federal district courts
1. The primary trial courts in the federal system
2. Have original jurisdiction over most federal questions
3. Have the power to review decisions of some administrative agencies
4. Each state has at least one
5. Some states have several
6. Cases not heard in one of the district courts are usually heard in one of the several specialized courts:
   a. U.S. Tax Court
   b. U.S. Court of Claims
   c. U.S. Court of International Trade

E. Bankruptcy court
1. Federal judicial districts handle bankruptcy matters and in almost all districts, bankruptcy cases are filed in the bankruptcy court.
2. Bankruptcy cases cannot be filed in state court.

Bibliography

American Nurses Association, Congress for Nursing Practice. (1980). *Nursing: A social policy statement.* Kansas City, MO: American Nurses Association.

American Nurses Association and International Association of Forensic Nurses. (1997). *Scope and standards of forensic nursing practice.* Washington, DC: American Nurses.

American Psychiatric Association. (2000). *Diagnostic and statistical manual of mental disorders* (4th ed., text revision). Washington, DC: Author.

Anderson, J. (Ed.). (2004, March). Vicarious trauma and its impact on advocates, therapists and friends. *Research and Advocacy Digest, 612,* 9–14.

Austin, S. (2008). Safe nursing practice. *Nursing2008,* 35–39.

Bailey, B. A. M. (2008, February/March). Forensic art: Project EDAN and the Doe Network. *Forensic Magazine, 3*(2), 18–22.

Bober, T., & Regehr, C. (2006). Strategies for reducing secondary or vicarious trauma: Do they work? *Brief Treatment and Crisis Intervention, 6,* 1–9.

Bongar, B. M. (2002). *The suicidal patient: Clinical and legal standards of care.* Washington, DC: American Psychological Association.

Brenner, J. (2002). *Forensic science: An illustrated dictionary.* Boca Raton, FL: CRC Press.

Brodsky, S. L. (1999). *Expert witness: More maxims and guidelines for testifying in court.* Washington, DC: American Psychological Association.

Burgess, A. W. (2002). *Violence through a forensic lens.* King of Prussia, PA: Nursing Spectrum, pp. 371–381.

Butts, J. B., & Rich, K. L. (2008). *Nursing ethics across the curriculum and into practice* (2nd ed.). Sudbury, MA: Jones and Bartlett.

Cashin, A., & Potter, E. (2006). Research and evaluation of clinical nurse mentoring: Implications for the forensic context. *Journal of Forensic Nursing, 2*(4), 189–193.

Clark, S. C., Ernst, M. F., Haglund, W. D., & Jentzen, J. M. (1996). *Medicolegal death investigator: A systematic training program for the professional death investigator, training text.* Big Springs, MI: Occupational Research and Assessment.

Cochran, M. (1999). The real meaning of patient-nurse confidentiality. *Critical Care Quarterly: Confronting Forensic Issues, 22*(1), 41–50.

Crewe, B. R. B. (2006). Overview of the American Justice System. In Hammer, R. M., Moynihan, B., & Pagliaro, E. M. (Eds.). *Forensic nursing: A handbook for practice* (pp. 178–213). Sudbury, MA: Jones and Bartlett.

Death investigation: A guide for scene investigators. (1996). Big Springs, MI: Occupational Research and Assessment.

Dudley, M. H. (2003). *Forensic medical investigation: Certification exam questions.* Wichita, KS: Dudley.

Eckert, W. G. (Ed.). (1997). *Introduction to forensic sciences* (2nd ed.). Boca Raton, FL: CRC Press.

Garner, B. A. (2006). *Black's law dictionary* (8th ed.). New York: Thomson Reuters.

Geberth, V. J. (1996). *Practical homicide investigation: Tactics, procedures, and forensic techniques* (3rd ed.). Boca Raton, FL: CRC Press.

Girard, J. E. (2008). *Criminalistics: Forensic science and crime.* Sudbury, MA: Jones and Bartlett, pp. 9–12.

Goll-McGee, B. (1999). The role of the clinical forensic nurse in critical care. *Critical Care Quarterly, 22*(1), 8–17.

Happel, R. (2003). Consideration of psychiatric case reviews. *Journal of Legal Nurse Consulting, 14*(2), 3–4.

Herdman, H. T., Health, C., Meyer, G., Scroggins, L., & Vassallo, B. (Editorial Committee). NANDA International. (2007). *NANDA-I nursing diagnoses: Definitions and classifications, 2007–2008.* Philadelphia: NANDA International.

Hoyt, C. A. (1999). Evidence recognition and collection in the clinical setting. *Critical Care Quarterly, 22*(1), 19–22.

Hoyt, C. A., & Spangler, K. A. (1996). Forensic nursing implications and the forensic autopsy. *Journal of Psychosocial Nursing and Mental Health Services, 34*(10), 24–31.

James, S. H., & Nordby, J. J. (Eds.). (2005). *Forensic science: An introduction to scientific and investigative techniques.* Boca Raton, FL: CRC Press.

Knight, B. (1991). *Forensic pathology.* New York: Oxford University Press.

Lee, H. C. (2000). *Physical evidence in forensic science.* Tucson, AZ: Lawyers and Judges.

Lynch, V. (2006). *Forensic nursing.* St. Louis, MO: Mosby.

McCann, I. L., & Pearlman, L. A. (1990). Vicarious traumatization: A framework for understanding the psychological effects of working with victims. *Journal of Traumatic Stress, 3*(1), 131–149.

Mosby's surefire documentation: How, what, and when nurses need to document (2nd ed.). (2006). St. Louis, MO: Mosby Elsevier.

Nurses's legal handbook (5th ed.). (2004). Sudbury, MA: Jones and Bartlett.

Porth, C. M. (2002). *Pathophysiology: Concepts of altered health states* (6th ed.). Hagerstown, MD: Lippincott Williams & Wilkins.

Quinn, C. (2005), *The medical record as a forensic resource.* Sudbury, MA: Jones and Bartlett.

Randolph, C. (2003). *How to give a winning deposition.* 14(1):17. Glenview, IL: American Association of Legal Nurse Consultants.

Silvia, A. J. (1999). Mechanism of injury in gunshot wounds: Myths and reality. *Critical Care Quarterly, 22*(1), 69–70.

Souryal, S. S. (2007). *Ethics in criminal justice: In search of the truth* (4th ed.). Newark, NJ: LexisNexis Group; Bender.

Spitz, W. U., Spitz, D., & Clark, R. (Eds.). (2006). *Spitz and Fisher's medicolegal investigation of death: Guidelines for the application of pathology to crime investigation* (4th ed.). Springfield, IL: Thomas.

Sung Tz'u. *The washing away of wrongs: Science, medicine, and technology in East Asia 1.* McKnight, B. E. (Trans.). (1981). Ann Arbor, MI: Center for Chinese Studies, University of Michigan.

U.S. Department of Justice Office for Victims of Crime. (2007, April 19). *Victim needs from a faith-based perspective; vicarious trauma* (pp. 1–2). Rockville, MD: National Institute of Justice.

Winfrey, M. E., & Smith, A. R. (1999). The suspiciousness factor: Critical care nursing and forensics. *Critical Care Quarterly, 22*(1), 1–6.

Forensic Nurse as an Expert Witness

15

DONNA GARBACZ BADER

I. Expert Witness Testimony
   A. *Frye v. United States*, 1923
      1. Established the standards of acceptance regarding expert witness testimony
      2. The standard states that the court can accept expert testimony on "well recognized scientific principle and discovery" if it is "sufficiently established and has achieved "general acceptance" in the scientific community.
      3. This ruling enables a new scientific test to be presented only after it has been thoroughly tested and accepted.
      4. The court refused to admit the blood pressure reading obtained during a polygraph test.
      5. In the court's opinion, the polygraph test had not gained enough scientific recognition to justify the result as admissible evidence in a court of law.
   B. *Daubert v. Merrell Dow Pharmaceuticals, Inc.*, 1993
      1. Rule 702 in the Federal Rules of Evidence
      2. The U.S. Supreme Court held that the "general acceptance" clause in *Frye v. United States* was not absolute.
      3. This case states that judges may use their discretion to admit expert testimony to "understand the evidence" and to "determine a fact in issue."
      4. The case states that for a new scientific technique or theory to be acceptable to the court, it must
         a. Be subject to testing and peer review
         b. Be standardized with a recognized maintenance of standards
         c. Must have a known and accepted rate of error
         d. Must attain widespread acceptance

II. Forensic Nurse as an Expert Witness
   A. Role
      1. Must maintain expertise in a particular area of nursing

2. Have the ability to translate nursing knowledge into an expert legal opinion
3. Have a broad knowledge of legal principles and communication skills
4. Must be aware of the limitations of his or her scope and standards of practice:
   a. State board rules and regulations, scope and standards of practice
   b. American Nurses Association (ANA) and International Association of Forensic Nurses (IAFN)
B. Responsibilities
   1. Prior to presenting testimony, forensic nurses should review the
      a. Precise scientific facts or definitions
      b. Specific standards of care addressed in each specific case
      c. Institution-based policies and procedures
      d. Chain of custody
      e. Evidence identification and collection
      f. Documentation
      g. Provision of medical care and treatment
      h. Care of the deceased victim or perpetrator
      i. Appropriate pharmacology, pathophysiology, anatomy
C. Qualifications
   1. Knowledge
   2. Skill
   3. Education
   4. Training
   5. Experience
   6. Credentials
D. Testimony
   1. When testifying, the forensic nurse must
      a. Present testimony clearly
      b. Relate nursing education and experience as an essential part of his or her nursing practice
      c. Establish the relationship between the practice of nursing and the practice of forensic nursing
      d. Be familiar with the judicial system and the rules and procedures for the jurisdiction in which the trial is held
      e. Base testimony on the reliability of accepted principles and methods
      f. Base testimony on sufficient facts or data
      g. Apply the principles and methods to the facts

      h. Be qualified to provide expert opinions in courts within the United States

      i. Anticipate that the specific science of forensic nurse opinion may be reviewed by the court and found to be reliable; the forensic nurse should expect the opposing attorney to ask questions regarding the forensic nurse's

        (1) Credentials

        (2) Training

        (3) Experience

        (4) Areas of expertise

        (5) Teaching positions

        (6) Publications in the field of forensic nursing

        (7) Any additional information that will validate expertise

2. The forensic nurse as a teacher for the judge and jury

    a. Identifies the holistic aspects of victim care

    b. Correlates the victim's injury to the evidence collected

    c. Carefully describes and defines medical terminology in a manner that allows both judge and jury to understand the issues related to the crime, injuries, and nursing care

E. Expert witness courtroom guidelines:

---

1. Dress professionally.
2. Maintain even voice level.
3. Sit straight.
4. Look attentive.
5. Listen to each question carefully.
6. Double negatives in a question may result in an incorrect reply.
7. Carefully consider questions such as, "Would you agree/disagree … ?" "Is it possible for … ?" "Would a reasonable and prudent nurse/forensic nurse … ?"
8. Speak clearly and audibly.
9. Be honest and believable.
10. Answer questions with clarity.
11. Be concise.
12. Use correct English.
13. Questions *do not* need to be answered immediately Answer a question with a verbal response only, such as "Yes," "No," "I don't understand the question," or "Could you please repeat the question?"

Continued

14. Avoid nonverbal responses (e.g., nodding, shrugging shoulders, rolling eyes, smiling inappropriately).
15. Avoid the use of slang or joking or sarcastic responses.
16. Avoid the use of incriminating words (e.g., "blame," "caused," "fault," "malpractice," "judgment," "criminal," "negligent").
17. Utilize written material when accurate or specific information is required.
18. Take time to carefully consider the question and compose an appropriate response.
19. Maintain eye contact when questioned.
20. Maintain eye contact with jury when answering.
21. Exude confidence.

    F. Incomplete charting loses cases.

III. The Jury
    A. Trial by an impartial jury of one's peers is guaranteed by the Sixth Amendment to the U.S. Constitution.
    B. *Peers*, as defined by the U.S. Supreme Court, means that the group of people selected to compose a jury must represent the community.
    C. Principal purpose of a jury is to employ commonsense judgment regarding the facts presented.
    D. The jury selection process of voir dire may be conducted by the attorneys or the judge.
       1. Attorneys and judges eliminate potential jurors through challenges (questions).
       2. Only a certain number of challenges (questions) are allowed.
       3. The number of people on a jury in criminal cases may vary among jurisdictions and per the severity of the offense.
       4. The jury eventually selected comes from diverse backgrounds, education, life experiences, and professions.
    E. Trial by jury versus trial by judge:
       1. Defendant may choose trial by judge over trial by jury
       2. The Sixth Amendment was interpreted to allow this choice by the U.S. Supreme Court in 1930.
       3. A question of guilt relating to a legal issue may prompt the defendant to waive the right of a jury trial, for example, plead that the criminal offense was
          a. Committed as a result of legal insanity
          b. Self-defense
          c. Accidental

  F. Jury deliberation is the exchange of opinions and ideas based on the facts presented during the trial in order to reach a verdict.

   1. Prior to deliberation, the judge provides the jury with instructions regarding application of the law to the evidence presented.

   2. Types of verdicts:

    a. Guilty: The defendant is legally judged to have committed the offense

    b. Not guilty: The defendant is legally judged not to have committed the offense.

    c. Mistrial: The jury is deadlocked and cannot reach a verdict.

    d. Jury nullification: A jury reaches a verdict that is inconsistent with the evidence presented; in a criminal case, the judge is required to enter a not guilty verdict of the jury. This prohibits the case from any further prosecution.

 G. Federal rules of evidence:

   1. The rules by which courts determine what evidence is admissible at a trial

   2. In determining what evidence is admissible, initially focus on the importance of the evidence presented

   3. Allocate between the parties the burden to produce evidence and the burden of convincing the court

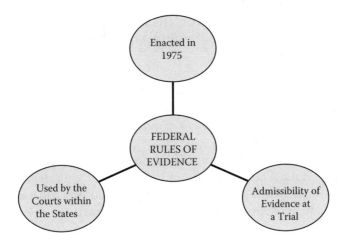

IV. Forensic Evidence Presented at Trial

 A. Methods by which evidence is presented to a jury in a manner that is understandable to the members

   1. Visual aids

   2. Video footage

   3. Still photographs

   4. Exhibits, which are cataloged pieces of evidence
   5. Audio recordings
   6. Transcripts of conversations
   7. Maps
   8. Handwriting
   9. Visit to the crime scene
 B. Fingerprint evidence
   1. Fingerprints are unique to each individual.
   2. It is difficult, if not impossible, to copy or forge fingerprints without altering the original.
   3. This evidence provides a means of proving the suspect's presence at the crime scene, especially if the crime scene is the secondary site and not the primary site where the crime occurred.
 C. Hair and fibers
   1. The presence of hair at the crime scene may be a source of evidence in that hairs are unique to each individual.
   2. Hair may contain DNA material, which will identify the individual and may not be duplicated or forged.
   3. Fibers may be useful in the identification of a specific weave or be unique to a particular brand or style.
 D. Computer evidence
   1. It is extremely difficult for an individual to dispose of his or her cybertrail.
   2. Specialized computer experts such as forensic computer technicians are able to reconstitute erased hard drives and to reassemble erased files.
 E. DNA evidence
   1. Specific type of evidence: A genetic fingerprint
   2. Cannot be altered, manipulated, or forged in any way
   3. Is recognized as one of the most accurate means of identifying a suspect
 F. For evidence to be admitted into court and presented before a jury, it must be proved that it was obtained, collected, and preserved according to established policy and procedure and that the chain of custody was properly maintained.

Bibliography

American Nurses Association, Congress for Nursing Practice. (1980). *Nursing: A social policy statement.* Kansas City, MO: American Nurses Association.

American Nurses Association and International Association of Forensic Nurses. (1997). *Scope and standards of forensic nursing practice.* Washington, DC: American Nurses.

American Psychiatric Association. (2000). *Diagnostic and statistical manual of mental disorders* (4th ed., text revision). Washington, DC: Author.

Anderson, J. (Ed.). (2004). Vicarious trauma and its impact on advocates, therapists and friends. *Research and Advocacy Digest, 612,* 9–14.

Bailey, B. A. M. (2008, February/March). Forensic art: Project EDAN and the Doe Network. *Forensic Magazine,* pp. 18–22.

Bober, T., & Regehr, C. (2006). Strategies for reducing secondary or vicarious trauma: Do they work? *Brief Treatment and Crisis Intervention, 6,* 1–9.

Bongar, B. M. (2002). *The suicidal patient: Clinical and legal standards of care.* Washington, DC: American Psychological Association.

Brenner, J. (2002). *Forensic science: An illustrated dictionary.* Boca Raton, FL: CRC Press.

Brodsky, S. L. (1999). *Expert witness: More maxims and guidelines for testifying in court.* Washington, DC: American Psychological Association.

Burgess, A. W. (2002). *Violence through a forensic lens.* King of Prussia, PA: Nursing Spectrum, pp. 371–381.

Butts, J. B., & Rich, K. L. (2008). *Nursing ethics across the curriculum and into practice* (2nd ed.). Sudbury, MA: Jones and Bartlett.

Cashin, A., & Potter, E. (2006). Research and evaluation of clinical nurse mentoring: Implications for the forensic context. *Journal of Forensic Nursing, 2*(4), 189–193.

Clark, S. C., Ernst, M. F., Haglund, W. D., & Jentzen, J. M. (1996). *Medicolegal death investigator: A systematic training program for the professional death investigator, training text.* Big Springs, MI: Occupational Research and Assessment.

Cochran, M. (1999). The real meaning of patient-nurse confidentiality. *Critical Care Quarterly: Confronting Forensic Issues, 22*(1), 41–50.

Committee on the Judiciary House of Representatives. (2004, December 31). *Federal rules of evidence.* Washington, DC: U.S. Government Printing Office.

Daubert v. Merrell Dow Pharmaceuticals, 509 U.S. 579 (1993). Retrieved Jan. 10, 2008 from http://supct.law.cornell.edu/supct/html/92-102.ZS.html

Death investigation: A guide for scene investigators. (1996). Big Springs, MI: Occupational Research and Assessment.

Dudley, M. H. (2003). *Forensic medical investigation: Certification exam questions.* Wichita, KS: Dudley.

Eckert, W. G. (Ed.). (1997). *Introduction to forensic sciences* (2nd ed.). Boca Raton, FL: CRC Press.

Frye v. United States. Retrieved Jan. 10, 2008 from http://law.jrank.org/pages/12871/Frye-v-United-States.html

Geberth, V. J. (1996). *Practical homicide investigation: Tactics, procedures, and forensic techniques* (3rd ed.). Boca, Raton, FL: CRC Press.

Girard, J. E. (2008). *Criminalistics: Forensic science and crime.* Sudbury, MA: Jones and Bartlett, pp. 9–12.

Goll-McGee, B. (1999). The role of the clinical forensic nurse in critical care. *Critical Care Quarterly, 22*(1), 8–17.

Hammer, R. M., Moynihan, B., & Pagliaro, E. M. (Eds.). (2006). *Forensic nursing: A handbook for practice.* Sudbury, MA: Jones and Bartlett, pp. 200–202.

Herdman, H. T., Heath, C., Meyer, G., Scroggins, L., & Vassallo, B. (Editorial Committee). NANDA International. (2007). *NANDA-I nursing diagnoses: Definitions and classifications, 2007–2008.* Philadelphia: NANDA International.

Hoyt, C. A. (1999). *Evidence recognition and collection in the clinical setting. Critical Care Quarterly, 22*(1), 19–22.

Hoyt, C. A., & Spangler, K. A. (1996). Forensic nursing implications and the forensic autopsy. *Journal of Psychosocial Nursing and Mental Health Services, 34*(10), 24–31.

James, S. H., & Nordby, J. J. (Eds.). (2005). *Forensic science: An introduction to scientific and investigative techniques.* Boca Raton, FL: CRC Press.

Knight, B. (1991). *Forensic pathology.* New York: Oxford University Press.

Lee, H. C. (2000). *Physical evidence in forensic science.* Tucson, AZ: Lawyers and Judges.

Lilly, G. C. (1996). *An introduction to the law of evidence.* Retrieved Jan. 10, 2008 from http://west.thomson.com/product/22093675/product.asp

Lynch, V. (2006). *Forensic nursing.* St. Louis, MO: Mosby.

McCann, I. L., & Pearlman, L. A. (1990). Vicarious traumatization: A framework for understanding the psychological effects of working with victims. *Journal of Traumatic Stress, 3*(1), 131–149.

Mosby's surefire documentation: How, what, and when nurses need to document (2nd ed.). (2006). St. Louis, MO: Mosby Elsevier.

Nurses's Legal Handbook (5th ed.). (2004). Sudbury, MA: Jones and Bartlett.

Porth, C. M. (2002). *Pathophysiology: Concepts of altered health states* (6th ed.). Hagerstown, MD: Lippincott Williams & Wilkins.

Quinn, C. (2005). *The medical record as a forensic resource.* Sudbury, MA: Jones and Bartlett.

Randolph, C. (2003). *How to give a winning deposition.* 14(1):10–17. Glenview, IL: American Association of Legal Nurse Consultants.

Silvia, A. J. (1999). Mechanism of injury in gunshot wounds: Myths and reality. *Critical Care Quarterly, 22*(1), 69–70.

Souryal, S. S. (2007). *Ethics in criminal justice: In search of the truth* (4th ed.). Newark, NJ: LexisNexis Group; Bender.

Spitz, W. U., Spitz, D., & Clark, R. (Eds.). (2006). *Spitz and Fisher's medicolegal investigation of death: Guidelines for the application of pathology to crime investigation* (4th ed.). Springfield, IL: Thomas.

Sung Tz'u. *The washing away of wrongs: Science, medicine, and technology in East Asia 1.* McKnight, B. E. (Trans.). (1981). Ann Arbor, MI: Center for Chinese Studies, University of Michigan.

U.S. Department of Justice Office for Victims of Crime. (2007, April 19). *Victim needs from a faith-based perspective; vicarious trauma*, pp. 1–2.

Winfrey, M. E., & Smith, A. R. (1999). The suspiciousness factor: Critical care nursing and forensics. *Critical Care Quarterly, 22*(1), 1–6.

The Perpetrator
A Victim and a Patient

16

DONNA GARBACZ BADER

I. Care for the Suspected and Convicted Offender
   A. The perpetrator of a crime is also likely to become a victim.
   B. Injury or death may occur
      - During or after commission of the crime
      - When victims attempt to defend themselves
      - When suicide is attempted after commission of the crime
      - During the arrest process
      - During incarceration
      - In an altercation with a crime partner
   C. Providing health care to the perpetrator who has committed a violent act may cause some health care professionals to question their individual ethical and moral values.
   D. It is necessary to remember the basic premise of the nursing profession, that of providing care that promotes a state of physical and mental wellness to those suffering from illness or injury and to help them return to a functional state of being.
   E. The injured and deceased victims (or perpetrator) of violent trauma or crime are varied in background and ideology, which should have no bearing on degree of health care and treatment available and received. Refer to the following:
      1. Fourth Amendment to the Constitution: Right to privacy
      2. American Hospital Association (1973): Statement on a Patient's Bill of Rights
      3. Hospice Association of America: Rights for Hospice Patients
      4. Joint Commission on the Accreditation of Healthcare Organizations
      5. American Civil Liberties Union
   F. When a suspected criminal presents to the health care facility for treatment, the forensic nurse must understand that the basic premise regarding the Fourth Amendment to the U.S. Constitution protects against unlawful search and seizure.
      1. The Fourth Amendment does not definitely prohibit all search and seizures; it only identifies unreasonable search and seizure.

    2. This exclusion is the most common rule that may affect the forensic nurse or nurse in relation to the suspected offender and the victim.

    3. In the case of *Mapp v. Ohio* (1961), the U.S. Supreme Court stated that evidence obtained through an unreasonable or unlawful search cannot be used against the person whose rights have been violated.

II. Direct Evidence Collection

  A. Blood test evidence

    1. The blood sample must be drawn in a medically reasonable manner; see *People v. Kraft* (1970).

    2. According to *Commonwealth v. Gordon* (1968), blood tests are admitted as evidence when the tests are medically necessary and not requested by police.

  B. Note: A forensic nurse or nurse or a physician who draws blood without the patient's consent may be liable for committing battery even if the patient is a suspected offender and the blood is necessary for medical purposes.

  C. Implied consent laws have been enacted in many states as part of the motor vehicle laws.

    1. These laws state that when an individual applies for a driver's license, the person implies consent to submit to a blood alcohol test if arrested for driving drunk.

    2. The forensic nurse must be aware of the state law arrests for drunk driving and if the implied consent law applies.

  D. When evidence is obtained during a surgical procedure or nonsurgical invasive procedure, immediately handing over the evidence to law enforcement may result in the evidence being inadmissible in a court of law.

    1. In 1985, the U.S. Supreme Court ruled that the constitutionality of court-ordered surgery to acquire evidence must be decided on a case-by-case basis

    2. Individual privacy and security interests must be weighed against the interest of society in the collection of evidence.

    3. Contraband may be swallowed by drug couriers to prevent detection or arrest and may be recovered after elimination.

    4. The U.S. Supreme Court in *United States v. Montoya de Hernandez* ruled that police may lawfully detain drug couriers until the swallowed item is recovered and seized.

    5. The forensic nurse must be cautious when assisting law enforcement in obtaining evidence from the offender,

especially if the offender does not give consent. Law enforcement must be able to prove that there is reasonable suspicion that the individual is a drug courier and that there is reasonable cause to suspect that contraband has been ingested.

E. When a forensic nurse/nurse removes evidence and later hands it over to law enforcement without a request, it is admissible as evidence (*State v. Perea*, 1981) since no government intrusion was involved, and there was no violation of the offender's Fourth Amendment rights.

F. When the forensic nurse or nurse examines an unconscious patient and discovers evidence, this evidence is admissible in court (*United States v. Winbush*, 1970) because the search was conducted to obtain identification of the patient and any available medical history.

III. Forensic Nursing in a Health Care Facility

A. The patient has a right to confidentiality and privacy regarding his or her medical information as well as any privileged information the patient chooses to discuss.

B. The Federal Privacy Act of 1974 states that any unauthorized or improper disclosure of medical information can be a legal misdemeanor or felony with punishment consisting of a fine or imprisonment.

C. The forensic nurse may place his or her professional license in jeopardy if confidentiality is breached.

D. It is necessary to differentiate if an incriminating statement is a "dying confession" or a violation of Fifth Amendment rights against self-incrimination.

E. In addition to constitutional rights, the American Nurses Association Code for Nurses states that the nurse will safeguard the patient's right to privacy by protecting confidential information. Only pertinent information related to the patient's treatment and welfare may be disclosed and disclosed only to those directly involved in the patient's care.

F. According to the *Scope and Standards of Forensic Nursing Practice*, Standards of Professional Practice: Standard V (American Nurses Association and International Association of Forensic Nurses, 1997), ethics defines the forensic nurse's decisions, actions are determined in an ethical manner, and each forensic nurse is aware of and adheres to local, state, and federal laws governing practice.

   G. Each health care facility has established safety policies and pro-
      cedures for the forensic nurse and other health care providers to
      follow when providing care and treatment to the patient who is
      detained for legal purposes.
   H. Safety measures are a part of health care facility policies to main-
      tain a safe environment for those providing care.
   I. All competent patients have the right to refuse any care, treat-
      ment, and medication regardless of their legal status.
   J. It is also very important to understand that there may be excep-
      tions to some policy or procedure based on individual circum-
      stances. These exceptions may revolve around legal, social, safety,
      and health issues, to mention only a few.

IV. Forensic Health in the Correctional Environment
   A. After conviction, an offender does not forfeit all constitutional
      rights.
   B. The Eighth Amendment protects the incarcerated offender
      against cruel and unusual punishment.
      1. Prison officials and health care workers cannot knowingly or
         intentionally ignore a prisoner's medical needs.
      2. The state has an obligation to provide medical care for those
         imprisoned.
   C. The correctional environments are some of the most controver-
      sial and stress producing in society.
   D. The forensic correctional population is varied, ranges from the
      young to the old, and includes both males and females, victims
      and perpetrators.
   E. Basic types of correctional facilities include
      1. Federal prison
      2. State prison
      3. Jail (local)
   F. The most common barrier to the patient seeking medical or men-
      tal health care is the culture, especially within the prison system:
      1. The correctional environment does not allow, accept, or tol-
         erate any signs of weakness, either physical or psychological.
      2. Prison society values order, compliance, and submission.
      3. Normal behavior includes use of drugs and physical and
         mental abuse among the prison population.

V. Nursing Care
   A. Nurses represent the largest group of health care professionals
      practicing in forensic mental health and correctional settings.

B. Working daily with offenders can be physically and psychologically demanding.

C. Offenders may be abusive, manipulative, and hostile toward the nurse and other health care providers.

D. A competent offender may refuse medical treatment; however, the offender does not have the right to refuse lifesaving measures, such as oxygen, hemodialysis, and insulin (*Commissioner of Correction v. Myers*, 1979). If an offender refuses lifesaving measures, the forensic nurse must immediately inform the administration of the facility.

E. For the forensic nurse to provide appropriate nursing care, the nurse must follow the guidelines of the profession relating to providing care in a manner of respect, ethical practice, legal considerations, and positive outcomes.

1. Understand and adapt to the culture of the specific facility
2. Be highly focused and objective
3. Be confident of personal assessment skills
4. Be familiar with the facility policies and procedures regarding organizational structure and those regulating the provision of health care
5. Be familiar with own duties and responsibilities when providing physical or psychological care
6. Understand and respect the various cultures and beliefs
7. Provide treatment based on individual assessment and evidence
8. Provide objective and complete documentation

VI. Mental Health and Risk for Violence

A. Confidentiality and privacy issues in the patient suffering from a diagnosed mental disability are varied based on the individual level of competence.

B. Offenders suffering with mental illness represent a majority of those in correctional facilities.

C. Being incarcerated is a significantly stressful event for those who do not suffer from mental illness and produces an exacerbation of symptoms in those suffering from mental illness.

D. The issue of placing offenders with a known mental illness within the criminal justice system has been the subject of current and future planning to improve the jail and prison system.

E. Society as a whole continues to view prisons and jails as the most appropriate venue to place offenders with mental illness and demands that federal and state governments develop and provide a system of care and treatment for these offenders separate from the general population.

F. A thorough forensic mental health examination is essential to rule out or confirm the presence of any other mental health symptoms and identify a diagnosis based on the current *Diagnostic and Statistical Manual of Mental Disorders* (*DSM-IV-TR*; American Psychiatric Association, 2000).

G. *DSM-IV-TR* disorder classifications

---

1. Disorders Usually Diagnosed in Infancy, Childhood, or Adolescence
2. Delirium, Dementia, and Amnestic and Other Cognitive Disorders
3. Mental Disorders Due to a General Medical Condition
4. Substance Abuse Disorders
5. Schizophrenia and Other Psychotic Disorders
6. Mood Disorders
7. Anxiety Disorders
8. Somatoform Disorders
9. Factitious Disorders
10. Dissociative Disorders

11. Sexual and Gender Identity Disorders
12. Eating Disorders
13. Sleep Disorders
14. Impulse-Control Disorders
15. Adjustment Disorders
16. Personality Disorders
17. Other Conditions That May Be a Focus of Attention
18. Additional Codes-Not Otherwise Specified
19. Multiaxial System

From: DSM-IV-TR, 2000, pp. 13–26.

H. Risk factors for violent behavior

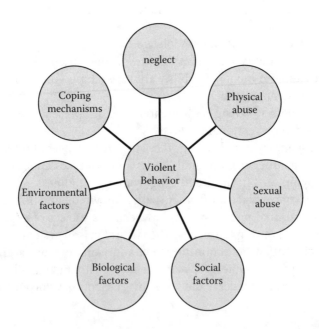

1. There is no single factor that can identify an individual as a potential offender; rather, there are a multitude of factors that contribute to development of offenders.
2. The U.S. Department of Justice, Federal Bureau of Investigation, found that the perpetrators of violent crime have the right biological predisposition, framed by their psychological makeup, that exists at a critical time in that person's social development.
3. Not all offenders of frequent violent crime (serial murders) are psychopaths; however, psychopathy alone does not explain the motivation for the violent criminal offenses.

I. Post-traumatic stress disorder (PTSD)
   1. The most common mental health disorder used in a criminal defense is PTSD.
   2. It is essential that the forensic examiner be familiar with the *DSM-IV-TR* definition of PTSD and the various traumatic stressors that may precipitate symptoms.
   3. For a PTSD defense to be valid, the defense must prove adherence to the *DMS* criteria.
   4. In many cases, the primary goal of the defendant is to try to convince the forensic examiner that the act committed is due to the PTSD condition, thus prompting a more lenient sentence.
   5. Traumatic memories must be correlated with objective evidence.

J. Dual diagnoses: Offenders are often diagnosed after incarceration with dual diagnoses.
   1. Substance abuse is most often a major factor in dual diagnosis and is usually associated with
      a. Antisocial personality disorder
      b. Bipolar disorder
      c. Schizophrenia
      d. Mood disorders
   2. Substance abuse can and does lead to increased aggression and violence.
   3. Developmental disabilities and mental illness.

K. Criminal profiling: A tool for criminal investigation
   1. The basic premise of criminal profiling is that behavior reflects personality.
   2. Criminal profiling is used most extensively by behavioral scientists and law enforcement in an investigation to narrow the field of suspects who possess certain behavioral and personality features that are discovered in the way a crime is committed.

3. In interpreting the offender's behavior at the crime scene, certain traits and characteristics can be attributed to the unknown offender.

4. The most valuable data consist of a combination of crime scene examination, investigative experience, an understanding of offender and victim behavior, knowledge of wound patterns, and forensic evidence.

5. An additional use of a profile is to request assistance from the public by providing specific information displayed by the unknown offender that may have been observed by another person.

6. As a result of psychological criminal profiling, a significant aspect of the developmental process of violent offenders has emerged and is now accepted as evident to some degree in all offenders who commit multiple violent criminal acts (serial murder); it is called the *homicidal triad*.

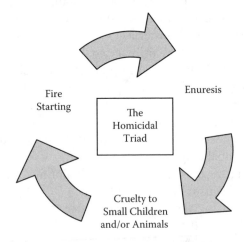

Fire Starting

Enuresis

The Homicidal Triad

Cruelty to Small Children and/or Animals

L. Legal aspects of mental health

1. Understanding an offender's state of mind has incredible bearing on the legal proceeding that plays an important part in determining the offender's guilt or innocence.

2. The goal of a thorough psychiatric assessment is to uncover any psychiatric disorder and to establish the offender's thought processes and cognitive abilities.

3. In addition to the psychiatric assessment, the forensic nurse must perform a thorough physical assessment.

4. Medical disorders and their treatment may alter cognition and behavior, just as psychiatric disorders and their treatments may alter an active medical disorder.

5. Physical and psychiatric assessments should also include the individual's past history (both medical and social). Observe nonverbal communications, vocal tone, overall appearance, and behavior. Does the behavior match the story? Does the story match the behavior?

6. Competency to stand trial relates to the current mental state of the defendant and the defendant's current ability to make a defense in court.

7. An insanity defense relates to the state of mind of the defendant at the time of the offense.

8. A finding of guilty but mentally ill means that the offender is found guilty but as a result of the plea that the mental illness caused the individual to commit the crime, the offender is sent to prison and treated for that mental illness.

VII. Nursing Diagnosis and Forensic Nursing Care
   A. Simply by being in the wrong place at the wrong time, the suspected or convicted offender or perpetrator is just as susceptible to becoming a victim of crime as the victim who survived a drive-by shooting.
   B. The professional forensic nurse sees no difference in the two victims; both receive the best possible nursing care and treatment, the most competent medical care and treatment with the same respect and dignity deserving of any person suffering either mentally or physically.
   C. The nursing process identifies a specific nursing diagnosis, and provides the forensic nurse with an organized and appropriate guideline for the provision of care and evaluation of outcomes and both long- and short-term goals.

Bibliography

American Hospital Association (1973/Rev. 1992). *A patient's Bill of Rights.* Retrieved Jan. 10, 2008 from http://www.aha.org/resource/pbillofrights.html

American Nurses Association, Congress for Nursing Practice. (1980). *Nursing: A social policy statement.* Kansas City, MO: American Nurses Association.

American Nurses Association and International Association of Forensic Nurses. (1997). *Scope and standards of forensic nursing practice.* Washington, DC: American Nurses.

American Psychiatric Association. (2000). *Diagnostic and statistical manual of mental disorders* (4th ed., text revision). Washington, DC: Author.

Anderson, J. (Ed.). (2004, March). Vicarious trauma and its impact on advocates, therapists and friends. *Research and Advocacy Digest, 612,* 9–14.

Bailey, B. A. M. (2008, February/March). Forensic art: Project EDAN and the Doe Network. *Forensic Magazine*, pp. 18–22.

Bober, T., & Regehr, C. (2006). Strategies for reducing secondary or vicarious trauma: Do they work? *Brief Treatment and Crisis Intervention, 6*, 1–9.

Bongar, B. M. (2002). *The suicidal patient: Clinical and legal standards of care.* Washington, DC: American Psychological Association.

Brenner, J. (2002). *Forensic science: An illustrated dictionary.* Boca Raton, FL: CRC Press.

Brodsky, S. L. (1999). *Expert witness: More maxims and guidelines for testifying in court.* Washington, DC: American Psychological Association.

Burgess, A. W. (2002). *Violence through a forensic lens.* King of Prussia, PA: Nursing Spectrum, pp. 371–381.

Butts, J. B., & Rich, K. L. (2008). *Nursing ethics across the curriculum and into practice* (2nd ed.). Sudbury, MA: Jones and Bartlett.

Cashin, A., & Potter, E. (2006). Research and evaluation of clinical nurse mentoring: Implications for the forensic context. *Journal of Forensic Nursing, 2*(4), 189–193.

Clark, S. C., Ernst, M. F., Haglund, W. D., & Jentzen, J. M. (1996). *Medicolegal death investigator: A systematic training program for the professional death investigator, training text.* Big Springs, MI: Occupational Research and Assessment.

Cochran, M. (1999). The real meaning of patient-nurse confidentiality. *Critical Care Quarterly: Confronting Forensic Issues, 22*(1), 41–50.

Criminal profiling. Retrieved from http://www.mytholyoke.edu/~mlyount/MySites/Forensic Psychology/CriminalProfiling.html

Death investigation: A guide for scene investigators. (1996). Big Springs, MI: Occupational Research and Assessment.

Douglas, J. E. (1993). *The criminal profiler* (Vol. 1) [A&E Collector's Choice Video, VHS]. Documentary. New York.

Douglas, J. E., et al. (1986). Criminal profiling from crime scene analysis. *Behavioral Science Law, R,* 401.

Dudley, M. H. (2003). *Forensic medical investigation: Certification exam questions.* Wichita, KS: Dudley.

Eckert, W. G. (Ed.). (1997). *Introduction to forensic sciences* (2nd ed.). Boca Raton, FL: CRC Press.

Fortinash, K., & Holoday Worret, P. (2008). *Psychiatric mental health nursing* (4th ed.). St. Louis, MO: Mosby/Elsevier, pp. 164–165.

Geberth, V. J. (1996). *Practical homicide investigation: Tactics, procedures, and forensic techniques* (3rd ed.). Boca, Raton, FL: CRC Press.

Girard, J. E. (2008). *Criminalistics: Forensic science and crime.* Sudbury, MA: Jones and Bartlett, pp. 9–12.

Gold, L. (2005). The role of PTSD in litigation. *Psychiatric Times, 23*(14). Retrieved August 23, 2008, from http://www.psychiatrictimes.com/display/article/10168/47651

Goll-McGee, B. (1999). The role of the clinical forensic nurse in critical care. *Critical Care Quarterly, 22*(1), 8–17.

Herdman, H., Heath, C., Meyer, G., Scroggins, L., & Vassallo, B. (Editorial Committee). NANDA International. (2007). *NANDA-I nursing diagnoses: Definitions and classifications, 2007–2008.* Philadelphia: NANDA International.

Hospice Association of America. *Hospice patient (2007–2008). Bill of Rights.* Retrieved Jan. 10, 2008 from http://www.nahc.org/haa/attachments/billofrights.pdf.

Hoyt, C. A. (1999). Evidence recognition and collection in the clinical setting. *Critical Care Quarterly, 22*(1), 19–22.

Hoyt, C. A., & Spangler, K. A. (1996). Forensic nursing implications and the forensic autopsy. *Journal of Psychosocial Nursing and Mental Health Services, 34*(10), 24–31.

Hufft, A., & Kate, M. (2003). Vulnerable populations and cultural perspectives for nursing care in correctional system. *Journal of Multicultural Nursing and Health, 9*(1), 18–26.

Hufft, A., & Peternelj-Taylor, C. (2000). Forensic nursing. In J. T. Catalano (Ed.), *Contemporary professional nursing* (2nd ed.). Philadelphia.

Knight, B. (1991). *Forensic pathology.* New York: Oxford University Press.

Lee, H. C. (2000). *Physical evidence in forensic science.* Tucson, AZ: Lawyers and Judges.

Lynch, V. (2006). *Forensic nursing.* St. Louis, MO: Mosby.

McCann, I. L., & Pearlman, L. A. (1990). Vicarious traumatization: A framework for understanding the psychological effects of working with victims. *Journal of Traumatic Stress, 3*(1), 131–149.

Mosby's surefire documentation: How, what, and when nurses need to document (2nd ed.). (2006). St. Louis, MO: Mosby Elsevier.

National Alliance for the Mentally Ill (NAMI)—New York State and the Urban Justice Center Mental Health Project. (2001). *How to help when a person with mental illness is arrested.* Albany, NY, pp. 17–19, 27.

National Institute of Correction. Retrieved Jan. 10, 2008 from http://www.nationalinstituteofcorrections.gov/Features/Library/?CORP=National%20Institute%20of%20Corrections%20(Washington,%20DC)

National Institute of Justice. (2006). *Corrections: Improving programs and practices.* National Institute of Justice 2006 Annual Report, pp. 37–40.

National Institute of Justice. Retrieved Jan. 10, 2008 from http://www.ojp.usdoj.gov/nij/topics/forensics/welcome.htm

Nurses's legal handbook (5th ed.). (2004). Sudbury, MA: Jones and Bartlett.

Peternelj-Taylor, C. (2005). Mental health promotion in forensic and correctional environments. *Journal of Psychosocial Nursing, 43*(9), 8–9.

Porth, C. M. (2002). *Pathophysiology: Concepts of altered health states* (6th ed.). Hagerstown, MD: Lippincott Williams & Wilkins.

Quinn, C. (2005). *The medical record as a forensic resource.* Sudbury, MA: Jones and Bartlett.

Silvia, A. J. (1999). Mechanism of injury in gunshot wounds: Myths and reality. *Critical Care Quarterly, 22*(1), 69–70.

Souryal, S. S. (2007). *Ethics in criminal justice: In search of the truth* (4th ed.). Newark, NJ: LexisNexis Group, Bender.

Sung Tz'u. *The washing away of wrongs: Science, medicine, and technology in East Asia 1.* McKnight, B. E. (Trans.). (1981). Ann Arbor, MI: Center for Chinese Studies, University of Michigan.

Turvey, B. *Criminal profiling: An introduction to behavioral evidence analysis.* Retrieved Jan. 10, 2008 from http://www.ajp.psychiatryonline.org/cgi/content/full/157/9/1532

U.S. Department of Justice, Federal Bureau of Investigation, Behavioral Analysis Unit National Center. (2005, August). The Analysis of Violent Crime Symposium, San Antonio, TX (pp. 11–18). Rockville, MD: National Institute of Justice.

U.S. Department of Justice Office for Victims of Crime. (2007, April 19). Victim needs from a faith-based perspective. *Vicarious Trauma* (pp. 1–2).

Winfrey, M. E., & Smith, A. R. (1999). *The suspiciousness factor: Critical care nursing and forensics. Critical Care Quarterly, 22*(1), 1–6.

Ethics and Forensic Nursing Practice

17

DONNA GARBACZ BADER

I. Law versus Ethics
   A. Laws are compulsory rules of conduct that are enforced by authority.
   B. Ethics examine values, actions, and choices to establish right and wrong.
   C. Occasionally, law, ethics, and best practice do not agree.
   D. Based on one's individual philosophy and perceptions, certain actions may be considered morally or legally vague.

II. Ethics Related to Forensic Nursing/Nursing Practice
   A. Ethics supply tools for solving dilemmas based on personal or social values.
   B. Clinical ethics guide the clinician relating to ethical behavior.
   C. Health care ethics are related to the law.
   D. Ethics in relation to forensic nursing practice should reflect
      1. Respect for persons
      2. Beneficence
      3. Justice
      4. Respect for community or society
      5. Caring

III. Ethical Issues Arising in Forensic Nursing
   A. Victims or perpetrators may be labeled based on factors specific to disease, occupation, lifestyle, mental capacity, gender, or any number of physical and psychological factors.
   B. The practice of forensic nursing places the nurse into relationships involving criminal activities and the victims injured or killed by criminal actions.
   C. Relationships with perpetrators may expose the nurse to violence, and behaviors of the perpetrator may result in nursing decisions that are not legally or ethically sound.
   D. Problems in developing a helpful and caring relationship may be altered when the patient is the victim.

E. Sympathy may prevail over empathy when caring for the victim.
F. Accept the concept of victim responsibility and consequence
  1. For recommended care and follow-up
  2. To the court if possible
  3. To society
G. Accept the concept of perpetrator responsibility and consequences
  1. For criminal action
  2. For actions for own care and healing

IV. Ethical Issues Relating to Forensic Nursing
  A. Decisions in forensic nursing practice need to consider the most appropriate course of action based on the patient's immediate needs.
  B. Regarding treatment versus confinement:
    1. Is the care and treatment of the patient secondary to maintaining the safety of the patient and nurse?
    2. Is care and treatment essential to maintain life, and is sedation or restraint necessary to provide immediate care?
  C. Privacy and confidentiality vary depending on the situation and circumstances:
    1. Working within the jail, prison, or detention center
    2. Providing care and treatment to a prisoner in a clinical setting

V. Moral Ethical Dilemmas
  A. Are ethical problems that cause a conflict of right, responsibilities, and values
  B. Cause a great deal of individual stress and anxiety
  C. May be complicated by psychological pressures and personal emotions
  D. May involve choices about justice or fairness

VI. Types of Moral Dilemmas

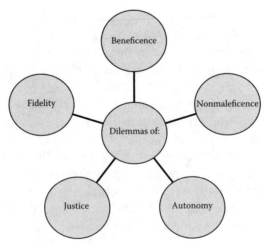

VII. Ethical Decisions
    A. The following criteria are necessary to make an ethical decision:
        1. Should be best clinical practice
        2. Should be within the scope of practice
        3. Should be within established policies and procedures
        4. Should be legal
        5. Should be the right moral action to take
    B. Understand that value conflicts occur among forensic nurses, nurses, physicians, clients, families, law enforcement personnel, established law, all forensic investigative team members.
    C. The forensic nurse needs to clarify personal values.

VIII. Forensic Nursing Practice
    A. The *Scope and Standards of Forensic Nursing Practice Standard V* (American Nurses Association and International Association of Forensic Nurses, 1997)
        1. Identifies the forensic nurse's responsibility to the victim, perpetrator, family, and community
        2. Identifies the need for respect, integrity, and justice for the victim in investigating and caring for the victim of crime
    B. International Association of Forensic Nurses (IAFN) *Code of Ethics* (2006)
        1. Was revised as a separate document in 2006
        2. Identifies five basic ethical concepts
            a. Responsibility to the public and the environment
            b. Obligation to science
            c. Care of the profession
            d. Dedication to colleagues
            e. Fidelity to clients

IX. The Nursing Process and Ethical Decisions
    A. The systematic organizational and objective approach of the nursing process can be used effectively when making ethical decisions:

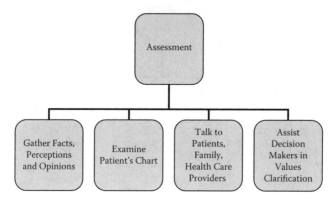

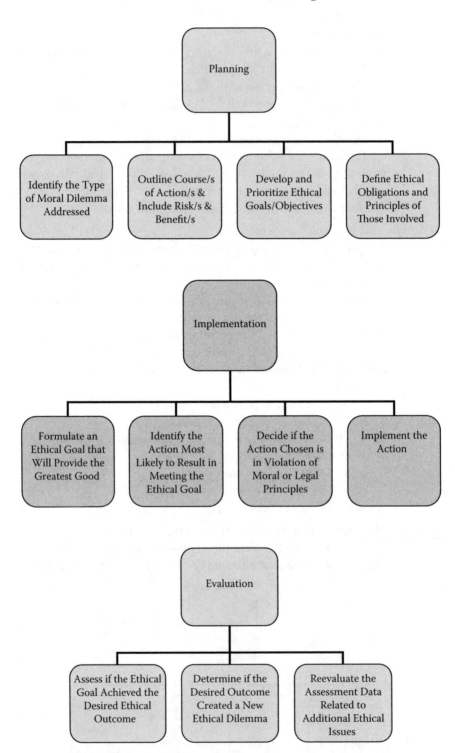

B. It is important to remember when addressing ethical and moral dilemmas that individual values and morals may result in planning goals that may not be for the greater good of the patient; professional ethics and legal responsibility must remain the primary focus in the decision-making process.

C. As a result of the numerous issues regarding ethical dilemmas, the nursing process offers the forensic nurse an organized outline for identifying issues and for planning toward an outcome that will provide for the greater good.

Bibliography

American Nurses Association. (2001). *Code of ethics for nurses with interpretive statements*. Silver Springs, MD: Author, pp. 7–9.

American Nurses Association, Congress for Nursing Practice. (1980). *Nursing: A social policy statement*. Kansas City, MO: American Nurses Association.

American Nurses Association and International Association of Forensic Nurses. (1997). *Scope and standards of forensic nursing practice*. Washington, DC: American Nurses.

Butts, J. B., & Rich, K. L. (2008). *Nursing ethics across the curriculum and into practice* (2nd ed.). Sudbury, MA: Jones and Bartlett.

Cashin, A., & Potter, E. (2006). Research and evaluation of clinical nurse mentoring: implications for the forensic context. *Journal of Forensic Nursing, 2*(4), 189–193.

Cochran, M. (1999). The real meaning of patient-nurse confidentiality. *Critical Care Quarterly: Confronting Forensic Issues, 22*(1), 41–50.

Goll-McGee, B. (1999). The role of the clinical forensic nurse in critical care. *Critical Care Quarterly, 22*(1), 8–17.

Hammer, R. M., Moynihan, B., & Pagliaro, E. M. (Eds.). (2006). *Forensic nursing: A handbook for practice*. Sudbury, MA: Jones and Bartlett, pp. 200–202.

Herdman, H., Heath, C., Meyer, G., Scroggins, L., & Vassallo, B. (Editorial Committee). NANDA International. (2007). *NANDA-I nursing diagnoses: Definitions and classifications, 2007–2008*. Philadelphia: NANDA International.

International Association of Forensic Nurses. (2006). *International Association of Forensic Nurses code of ethics: The forensic nurse's code of ethics*. Arnold, MD: Author.

Lynch, V. (2006). *Forensic nursing*. St. Louis, MO: Mosby.

Mosby's surefire documentation: How, what, and when nurses need to document (2nd ed.). (2006). St. Louis, MO: Mosby Elsevier.

Sung Tz'u. *The washing away of wrongs: Science, medicine, and technology in East Asia 1*. McKnight, B. E. (Trans.). (1981). Ann Arbor, MI: Center for Chinese Studies, University of Michigan.

Psychosocial Aspects of Crime

18

DONNA GARBACZ BADER

I. Psychological Response and Considerations
   A. The physical and psychological health and safety of each victim should always be the forensic nurse's first priority.
   B. The care and treatment provided by the forensic nurse may affect the victim for the rest of his or her life.
   C. All patients, victims, and perpetrators have emotional, psychological, and spiritual sides.
   D. Emotions are a part of the human makeup, and many traumatic events produce a fear of possible death or physical incapacity, leading to an emotional response that may result in further injury to the victim as well as to the health care providers.

II. The Forensic Nurse
   A. Care of self
      1. The forensic nurse needs to be aware of his or her emotional response to the constant exposure of working with victims, perpetrators, and the effects of violence, crime, disasters, and any traumatic event that becomes part of the forensic nurse's "work."
      2. The professional field of nursing carries numerous responsibilities and expectations, including those from
         a. Patients, clients, or victims
         b. Medical staff
         c. Administration
         d. Peers
         e. Families, friends, or support system
         f. The nurse himself or herself
      3. Positive outcomes related to nursing actions are the expectation.
      4. The forensic nurse or nurse realizes the need to relieve pain (physical and emotional) and to seek justice for those unable to speak for themselves, such as the dead, the mentally or physically impaired, and the innocent.

5. The nurse's expectations for his or her responsibilities prove to be the most common cause of stress.
6. Feelings of guilt may develop when caring for a patient who is also the perpetrator and who has intentionally caused injury or death to another.
7. Feelings of fear and repulsion toward perpetrators and the nature of the crimes may induce symptoms of severe depression and loss of confidence in the nurse's own forensic and nursing skills.

III. Vicarious Trauma
   A. Vicarious trauma is a stress reaction experienced by a provider who is continually exposed to the effects of witnessing and listening to descriptions of traumatic images and assisting victims of adult and child sexual abuse and domestic violence and those who have died.
   B. Vicarious trauma is a natural reaction.
   C. Vicarious Trauma is
      1. Not direct trauma
      2. Caused by second-hand exposure
      3. An accumulation of constant exposure to other people's trauma
   D. The most important aspects of coping with the intensity of this type of work are to acknowledge that you will be affected and to give yourself permission to distance yourself from the circumstances and focus on providing appropriate care and treatment.
   E. As a result of the distinctive impact of treating trauma victims, vicarious trauma is only common in trauma-related occupations.
   F. Vicarious trauma is also called
      1. Compassion fatigue
      2. Secondary trauma
      3. Secondary traumatic syndrome
      4. Secondary traumatic stress disorder
      5. Empathy stress
   G. Factors that may increase the probability of developing vicarious trauma symptoms are
      1. The degree of empathy that the forensic nurse feels for the victim's suffering
      2. Unexpected or repeated exposure to trauma
      3. Lack of experience working with trauma victims
      4. One's own unresolved emotional issues

H. The impact of vicarious trauma on the forensic nurse may
   1. Overwhelm coping mechanisms
   2. Reduce effectiveness of providing appropriate care and treatment
   3. Produce a feeling of helplessness
   4. Cause detachment from other coworkers not involved in providing forensic care
   5. Cause detachment from family and friends
   6. Decrease tenure as a forensic nurse
I. Symptoms of vicarious trauma resemble those of post-traumatic stress disorder (PTSD).
   1. Based on individual life experiences, the forensic nurse may have been exposed to a traumatic event, either as a victim or as a witness, and thus become a greater risk for the development of PTSD.
   2. Symptoms of PTSD may become evident when the forensic nurse is caring for a victim, living or deceased, who has suffered from the same or similar injuries under similar conditions.
   3. The traumatic event is frequently reexperienced by
      a. Frequent investigation of sexual assault victims
      b. Frequent investigation of death scenes in which the victim sustained similar injuries but survived
      c. Frequent interaction with perpetrators in an environment that the nurse perceives as threatening (further discussion related to PTSD is in Section VI, The Victim and Perpetrator).
J. Three categories of symptoms of vicarious trauma

Intrusions	Avoidance	Hyperarousal
• Flashbacks • Nightmares • Loss of safety and control • Loss of compassion • Loss of trust	• Isolation • Disconnection from people or situations that produce intrusive symptoms • Feelings of despair • Low self-esteem • Feelings of powerlessness	• Hypervigilance • Sleeplessness • Increased startle response • Increased anxiety • Increased anxiety attacks

K. If the forensic nurse, peer, coworker, friend, or family member identifies symptoms related to ineffective coping, it is imperative for that person to seek assistance as to what action should be taken to provide an appropriate intervention for the nurse affected by vicarious trauma.

L. Coping strategies for vicarious trauma are as follows:

Therapeutic Coping Strategies	Personal Coping Strategies
• Limit exposure to traumatic material • Accept your reaction as a normal response to specialized work • Develop supportive environment • Recognize that vicarious trauma is an occupational hazard of working with trauma victims	• Engage in activities that promote physical health • Engage in leisure activities • Seek both emotional and active support • Take occasional mental health days • Seek experiences that provide comfort and hope

M. If the forensic nurse, peers, coworkers, friends, or family members identify symptoms related to ineffective coping, it is imperative that the nurse be removed from the immediate environment and care be transferred to another forensic nurse, professional nurse, or appropriate professional health care or mental health care provider.

IV. Victimology
   A. *Victimology* is the study of the victim's characteristics by establishing a measure of that person's risk of becoming a victim as a result of his or her personal, professional, and social life.
   B. As a result of an increase in victim research, two classifications of victimology have developed:
      1. Forensic victimology: The study of the victims of violent crime for the purpose of criminal investigation

---

FORENSIC VICTIMOLOGY INVOLVES

A critical and objective description of a victim's lifestyles and the circumstances and events that led up to an injury and the exact nature of any harm, suffering, or death

---

PRINCIPLES OF FORENSIC VICTIMOLOGY

1. Developing a through understanding of the victims and their situation provides information sufficient to interpret the nature of injury or death and the perpetrator, correlating this information to the crime
2. Develop a victim profile
3. Develop a criminal profile

FORENSIC VICTIMOLOGY INVESTIGATION

As a specialty within the field of forensic science, the scientific method is the structural tool or process used in the investigative process.

PURPOSE OF FORENSIC VICTIMOLOGY

To provide justice by presenting to the court all investigative evidence and proof to establish that a crime was committed and that there is or was a victim.

2. General victimology: The study of all individuals who have become victims regardless of the situation

GENERAL VICTIMOLOGY

Those injured or killed by accident or natural or human-made disasters

C. The goal of developing sufficient victimology is to be able to determine if the victim's lifestyle was a contributing factor to victimization.
D. By learning the victim's personality, lifestyle, habits, attitudes, and perspectives; the crime scene and the offense can be analyzed and evaluated to get an understanding of the behavior that was evident and correlate that information to the reason that the crime was committed.
E. Victimology data are so vital to the investigative process and resolution of the crime that detailed attention to this aspect of the investigation begins at the outset.
F. Presence of three or more of six identified variables significantly increases the risk of victimization:

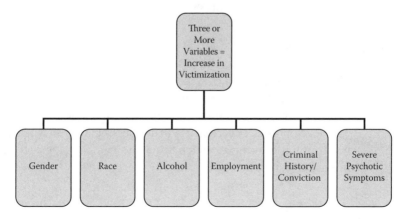

    G. Women are significantly more likely to be victimized.

  V. Psychological Aspects Associated with Becoming a Victim
    A. Becoming a victim of crime produces a major life stressor for the victim.
    B. The victim suffers numerous feeling of guilt, loss, and invasion, and these feelings may not appear for several days or weeks after the incident.

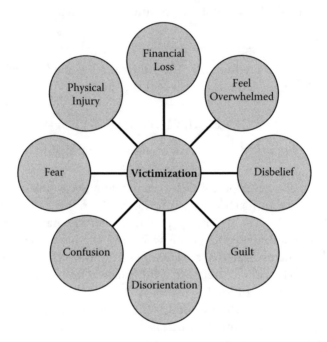

    C. As the psychological symptoms of victimization become more apparent, they fall into the category of those most often seen in victims suffering from PTSD.

  VI. The Victim and Perpetrator
    A. Post-traumatic stress disorder (PTSD)
        1. PTSD is a serious anxiety condition that a victim, family, friend, forensic nurse, or any member of the crime scene investigation team, emergency personnel, and rescue workers can develop after experiencing or witnessing an overwhelming traumatic event at which time the person experienced intense fear, helplessness, or horror.

2. As defined in the *Diagnostic and Statistical Manual of Mental Disorders, Fourth Edition, Text Revision* (*DSM-IV-TR*; American Psychiatric Association, 2000), PTSD symptoms develop following exposure to an extreme traumatic stressor involving direct personal experience of an event that involves actual or threatened death or serious injury or other threat to one's physical integrity; or witnessing an event that involves death, injury, or a threat to the physical integrity of another person; or learning about unexpected or violent death, serious harm, or threat of death or injury experienced by a family member or other close associate.
3. Traumatic events are classified as follows:

Abuse	Catastrophe	Violent Attack	War, Battle, and Combat
Mental	Fatal accidents	Animal attack	Death
Physical	Seriously harmful accidents	Assault	Explosion
Sexual	Natural disasters	Battery	Gunfire
Verbal	Terrorism	Domestic violence	"Shell shock"
		Rape ("postrape syndrome")	"Battle fatigue"

4. Common responses to experiencing a traumatic event may include
   a. Shock
   b. Anger
   c. Nervousness or anxiety
   d. Fear
   e. Possible guilt
5. Responses may diminish and resolve over time; degree of response is dependent on a variety of individual factors: if the diagnosis of PTSD is substantiated; if their feelings persist and are increasingly strong to the point at which the individual is unable to conduct his or her activities of daily living, suffers from an alteration the thinking process; and if the individual exhibits symptoms lasting more than 1 month.
6. Symptoms of PTSD most often appear within 3 months of the event. In some cases, symptoms do not begin to appear until 5 or even 10 years after the event.
7. Severity and duration of the symptoms vary with each individual, from 6 months to several years; some individuals may never recover.

8. The classic features of PTSD are as follows:

Reliving	Avoidance Mechanisms	Increased Arousal	Physical Symptoms
Flashbacks	Of people	Difficulty relating to others	Hypertension
Hallucinations	Of situations		Tachycardia
Nightmares	Detachment	Failure to show emotion	Increased respiratory rate
	Isolation	Difficulty falling and staying asleep	Muscular tension
	Anhedonia	Irritability	Nausea
		Outbursts of anger	Diarrhea
		Lack of concentration	Anorexia or Increased food intake
		Easily startled	

B. Care of the victim and perpetrator suffering from PTSD
   1. The victim
      a. Establish a positive rapport.
      b. Promote physical comfort.
      c. Allow the victim to discuss his or her account of the trauma.
      d. Listen and document any changes in the tone of voice.
      e. Observe and document nonverbal behaviors.
      f. Encourage the victim to discuss emotions and feelings related to the trauma.
      g. Do not hurry the victim; allow for periods of silence.
      h. Avoid inserting your own words or feelings into the victim's experience.
   2. The incarcerated perpetrator.
      a. A forensic nurse needs to understand the social environment of confinement and risk factors that identify populations more susceptible to be victims of violence.
      b. The perpetrator is exposed to an increased risk for trauma and to witness traumatic events.
      c. The perpetrator may become a victim and thus may be hesitant to discuss or acknowledge trauma or traumatic events, which would identify the perpetrator as weak and vulnerable.
      d. Exhibited behaviors may not be associated with the crime committed; therefore, underlying problems with past abuse or drug and alcohol abuse need to be explored and may contribute to development of PTSD.
      e. The perpetrator's coping and behavior mechanisms may become evident when malingering may be suspected so

the perpetrator can be removed from the immediate environment.

    f. The forensic nurse needs to be objective to perform an accurate assessment.

C. Documentation related to victims of crime suffering from PTSD

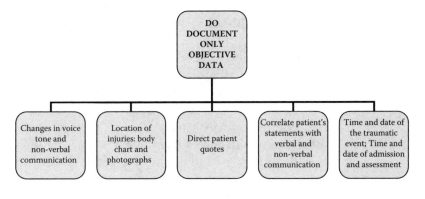

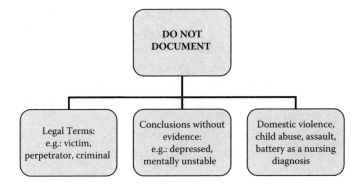

D. Treatment options for PTSD
    1. Most effective treatment is attained when a combination of therapies is utilized:
        a. Cognitive-behavioral therapy
        b. Psychodynamic therapy
        c. Group therapy
        d. Pharmacotherapy

E. Nursing diagnosis for the forensic nurse and victim and perpetrator diagnosed with PTSD or suffering from vicarious trauma
    1. Most frequently identified nursing diagnoses:
        a. Risk for suicide
        b. Ineffective coping
        c. Disturbed sleep pattern
        d. Dysfunctional grieving

      e. Anxiety

      f. Post-trauma syndrome

      g. Risk for post-trauma syndrome

      h. Risk for self-directed violence

      i. Imbalanced nutrition: less than body requirements

      j. Noncompliance

      k. Risk-prone health behaviors

      l. Disturbed body image

      m. Rape-trauma syndrome

2. Additional patient nursing diagnoses dependent on severity of the PTSD symptoms when the examiner has concerns regarding personal safety:

    a. Risk for other-directed violence

    b. Other nursing diagnoses identified based on the severity of the symptoms and unknown/potential preexisting mental health symptoms or mental health diagnosis

F. Homicide and the survivors

1. The major focus of concentration for the victim of a fatal crime tends to be the victim, the crime scene, the suspected offender, and family and friends.

2. Homicide is the second leading cause of death among the population aged 15–24 years old.

3. Psychological studies have demonstrated that family members of homicide victims are at high risk for developing symptoms of PTSD.

4. Patterns of family disruption after a homicide cause members to feel overwhelmed and unable to support each other or the victim's friends.

5. Changes appear in communication and role function.

6. Increases in stress and coping are further evident when a family member is the perpetrator.

7. Research has identified the following initial emotions evident in family responses when notification of sudden death caused by an act of violence was received:

    a. Sense of violation related to the act of murder

    b. Numbness and disbelief

    c. Intense sadness

    d. Anger, rage

8. The family may experience a secondary victimization associated with interactions in the criminal justice system and the lack of understanding of others.

9. Forensic nursing implications and nursing diagnosis for survivors involve the following:

- Spiritual distress
- Readiness for enhanced spiritual well-being
- Decisional conflict
- Acute confusion
- Disabled family coping
- Ineffective denial
- Complicated grieving
- Hopelessness
- Ineffective role performance
- Stress overload
- Risk for other-directed violence

10. Additional nursing diagnoses may address physical issues as well as mental health issues.
11. Forensic nurses must recognize the long-term physiological and psychological effects associated when the victim is the survivor of a loss resulting from a homicide.
12. Planning and follow-through are an essential part of the forensic nurse's responsibility to those who survive and will feel the loss for a short time or as long as they live.
13. Care of the homicide survivor should be as important as the care of the victim and working the crime scene investigation; it is impossible to separate the victim from the survivors regardless of their role within the family and the community.

G. Forensic nurse psychological well-being: Two major themes are incorporated in the American Nurses Association *Code of Ethics for Nurses* (2001) and the International Association of Forensic Nurses *Code of Ethics for the Forensic Nurse* (2006) as related to the mental and physical well-being of the nurses or forensic nurses and their responsibilities in providing care for victims of trauma and those accused or found guilty by a court of law of committing a criminal offense.

1. The first and foremost concern of any nurse is commitment to the patient, whether they are victims or perpetrators, family, individual groups, or a community.
2. The nurse owes the same care and responsibilities to the self as is provided to individuals receiving mental and physical nursing care as a result of a trauma or criminal event. To provide the best nursing care possible, the forensic nurse must be aware of his or her own feelings and emotions, which may hinder a crime scene investigation, and recognize the need to seek assistance.

Bibliography

American Nurses Association. (2001). *Code of ethics for nurses with interpretive statements*. Silver Springs, MD: Author, pp. 7–9.

American Nurses Association, Congress for Nursing Practice. (1980). *Nursing: A social policy statement*. Kansas City, MO: American Nurses Association.

American Nurses Association and International Association of Forensic Nurses. (1997). *Scope and standards of forensic nursing practice*. Washington, DC: American Nurses.

American Psychiatric Association. (2000). *Diagnostic and statistical manual of mental disorders* (4th ed., text rev.). Washington, DC: Author, pp. 13–26, 463–470.

Anderson, J. (Ed.). (2004, March). Vicarious trauma and its impact on advocates, therapists and friends. *Research and Advocacy Digest, 612*, 9–14.

Baliko, B., & Tuck, I. (2008). Perceptions of survivors of loss by homicide: Opportunities for nursing practice. *Journal of Psychosocial Nursing, 46*(5), 27–34.

Bober, T., & Regehr, C. (2006). Strategies for reducing secondary or vicarious trauma: Do they work? *Brief Treatment and Crisis Intervention, 6*, 1–9.

Bongar, B. M. (2002). *The suicidal patient: Clinical and legal standards of care*. Washington, DC: American Psychological Association.

Budur, K., Falcone, T., & Franco, K. (2006). Diagnosing and managing posttraumatic stress disorder. *Cleveland Clinical Journal of Medicine, 73*(1), 121–124.

Busko, M. (2007). *Early psychotherapy, not SSRI therapy, prevents chronic PTSD in large trial*. Retrieved September 1, 2008, from http://www.medscape.com/viewarticle/567859

Center for Mental Health Services. (2004). *Mental health response to mass violence and terrorism: A training manual*. Rockville, MD: U.S. Department of Health and Human Services.

Fortinash, K. M., & Holoday Worret, P. A. (2008). *Psychiatric mental health nursing* (4th ed.). St. Louis, MO: Mosby Elsevier.

International Association of Forensic Nurses. (2006). *International Association of Forensic Nurses code of ethics: The forensic nurse's code of ethics*. Arnold, MD: Author.

Lam, J., & Rosenheck, R. (1998). The effect of victimization on clinical outcomes of homeless persons with serious mental illness. *Psychiatric Services 40*, 678–683.

Lynch, V. (2006). *Forensic nursing*. St. Louis, MO: Mosby.

McCann, I. L., & Pearlman, L. A. (1990). Vicarious traumatization: A framework for understanding the psychological effects of working with victims. *Journal of Traumatic Stress, 3*(1), 131–149.

Mora, J. (2008, Spring). PTSD—The application of forensic nursing. *On the Edge, 14*(1).

Morgan, C., Feuerstein, S., Fortunati, F., Coric, V., Temporini, H., & Southwick, S. (2005, October). Forensic files: Posttraumatic stress disorder within the forensic area. *Psychiatry, 2*(10), 21–24.

Mosby's surefire documentation: How, what, and when nurses need to document (2nd ed.). (2006). St. Louis, MO: Mosby Elsevier.

Muscari, M. (2008). Victimization. *Advance Newsmagazine*. King of Prussia, PA: Merion. Retrieved September 12, 2008, from http://www.advanceweb.com

NANDA International. (2007). *NANDA-I Nursing diagnoses: Definitions and classifications, 2007–2008*. Philadelphia: NANDA International

National Institute of Mental Health. (2002). *Mental health and mass violence: Evidence-based early psychological intervention for victims/survivors of mass violence. A workshop to reach consensus on best practices* (NIH Publication No. 02-5138). Washington, DC: U.S. Government Printing Office. Retrieved Feb. 8, 2008 from http://www.nimh.nih.gov/research/massviolence.pdf

National Organization for Victim Assistance. (2005). *Victim assistance programs.* Retrieved Feb. 15, 2008 from http://www.trynova.org

Office for Victims of Crime and the American Red Cross. (2006). *Responding to victims of terrorism and mass violence crimes.* Washington, D.C.: U.S. Department of Justice Office of Justice Programs.

Posttraumatic stress disorder. (2007), Retrieved August 2008 from http://www.nlm.nih.gov/medlineplus/posttraumaticstressdisorder.html

Renaud, E. (2006). Post-traumatic Stress Disorder: An overview of theory, treatment, and forensic practice considerations. In Hammer, R. M., Moynihan, B., & Pagliaro, E. M. (Eds.). *Forensic nursing: A handbook for practices* (pp. 355–395). Sudbury, MA: Jones and Bartlett.

Souryal, S. S. (2007). *Ethics in criminal justice: In search of the truth* (4th ed.). Newark, NJ: LexisNexis Group, Bender.

Stokowski, L. (2008). *Forensic nursing: Part 2. Inside forensic nursing.* Retrieved April 30, 2008, from http://www.medscape.com/viewarticle/571555

Turvey, B. E., & Petherick, W. (2009). *Forensic victimology: Examining violent crime victims in investigative and legal contexts.* San Diego, CA: Elsevier Academic Press.

U.S. Department of Justice, Office of Justice Programs. (2006). *National crime victimization survey: Criminal victimization, 2005* (Bureau of Justice Statistics Bulletin, September 2006, NCJ 214644). Washington, DC.

U.S. Department of Justice Office for Victims of Crime. (2007, April 19). Victim needs from a faith-based perspective. *Vicarious Trauma* (pp. 1–2). Rockville, MD: National Institute of Justice.

Deaths in Nursing Homes

19

VINCENT J. M. DI MAIO
AND THERESA G. DI MAIO

Contents

Introduction

There are between 16,000 and 17,000 nursing homes in the United States, with approximately 1.5 million patients over the age of 65 years. It is estimated that approximately 20% of all deaths occur in nursing homes. Deaths in nursing homes are, for the most part, natural. There are exceptions, with occasional deaths due to trauma. Unfortunately, there are virtually no data on the number of deaths due to homicide, suicide, or accident in nursing homes.

1. Homicides
    a. These are uncommon.
    b. The perpetrators of the homicides may be nursing home personnel, visiting family members, or fellow patients.
    c. Usually, homicides are committed by visitors (e.g., spouses of patients with a chronic or fatal disease who come in, kill the patient, and then often kill themselves).
    d. When patients are involved, the assailant is often suffering from dementia or severe mental disease.

2. Suicides
    a. These are rare even though statistics on suicide identify older adults as a high-risk population.

  b. There are virtually no published data on this type of death.

  c. The low suicide rate may be due to a controlled environment with minimum access to weapons or large quantities of drugs; poor health of the patients, which inhibits physical activity; and lack of privacy.

 3. Accidents not involving medications

  a. It is not uncommon for the nursing home staff to attempt to conceal a fatal accident.

  b. Falls produce the largest number of deaths.

  c. Second in frequency are asphyxial deaths caused by bed rails, restraint vests, and too small mattresses.

  d. Other causes are drinking of cleaning fluids by senile patients, burns caused by immersion in hot bath water, and the like.

 4. Drug overdoses

  a. Such deaths may be either inadvertent or intentional.

  b. Typically, most nursing homes are understaffed. It is probably not uncommon for a patient to get either too much of a medication or the wrong medication.

  c. When death does occur, the nursing home is probably often unaware of the mixup and assumes the death to be natural.

  d. In most of the cases we have seen, deaths due to overdoses were not reported by the institution but surreptitiously by an employee who notified the medical examiner or the family. In other cases, the overdose was discovered by chance when the patient was seen in a hospital or, if they died, in a medical examiner's office for autopsy.

  e. Rarely, the drug overdose is intentional. A number of cases of health care workers who believed it their calling to end "suffering" by killing a patient have been reported.

 5. Gross neglect of patients

  a. Nursing homes or personnel have been charged with homicide for improper and inadequate care of patients.

  b. In one case involving a death resulting from infected decubitus ulcers (pressure sores), the care-home provider was convicted of manslaughter.

  c. In another case, an attending nurse pled guilty to the felony offense of injury to an elderly individual, second degree, because she did not promptly notify a physician or summon emergency medical services personnel when a patient was obviously suffering a heart attack.

  d. In all probability, the number of cases for which individuals and perhaps institutions will be charged with homicide in the death of patients will increase.

The biggest problem in many, if not most, nursing homes is staffing:

1. Unskilled individuals are hired at very low salaries to minister to sick, debilitated, and often confused patients.
2. Employees may not be adequately screened, and it is not uncommon for individuals with criminal records to be hired.
3. Training is minimal.
4. Staffing is often inadequate.
5. Staffing with registered nurses, the core of good nursing care, is minimum, often just enough to satisfy the regulations.

Records of the administration of care should always be approached with caution: Records will show

1. Patients are turned every 2 hours and kept clean, but decubitus ulcers develop.
2. Patients eat all their meals but lose weight.
3. Medications are always given, even when it turns out that they were not available.
4. In some instances, care is documented as given even after the patient has died.

Gross Neglect of Patients

Signs of neglect are

- Contractures
- Malnutrition
- Dehydration
- Pressure sores (decubitus ulcers)

Contractures

1. A contracture is an abnormal, often permanent, condition characterized by flexion and fixation of a limb at a joint that leaves the joint in a nonfunctional position, resistant to bending.
2. They are caused by atrophy and abnormal shortening of muscle fibers.
3. Their primary cause is disuse. The muscles become weak, atrophy, change shape, and shorten with disuse.
   a. The muscle decreases in diameter and in the number of muscle cells.
   b. Eventually, there may be replacement with fibrous connective tissue.

4. These are seen in nursing home patients with impaired sensoria who are confined to bed.
5. In such patients, a nurse should administer passive range-of-motion exercises on a daily basis to prevent development of contractures.
6. Development of contractures indicates poor nursing care.
7. Approximately 20% of nursing home residents nationwide have contractures.

Malnutrition

1. Malnutrition involves a deficit, excess, or imbalance in essential components of a balanced diet.
2. The type of malnutrition seen in nursing homes is usually protein-caloric malnutrition.
3. Malnutrition in nursing home patients can be caused by
   a. Chronic disease conditions that make eating difficult (e.g., paralysis caused by a stroke; dementia)
   b. Increased caloric or protein requirements due to infection or the healing of wounds
   c. Medications that impair the desire to eat (e.g., psychotropic drugs)
   d. Failure of the nursing home to supply adequate nutrition or feed the patients

4. Of patients in nursing homes, 35–80% are malnourished, with 30–40% of patients substandard in weight.
5. A weight loss of 5% or greater in 30 days, 7.5% in 3 months, and 10% in 6 months indicates a patient's nutrition should be evaluated.
6. The amount of nutrition required by a person to live depends on body size, age, health, the environment, and degree of activity.
7. Malnutrition predisposes an individual to the development of decubitus ulcers and infection. These in turn lead to increased caloric and protein requirements, thus making the malnutrition worse, which again predisposes to decubitus ulcers and infection.
8. The number of calories required by a person increases with activity and health problems.
   a. Stress caused by infections or decubitus ulcers can increase the caloric requirement by a factor of 1.2 to 1.6.
   b. The basal metabolic rate (BMR) increases 5% for every 1°F rise in body temperature, which necessitates an increase in caloric intake.
   c. Daily protein intake is normally 0.8 to 1.0 g/kg. With infection or decubitus ulcers, this can increase to 1.2 to 1.5 g/kg.

9. The easiest way of determining chronic malnutrition, aside from severe weight loss, is by measuring serum albumin.
   a. Albumin accounts for more than 50% of serum proteins.
   b. The main purpose of albumin within blood is to maintain colloidal osmotic pressure, which keeps fluid within the vascular space.

10. Regarding serum albumin:
    a. Low levels of albumin reflect long-standing malnutrition.
    b. Low levels are associated with protein deprivation or chronic disease, infection, surgical stress, and trauma, all of which result in demand for more protein.
    c. The half-life of albumin is 12 to 20 days but is shortened in the presence of infection.
    d. Thus, low levels of albumin generally reflect what happened to the patient 1–2 months in the past.
    e. Individuals in nursing homes suffering from these conditions should be given additional food (calories and protein).
    f. Values are as follows (there is some variation in normal ranges among laboratories):

Normal	3.5–4.5 g/dl
Mild protein depletion	3.0–3.4 g/d
Moderate depletion	2.5–2.9 g/dl
Severe depletion	<2.5 g/dl

11. Prealbumin has a much shorter half-life, approximately 2 days.
    a. The name *prealbumin* is a misnomer as it implies that it is a precursor for albumin, which it is not.
    b. Because of its short (2-day) half-life, it is sensitive to acute changes in nutrition.
    c. The normal value for prealbumin is 15 to 35 mg/dl.
    d. It provides the best monitor of current protein status.
    e. Prealbumin levels can be drawn once or twice per week and used as a sensitive monitor of nutritional progress.

Dehydration

1. Dehydration is common in nursing home patients.
2. It is caused by illness (diarrhea, fever, infection); the effects of medications (e.g., diuretics); and decreased fluid intake.
3. When personnel do not monitor the intake of fluid and provide extra fluids when required, dehydration develops.

Pressure Sores (Decubitus Ulcers)

1. The prevalence of pressure ulcers among patients in long-term care facilities has been reported as 2.3–28%.
2. Under most circumstances, elderly nursing home patients should not develop pressure sores. Their presence indicates poor nursing care.
3. Factors predisposing to pressure sores are
   a. Depressed sensory or motor function
   b. Altered consciousness
   c. Pressure over bony prominences
   d. Malnutrition
   e. Shearing forces
   f. Moisture (fecal and urinary incontinence)

4. The most common factor leading to development of decubitus ulcers is pressure, usually over bony prominences, in an individual with altered consciousness or impaired motor activity.
   a. The inability to shift one's body because of depressed sensory or motor function or unconsciousness leads to abnormal pressure and thus development of decubitus ulcers.
   b. When the pressure on soft tissue is greater than 32 mm of mercury, it closes capillary blood flow.
   c. This results in deprivation of oxygen to the tissue in this area and accumulation of metabolic end products.
   d. If these continue to accumulate for more than 2 hours, there is irreversible tissue damage.

5. The most common sites are the sacrum, the coccygeal areas, and the greater trochantars from lying in bed as well as the ischial tuberosities if the patient is able to sit.
6. A major cause of decubitus ulcers is malnutrition.
   a. This results in muscle atrophy and a decrease in subcutaneous tissue, reducing the padding over the muscles, making the pressure more significant and producing ulcers.
   b. Obesity also contributes to pressure ulcers. A normal amount of fat protects the skin by acting as a cushion. Large quantities of fat, however, lead to ulceration because the adipose tissue is poorly vascularized, and the underlying tissue then becomes more susceptible to ischemia.

7. Another major factor causing ulcers is shearing forces.
   a. There is sliding of one tissue layer over another with stretching and angulation of blood vessels, which results in injury and thrombosis.

b. This commonly occurs when the head of the bed is raised too high and the individual's body tends to slide downward.

c. Friction and perspiration cause fixation of the skin and the superficial fascia to the sheets, while the deeper fascia slides down.

d. Shearing forces in the elderly are aggravated by the loose skin common in the elderly because of loss of subcutaneous tissue and dehydration.

8. Moisture, usually caused by urinary and fecal incontinence, predisposes to development of pressure sores. Moisture reduces skin resistance to the other factors and increases the possibility of decubitus ulcers fivefold.

Decubitus ulcers (pressure sores) are divided into four stages based on their clinical appearance and extent:

1. Stages

a. Stage 1: The initial lesion seen following compression of skin and tissue is reactive hyperemia (reddening of the skin).

(1) The redness is caused by sudden increase in blood flow to the area compressed; after relief from the pressure of compression if there is no injury to the tissue, the redness will disappear in less than 1 hour.

(2) If the compression is long enough to produce ischemia but not irreversible injury, then you have an abnormal reactive hyperemia, which can last several hours.

(3) If the pressure is maintained long enough, one then has a stage 1 pressure sore manifested by erythema that lasts longer than 24 hours, does not blanch on pressure, and shows induration of the tissue caused by edema.

(4) These sores can occur in a matter of a few hours. Stage 1 pressure sores are an indication of a potential problem; they do not in themselves indicate neglect. They are readily treatable and should not progress.

b. Stage 2: These range in severity from a blister to ulceration of the skin. They may involve the full thickness of the skin but do not penetrate into the subcutaneous fat. These lesions are in a gray zone as indicators of neglect. They should not occur, but do. They are readily treatable.

c. Stage 3: These are full-thickness ulcers extending through the skin and subcutaneous fat up to the fascia. There is usually undermining of the skin. The base of the ulcer is usually necrotic, foul smelling, and infected.

    d. Stage 4: The ulcer extends through the fascia into muscle, often to the bone. Osteomyelitis may develop.

2. Stage 3 and Stage 4 ulcers, in elderly nursing home patients, usually indicate poor or lack of nursing treatment and thus neglect.
   a. Preventive measures involve basic nursing techniques.
   b. The patient should be turned or repositioned at least every 2 hours and when in wheelchairs every hour.
   c. Adequate nutrition and hydration should be given.
   d. The skin must be kept dry by preventing patients from lying in their urine and feces.
   e. The head of the bed should not be raised to such a degree that the patient will slide down.
   f. If necessary, extra padding over bony prominences should be provided.
   g. If a sore develops, the physician should be notified immediately.

3. The incidence of pressure sores in individuals in nursing homes varies from study to study. A conservative approximation is 7–8%. Tsokos, Heinemann, and Puschel (2000) conducted a prospective study of 10,222 bodies from nursing homes, hospitals, and private residences.
   a. Pressure sores were observed in 11.2% of the individuals: 6.1% stage 1, 2–3% stage 2, 1.1% stage 3, and 0.9% stage 4.
   b. Stage 3 and 4 sores were found principally on the sacrum (69.6%).
   c. Of all stage 4 sores, 73% were in individuals 80 years of age and older.

4. Both the presence of pressure sores and deaths caused by them are underreported.
5. Pressure sores are dismissed as inevitable by many physicians.
6. Decubitus ulcers (stages 2–4) lose both fluids and proteins.
7. Open sores are invariably colonized by bacteria. The resultant infection can cause septicemia.
8. Individuals have been charged with homicide, with at least one conviction, in deaths resulting from decubitus ulcers due to gross neglect or failure to provide the most basic nursing services.

Deaths Caused by Hospital Bed Side Rails

1. Bed side rails are intended to prevent patients from injuring themselves. They are not suitable for and will not restrain individuals who are active or ambulatory, no matter the mental status.

2. Bed rails cause injury indirectly in that most falls from beds in elderly individuals occur when they attempt to climb over the rails.

3. Bed rails may cause death directly by entrapment.

   a. The Food and Drug Administration (FDA) received approximately 691 entrapment reports over a period of 21 years from January 1, 1985, to January 1, 2006, with 413 deaths, 120 injury victims, and 158 near-miss events with no serious injury as a result of intervention.

   b. The entrapment occurred in openings within the bed rails, between the bed rails and mattresses, under bed rails, between split rails, and between the bed rails and head- or footboards.

   c. The majority of such cases involve nursing homes, where the patients are elderly and tend to have cognitive and physical disabilities.

4. Parker and Miles (1997) reviewed 74 deaths attributed solely to bed rails.

   a. In 70%, there was entrapment between the mattress and bed rail, with the face pressed against the mattress.

   b. In 18%, the deaths were caused by entrapment of the neck within the rails.

   c. Death occurred for 12% when they slid partially off the bed, resulting in suspension by either the head or pelvis.

5. The U.S. Department of Health and Human Services (2006) has produced a document offering recommendations relating to hospital beds that are intended to reduce life-threatening entrapment. They identified seven areas in the bed system where there is a potential for entrapment:

   a. Within the rail

   b. Under the rail, between the rail supports, or next to a single rail support

   c. Between the rail and the mattress

   d. Under the rail, at the ends of the rail

   e. Between split bed rails

   f. Between the end of the rail and the side edge of the head- or footboard

   g. Between the head- or footboard and the mattress end

6. The FDA is recommending dimensional limits for the first four areas because it is believed that the majority of the entrapments reported have occurred in these areas.

   a. Area 1: This is any open space within the rail. Openings in the rail should be small enough to prevent the head from entering.

The FDA is recommending less than 120 mm (4¾ inches) as the dimensional limit for any open space within the rail. This dimension encompasses the fifth percentile female head breadth.

b. Area 2: This space is the gap under the rail between a mattress compressed by the weight of a patient's head and the bottom edge of the rail at a location between the rail supports or next to a single rail support. Preventing the head from going under the rail would prevent neck entrapment in this space. The FDA recommends that this space be small enough to prevent head entrapment, that is, less than 120 mm (4¾ inches).

c. Area 3: This area is the space between the inside surface of the rail and the mattress compressed by the weight of a patient's head. The space should be small enough to prevent head entrapment, taking into account the mattress compressibility, any lateral shift of the mattress or rail, and any play from loosened rails. The FDA recommends that this space be small enough to prevent head entrapment, that is, less than 120 mm (4¾ inches), for the area between the inside surface of the rail and the compressed mattress.

d. Area 4: This space is the gap that forms between the mattress when compressed by the patient and the lowermost portion of the rail, at the end of the rail. Factors that increase the gap size are mattress compressibility, lateral shift of the mattress or rail, and degree of play from loosened rails. The space poses a risk for entrapment of a patient's neck. Based on neck diameter dimensions, the FDA recommends less than 60 mm (2-⅜ inches) between the mattress support platform and the lowest portion of the rail at the rail end.

Deaths Caused by Restraining Devices

Restraints are mechanical devices, materials, or equipment that restrict individuals' freedom of movement or normal access to their bodies.

1. If individuals attempt to escape from such devices, they run the danger of ligature strangulation or traumatic or positional asphyxia.
2. Miles and Irvine (1992) reviewed 122 deaths caused by vest and strap restraints.
   a. Of these, 85% occurred in nursing homes.
   b. The victims were elderly, with a median age of 81 years.
   c. Victims were found suspended from chairs in 58% of the cases and from beds in 42%.

3. Typically, there was a history of sliding down in or escaping from restraints.
4. The victims were placed in a vest or strap restraint and left alone.
   a. They then slid off the bed or chair, with the restraint catching them across the chest or, less commonly, under the chin.
   b. If they do not slide down far enough to reach a weight-bearing surface, they may die of asphyxia due to strangulation or traumatic asphyxia.

Bibliography

Burger, S. G., Kayser-Jones, J., & Bell, J. P. (2000, June). *Malnutrition and dehydration in nursing homes: Key issues in prevention and treatment.* Research supported by the Commonwealth Fund. Retrieved June 1, 2009 from http://www.commonwealthfund.org/content/publications/fund-reports/2000/jul/malnutrition-and-dehydration-in-nursing-homes--key-issues-in-prevention-and-treatment.aspx.

Collins, N. (2001). The difference between albumin and prealbumin. *Advances in Skin and Wound Care, 14*(5), 235–236.

Di Maio, V. J. M., and Di Maio, T. G. (2002). Homicide by decubitus ulcers. *American Journal of Forensic Medicine and Pathology, 23*(1), 1–4.

Kuszajewski, M. L., & Clontz, A. S. (2005). Prealbumin is best for nutritional monitoring. *Nursing, 35*(5), 70–71.

Miles, S. H., & Irvine, P. (1992). Deaths caused by physical restraints. *Gerontologist, 32*, 762–766.

Parker, K., & Miles, S. H. (1997). Deaths caused by bed rails. *Journal of the American Geriatrics Society, 45*(7), 797–802.

Suominen, K., Henriksson, M., Isometsä, E., Conwell, Y., Heilä, H., & Lönnqvist, J. (2004). Nursing home suicides: A psychological autopsy study. *International Journal of Geriatric Psychiatry, 18*(12), 1095–1101.

Todd, J. F., Ruhl, C. E., & Gross, T. P. (1997). Injury and death associated with hospital bed side-rails: Reports to the U.S. Food and Drug Administration from 1985 to 1995. *American Journal of Public Health, 87*(10), 1675–1677.

Tsokos, M., Heinemann, A., & Puschel, K. (2000). Pressure sores: Epidemiology, medicolegal implications and forensic argumentation concerning causality. *International Journal of Legal Medicine, 113*, 283–287.

U.S. Department of Health and Human Services, Food and Drug Administration, Center for Devices and Radiological Health, Division of Device User Programs and Systems Analysis (HFZ-230) Office of Communication, Education, and Radiation Programs, Division of Postmarket Surveillance (HFZ-520), Office of Surveillance and Biometrics Guidance for Industry and FDA. (2006). *Staff hospital bed system dimensional and assessment guidance to reduce entrapment.* Retrieved June 1, 2009 from http://www.fda.gov/medicaldevices/deviceregulationandguidance/guidancedocuments/ucm072662.htm.

Excited Delirium Syndrome (EDS)

20

THERESA G. DI MAIO
AND VINCENT J. M. DI MAIO

Contents

Introduction

Delirium involves an acute (minutes to hours), transient disturbance in consciousness and cognition. It is manifested by:

1. Disorientation
2. Disorganized and inconsistent thought processes
3. Inability to distinguish reality from hallucinations
4. Disturbances in speech; disorientation to time and place; misidentification of individuals
5. Termed *excited delirium* when it involves combative or violent behavior

Excited delirium syndrome (EDS) involves the sudden death of an individual during or following an episode of excited delirium and for which an autopsy fails to reveal evidence of sufficient trauma or natural disease to explain the death. In virtually all such cases, the episode of excited delirium is terminated by

1. A struggle with police or medical personnel
2. The use of physical restraint

In regard to the individual dying of EDS,

1. The individual may go into cardiopulmonary arrest during or within minutes following cessation of the struggle, rarely a few hours later.
2. Attempts at resuscitation are unsuccessful.
3. If a cardiac monitor is available, the rhythm noted is usually pulse-less electrical activity (PEA) or asystole or less commonly severe bradycardia.

History

Excited delirium syndrome was first described in a chronic form in individuals with mental disease by Luther Bell in 1849. It then became known as *Bell's mania*. The characteristics of Bell's mania were

1. Women as majority of victims
2. Mental illness
3. Sudden onset of symptoms
4. Delirium
5. Extreme agitation
6. Violence with no disposition to yield to overwhelming force
7. The need to use physical restraint to control
8. Chronic course (days to weeks before death)
9. Acute cases uncommon
10. Negative findings at autopsy

Bell's mania was reported repeatedly in the psychiatric literature from 1849 to 1949. It disappeared from the literature with the introduction of phenothiazines for treatment of mental illness in the 1950s.

Present

Bell's Mania, now known most commonly as EDS, reappeared in an acute form in the early 1980s with the widespread use of illegal stimulants. It is characterized by

1. Acute onset of symptoms (minutes to hours)
2. Delirium with
   a. Acute, transient disturbance in consciousness and cognition
   b. Disorientation
   c. Disorganized and inconsistent thought processes
   d. Inability to distinguish reality from hallucinations
   e. Disturbances in speech
   f. Disorientation to time and place
   g. Misidentification of individuals

2. Combative or violent behavior
3. Male victims predominantly
4. Predominant occurrence in chronic abusers of cocaine, methamphetamine; less commonly seen in association with diphenhydramine, alcohol withdrawal, phencyclidine (PCP), Ecstasy
5. Deaths still occur in mental patients
   a. Deaths occurring in psychiatric patients not on illegal stimulants may be associated with underlying natural disease or the presence of psychotropic drugs.
   b. Many of the antipsychotic medications are cardiotoxic, with some having effects on the cardiovascular system similar to cocaine.
   c. In some cases, the individuals are also on illegal stimulants.

6. Presentation the same for individuals with mental disease and those using illegal stimulants
7. The need to use physical restraint to control
8. Sudden cardiac death
9. Occurrence of most deaths when police or medical personnel try to restrain the individual
10. Lack of response to cardiopulmonary resuscitation even if medical personnel are present at time of arrest
11. Negative findings at autopsy

Because most such deaths occur in the community following bizarre behavior, the police are inevitably summoned and are the first to encounter such individuals. Whether the police want to transport these individuals to jail or a medical facility, they must first either gain their cooperation or restrain them. Thus, the possible courses of action for the police are

1. Verbal deescalation
2. Chemical/electrical restraint
3. Physical restraint

Since the individual is in a state of delirium, verbal deescalation usually does not work. The police will often then try to incapacitate the individual with chemical sprays such as pepper spray or by use of a device such as a Taser®. Unfortunately, many individuals in the throes of excited delirium appear to be resistant to both chemical sprays and electromuscular disruption (EMD) devices such as the Taser.

Alleged Causes of Death in EDS

Since deaths due to EDS almost always occur after restraint is either instituted or attempted, the cause of death was initially attributed to the actions of police and medical personnel.

1. There were often charges of police or medical misconduct.
2. When no physical cause for the death was found at autopsy, this was ascribed to a coverup.
3. In regard to trauma, the usual findings were minor abrasions and contusions explainable by the struggle that preceded death.

Traditionally, two explanations have been put forth to explain deaths due to EDS: use of neck holds or positional or restraint asphyxia.

Neck Holds

1. Compression of the airway usually does not occur and is not necessary for a neck hold to be effective.
   a. Two thirds to three quarters of the blood supply to the brain is provided by the carotid arteries, with the remainder supplied by the vertebral arteries.
   b. Compression of the carotid arteries for 10–15 seconds produces cerebral hypoxia and loss of consciousness.
   c. After the choke hold is released, the victim should regain consciousness within 20–30 seconds.

2. The carotid arteries have to be continuously occluded for 2–3 minutes or more for death to occur. This action would be clearly obvious to any observer.
3. If during a struggle the individual was either hit in the neck or an arm placed around it, hemorrhage in the neck may be present.
   a. In rare instances, fractures of the superior horns of the thyroid cartilage or the hyoid bone occur.
   b. This leads some individuals to contend that manual strangulation has occurred (i.e., prolonged use of the neck hold).
   c. What they fail to realize is that both hemorrhage in the neck and the aforementioned fractures do not equate to death due to

strangulation They are only *markers* indicating that pressure or a blow to the neck has occurred.

d. Death from manual strangulation involves constant pressure to the neck over a number of minutes, generally more than 2 minutes.

Positional or Restraint Asphyxia

Regarding positional or restraint asphyxia, in 1988 Reay, Howard, Fligner, and Ward conducted a series of experiments to determine the effects on peripheral oxygen saturation and heart rate when an individual was hog-tied and placed prone following exercise.

1. They concluded that hog-tie restraint prolongs recovery from exercise as determined by changes in peripheral oxygen saturation and heart rate.
2. They speculated that restriction of thoracic respiratory movements could be one of the mechanisms for this occurrence.
3. Even with the elimination of hog-tying, however, the number of deaths due to EDS continued, if not increased.
4. Following this, whenever anyone was restrained and died, positional asphyxia was said to be the cause of death, whatever the position of the deceased, the method of restraint, or the presence of drugs
5. In 1993, O'Halloran and Lewman codified the association of restraint and asphyxiation from hog-tying and death under the term *restraint asphyxia* or *positional asphyxia*.
6. The problem was that Reay et al.'s (1988) original findings were wrong. Their equipment was inadequate for the task and the analysis flawed.

In 1997, Chan, Vilke, Neuman, and Clausen published their studies on restraint asphyxia.

1. Chan et al. repeated the experiments of Reay et al. (1988) using a more systematic approach and more sophisticated technology.
2. Pulmonary function testing (PFT: forced vital capacity, forced expiratory volume in 1 second, and maximal voluntary ventilation) was performed on individuals in the sitting, supine, prone, and restraint (hog-tied) positions. The subjects were then subjected to exercise.
3. Determinations of arterial blood gas, pulse rate, oxygen saturation by CO-oximetry and pulse oximetry, and PFT were performed.
4. Chan et al. found the following:
   a. Placing individuals in the restraint position after exercise resulted in restrictive pulmonary functioning as measured by PFT.
   b. The PFT changes, although statistically significant, were not clinically relevant.

    c. There was no evidence of hypoxia in the restraint position after exercise and no evidence of hypercapnia either during exercise or in restraint.

5. Chan et. al concluded that there was no evidence that body position while in the hog-tied or "hobble" restraint position, in and of itself, causes hypoventilation or asphyxiation.

Some individuals claim that death in EDS is due to compromise in ventilation occurring when a police officer or medical worker applies body weight to the upper torso of an individual in an attempt to restrain the individual or prevent further struggle. This is usually accomplished by lying across an individual's back or applying pressure on the back with a knee or hands.

Michalewicz et al. conducted a series of experiments published in 2007. They investigated ventilatory and metabolic demands in healthy adults placed in the prone maximal restraint position (PMRP) (i.e., hog-tie restraint).

1. Maximal voluntary ventilation (MVV) was measured in seated subjects, in the PMRP, and when prone with 90.1–102.3 kg (198–225 lb) of weight on the back.
2. Twenty-seven subjects were then placed in the PMRP and struggled vigorously for 60 seconds.
3. The authors found no clinically important restriction of ventilatory reserve when subjects were placed in the PMRP or when prone with up to 90.2 or 102.3 kg of weight on their back.
4. When subjects were maximally struggling for 60 seconds while in the PMRP, there were no clinically important limitations of metabolic or ventilatory functions.
5. The authors concluded: "Based on these findings, as well as previously published studies, we suggest that factors other than ventilatory failure associated with the restraining process may be responsible for the sudden unexpected deaths of restrained individuals."

What Is the Cause of EDS?

Death occurring from EDS, whether due to intrinsic mental disease or use of stimulants, is due to a combination of

1. The normal physiologic changes seen in an individual whose sympathetic nervous system is activated by
    a. Emotional stress (delirium)
    b. Physical exertion
    c. A struggle

2. In combination with, depending on the case,
   a. The use of illicit drugs
   b. Medications
   c. Natural disease
   d. In some individuals, possibly polymorphism of cardiac adreno-receptors with resultant exacerbation of the normal responses to violent physical activity

The sympathetic nervous system is the controller of the "fight-or-flight" response. Whenever an individual is exposed to stress, there is a widespread physiological reaction throughout the body.

1. This stress can be physical or psychological.
2. The reaction of the body to stress is integrated in the brain through the hypothalamus.
3. Signals are transmitted downward from the hypothalamus through the brain stem, into the spinal cord.
4. Then, the signals go to organs such as the heart, producing massive sympathetic discharge with release of the neurotransmitters norepinephrine (noradrenalin) and epinephrine (adrenalin).

Neurotransmitters are substances that travel through synapses (a space between the end of the nerve fiber and the cell of the organ) to deliver information to other neurons or cells.

1. They are produced within neurons (nerve cells), stored in vesicles at the end of the axons, and released into the synapse on nerve stimulation.
2. The neurotransmitters we are concerned with are the catecholamines: The principal catecholamines are epinephrine, norepinephrine, and dopamine.
3. The main catecholamines in the brain are norepinephrine and dopamine; outside the brain, they are norepinephrine and epinephrine.
4. Outside the brain, sympathetic neurons release norepinephrine, and the adrenals release both norepinephrine and epinephrine.

Norepinephrine is released from nerve fibers (axons) into the synapse (a space between the end of the nerve fiber and the cell of the organ).

1. The norepinephrine interacts with receptors on the cells known as adrenoceptors.
2. *Adrenoceptors* are sites on cell membranes through which norepinephrine and epinephrine act as neurotransmitters in the brain, the cardiovascular system, and other organs.

3. The sympathetic nervous system influences the cardiovascular system through changes in the release of norepinephrine from sympathetic nerve terminals and norepinephrine and epinephrine from the adrenals.
4. Reuptake mechanisms such as transport systems, specific enzymes, or diffusion out of the synapse rapidly inactivate the neurotransmitters released into the synapse. This controls the degree of excitation.
5. Virtually all neurotransmitters are recaptured by transport systems located at the nerve terminals of the releasing neurons.

The membrane receptors responsible for mediating responses to catecholamines were initially divided into α- and β-adrenoceptors.

1. α-Adrenoceptors are differentiated into α_1-adrenoceptors and α_2-adrenoceptors. Both α_1- and α_2-adrenoceptors can in turn be divided into three subtypes: α_{1A}-, α_{1B}-, and α_{1D}- and α_{2A}-, α_{2B}-, and α_{2C}-adrenoceptors, respectively.
2. There are three β-adrenoceptors: β_1, β_2, and β_3.
   a. The predominant receptor in heart cells is the β_1 subtype.
   b. Release of catecholamines causes an increase in the heart rate and force of contraction by way of β_1-receptors in heart cells.

The small coronary arteries and arterioles are the principal determinants of coronary artery resistance.

1. Both α_1- and α_2-adrenoceptors mediate coronary vasoconstriction, with α_1 predominating in the larger vessels and α_2 in the microcirculation.
2. Sympathetic activation of normal coronary arteries by either stress or physical activity results in vasodilation of epicardial vessels and, in some circumstances, vasoconstriction of the microvessels.
3. In the presence of atherosclerosis or endothelial dysfunction, there is vasoconstriction of epicardial and microvessels.
4. This can be sufficient to produce myocardial ischemia.
5. The fact that vasoconstriction occurs in the presence of atherosclerosis or endothelial dysfunction is significant in that accelerated development of atherosclerosis and endothelial injury are produced by chronic use of cocaine and methamphetamine. Individuals dying of EDS are typically chronic users of these stimulants.

On stimulation of the adrenal glands by the sympathetic nervous system, there is release into the blood of both norepinephrine and epinephrine, with epinephrine predominating (80% epinephrine and 20% norepinephrine).

1. These are carried by the blood to the organs, where they have basically the same effect as does direct sympathetic stimulation.
2. The only difference is that the effects last 5–10 times as long because these substances are slowly removed from the blood over a period of 1–3 minutes.

We can see that stimulation of the sympathetic nervous system causes the following:

1. Norepinephrine is released at the synapses and norepinephrine and epinephrine into the blood from the adrenals
2. The norepinephrine works on the β_1-myocytes of the heart to cause it to beat harder and faster.
3. This in turn results in greater demand for oxygen by the myocardium.
4. If the coronary arteries have either endothelial injury or atherosclerosis, typical complications resulting from chronic use of cocaine and methamphetamine, there will be contraction of the coronary arteries with decreased supply of oxygenated blood to the myocardium at a time when increased amounts are needed.
5. All this predisposes to development of a cardiac arrhythmia.

In EDS, death often occurs immediately after the individual is restrained and struggling ceases. This time frame corresponds to the time of "postexercise peril" described by Dimsdale, Hartley, Guiney, Ruskin, and Greenblatt (1984). It is when an individual is unusually susceptible to developing a fatal cardiac arrhythmia.

Dimsdale et al. (1984) found that during exercise the following occurred:

1. An individual's blood norepinephrine and epinephrine increased, with norepinephrine increasing more sharply.
2. Peak levels of these catecholamines did not occur during the struggle, however, but in the 3 minutes immediately following cessation of the exercise.
3. Following cessation of exercise, epinephrine and norepinephrine continued to rise, with norepinephrine levels more than 10-fold above baseline levels and epinephrine threefold above.
4. Young, Srivastava, Fitzovich, Kivlighn, and Hamaguchi (1992) found that the highest levels of plasma catecholamines occurred during the 3 minutes postexercise. In their studies, epinephrine

levels peaked 1 minute after cessation of exercise, at which point the mean value was more than eightfold the mean resting level.

Compounding the physiological actions of elevated levels of catecholamine are changes in blood potassium levels. Young et al. (1992) found the following during exercise:

1. The mean plasma potassium increased slightly more than 1 mEq/L.
2. There is little evidence, however, that these extremely high levels of potassium due to exercise adversely affect cardiac functioning.
3. Studies suggested that exercise-induced increases in blood catecholamines have a cardioprotective effect on hyperkalemia.
4. Following cessation of exercise, the potassium level fell rapidly, returning to approximately normal levels in 5 minutes.
5. The maximum rate of fall occurred within the first or second minute postexercise.
6. It is felt that it is the rapid drop to low levels following cessation of exercise that produces an arrhythmia. This hypokalemia predisposes to prolongation of the QT interval, development of *torsade de pointes*, and sudden cardiac death.

Drugs: Therapeutic and Illicit

The catecholamines normally present in circumstances of stress, both emotional and physical, are supplemented and aggravated by

1. Catecholamines produced due to ingestion of illicit stimulants such as cocaine and methamphetamine
2. Catecholamines produced by the ingestion of some antipsychotic medications
3. Catecholamines that accumulate in the synapse due to blockage of the transport system by cocaine
4. The directly cardiotoxic properties of certain drugs (e.g., cocaine, diphenhydramine) on the myocardium
5. Possibly polymorphism of the α- and β-receptors

The stimulants most commonly associated with death due to EDS are

1. Cocaine and methamphetamine
2. Occasionally PCP, diphenhyramine, and Ecstacy
3. Occasionally in association with acute and chronic alcoholism, diphenhydramine, and Ecstasy

Cocaine is a powerfully addictive drug of abuse whose major routes of administration are sniffing (snorting), injection, and smoking (including free-base and crack cocaine). Less commonly, it is taken orally.

1. High doses of cocaine or prolonged use can trigger paranoia; bizarre, erratic, or violent behavior; and delusions.
2. It activates the sympathetic nervous system both centrally and peripherally.
3. It interferes with the reuptake of dopamine in the brain by strongly binding to the dopamine reuptake transporters (DATs).
    a. This impairs transport of dopamine back into the nerve terminals after release, with resultant increase in dopamine at the synapse.
    b. The resultant elevated levels of dopamine produce the high that characterizes cocaine use.

4. Chronic cocaine abusers have increased density of DAT binding sites in the limbic striatum of the brain.
    a. In chronic cocaine abusers dying in excited delirium, the number of dopamine DATs have been found not to be increased.
    b. This possibly explains the occurrence of excited delirium in these individuals.

5. The central nervous system stimulation from cocaine causes increased release of norepinephrine at the peripheral synapses and epinephrine from the adrenals.
6. Peripherally, cocaine acts to produce inhibition of norepinephrine reuptake at the synapses.
7. Thus, directly by central nervous stimulation and indirectly by blocking the reuptake of norepinephrine, cocaine causes increased concentrations of norepinephrine at the synapses between the nerve terminals and the receptors on the organs.
8. Myocardial ischemia due to the effects of markedly elevated catecholamine levels is the cause of a fatal arrhythmia in individuals with EDS due to cocaine. The ischemia is due to:
    a. An increase in myocardial oxygen demand resulting from increased heart rate, blood pressure, and myocardial contractility due to increased levels of epinephrine and norepinephrine at the postganglionic synapses of the heart
    b. In conjunction, a decrease in the supply of oxygen to the myocardium due to vasoconstriction of the coronary vasculature resulting from increased α-adrenergic stimulation

Methamphetamine is an addictive stimulant drug that may be taken orally, intranasally (snorting), intravenously, and by smoking.

1. It is related chemically to amphetamine, but the central nervous system effects are greater.
2. Euphoria appears similar to that produced by cocaine, but the effects may last much longer.
3. High doses or chronic use result in agitation, confusion, hallucinations, paranoia, and aggressiveness.
4. It stimulates the sympathetic nervous system both centrally and peripherally by increasing levels of dopamine and norepinephrine.
5. Acting on the brain, it causes the accumulation of high levels of the neurotransmitter dopamine by decreasing the number and activity of dopamine transporters.
6. The mechanism of death in EDS due to methamphetamine is the same as with cocaine: myocardial ischemia due to the effects of markedly elevated catecholamine levels.

Psychotropic Drugs

1. Psychotropic drugs include antipsychotics, neuroleptics, antidepressants, stimulants, and antianxiety agents.
2. These may cause cardiac arrhythmias and sudden death.
3. Control of the duration of the action potential of ventricular myocytes (heart cells) is based on an equilibrium between inward and outward currents of ions across the cell membrane.
   a. These drugs may block outward movement of K^+ and thus repolarization or inhibit inward ionic currents, especially Na^+ and Ca^{2+} in heart cells.
   b. Imbalance in the flow can cause QT prolongation.

4. Prolongation of the QT interval is associated with the ventricular tachyarrhythmia *torsade de pointes* and sudden death.
5. Thus, these drugs, in conjunction with a hyperadrenergic state caused by the delirium and struggle and in conjunction with hypokalemia, may produce a fatal arrhythmia.

Polymorphism

1. Small, Wagoner, Levin, Kardia, and Liggett (2002) demonstrated that in some individuals a polymorphic α_{2c}-receptor (α_{2c}-Del 322–325) produced a substantial loss of the normal negative feedback such that there was an increase in synaptic norepinephrine release.

2. In addition, a variant of the β_1-receptors (β_1-Arg 389) enhances β_1-receptor activity.
3. The combination of the two receptor variants in the same individual, resulting in an increase in norepinephrine release and enhanced β_1-receptor function at the cardiac myocyte, appeared to act synergistically to increase the risk of heart failure.
4. The presence of polymorphic α_2- and β_1-receptors may explain why some individuals die following the physical stress of EDS while the bulk of the population does not.

Prevention of Deaths Due to EDS

The Police

To prevent deaths from EDS, the police must

1. Identify individuals in excited delirium
2. Attempt to deescalate the situation and calm the individual in excited delirium down
3. Use overwhelming force if restraint must be used
4. After being restrained, monitor the individual in excited delirium at the scene and during transport
5. Immediately transport the individual with excited delirium to a hospital for treatment or observation

Deescalating the Situation

1. Environmental options
   a. Scan the scene to remove potentially hazardous objects
   b. Remove bystanders who might escalate the individual's level of distrust and agitation
   c. Ask others to move away from the individual to reduce stimulation
   d. Attempt to reduce the noise level

2. Personnel
   a. The officers should remain calm and restate requests until compliance is attained.
   b. No action should be taken unless there is an immediate threat to the individual or others.
   c. Statements should always be phrased in a positive manner with offers to help and assist.
   d. Be patient. It takes time for a highly agitated individual to calm down.
   e. Keep a safe distance, 10–15 feet from the individual.

f. Never turn one's back on a violent psychotic individual.
g. If a verbal intervention does not work, then one must resort to restraint.

Restraint

1. Any attempt to restrain or gain physical control of a highly agitated and aggressive individual suffering from excited delirium brings with it the possibility of death to the individual.
2. By reducing the time of struggle, the effects of the continued physiological catecholamine surge inherent in the struggle will be reduced, and one may prevent death from occurring.
3. Quick physical control can only be gained by use of overwhelming force.
4. If emergency medical services units are at a scene, once the individual is restrained, they should administer a sedative or tranquilizing agent.
5. All individuals in excited delirium should be taken immediately to a medical facility.
    a. At the scene or during transport, face-to-face monitoring of the individual's breathing status must be done by police or emergency medical services personnel until arrival at a hospital facility.
    b. Any diminished respiratory status or rapid elevation of core body temperature may signal a danger warning for sudden cardiac arrest from EDS.
    c. Be ready to immediately begin cardiac resuscitation procedures.

Hospital Setting

1. Initial use of verbal deescalation as well as the offering of sedative medications is recommended to reduce agitation.
    a. When attempting deescalation by verbal intervention, it is vitally important that staff members display calm and nonthreatening behavior toward the patient.
    b. No rapid movements toward the patient should be attempted. Psychotic agitated patients are difficult to deal with and dangerous. Staff cannot expect them to cognitively interpret, rationalize, and respond to requests in a "normal" time or manner.
    c. If conservative measures are not successful or not possible, then the staff must use physical restraint.
2. The use of restraint must only be initiated with a clear understanding that there is a potential for sudden death.
    a. If physical restraint is necessary, approximately six individuals trained in approved physical restraint techniques should be used.

b. This will reduce the time of struggle, thus reducing the cascading physiological response mechanisms inherent in EDS.

3. As soon as the individual is restrained, medication should be administered to calm the patient. The intravenous route is the most rapid.

Bibliography

Bell, L. V. (1849). On a form of disease resembling some advanced stages of mania and fever. *American Journal of Insanity, 6,* 97–127.

Chan, T. C., Vilke, G. N., Neuman, T., & Clausen, J. L. (1997). Restraint position and positional asphyxia. *Annals of Emergency Medicine, 30,* 578–586.

Di Maio, T. G., & Di Maio, V. J. M. (2006). *Excited delirium syndrome.* Boca Raton, FL: CRC Press.

Di Maio, V. J. M., & Di Maio, D. (2001). *Forensic pathology* (2nd ed.). Boca Raton, FL: CRC Press.

Dimsdale, J. E., Hartley, G. T., Guiney, T., Ruskin, J. N., & Greenblatt, D. (1984). Post-exercise peril: Plasma catecholamines and exercise. *Journal of the American Medical Association, 251,* 630–632.

Fishbain, D. A., & Wetli, C. V. (1981). Cocaine intoxication, delirium and death in a body packer. *Annals of Emergency Medicine, 10,* 531–532.

Lange, R. A., & Hillis, L. D. (2001). Cardiovascular complications of cocaine use. *New England Journal of Medicine, 345*(5), 351–358.

Mash, D. C., Pablo, J., Ouyang, Q., Hearn, W. L., & Izenwasser, S. (2002). Dopamine transport function is elevated in cocaine users. *Journal of Neurochemistry, 81,* 292–300.

Michalewicz, B. A., Chan, T. C., Vilke, G. M., Levy, S. S., Neuman, T. S., & Kolkhorst, F. W. (2007). Ventilatory and metabolic demands during aggressive physical restraint in healthy adults. *Journal of Forensic Science, 52*(1), 171–175.

O'Halloran, R. L., & Lewman, L. V. (1993). Restraint asphyxiation in excited delirium. *American Journal of Forensic Medicine and Pathology, 14*(4), 289–295.

Reay, D. T., Howard, J. D., Fligner, C. L., & Ward, R. J. (1988). Effects of positional restraint on oxygen saturation and heart rate following exercise. *American Journal of Forensic Medicine and Pathology, 9*(1), 16–18.

Small, K. M., Wagoner, L. E., Levin, A. M., Kardia, S. L. R., & Liggett, S. B. (2002). Synergistic polymorphisms of B_1 and alpha$_{2c}$ adrenergic receptors and the risk of congestive heart failure. *New England Journal of Medicine, 347*(15), 1135–1142.

Wetli, C. V., & Fishbain, D. A. (1985) Cocaine-induced psychosis and sudden death in recreational cocaine users. *Journal of Forensic Science, 30*(3), 873–880.

Young, D. B., Srivastava, T. N., Fitzovich, D. E., Kivlighn, S. D., & Hamaguchi, M. (1992). Potassium and catecholamine concentrations in the immediate post exercise period. *American Journal of Medical Science, 304,* 150–153.

Blunt Force Injuries

21

SUE GABRIEL

I. Blunt Force Injury
   A. Is the force of an object striking the body or the force of a body striking an object
   B. Examples of this would be
      1. The force exerted by a person swinging a baseball bat that is used to strike a person
      2. For a person who jumps from a roof, the force of gravity combines with the body weight of the person who falls and comes in contact with the pavement
   C. Severity of injury determined by the force applied
      1. Broad, flat weapons deliver the force over a broad area, which causes the force to be distributed over yet a larger area. This can be referred to as the *ripple effect.*
      2. An example would be a flat 4-inch wide board that would cause injury to a more diffuse surface area than just the 4 inches at the point of impact.
   D. Size of the weapon
      1. A smaller weapon that either deteriorates when it comes in contact with an object or is misshapen will deliver less direct impact to the area.

         As an example, striking someone on the head with a bottle would cause the bottle to break on impact, thus causing less applied force to the area.
      2. A small weapon can deliver a devastating impact if the force is strong and the impact is to a small bony area, such as a skull, nose, or chin.

         As an example, a forceful fist that comes in contact with a nose would be force applied to a smaller surface area, thus causing serious damage.
   E. Length of time force is applied
      1. If the force increases over a length of time, the injury is less than if the amount of force comes in a single given event.

For example, if an engine is lowered onto the chest of a person over a long period of time, the injuries would be less than if the engine were dropped onto the chest of a person in a single, swift event.

II. Injuries Caused by Blunt Force Trauma
  A. Abrasions
    1. Superficial epithelial tissue (top layer of skin) is removed via the body coming in contact with a rough surface.
    2. There are two kinds of abrasions:
      a. Superficial abrasions are like the skinned knees of children who fall on rough surfaces of sidewalks or streets.
      b. Deep abrasions are seen in motorcycle accidents when the rider is thrown from the cycle and comes in contact with a rough surface while continuing in motion. The combination of motion and rough surface causes deeper abrasions.
  B. Contusion (also known as a bruise)
    1. A contusion is caused from bleeding into the skin and/or soft tissue.
    2. A contusion can be superficial and seen by the naked eye, or it may be deep and occur to internal organs, which would only be seen via a surgical procedure or autopsy.
    3. Blood can be confined or localized to a specific area, which is known as a *hematoma*. This can occur in soft tissues and organs.
    4. There may be a "pattern" to the contusion, indicating the shape of the instrument that caused the contusion
      a. If a person was stomped, the imprint of the sole of the shoe would be present on the skin within the contused soft tissue.
      b. Spanking a child with a belt often leaves the imprint of the buckle, strap, or belt decoration on the skin.
    5. Many contusions may not appear for several days after the incident, especially if they are deep in the soft tissue.
    6. Contusions that are deep can cause internal bleeding to organs and have no visible bruising on the skin.
    7. Before assaultive injury can be determined, always be mindful that
      a. Medical conditions of the victim can cause spontaneous bruising.
      b. Elderly individuals bruise more easily due to the frailty of their skin.

      c. Children tend to bruise more easily, and bruising normally occurs over bony prominences such as elbows, knees, shins, foreheads, and chins.

      d. Medications can cause bruising at any age.

  8. The following are color changes of a contusion:

      a. Color is *not* accurate in determining age of a contusion. Remember people see colors, hues, and shades differently. Accurate dating of contusions can only be done by microscopic examination of the involved tissue.

      b. Immediate discoloration of the contused tissue can be reddish, purple, blue, or a combination thereof. This occurs from blood escaping into the tissue.

      c. Colors then progress to green, shades of yellow, and finally tan. This occurs as the free hemoglobin is broken down in the tissue and absorbed.

      d. *Never* document a contusion by the number of days.

      e. *Always* document the color of the contusion.

Estimating the Age of a Contusion

Red and Swollen 0–2 days	Dark blue/purple 2–5 days	Green 5–7 days	Yellow 7–10 days	Tan 10–14 days	Gone 2–4 weeks

C. Lacerations

  1. These occur when blunt force is applied to the skin, particularly over bony prominences, causing the skin to stretch beyond its capacity, resulting in the skin tearing apart.

  2. Lacerations are characterized by ragged edges with tissue bridging.

      a. Tissue bridging is small threadlike strands of tissue that are present and stretch from one side of the laceration to the other.

      b. Abrasions and contusions can be present at the outer margins of a laceration.

      c. An example would occur when a child falls onto the edge of a table, causing a laceration above the eyebrow with contusions and abrasions around the laceration.

D. Crushing injuries

  1. The tissue or bone is crushed by impact of a force.

  2. An example would be getting an arm caught in farm machinery, such as an auger, causing tissue and bone to be crushed.

E. Avulsion injuries
   1. Skin can be stripped off bone, along with pieces of body parts.
   2. Common avulsion injuries occur when people who operate machinery wear a wedding band. The band gets caught in the machinery, and the force pulls the band and skin from the finger.
   3. Avulsion injuries frequently occur when people operate snowblowers. A glove becomes caught when they reach in to remove snow packed in the auger. The auger pulls the glove in along with the hand. The person applies countertraction to pull the glove and hand out, often resulting in loss of skin and bone.
F. Sheared injuries: Surface tissue and deeper tissue are removed by applying force or pressure to an area.
G. Fractures
   1. Ribs
      a. Can be pathogenic in nature; caused by a disease process such as osteoporosis, osteogenesis imperfecta, tumors, carcinogenic metastasis
      b. Can be the result of medical treatment during cardiopulmonary resuscitation (PR)
      c. May occur due to direct trauma
         (1) May happen at the point of impact
         (2) Realize ribs may splinter and lacerate internal organs
         (3) Be wary of which organs are possibly involved given the location of the rib fracture
             An example may be impact of a steering wheel to the chest in a motor vehicle crash (MVC)
      d. May occur due to indirect trauma
         (1) Squeezing or compression of the chest may cause rib fractures as in child abuse or shaken baby.
         (2) Rib fractures of this nature depend on which angle the force was exerted: back to front, front to back, or side to side.
         (3) Rib fractures can result in flail chest.
   2. Sternum
      a. May be due to direct trauma such as in a motor vehicle crash, a blow to the chest with a fist, or some other type of blunt force
      b. May be due to medical intervention during cardiopulmonary resuscitation (CPR)

3. Skull: May be due to direct trauma such as a blow to the head with a weapon (tire iron, pipe), motor vehicle crash, a fall, or another type of blunt force

4. Extremities (arms, legs)
    a. Fractures may be due to direct trauma such as a blow to the extremity with a weapon, motor vehicle crash, or a fall.
    b. Focal fractures result from a small force striking a small area.
    c. Crushing fractures result from pressure or weight applied to the extremity. Soft tissue involvement may also be seen.
    d. Pathogenic fractures: These are caused by a disease process such as metastatic cancer, osteoporosis, and osteogenesis imperfecta.
    e. Penetrating fractures may occur from
        (1) A gunshot wound
        (2) A stab wound
        (3) Impalement of an object
    f. Indirect fractures may occur as follows:
        (1) The bone is pulled apart, which is known as a *traction fracture*.
        (2) An *angulation fracture* is when the bone is bent until it snaps.
        (3) A *rotational fracture* is when the bone is twisted and fractures in a spiral manner. This is also known as a *spiral fracture* and is a frequent fracture of long bones in child abuse injuries.
        (4) *Vertical compression fractures* of a long bone occur in airplane crashes or falls from a high location.
        (5) Vertebral factures are seen as a result of falls, medication, or disease.
        (6) There may be a combination of any fractures listed.
    g. Lower extremity fractures are either direct or indirect:
        (1) Pelvic fractures may occur from
            (a) Motor vehicle crashes
            (b) Airplane crashes
            (c) Skydiving
            (d) Falling or jumping from heights
        (2) Bumper fractures: from car-pedestrian accidents
        (3) Ankle fractures: from a motor vehicle crash when a foot gets caught under the accelerator
        (4) Knee and patellar fractures: from motor vehicle crashes when the knee strikes the dash

      h. Upper extremity fractures: Wrist and forearm fractures may occur from falls, motor vehicle crashes, altercations with another person (assaults).

H. Internal injuries from blunt force trauma

    1. Heart and pericardium

      a. Direct force, in the case of motor vehicle crashes when the steering wheel strikes the thorax

      b. Compression injuries from the weight of an object on the chest or abdomen

      c. Blasts or explosions that cause debris to strike the upper chest or abdomen

    2. Myocardial contusion from severe direct trauma

    3. Myocardial laceration: laceration to ventricles, vessels, aorta, atria, valves, or a combination of these

    4. Cardiac tamponade: blunt force to the upper chest

    5. Commotio cortis: sudden forceful impact to the midchest causing ventricular fibrillation, such as a when a baseball strikes the midchest

    6. Diaphragmatic injury

      a. Blunt force trauma to the chest such as a when a steering wheel impacts the chest in a motor vehicle crash

      b. Increased intra-abdominal pressure with upward displacement of viscera in the case of a crushing injury

    7. Pulmonary injury: Usually caused by a puncture or a laceration from rib fractures, resulting in

      a. Pneumothorax

      b. Hemorrhage to the lung

      c. Pulmonary contusions

    8. Abdominal organ injury: The most common organs injured are the liver, spleen, gastrointestinal tract, bladder, stomach, external male and female genitalia, as well as uterine rupture in a pregnant female.

I. Head injuries from blunt force trauma

    1. Scalp

      a. Contusions

      b. Lacerations

      c. Abrasions

      d. Hematomas

    2. Skull fractures are dependent on

      a. The force of the object used to cause the fracture

      b. Amount of head hair at impact location

       c. Whether the head was covered (by a hat, turban, etc.)
       d. Age of the victim
       e. Thickness of the scalp at impact location
       f. Shape of the skull at the impact location
       g. Can occur with minimal to excessive force, depending on the location

3. Types of skull fractures
    a. Linear or straight line
      (1) From a fall
      (2) From blunt force trauma
    b. Depressed or indentation in the skull
      (1) Example occurs when hit with the round end of a hammer
      (2) From a gunshot wound
    c. Multiple linear: from repeated blows to the head

4. Intracranial injuries from blunt force trauma
    a. Epidural bleed
      (1) The area between the inner skull and the covering of the brain (dura)
      (2) Can result in a hematoma
    b. Subdural
      (1) The area between the brain and the tough covering of the brain (dura)
      (2) Can result in a hematoma
    c. Subarachnoid
      (1) Very thin covering of the brain and spinal cord; area between the dura and the brain
      (2) Bleeding perhaps caused by blunt force trauma, either minor or severe, to head or neck

5. Intracerebral
    a. Bleeding into the brain
    b. Can be localized to a single area or occur in many areas
    c. Contusions
      (1) Bruising to the brain (cerebrum)
      (2) Blunt force trauma with coup and countercoup motion or the brain impacting the front then the back of the skull with force
        (a) Bruising on the opposite side of impact
        (b) From falls, sports accidents, shaking, motor vehicle crashes
    d. Lacerations: occur with or without skull fractures

    e.   Diffuse axonal injuries: sudden acceleration and decel-
eration injuries causing stretching, tearing of nerves and
blood vessels in the brain

6. Concussion

    a.   Blow to the head with or without loss of consciousness

    b.   Can be severe enough to cause amnesia

7. Edema (swelling of the brain) can occur as a result of

    a.   Blunt force trauma to the head

    b.   Infection

    c.   Tumors

    d.   Toxins

        (1) Causes vessel dilation and more fluid volume

        (2) Skull cannot expand, so brain tissue is compressed,
often causing tissue death

J. Neck injuries from blunt force trauma

1. Head moves forward (chin to chest)

2. Fracture/dislocation

3. Overflexes neck (hyperflexion)

    a.   The head moves backward (hyperextension), causing

        (1) Ligament tears

        (2) Subluxation

        (3) Crushing injuries to the neck/vertebrae

        (4) Twisting (torsion)

        (5) Fractures and ligament tears

    b.   Stretching injuries result in spinal cord severing.

    c.   Most neck injuries occur in the cervical section.

Appendix 1

Blunt Force Injuries

Laceration

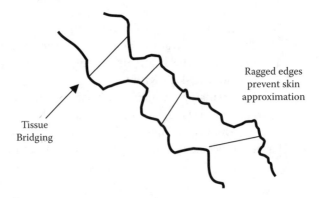

Tissue
Bridging

Ragged edges
prevent skin
approximation

Appendix 2

Blunt Force Injuries

Multiple Linear Skull Fractures: Which Came First?

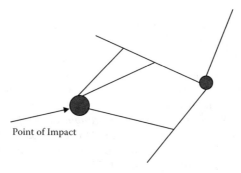

Point of Impact

Appendix 3

Blunt Force Injury

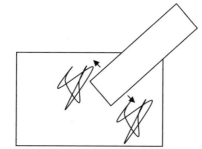

Ripple effect when wide object is used to strike a large surface

Appendix 4

Blunt Force Trauma

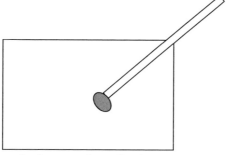

Focal impact with a smaller object

Bibliography

Besant-Matthews, P. E. (2006). In Lynch, V. A. (with Duval, J. B.). *Forensic nursing.* St. Louis, MO: Elsevier Mosby, pp. 190–196.

Di Maio, V. J. M., & Dana, S. E. (1998). *Handbook of forensic pathology.* Boca Raton, FL: CRC Press, pp. 65–94.

Di Maio, V. J., & Di Maio, D. (2001). *Forensic pathology* (2nd ed.). Boca Raton, FL: CRC Press, pp. 117–130.

Dudley, M. H. (Ed.). (2002). *Forensic medical investigation: A comprehensive review.* Albuquerque, NM, and Wichita, KS: Dudley, pp. 2.2–2.5.

Geberth, V. J. (1996). *Practical homicide investigation: Tactics, procedures, and forensic techniques* (3rd ed.). Boca Raton, FL: CRC Press, pp. 301–302.

Geberth, V. J. (2006). *Practical homicide investigation: Tactics, procedures, and forensic techniques* (4th ed.). Boca Raton, FL: CRC Press, pp. 336–339.

Spitz, W. U. (2006). In Spitz, W. U., & Spitz, D. J. (Eds.). *Spitz and Fisher's medicolegal investigation of death* (4th ed.). Springfield, IL: Thomas, pp. 460–531.

Wright, R. K. (2005). In James, S. H., & Nordby, J. J. (Eds.). *Forensic science: An introduction to scientific and investigative techniques* (2nd ed.). Boca Raton, London: Taylor & Francis Group, pp. 46–52.

Sharp Force Trauma

22

SUE GABRIEL

I. Types of Sharp Force Trauma: Incised, Chopping, Stab
   A. Incised wounds
      1. Have clean margins like a surgical incision
         a. No tissue bridging as seen in lacerations
         b. No ragged margins as seen in lacerations
      2. Incised wounds are longer than they are deep
      3. The point of origin is often the deepest portion of the wound and becomes shallower at the stopping point
      4. Incised wounds are made with a sharp instrument
         a. Knife
            (1) Single-edge blade
            (2) Double-edge blade
            (3) Serrated blade
         b. Piece of broken glass
         c. Sharp piece of metal
      5. Usually they are not fatal unless the incised area is over a superficial vessel
         a. In the neck
         b. Over the wrists, arms, legs
      6. Types of incised wounds
         a. Surgical
            (1) Performed by a medical professional during a surgical procedure
            (2) Can be performed by a skilled layperson with some knowledge of surgical procedures
         b. Self-inflicted (suicide wounds): often seen are both hesitation wounds and the fatal incised wound
         c. Hesitation wounds are
            (1) Self-mutilation wounds
            (2) Often seen in those who have thoughts of suicide
            (3) Especially seen on forearms and wrists
            (4) Can also be inflicted by a perpetrator
               (a) As a means of torture
               (b) As a victim tries to get away from a perpetrator with a sharp weapon

   (5) Hesitation marks are usually parallel to each other (nonfatal)

   (6) Nonfatal wounds can be seen in conjunction with deeper, fatal wounds appearing about the neck or arms (wrists, antecubital, and inguinal areas)

  d. Perpetrator-inflicted fatal incised wounds

   (1) When a victim is grabbed from behind, the incised neck wound will have its origin on the opposite side of the neck from the hand in which the weapon is held. For example, if the perpetrator is right handed and approaches the victim from behind, the initial incised wound will originate on the left side of the victim's neck.

   (2) The incision on the side of the neck where the initial incision occurs is usually the deepest, then becomes shallower as it crosses the neck to the other side.

   (3) The same is true when the perpetrator stands in front of the victim. The incised wound, however, may be angled across the neck from a higher to a lower point or more horizontal when from the back.

  e. Defensive incised wounds: These wounds occur on the palms, lower arms, upper arms, and backs of hands. For example, the victim holds his or her hands or arms up in front of his or her face to afford protection from an assailant. The victim may also grab at the weapon, suffering incised wounds to palms and fingers The incised wounds are often angled in these areas as either the victim or assailant moves about as slashing motions are attempted by the assailant.

  f. Fatal accidental incised wounds: These are really not seen too often, but do happen. For example, the victim falls down the stairs, hitting a framed picture and breaking the glass. The glass severs a major vessel and exsanguination (total loss of blood) occurs.

B. Chopping wounds

 1. Weapons used in chopping type wounds are heavy with sharp sides.

 2. Incised wounds of this nature are deep.

  a. This is due to the force and weight of the weapon as it comes in contact with an object or person.

  b. They usually go deep enough to make wedge-shaped cuts into the bone and tissue or completely sever the bone.

  c. This is true if the weapon has a sharp edge, such as a machete, axe, cleaver, and hatchet.

3. Wounds may be made by chopping with a dull-edged weapon.
   a. Shovels, ice chippers, hoe
   b. The wound resembles more of a laceration with jagged edges
4. Boat or plane accidents involving a propeller leave a wound that appears like a chopping wound.

C. Stab wounds
   1. These are made with a sharp or pointed weapon: knife (single or double bladed); two-pronged meat fork; ice pick; scissors; tools such as screwdrivers, awls; common household objects such as forks, steak knives, tent stakes, crochet and knitting needles, and pens or pencils, for example
   2. The depth of the wound is greater than its length.
   3. A single-bladed knife leaves an incised-looking wound.
   4. A double-bladed knife leaves more of a "V"-shaped wound.

II. Langer's Lines (Cleavage Lines)
   A. Langer's lines correspond to crease lines over the skin's surface and run obliquely in the area of greatest stretch. When incisions are made parallel to these lines, there is less scarring.
   B. When stab wounds are made parallel to cleavage lines, the wound may appear as a narrow slit, sometimes unrecognizable, or unnoticed by healthcare professionals.
   C. When stab wounds are made perpendicular to these lines, the wound appears to be a gaping wound.
   D. Other factors affecting the size and shape of the wound are clothing the weapon must penetrate, toughness of the skin, and thickness of the skin.

III. Patterned Abrasion Marks
   A. Patterned abrasions may appear on the skin at one end of the incised wound.
   B. This pattern may be caused by the hilt of the knife (where the blade attaches to the handle). When there is significant force as the blade penetrates, the hilt will leave a patterned injury indicative of blunt force.

IV. Never Make Assumptions

Never assume that because the weapon was "just a pocket knife" or something with a short blade that the penetration is not deep. This depends on the force applied and the location of the stab wound. For instance, a 3-inch pocket knife can penetrate to a depth of 6 inches or more, depending on the force and location it is used, as in the soft abdominal tissue that "gives" versus over a bony prominence such as a head or arm.

V. Need for X-Rays

Multiple stab wounds will often penetrate or chip bones. This can lead to portions of the blade being left in the bone. This is why victims should be X-rayed.

Incised wound: Margins are clean and straight. Initial contact starts out deeper and then ends more shallowly.

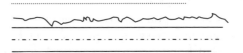

Hesitation marks: These are superficial and usually parallel. Margins may be clean and straight or rough, depending on what sharp object was used to inflict the injury

Stab wounds: When the wound goes with the cleavage or lines of Langer, it appears as a slit compared to the stab wound going against the cleavage, which appears as a gaping wound.

Skin surface

Chopping wound: This will appear as a "V"-shaped wound.

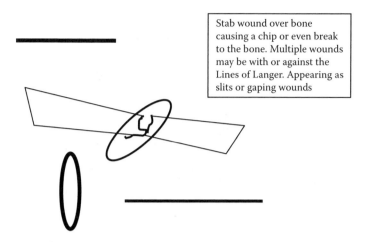

Stab wound over bone causing a chip or even break to the bone. Multiple wounds may be with or against the Lines of Langer. Appearing as slits or gaping wounds

Multiple stab wounds with chips to the bone.

Bibliography

Besant-Williams, P. E. (2006). In Lynch, V. A. (with Duval, J. B.). *Forensic nursing.* St. Louis, MO: Elsevier Mosby, pp. 196–200.

Di Maio, V. J. M., & Dana, S. E. (1998). *Handbook of forensic pathology.* Boca Raton, FL: CRC Press, pp. 95–105.

Di Maio, V. J., & Di Maio, D. (2001). *Forensic pathology* (2nd ed.). Boca Raton, FL: CRC Press, pp. 187–228.

Dudley, M. H. (Ed.). (2002). *Forensic medical investigation: A comprehensive review.* Albuquerque, NM, and Wichita, KS: Dudley, pp. 2.5–2.12.

Geberth, V. J. (1996). *Practical homicide investigation: Tactics, procedures, and forensic techniques* (3rd ed.). Boca Raton, FL: CRC Press, pp. 297–301.

Geberth, V. J. (2006). *Practical homicide investigation: Tactics, procedures, and forensic techniques* (4th ed.). Boca Raton, FL: CRC Press, pp. 331–338.

Spitz, W. U. (2006). In Spitz, W. U., & Spitz, D. J. (Eds.). *Spitz and Fisher's medicolegal investigation of death* (4th ed.). Springfield, IL: Thomas, pp. 532–606.

Wright, R. K. (2005). In James, S. H., & Nordby, J. J. (Eds.). *Forensic science: An introduction to scientific and investigative techniques* (2nd ed.). Boca Raton, FL: Taylor & Francis, pp. 45–46.

Gunshot Wounds

SUE GABRIEL

23

I. In general, the most common gunshot wounds are from small firearms:
   A. Handguns
      1. Revolvers
      2. Autoloading guns
         a. Automatics
         b. Semiautomatics
   B. Other wounds come from shotguns and rifles (long guns). For the shotgun:
      1. When fired in close contact over a bony surface such as the head, it will leave a large entrance wound with pellets embedded deep in the tissue, which can be seen on X-ray.
      2. The further away the shotgun, the more buckshot will be in the surrounding skin adjacent to the entrance of the wound.

II. Rifling: What Is It?
   A. The internal portion of the barrel of a weapon has parallel spiral striations that are specific to each weapon.
   B. These striations are called *grooves.*
   C. *Lands* are the metal between the grooves.
      1. The spiral groove will go either right to left or left to right.
      2. Each handgun will have unique grooves and spiral directions that help to distinguish the make and caliber.
      3. As the bullet is fired and travels down the barrel, lands and grooves are etched in the bullet. Many gun barrels also have imperfections that make the markings on the bullets unique to *one* particular make and model of weapon.

III. Characteristic Makeup of a Gunshot
   A. A gun is fired.
   B. The bullet travels down the barrel.

C. Hot gas follows the exiting bullet from the weapon.

D. Particles of burning gunpowder are also expelled from the weapon.

E. Carbon and soot are present.

F. Metal shavings from the bullet are present.

G. All may come in contact with the shooter or the victim and their skin or clothing.

IV. Different Gunshot Wounds

A. The distance between the muzzle and body of the gun will influence the appearance of the wound and the amount of residue left on the shooter or the victim.

B. Regarding the contact wound:

1. Hard: The muzzle of the weapon is held against the skin or bony surface with a covering of thin skin (head) when fired.

2. The appearance from a contact wound is as follows:

   a. The skin around the wound is burned and blackened at the point of contact.

   b. The imprint of the barrel end is often left on the skin.

   c. A stellate (star-shaped) wound is left (most common when the barrel is pressed against bone with thin skin covering).

   d. With wounds to bone, the fragments usually follow the path of the bullet.

   e. On entrance, the bone fragments are pushed inward.

   f. On exit, the bone fragments project outward: The extent of injury depends on the caliber of the weapon.

   g. As for backspatter:

      (1) It is present with contact wounds.

      (2) Blood and tissue are forced back out of the entrance wound by hot gases.

      (3) Backspatter appears on the perpetrator, the weapon, the area around the victim, and on the victim.

      (4) Backspatter is dependent on the caliber of weapon used.

      (5) Larger calibers will emit more backspatter.

C. For the loose contact wound, there is

1. A slight gap between skin and muzzle

2. A ring of soot around the wound that can be washed off

D. Near contact wounds have a wider band of soot than loose contact wounds; distance is about ½ inch.

E. Regarding the intermediate distance wound:
  1. Tattooing or stippling occurs.
      a. Pinpoint hemorrhages are made by burning powder striking the skin as it emerges from the muzzle.
      b. This cannot be washed off.
      c. It surrounds the entrance of the wound.
      d. The area covered by tattooing depends on the weapon and type of powder.
  2. An intermediate distance is up to 2 feet.
  3. As for gunshot residue, soot emerging from the muzzle can settle on the hand and clothing of the shooter.
F. For a distant wound,
  1. No tattooing is found on the skin around the entrance wound.
  2. The wound is round to oval.
  3. The firing distance is 2 feet or greater.
  4. There is a seared margin around the entrance from the hot bullet passing through the skin; or abrasion rings may or may not be present around the wound, depending on the weapon and type of bullet used.
  5. The abrasion ring can be irregular in shape:
      a. The bullet enters at an angle.
      b. Skin irregularities occur as the bullet enters.
      c. The bullet is malformed.
      d. The bullet becomes unstable after being fired.
G. For the grazing wound,
  1. The bullet enters the skin at an angle and shallowly, searing and abrading the skin as it skids across the tissue.
  2. There can be a split in the skin at the exit.
H. Tangential wounds
  1. Enter the skin at a parallel angle and extend into the subcutaneous tissue
  2. Are slightly deeper than a graze

V. Exit Wounds
  A. Tend to be larger than entrance wounds
  B. More irregular
    1. Bullet has slowed.
    2. Bullet may have tumbled on its path so the point is not the first to exit the skin surface.
    3. Bullet may have become deformed from striking bone along its path to exit.

C. Size of exit wounds can vary from
   1. Small slit
   2. Stellate (star shaped) and large
   3. No abrasion ring
      a. With the exception of a shored exit wound
      b. When bullet hits an article of clothing (belt buckle, bra strap); skin pushed outward at exit point against a hard surface, causing the bullet to burn the edges of the rough tissue as it exits
   4. No tattooing on exit wounds

VI. General Information
   A. The size of the wound cannot determine the caliber of the weapon.
   B. The size of wound is dependent on the type of bullet, the range of fire, clothing the victim is wearing (both exterior and undergarments), and angle.
   C. Suicide by a gunshot is most common for both men and women in the United States.
      1. The handgun is most commonly used, especially by women.
      2. The majority of people are right handed, so the wound is often in the left temple area or mouth.

Hard contact leaves the imprint of the gun muzzle on the skin.

Seared ring with soot (light gray) around loose contact wound.

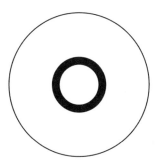

Seared ring with soot (light gray) around in near-contact wound; larger area of soot.

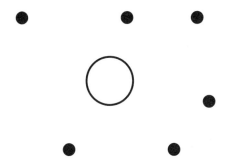

Scattered soot and tattooing.

Bibliography

Besant-Matthews, P. E. (2006). In Lynch, V. A. (with Duval, J. B.). *Forensic nursing.* St. Louis, MO: Elsevier Mosby, pp. 201–213.

Di Maio, V. J. (1999). *Gunshot wounds: Practical aspects of firearms, ballistics, and forensic techniques* (2nd ed.). Boca Raton, FL: CRC Press, pp. 65–151.

Di Maio, V. J. M., & Dana, S. E. (1998). *Handbook of forensic pathology.* Boca Raton, FL: CRC Press, pp. 107–136.

Dudley, M. H. (Ed.). (2002). *Forensic medical investigation: A comprehensive review.* Albuquerque, NM, and Wichita, KS: Dudley, pp. 2.62–2.74.

Geberth, V. J. (1996). *Practical homicide investigation: Tactics, procedures, and forensic techniques* (3rd ed.). Boca Raton, FL: CRC Press, pp. 283–297.

Geberth, V. J. (2006). *Practical homicide investigation: Tactics, procedures, and forensic techniques* (4th ed.). Boca Raton, FL: CRC Press, pp. 318–331.

Spitz, W. U. (2006). In Spitz, W. U., & Spitz, D. J. (Eds.). *Spitz and Fisher's medicolegal investigation of death* (4th ed.). Springfield, IL: Thomas, pp. 642–693.

Wright, R. K. (2005). In James, S. H., & Nordby, J. J. (Eds.). *Forensic science: An introduction to scientific and investigative techniques* (2nd ed.). Boca Raton, FL: Taylor & Francis, pp. 46–51.

Asphyxia

24

SUE GABRIEL

I. Asphyxia Definition
   A. Simply defined, asphyxia is lack of oxygen to brain and tissues.
   B. The causes can be due to various reasons

II. Types of Asphyxia
   A. Suffocation or failure of oxygen to reach the blood. The following are causes of suffocation (these can be accidental or intentional):
      1. Environmental lack of oxygen
         a. If a person is buried alive
         b. A person who is locked in a refrigerator
         c. When a victim is in a grain elevator accident and sinks beneath the grain
      2. Smothering, causing obstruction of nose/mouth
         a. Accidental in the case of overlaying when a person, often the mother, rolls on an infant, forcing the infant's face into the mattress and obstructing the nose and mouth
         b. In unshored trenches when the sides cave in, burying a person alive
      3. Homicide
         a. Gagging a victim with occlusion of the nose, which is often seen in home invasions and kidnappings
         b. Occlusion of the nose and mouth by placing a pillow over the face, using cupped hands over the mouth, or pinching the nose closed with fingers
            (1) Often seen in child deaths when a parent or caretaker is trying to quiet a crying baby or purposefully taking the infant's life
            (2) Confining or restraining victims in home invasions
      4. Suicide
         a. This can be an individual act or affect people en masse.
         b. A plastic bag is placed over the head and then secured with duct tape or another device.
            (1) This is often seen in elderly deaths because of chronic or terminal illness, depression, or financial loss or in a spousal suicide pact.

    c. This is also seen in cults with mass suicide casualties, as in the case of cult leader Jim Jones and Jonestown, Guyana, and Heaven's Gate mass suicide in San Diego, California.

5. Choking: Most often this occurs accidentally and causes a blockage of the air passages. Common offenders are

    a. Food

    b. A foreign object

    c. A large amount of alcohol consumption that causes the victim to choke on his or her vomit

    d. A disease process

    e. Acute epiglottitis (primarily seen in children) or other severe bacterial infections of the airway

6. *Mechanical asphyxia* is defined as

    a. Pressure exerted on the chest and abdomen that restricts movement of the diaphragm to inhale and exhale

       (1) This can occur when a victim is ejected from a motor vehicle and the vehicle lands on top of victim; the weight of the vehicle prevents inhalation or exhalation.

       (2) This can occur when a mechanic is working beneath a vehicle engine; the entire engine falls on the mechanic's chest, preventing the chest from rising and falling with normal breathing.

       (3) "Burking," homicidal mechanical asphyxia (William Burke, 1829), an accomplice would gather bodies for anatomical dissection by plying victim with alcohol and then sitting on the victim's chest while covering the nose and mouth.

    b. Overlaying can also fall into the category of mechanical asphyxia: Unknowingly, a parent rolls on top of an infant with his or her body, causing compression of the infant's chest, which causes impediment of normal respirations.

    c. Positional asphyxia occurs with the following:

       (1) When a person is in an immovable position and the airway becomes obstructed. One of the most common occurrences is due to alcohol intoxication. The victim may be slumped in such a position that causes the airway to become obstructed.

       (2) Another common occurrence is after an unwitnessed seizure. The victim may fall into a position that occludes the airway.

(3) In-custody deaths occur when a prisoner is restrained in a position that causes the airway to become blocked or prevents the diaphragm from moving during normal respirations.

B. *Strangulation* is the occlusion of vessels in the neck.

1. Manual strangulation can occur with the following:

   a. Eleven pounds of pressure. This will cause fatal occlusion of carotid arteries: Strangulation can occur if a victim hangs him- or herself from a doorknob. The weight of the head will put enough pressure on the carotids to cause death.

   b. Jugular veins will be occluded with 4.5 pounds of weight.

   c. Strangulation can occur at the hands of a perpetrator, which would be classified as a homicide. This can occur by

      (1) Kneeling on the neck

      (2) Use of the hands around the neck to apply pressure

2. Appearance of a victim of manual strangulation is as follows:

   a. Face is congested due to the restriction of circulating blood flow

   b. Petechiae (broken blood vessels) in sclera, conjunctiva, and periorbital area are apparent

   c. Possibly abrasions and contusions to neck, face, and under the jawline of the victim, which occur while the victim tries to become free from the assailant

   d. Possibly arc-shaped fingernail marks and fingerprint-shaped contusions left by the hands of the perpetrator

3. Regarding ligature strangulation,

   a. The ligature used is tightened by the hands of the perpetrator; often the ligature is applied from behind the victim by the perpetrator.

   b. Garroting is a form of ligature strangulation. An object such as a rod or stick is used in conjunction with a wire, rope, or piece of clothing to act as something the perpetrator grasps and uses to turn, causing the ligature to tighten. This type of device was used in the high-profile murder case of Jon Benet Ramsey, which was deemed a homicide.

   c. Accidental strangulation can occur when

      (1) A person gets a tie, scarf, or piece of clothing caught in a moving object, such as an escalator or piece of machinery. The object is tightened as the machinery pulls it forward.

(2) Children become victims of accidental strangulation during play. This can occur in playhouses when the child is looking out of a window and the window sash falls, catching the child's neck between the sash and the window ledge. Toy boxes with unhinged safety lids can fall and catch the child's neck between the edge of the toy box and the heavy lid. Many child deaths have occurred with the automatic windows in the car. The child is left alone in a running car and plays with the automatic windows. The child's neck becomes lodged between the window and frame of the car. The child is unable to reach the button to open the window.

    d. The appearance of victims of ligature strangulation is as follows:

      (1) Face is congested.

      (2) Petechiae are present in

        (a) Sclera

        (b) Conjunctiva

        (c) Periorbital area

      (3) Regarding ligature marks:

        (a) These create a furrow or depression in the neck.

        (b) These may appear slight to deep depending on what was used as the ligature.

        (c) *Never* untie the knot in the ligature; always cut the ligature a good distance (approximately 6 inches) from the knot.

        (d) Note and document with photos and drawings where the knot is located: right, left, below ear, to the back, or to the front.

4. Concerning hanging in suicides, accidental deaths, or homicides:

    a. The weight of the body tightens the noose around the neck.

    b. Full body weight is not necessary.

    c. The weight of the head (10–12 pounds) is enough to solicit hanging from a doorknob in a sitting position.

    d. Most hangings are self-inflicted; however, accidental hangings can occur in play. This is due to clothing becoming caught on something, such as the child jumping from a tree or falling from a tree house or getting clothing caught in a car door as the car takes off and the clothing becomes tightened around the neck. On escalators, as a parent bends over to aid in releasing a child's extremity or piece of clothing, inadvertently an article of clothing becomes caught that tightens around the parent's neck and causes the parent to be strangled.

   e. As for nooses:
- (1) They can be made from ropes, cords, clothing, belts, sheets, or chains.
- (2) They have a slipknot
- (3) They leave a furrow.
- (4) How deep and wide the furrow is depends on the item used for the noose.

   f. The hanging occludes the carotid arteries.

   g. If the victim is fully suspended,
- (1) Blood pools in extremities.
- (2) Petechiae will be present.
- (3) Tardieu spots (ruptured small blood vessels from the engorgement of dependent blood pooling) appear.

  5. Autoerotic hanging concerns the following:
- a. The victim is usually male.
- b. Self-induced transient cerebral hypoxia occurs.
- c. It increases sexual pleasure.
- d. When fatalities occur, the victim's escape or safety mechanism fails.
- e. Often, male victims are found in women's clothing.
- f. Bindings can be around genitalia.
- g. There may be pornographic paraphernalia nearby.

C. In chemical asphyxia, toxic gases cause the asphyxia.
  1. Carbon monoxide gas is a common causative agent.
- a. This causes accidental deaths in homes.
- b. This is used in suicide deaths with the most common mechanism being running a car in a closed garage.
- c. The skin will have a cherry red appearance

  2. Cyanide can be used.
- a. It may be used in suicide.
- b. It may be used to carry out the death penalty in some states.
- c. It has an almond odor.

  3. Hydrogen sulfide can be an agent.
- a. Maintenance workers in sewers suffer from this if poor ventilation and air quality are present.
- b. Accidental deaths may occur.

D. Choke holds are a cause.
  1. In-custody deaths can occur while this restraint is placed on an uncooperative inmate or person who is under arrest.

2. A choke hold causes compression of the airway.
3. An arm is placed around the neck of the victim to hold the victim in what is termed a *sleeper hold*.
4. The compression of the airway leads to death due to cerebral hypoxia.

Bibliography

Anderson, D. M., Keith, J., Novak, P. D., & Elliot, M. A. (2002). *Mosby's medical, nursing, and allied health dictionary* (6th ed.). St. Louis, MO: Mosby , p. 143. (Original work published 1982)

Di Maio, V. J. M., & Dana, S. E. (1998). *Handbook of forensic pathology.* Austin, TX: M. D. Press, pp. 137–144.

Di Maio, V. J., & Di Maio, D. (2001). *Forensic pathology* (2nd ed.). Boca Raton, FL: CRC Press, pp. 230–275.

Dudley, M. H. (2002). *Forensic medical investigation: A comprehensive review.* Albuquerque, NM, and Wichita, KS: Dudley, pp. 3.15–3.22.

Geberth, V. J. (1996). *Practical homicide investigation: Tactics, procedures, and forensic techniques* (3rd ed.). Boca Raton, FL: CRC Press, pp. 306–313.

Geberth, V. J. (2006). *Practical homicide investigation: Tactics, procedures, and forensic techniques* (4th ed.). Boca Raton, FL: CRC Press, pp. 339–348.

Rooms, R. R., & Shapiro, P. O. (2006). In Lynch, V. A. (with Duval, J. B.). *Forensic nursing.* St. Louis, MO: Elsevier Mosby, pp. 346, 362.

Spitz, W. U. (2006). In Spitz, W. U., & Spitz, D. J. (Eds.). *Spitz and Fisher's medicolegal investigation of death* (4th ed.). Springfield, IL: Thomas, pp. 783–845.

Wright, R. K. (2005). In James, S. H., & Nordby, J. J. (Eds.). *Forensic science: An introduction to scientific and investigative techniques* (2nd ed.). Boca Raton, FL: Taylor and Francis Group, pp. 56–57.

Child Abuse

25

SUE GABRIEL

I. Child Abuse
   A. Child abuse is defined as single or multiple nonaccidental injuries with a similar pattern occurring to a child.
   B. In dealing with children who may be victims of abuse, it is *very important* to know normal growth and development stages, including the following:
      1. Less than 25% of infants roll over before 3 months of age.
      2. Most do not crawl well before 9–10 months of age.
      3. The ability to turn a circular knob does not occur before 2 years of age.
      4. Falling from a height less than 3–4 feet does not commonly cause skull fractures.
   C. Injuries occurring on different planes of the body at the same time should raise suspicion for further investigation.
   D. Children are frontal explorers, so normal injuries should be frontal: bumps to the forehead, lip, nose.
   E. It is a natural instinct to protect the thorax, genitalia, abdomen, sides, and back during a fall or burn injury, so contusions, abrasions, burns, and lacerations to these areas should raise suspicion and warrant further investigation.
   F. Find out if there are any developmental delays in the child being assessed; if there are delays present, find out at what level the child functions, both cognitively and physically.
   G. Know that many child abuse cases result as fatalities or may become fatalities when treatment is delayed or when outward symptoms appear too late, causing medical intervention to be ineffective.
   H. Terminology to know when working with infants and children who are suspected victims of child abuse is as follows:
      1. Neonaticide: Killing of an infant less than 24 hours old
      2. Infanticide: Killing of an infant greater than 24 hours old
      3. Filicide: Killing of a child

I. Red flags for practitioners to be aware of in nonaccidental physical injuries are the following:

1. Bite marks anywhere on the body
   a. Ask how and why bite marks are present.
   b. Does the explanation fit what you are seeing and what a
      child at this developmental age is capable of doing?

2. Injuries to the external genitalia
   a. Are there bruises, abrasions, or bite marks present?
      (1) Look at the scrotum, penis, and anus in males.
      (2) Look at the labia (majora and minora), mons, and
          anus in females.
   b. Many times, abuse injuries to the genitalia may occur dur-
      ing the toilet training stage. In some cases, on examination,
      one may find strings, rubber bands, or other items tied
      around the penis as punishment for toileting accidents.
   c. When in doubt, call in a sexual assault nurse examiner
      or have the child seen at a child advocacy center to exam-
      ine the child for possible sexual abuse.
   d. Be aware that injures to the external genitalia can occur to
      either male or female children. Do not neglect to examine
      the genital area for abuse, no matter what the age of the child
      or infant and no matter what the child or adult tells you.

3. The following should be considered regarding lacerations and
   abrasions:
   a. These are normal for mobile children and usually occur
      over bony surfaces, such as the chin, nose, eyebrows,
      knees, shins, elbows, and head.
   b. You must know your developmental tasks for all ages:
      (1) It is *not* normal for a 3-month-old infant to have lac-
          erations or abrasions to knees from crawling.
      (2) It is *not* normal for a 6-month-old to crawl off the
          bed and sustain a skull fracture.
   c. Inquire and observe for deficient or delayed developmen-
      tal or cognitive skills.
   d. Does the explanation of how the child sustained the
      injury coincide with the injuries observed?

4. Look for bruising (contusions) in unusual places.
   a. It is highly unusual to sustain a bruise to the buttocks of
      diapered infants and children.
   b. Bruising on the back side anywhere should raise suspi-
      cion since children are frontal explorers.
   c. Bruises around the legs and arms could represent grab
      marks.

    d. Earlobe bruises may arise from being pinched repeatedly as punishment.

    e. Bruising may occur either individually or in clustered areas; notice if the clustered areas of bruising vary in color, meaning bruising is happening in the same area during various events

    f. Notice the color of contusions. This may vary from dark reddish purple (which is representative of a recent or newer bruise):

      (1) Progresses to green and yellow

      (2) Tan (represents the oldest bruising)

    g. Always document shape, color, size, location, and number of bruises if occurring in a cluster.

      (1) It is normal for kids to have bruising over knees, shins, elbows, and foreheads.

      (2) It is *not* normal for diaper-wearing infants and toddlers to have bruising to buttocks or other soft tissue.

      (3) Look for grab marks on arms.

5. Bruises may resemble the implement used to inflict the contusion. Some common implements are

    a. Belts and belt buckles

    b. Electric cords in the form of a loop

    c. Flyswatters

    d. Rulers

    e. Wooden spoons or paddles

    f. The human hand

6. Look for swelling and bruising to the face.

    a. Does the adult explain the injuries by a history of high incidence of "accidents" or "frequent injuries" or being clumsy?

    b. Check the inside of the mouth: Is there tearing of the frenulum or bruising about the gums, broken teeth, or lacerations or contusions to the cheeks or tongue or soft palate?

7. Fractures may be in unusual places and in different stages of healing when viewed on X-ray.

    a. Facial fractures are unusual.

    b. Rib fractures, anterior and posterior, may be present.

    c. Spiral fracture to long bones of arms and legs (humerus and femur) may occur.

    d. Any fractures in children should raise suspicion.

      (1) A thorough history and assessment are imperative.

      (2) When child abuse is suspected, full-body X-rays should be done.

      (3) In children, 50% of fractures are not accidental.

   e. Also look for numerous small bruises to the head.

   f. Black eyes without facial injuries may occur from "falling" on the face.

II. Physical Neglect

 A. Physical neglect can be defined as failure by a parent, guardian, or caretaker to provide food, clothing, shelter, or medical and dental needs for a child.

 B. Neglect is probably the most difficult to prove and prosecute.

  1. Documentation of what is seen and heard and the parent-child interaction is important.

  2. Document inconsistencies during the history taking and assessment.

 C. With neglect, there is often failure to seek care for the following:

  1. Medical issues.

  2. Dental needs such as extractions, caries, or other dental needs that could cause long-lasting medical conditions.

  3. Vision needs such as glasses or contagious eye infections.

  4. Illnesses that, if left untreated, could increase in severity, be life threatening, or cause future damage and illness. Such illnesses could be strep throat, pneumonia, lack of immunizations, asthma diagnosis with no medication, urinary tract infections, or skin diseases.

 D. Observe for signs of a neglectful parent.

  1. The parent is indifferent to the needs of the child.

  2. The parent appears apathetic or depressed.

  3. The parent may be abusing drugs or alcohol.

  4. The parent behaves irrationally or acts bizarre.

 E. Childhood risk factors for neglect are as follows:

  1. Premature birth

  2. Birth defects or anomalies

  3. In utero toxin (drugs, alcohol) experience

  4. Shy or difficult behavior

  5. Chronic/serious illness

  6. Cognitive or physical impairment

  7. Behavior problems

 F. Parental and family risk factors are as follows:

  1. Personality disorders

  2. Adults outside the family telling them how and what to do; parents are not allowed to think for themselves

  3. Depression

  4. Poor impulse control

  5. Lack of trust

   6. Feelings of insecurity
   7. Little attachment to own parents
   8. Were abused themselves
   9. Low tolerance for frustration
   10. Domestic violence present in the home
   11. Single-parent homes
   12. Age of the parent (younger parents are at a higher risk)
   13. Unrealistic expectations of child
G. Social and environment risk factors are as follows:
   1. Stressful life event that has happened
   2. Lower socioeconomic status
   3. Lack of access to medical care, health insurance, social services, child care, family support
   4. Unemployment
   5. Homelessness
   6. Poor schools
   7. Living in violent neighborhoods
   8. Experiencing social isolation
H. Children experience emotional abuse when there are the following:
   1. Screaming at or about the child
   2. Belittling the child in private or publicly
   3. Threatening the child with harm if he or she does not act in a certain way or speak in a certain way
   4. Degrading the child; telling the child how worthless he or she is
   5. Blaming the child for anything or everything that goes wrong in the family or life in general
   6. Making the child feel worthless
   7. Locking the child in a dark closet or basement for punishment or isolation
I. Sexual abuse or exploitation (each state has different definitions of what constitutes sexual abuse and exploitation; *know your state laws*) of a child can include the following, which are carried out by someone the child knows in the majority of cases:
   1. Fondling the child's genitalia or having the child fondle the adult
   2. Making the child watch pornography
   3. Having the child touch an adult for the adult's sexual gratification
   4. Filming a child performing sexual acts or in pornographic poses
   5. Penile/vaginal penetration

     6. Penile/oral penetration
     7. Penile/anal penetration
     8. Penetration with an object

III. Behavioral Signs and Symptoms of Abuse in a Child
   A. Depression and withdrawal
   B. Aggressive behavior
   C. Wariness of others
   D. Anger
   E. Fear or the lack of fear
   F. Manipulative behavior
   G. Lack of emotion

IV. Perpetrator's or Caregiver's Response Indicators of Abusive Behavior toward the Child
   A. A parent may show over- or underconcern.
   B. A parent may be aloof to others.
   C. The parent does not ask questions regarding the welfare of the child.
   D. The parent perceives an incident with the child as self-centered and caused by the child.
   E. The parent is belligerent, uncooperative, and resistant when someone tries to discus concerns regarding the child.
   F. *Always* look for more than one characteristic of abuse.

V. Medical Conditions Can Be Mistaken for Abuse
   A. Mongolian spots
   B. Car seat burns to the back of the legs
   C. Scalded skin syndrome (a staphylococcal infection)
   D. Impetigo (can be mistaken for cigarette burns)
   E. Chicken pox (can be mistaken for cigarette burns)
   F. Bleeding disorders
     1. Hemophilia
     2. Aspirin intoxication
     3. Liver disease
   G. Folk medicine or nontraditional medicine
     1. Cupping
       a. A small circular cup is heated and placed on the skin, usually on chest or upper back.
       b. It forms suction on the skin, which leaves a patterned or circular bruise.
       c. It is used to rid the body of illness or toxins, such as upper respiratory infections, colds, coughs.

      2. Coining
         a. Coining is used for the same purpose as cupping.
         b. A coin is dipped in oil and rubbed to create friction on the skin.
         c. The coin leaves abrasions, bruising, or petechiae.
         d. Coining is often seen on the back.

VI. Falls
   A. Falls less than 4 feet seldom cause injury.
   B. Find out the following:
      1. What was the distance that the child fell?
      2. Was it on carpet, tile, or a wood floor?
      3. Black eyes are seldom seen on just one side if the child fell on his or her face.
      4. The head is large in proportion to a child's body and pulls the child forward or backward.
         a. The head usually strikes the surface first.
         b. The nose sticks out the farthest from the face and would hit first. The nose should endure an injury if the child fell forward.

VII. Biggest Questions to Ask Yourself
   A. Does the injury that is seen fit the story that is told?
   B. Does the injury and the story fit the developmental tasks that the child should be or is capable of performing?
   C. These questions and their answers should guide the remainder of assessment, treatment, and the need for involvement of law enforcement

VIII. Shaken Baby Syndrome
   A. Shaken baby syndrome (SBS) is a form of child abuse.
   B. It is a collection of signs and symptoms from shaking an infant or child.
      1. Infants and young children have heavy heads and weak neck muscles.
      2. Infants and young children have a thin skull.
      3. There are soft cranial sutures.
      4. There are open fontanels.
      5. There is an increase of cerebral spinal fluid in the cranial vault.
   C. Shaking the child, which is most commonly done while holding the child around the chest with both hands, can cause the following:
      1. A subdural hematoma
      2. A subarachnoid hemorrhage

3. A retinal hemorrhage, which is the cardinal sign of a shaken baby
4. Fractured ribs
5. A coup and contracoup effect. With excess cerebral spinal fluid and a small brain and large cranium, the brain is literally slammed from front to back with each shake. This can cause hemorrhage to the brain.

IX. Munchausen Syndrome by Proxy
   A. Munchausen syndrome by proxy (MSBP) is a form of child abuse.
   B. It is difficult to detect even by highly trained health care providers.
   C. The parent, guardian, or caregiver exaggerates or fabricates a mysterious illness of the child and pursues doctor after doctor trying to find out what is causing the mysterious malady when in reality it is caused by the parent in most cases. The mother is most often found to be the offender.
   D. MSBP begins in infancy and is not often recognized until the child is 14 months to 3 years.
   E. Children less than 5 years are often fatalities of MSBP.
   F. The illness complaints begin to taper off at about 8 years, when the child is old enough to know what is happening to him or her.
   G. Examples of illnesses or symptoms in MSBP are the following:
      1. Mysterious rashes, which in reality are the result of
         a. Oven cleaner applied to the skin
         b. Lye applied to the skin
         c. Other skin irritants that would result in a rash or burn
      2. Mysterious infections that have no cure, such as
         a. High temperatures and seizures, which are found to be the result of feces injected into the skin of the child or slow poisoning
         b. Feces or urine or other body fluids injected into the intravenous tubing of a child in the hospital
      3. Blood work that is abnormal with dangerously low hemoglobin, which may be due to slow poisoning with a variety of chemical toxins
      4. Complaints by the parent of the infant experiencing apneic spells
         a. Actually, the parent is smothering the infant to the point of unconsciousness.
            (1) The parent then gives cardiopulmonary resuscitation to revive infant.
            (2) The parent is often seen by nursing staff as a model parent, even a hero.

b. Apneic episodes perhaps triggered by parent sticking objects into the trachea

5. Complaints by the parent that the child has chronic diarrhea, which in reality is achieved when the parent gives the child a laxative solution

6. Complaints of electrolyte imbalance and dehydration; induced by feeding saltwater solutions to the infant in conjunction with laxatives

H. Many children suffer unnecessary hospitalizations, surgeries, and procedures due to this elusive form of child abuse before it is discovered, if indeed it is. Many children die before MSBP is diagnosed.

X. Parents Who Take Abuse to the Next Level

Some parents take abuse to the next level and kill their children. Parents who kill their own child/children do so for the following reasons:

A. Altruism
1. The parent cannot care for the child but cannot give the child up. This often leads the parent to kill the child and him or herself, resulting in a homicide/suicide.
2. The parent may want to relieve suffering of the child. This many be real or imagined suffering.

B. Acute psychotic episodes: The parent may be under the influence of hallucinogenics.

C. Unwanted child: The parent no longer wants or never did want the child.

D. Accidental filicide: The infant is fatally maltreated unintentionally; for instance, the infant is not taken for medical attention soon enough when ill or the infant is accidentally injured and the injury goes unrecognized.

E. Spousal revenge: The life of the infant is taken to make the other spouse suffer.

F. Mercy killings: If an infant is truly suffering, the parent can no longer watch the infant suffer.

XI. Interventions for Dealing with Child Abuse
A. Legal interventions
1. Report any suspected child abuse. It is not actually necessary to prove it is abuse; all one needs to report is suspicion. This should be reported to the appropriate agency.
a. Abuse may be reported to law enforcement.
b. Abuse may be reported to social services (child protective services).

    c. Every state is different in definition and reporting of child abuse.

    d. Many states consider any person who holds a professional license to be a mandatory reporter.

    e. It is one's legal/moral responsibility to report any suspected child abuse to the authorities.

    f. One needs only to have a suspicion to report. It is up to others to investigate and collect evidence.

  B. Physicians receive little education on detecting and diagnosing child abuse. The American Academy of Pediatrics would like to make child abuse education for physicians and other health care providers a form of mandatory continuing education.

  C. Child abuse continues to occur in the privacy of the home. Many continue to hold the belief that children are the property of the parents. Even more disheartening and frightening, there are many who believe that children are replaceable commodities.

XII. Documentation

  A. Documentation is one of the most important tools used to build a good case against abusive and neglectful parents, guardians, and caregivers.

  B. Document what you see and hear.

  C. Document how the child acts with and without the parents around.

  D. Document how the parent or caregiver acts around the child.

  E. Document size, shape, color, location, and number of injuries.

    1. Use a point of origin (so many inches or centimeters from the top of the head to each injury and so many inches or centimeters to the right or left of the midline) so there is no question where the injury is located.

    2. Is the injury on the anterior or posterior plane or both?

    3. Is the injury located on the medial or lateral aspect of the location in question?

    4. Be objective in recording: Document only what is seen.

  F. Draw on a "person" diagram where you see the injury.

    1. Describe if it has a specific shape (horseshoe shaped, linear, circular, square, etc.).

    2. Describe or draw the pattern the injury resembles. The weapon that was used to inflict the injury may leave a pattern of itself on the skin. Photograph this pattern injury with a ruler beside it to indicate size.

G. Insist that law enforcement photograph the injury.
   1. Many have never investigated a child abuse case. Work together in gathering and documenting the evidence.
H. Use quotes to indicate what the victim or adult says; do not "clean up" the grammar, and quote it exactly as it was said.
I. *Do not* go into lengthy questioning of the child.
   1. Kids want to please adults.
   2. Persistent questioning may cause a child to say things that he or she thinks you want to hear versus what really happened. Do not question siblings for the same reason.
   3. There are forensic interviewers trained in working with children within the nearest child advocacy center.
J. *Remember:* The abuser may be present in the room with the child; try to elicit information when the parent or caregiver steps out for something.
K. Quote what the child says and how he or she describes what and how the injury took place. Do not change the language.
   1. Note the nonverbal behavior in your documentation, such as if the child cries and tries to run and hide when he looks at his parent/caregiver, or the verbal behavior if the child tells his parent/caregiver, "No, stay away from me, don't touch me."
   2. All of this information will be useful in helping the child find respite from an abusive situation.
   3. The health and welfare of children lie in the hands of health-care providers. Know what is normal, abnormal, or suspicious. These children are counting on you!

Bibliography

American Academy of Pediatrics and Committee on Child Abuse and Neglect. (2001). Distinguishing sudden infant death syndrome from child abuse fatalities. *Pediatrics, 107*(2), 437–441.
Bar, R. G., Trent, R. B., & Cross, J. (2006). Age-related incidence curve of hospitalized shaken baby syndrome cases: Convergent evidence for crying as a trigger to shaking. *Child Abuse and Neglect, 30*(1), 7–16.
Centers for Disease Control. (2002, March 8). *Fact sheet. Homicide risk among infants.* Retrieved September 13, 2004, from http://www.cdc.gov/od/media/presssrel/fs020208
Fulton, D. (2000a). Early recognition of Munchausen syndrome by proxy. *Critical Care Nursing Quarterly, 23*(2), 35–42.
Fulton, D. R. (2000b). Shaken baby syndrome. *Critical Care Nursing Quarterly, 23*(2), 43–50.
Lynch, V. A. (with Duval, J. B.). (2006). *Forensic nursing.* St. Louis, MO: Elsevier Mosby, pp. 249–259.

Mugavin, M. E. (2005). A meta-synthesis of filicide classification systems: Psychosocial and psychodynamic issues in women who kill their children [Electronic version]. *Journal of Forensic Nursing, 1*(2), 65–72.

National Clearinghouse on Child Abuse and Neglect Information. (2004, June 14). Recognizing child abuse and neglect: Signs and symptoms. In *National Clearinghouse on Child Abuse and Neglect* (pp. 1–2). Washington, DC: Administration for Children and Families: United States Department of Health and Human Services. (Original work published 2003) Accessed Feb. 3, 2005 from http://www.childwelfare.gov/pubs/factsheets/signs.CFM

Ragaisis, K., & Pearson, G. (2004). Case study: When the system works: Rescuing a child from Munchausen's syndrome by proxy. *Journal of Child and Adolescent Psychiatric Nursing, 17*(4), 173–176.

Schwartz, L. L., & Isser, N. K. (2007). *Child homicide: Parents who kill*. Boca Raton, FL: CRC Press.

Snyder, H. N., & Sickmund, M. (2006, March). *Juvenile offenders and victims: 2006 national report*. Washington, DC: National Center for Juvenile Justice, United States Office of Justice Programs, United States Office of Juvenile Justice and Delinquency Prevention.

Pasqualone, G. A. (1999). Munchausen by proxy syndrome: The forensic challenge of recognition, diagnosis, and reporting. *Critical Care Nursing Quarterly, 22*(1), 52–64.

Walsh, B. (2005, August). Portable guides to investigating child abuse. In: *Investigating child abuse fatalities* (pp. 1–31). Office of Justice Programs. Office of Juvenile Justice and Delinquency Prevention: United States Department of Justice.

Ziegler, D., Sammut, J., & Piper, A. C. (2005). Assessment and follow-up of suspected child abuse in preschool children with fractures seen in a general hospital emergency department. *Journal of Paediatrics and Child Health, 41*(5–6), 251–255.

Sexual Assault

SUE GABRIEL

26

I. Assessment of Sexual Assaults
  A. Sexual assault examiners are guided by standards of practice set forth by the International Association of Forensic Nurses (1996) and the standards of nursing practice according to the American Nurses Association, incorporating standards and principles of established nursing subspecialties.
  B. Sexual assault examinations are performed by registered nurses with advanced education and clinical practice.
  C. Exams are conducted within community agencies' policies and within medical protocol and legal structure.
  D. Sexual assault examiners vary in experience and educational and clinical preparation, granting each examiner professional autonomy and unique professional style while conforming to the standard of practice.
  E. The following are the goals and interventions of the sexual assault nurse examiner (SANE):
    1. Education of the client regarding his or her informed consent or refusal of the exam; if consent is given for the exam or parts thereof, then the examiner can proceed
    2. Assessment of injury
    3. Treatment by medical protocol or referring for medical treatment as necessary
    4. Objective documentation
    5. Detailed health history
    6. Nonjudgmental evaluation of the client's recount of the crime or personal medical history
    7. Collection and preservation of evidence
    8. Prevention of potential psychological and physical health threats developing from the assault
    9. Documentation of findings that are or are not consistent with a complaint of a sexual assault
    10. Referral to resources available to assess follow-up needs, both short and long term
  F. Adult victims of assault are
    1. Females, which are the most common clients.
    2. Males can also be victims.

      3. Any gender and a person with any sexual orientation can be subject to and a victim of sexual assault.

  G. The following describes the child client:

      1. Females may be victims.

      2. Males may be victims.

      3. For a child sexual assault, specially trained examiners, interviewers, law enforcement personnel, and advocates are utilized in working with children and a child advocacy program. Many areas have a child advocacy location where forensic exams and interviews are performed.

  H. The exam and length of time commitment should be explained to the client or adult accompanying a child.

      1. The client has the right to object to or to refuse any or all parts of the exam and collection of evidence.

      2. The client is the one in control.

  I. The multidisciplinary team approach (see Littel, 2004) involves the SART (sexual assault response team):

      1. SANE

      2. Law enforcement

      3. Advocate (adult or child)

      4. As needed, many others, including emergency department (ED) physician, county attorney, mental health providers, and other health services for follow-up care

  J. The examiner should introduce him- or herself.

      1. Explain what your role is.

      2. Explain what the exam entails.

      3. Explain why a permit is needed for the exam and obtain the permit if the client agrees after having been informed.

      4. The first thing done is a urine collection for pregnancy.

         a. Advise the client not to wipe the area.

         b. Advise the client not to wash his or her hands.

         c. If the client indicates feelings of a drug-facilitated rape, such as a large gap in memory of the events that have occurred, collect urine and blood according to your facility and lab protocol.

         d. The client should not eat or drink until the exam is completed.

      5. The examiner should explain the length of the exam in general.

         a. This will be dependent on the kit used, cooperation of the client, extent of injuries found on the exam, and collection and packaging of evidence.

         b. The exam can take 3–5 hours or longer.

6. Let the client know that you will be asking some very personal questions, but this is part of the forensic information gathering.
7. Explain to the client that he or she can stop and rest during the exam.
8. Explain to the client that he or she may ask the advocate to step out of the room at any time.
9. Explain to the client that he or she may have whomever they wish for support during the exam.
10. Explain what you are doing prior to doing it.
11. Let the client know when you will be touching him or her.
12. Offer sexually transmitted infection (STI) antibiotic prophylaxis and emergency contraception according to the Centers for Disease Control and Prevention (CDC) guidelines (see Web site in the Bibliography) and facility protocol, remembering that it is the client's choice.
13. After the exam, thank the client for coming in.
14. Give the client telephone numbers of agencies, such as the following, for follow-up care in 2 weeks and again in 4 weeks:
    a. Local county health department
    b. Voices of Hope or other local rape advocacy agencies
    c. Personal physician

K. The following pertains to the history of the event.
1. It is given to law enforcement by the client.
2. It is given to the SANE by law enforcement or the client.
    a. As the client tells his or her story, document word for word what is said; *do not* put the story in your own words to make it sound grammatically correct.
    b. Document in quotation marks the client's words, such as, "He told me to be quiet and it would be over soon." Think of your documentation as forensic evidence collection.
    c. Is this a drug-facilitated assault?
        (1) Does the client remember drinking something and then having little, if any, memory of what happened after that?
        (2) If so, follow national guidelines for specimen collection of blood and urine (Littel, 2004; see "National Protocol," pp. 101–104).
3. An advocate is there for support *only* and should not question the client for information.
4. Know that this entire exam, including history taking, is done at the client's pace, not that of anyone else.

    5. Find out if the client has
        a. Bathed or showered
        b. Defecated or urinated
        c. Douched
        d. Changed clothes
        e. Gargled
        f. Had consensual sex in the last 72 hours
    6. Describe the demeanor of the client.

II. The Exam
  A. Most often, the exam is performed in a designated exam room in the ED or free-standing facility.
    1. Remember that the client is in control and may opt for no exam or only segments of the exam; this is his or her choice.
    2. The SANE should explain to the client that this is the only time during which to gather evidence, and a decision can be made at a later date regarding whether he or she chooses to proceed with pressing charges.
    3. If the assault was over 72 hours ago, the possibility of gathering viable evidence is doubtful; however, a report should be filed with law enforcement.
    4. A sexual assault nurse should be called to visit with the client and find out what has taken place and whether some evidence may still be available.
  B. An appropriate sexual assault kit for the individual jurisdiction should be used.
    1. A consent form signed for the forensic exam and collection of evidence should be obtained.
        a. If the client is a minor or ward of the state or has a legal guardian, the parent or designated guardian must sign for the kit to be collected.
        b. This may vary with individual states.
    2. Once the kit's seal is broken and the examiner begins the exam, the chain of custody must be maintained. The kit and evidence should be in the examiner's possession at all times; it is *never* to be left unattended.
    3. Guidelines of the particular kit and your facility's policy and procedure should be followed.
    4. Anticipate other evidence not acknowledged in the kit.
        a. Such things as saliva, semen, blood, vomit, chewed food or gum, insects, jewelry, or fingerprints on areas of the client's body may contain forensic evidence.
        b. Collect and preserve the evidence.

    c. Use sterile water and sterile cotton applicators to swab bite marks and where the client was kissed or licked, and substances that fluoresce with a black light should be swabbed.

    d. Swabbing should be done with a rolling motion, not rubbing, so all surfaces of the swab touch the client's skin or object swabbed.

    e. If you suspect evidence to be on a removable object such as hair barrettes, jewelry, belly rings, chewing gum, or the like, collect the item in its entirety. It can be placed in a sterile urine cup with holes pierced in the lid with a sterile needle or a clean white envelope (see Section IV E., "After the Exam").

    f. How evidence is preserved may be dictated by your particular crime lab.

C. Do the following for the external exam:

    1. Perform a complete head-to-toe exam (looking for injuries such as abrasions, bruises, patterned injuries, lacerations, bite marks, intentional burns from objects such as cigarettes or other implements).

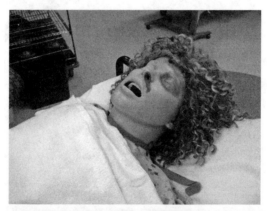

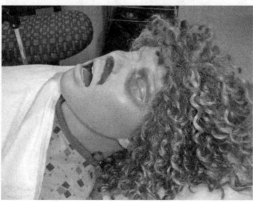

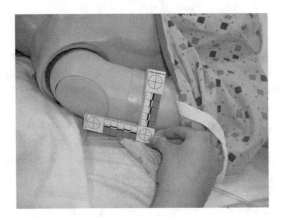

Use a forensic ruler to measure injuries.

2. Use a black light.

   a. Any protein substance (e.g., semen, saliva, vomit, or blood) will be fluorescently visible to the naked eye.

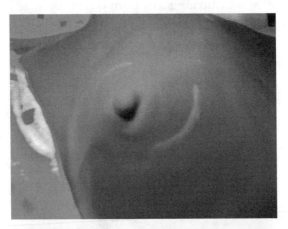

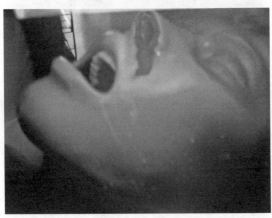

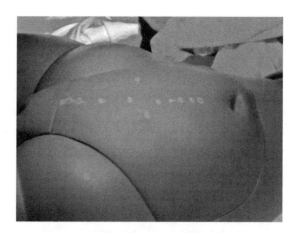

b. Any evidence found with the black light should be col-
    lected, and documentation should include where on the
    body or clothing the evidence was collected.

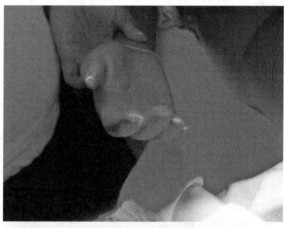

3. Photograph all external injuries on extremities, abdomen, back, and face with a 35-mm camera.
   a. Often, a digital camera is useful. You can see if your photo came out. You can download it to a computer to be saved or printed.
   b. However, your facility and law enforcement will decide how to handle photos in order to maintain chain of custody.
   c. Most important is how you will maintain chain of custody of your photos for future evidence in a court of law.
   d. Documentation regarding the location of each photograph should be completed. For instance, is it the right or left upper or lower arm?
   e. Measurements should be taken of each injury, using width and length, and then documented.
   f. While photographing injuries, a disposable forensic ruler (or one that can be sanitized after patient use) should be next to the injury to indicate size.
   g. If multiple injuries are in a condensed area, measure the largest to smallest.
   h. Also, note the color and document, for example, "a 3 cm × 2.5 cm bluish purple bruise located 7 cm down from the left shoulder on the lateral aspect of the distal left arm."
   i. Documentation needs to be objective and specific so there is no question where the injury is located.
4. Fingernail scrapings and swabs and clippings are collected.
5. Saliva from under the tongue, between the cheek and gum, tongue, and roof of the mouth is taken.
6. Head hair samples are taken.
   a. These are normally pulled from various locations on the head.
   b. 15–20 are needed.
7. Regarding head hair combings:
   a. Many times, trace evidence is available in the combings.
   b. Also, package the comb used; evidence is often found on the teeth of the comb used.
8. A blood sample is taken:
   a. Via a vial
   b. Or via finger poke, placing a drop of blood on a special filter paper provided in the kit
9. For pubic hair combing, remember to package the comb used.

10. Pubic hair samples should be pulled if available (or according to your crime lab's requirement). Many clients may be shaved, but still use comb provided to run over shaved area. Evidence may still be available on shaved clients.

11. Anal swabs should be completed along with photos of the anal rugae, documenting any tissue tears.

12. Penile and scrotum swabs should be completed on males.

13. For the external genitalia examination of a female,
    a. Begin with the external genitalia (female) and work inward, noting any injury to
    b. Clitoral hood
    c. Clitoris
    d. Labia majora
       (1) Left
       (2) Right
    e. Labia minora
       (1) Left
       (2) Right
    f. Urethral opening
    g. Vaginal opening
    h. Hymen
    i. Fossa navicularis
    j. Posterior fourchette
    k. Perineum
    l. Anus

14. For the male external genitalia, examine the following:
    a. Urethral meatus
    b. Glans
    c. Coronal sulcus
    d. Shaft
    e. Scrotum
    f. Perineum
    g. Anus
    h. Looking for the presence of blunt force trauma such as bruising, bite marks, abrasions, and lacerations as well as burns and patterned injuries on any client

15. An internal speculum exam for females is performed, observing for internal injuries of the vaginal wall and cervix.
    a. These exams are not normally done on children unless injury is suspected, and they are performed *only* under sedation or by a specially trained provider.

b. Female children who are prepubertal with unestrog-
    enized hymens will have a great deal of pain if a specu-
    lum exam or sterile swabbing is attempted.
c. Any female who has not reached menarche or who has
    not yet had a speculum exam by a licensed provider
    should not receive a speculum exam by the examiner.
d. Collect cervical and vaginal swabs, age permitting.
e. View vaginal walls left and right and the cervical os for
    injury.
f. There are many techniques for visualizing the hymen in
    children without the use of a speculum for visualization:
    (1) Use the knee chest position.
    (2) Use the frog leg position.
    (3) Use labial traction (grasp each side of the labia
         majora between finger and thumb of each hand and
         pull toward you and down). The child may want to
         do this for you.
    (4) Use warm sterile water or saline on the vaginal
         opening, which may also relax the hymen to afford a
         more optimal look.
g. Any seen or suspected STI should be cultured or treated
    with antibiotic coverage according to the CDC recom-
    mendations. Note that any STI noticed on exam will *not*
    be from the immediate incident.

III. Exam Documentation
    A. Documentation is done using the face of the clock for reference
       points.
    B. The clitoris (female) or urinary meatus (male) is located at
       12 o'clock position, and the anus is at the 6 o'clock position.
       1. Everything else is in between.
       2. As an example, document that "there is a 3-millimeter abra-
          sion to the hymen at 5 o'clock."
    C. Injuries should be documented by size and location.
    D. In female clients, pay special attention to the areas of the fossa
       navicularis and the posterior fourchette for abrasions and lac-
       erations. Remember that injuries can occur in any location.
    E. In males, look for bite marks or bruising to penis and scrotum
       and lacerations in the folds of the anal opening.
       1. Remember that you are assessing circumferentially, so all
          surfaces of the penile shaft are examined.
       2. Utilize body diagrams to indicate the location and size of the
          injuries.

F. Regarding the colposcope:
1. This is a specialized camera that takes magnified photographs of the external and internal genitalia.
2. Begin your pictures at the top or 12 o'clock position (mons for female) and at the urinary meatus (male) and work your way to the anus in a systematic order utilizing the face of the clock to designate injuries.
3. At the anus, spread the rugae of the anal opening to check for any lacerations, bruising, or abrasions that may be hidden in the folds. Also use the face of a clock to document any injuries.
4. Injuries are easier to detect with a colposcope than with the naked eye.
5. Pictures can be printed from a computer or saved directly to the computer or disk and stored in a secure location.
6. Many colposcopes have colored filters available to aid in the detection of injuries.
7. Magnified photos can be taken and filtering added to enhance definitive injuries on the same magnified photo (thus showing with or without filter color).
8. Know that your crime lab and law enforcement may have certain ways they prefer to have collections done.
9. If you are instituting a new program in your area, you can refer to the national sexual assault guidelines (see reference list).
10. Refer to the CDC recommended treatment guidelines for STIs (http://www.cdc.gov/std/treatment/).
11. Inquire about the client's safety to return home.

IV. After the Exam
A. Answer any questions the client may have.
B. For storing and sealing of evidence and the kit:
C. Each envelope should be sealed with tamperproof tape and initialed and dated by the collector.
D. If additional evidence is collected in extra envelopes, swab cartons, or urine containers with lids, make sure these have the same type of seals with name, date, and initials of the person who collected the evidence.
E. Any evidence that is wet should be air dried prior to packaging. If urine containers are used for evidence, poke holes in the lid with a sterile needle to help prevent bacteria growth from destroying the evidence.
1. *Never* store any evidence in plastic bags; always use paper.
2. If clothing is wet when collected, store in paper bags until it can be air dried in the law enforcement's evidence room.

3. After all evidence is collected, packaged, sealed, dated, and initialed, it is placed in the kit. The kit is then sealed in the same manner and handed to law enforcement with a signature to ensure the chain of custody is maintained.

4. Clothes are normally collected separately in paper bags, sealed in the same manner, and handed to law enforcement in the same manner in which the kit was transferred.

5. Make sure you as the collector of evidence notify law enforcement that there is wet material or drawn blood in the kit so that they know that it needs to be air dried or refrigerated.

F. For dismissal instructions:
1. Educate the client on the necessity of follow-up care with the local county health department, clinic, or family care provider within 2–4 weeks or before if necessary.
2. A visit for follow-up should be made to the health department, clinic, or care provider again in 6 weeks.
3. Make sure immunizations are up to date (e.g., tetanus).

G. The advocate will help the client with information regarding restraining orders, counseling, and temporary safe accommodations.

H. Always thank the client for coming in for the exam.

V. Many Victims of Sexual Assault Will Exhibit Symptoms of Rape Trauma Syndrome:
A. Immediate reaction
1. Crying
2. Hysteria
3. Shock and disbelief
4. Tearfulness
5. Tenseness
6. Controlled affect
7. Anxious smiles to laughter
8. All or none of the above

B. Physical reactions: Pain and discomfort
1. Localized
2. Generalized

C. Sleep disturbances
1. Disorganized sleep: May wake up once he or she gets to sleep and cannot go back to sleep
2. Difficulty falling asleep
3. Talking or screaming out in sleep
4. Night terrors

  D. Eating disturbances
    1. No appetite
    2. Weight loss
    3. Nausea
  E. Discomfort to the area of attack
    1. Oral: Mouth and throat irritation
    2. Vaginal
      a. Generalized pain
      b. Itching
      c. Burning
      d. Discharge
    3. Anal
      a. Rectal pain
      b. Bleeding
  F. Emotions
    1. Fear of dying
    2. Fear of injury
    3. Fear of mutilation
    4. Other emotions that occur in conjunction with fear
      a. Shame
      b. Humiliation
      c. Guilt
      d. Self-blame
      e. Degradation
      f. Embarrassment
      g. Anger
      h. Need for revenge
    5. Cautious or fearful of people
  G. Thoughts of how this situation can be undone
  H. Long-term effects
    1. Dreams
    2. Nightmares
    3. Vague physical complaints
    4. Phobias
    5. Social self-isolation
      a. Go to work or class
      b. Little socialization after work or class
      c. May not be able to leave the house at all
    6. Sexual intimacy may become difficult
    7. Clients who do not report:
      a. Individuals may keep it all to themselves.
      b. Individuals may keep it silent.

   c. Many keep the secret silent until they can carry the bur-
       den no longer.
   d. Many never disclose but have a lifetime of medical, emo-
       tional, and mental health conditions associated with the
       actual event.
8. Crisis counseling
   a. Is important
   b. Should be encouraged

VI. At-Risk Population
   A. Elder sexual assault may occur.
      1. Occurs in private homes
      2. Occurs more often in long-term care facilities
         a. A caregiver may be the offender.
         b. Another client, who may or may not understand what he
             or she is doing, may be the offender.
         c. The client may or may not be cognitively able to describe
             what has happened.
      3. The client may have a power of attorney who will sign for
          medical issues, such as for the sexual assault kit.
   B. Cognitively impaired individuals may be involved.
   C. Special needs children and adults may be involved.
      1. May be speech, hearing, sight impaired
      2. May be nonambulatory
      3. May be developmentally and cognitively disabled
      4. The following may be needed:
         a. Sign language interpreter
         b. Written communication
         c. Braille communication device
   D. In a nonambulatory population, the examiner needs to distin-
       guish between new and old injuries, such as pressure sores versus
       burns, blunt force trauma.
   E. The same samples should be obtained, but this may take longer
       and more care in explaining and understanding for the client.
   F. The at-risk population may also be a ward of the state or have
       a legal guardian. The individual's caseworker or legal guardian
       would need to sign the permit for use of a sexual assault kit.

Bibliography

American Nurses Association and the International Association of Forensic Nurses
   (1997). McHugh, J. and Leake, D. (Eds.) *Scope and Standards of Forensic Nursing
   Practice.* Washington, DC: American Nurses Publishing, pp. 1–40.

American Nurses Association (Congress on Nursing Practice and Economics) (2004, February). *Recognition of a Specialty, Approval Scope Statements, and Acknowledgement of Nursing Practice Standards,* pp. 1–18.

Bolen, R. M. (2003). Child sexual abuse: Prevention or promotion? *Social Work, 48*(2), 174–185.

Burgess, A. W. (2002). *Violence through a forensic lens.* King of Prussia, PA: Nursing Spectrum, pp. 69–143.

Hazelwood, R. R., & Burgess, A. W. (2001). *Practical aspects of rape investigation: A multidisciplinary approach.* Boca Raton, FL: CRC Press.

Hufft, A. (2004). *International Association of Forensic Nurses Care Curriculum for Advanced Practice Forensic Nursing,* pp. 1–5.

International Association of Forensic Nurses. (1996). *Sexual assault nurse examiner standards of practice.* Arnold, MD: IAFN Publishers, pp. 1–16.

Littel, K. (2004, September). *A national protocol for sexual assault medical forensic examinations: Adults/adolescents* (NCJ 206554). Washington, DC: United States Department of Justice, Office On Violence Against Women. Retrieved January 4, 2008, from http://www.ncjrs.gov/pdffiles1/ovw/206554.pdf

Patterson, D., Campbell, R., & Townsend, S. M. (2006). Sexual assault nurse examiner (SANE) program goals and client care practices. *Journal of Nursing Scholarship, 38*(2), 180–185.

Perry, B. D. (n.d.). Sexual abuse of infants [Abstract]. *Child Trauma Academy Materials.* Retrieved May 8, 2004, from http://www.childtrauma

Ray, S. L. (2001). Male clients' perspectives of incest/sexual abuse. *Perspectives in Psychiatric Care, 37*(2), 49–59.

Sommers, M. S., Zink, T., Baker, R. B., Fargo, J. D., Porter, J., Weybright, D., et al. (2006). The effects of age and ethnicity on physical injury from rape. *Journal of Obstetrics, Gynecologic, and Neonatal Nursing, 35*(2), 199–207.

Stermac, L., Dunlap, H., & Bainbridge, D. (2005). Sexual assault services delivered by SANEs. *Journal of Forensic Nursing, 1*(3), 124–128.

United States Centers for Disease Control and Prevention. (2006, August 4). Sexually transmitted diseases: Treatment guidelines 2006: Sexual assault and STDs. *MMWR Morbidity and Mortality Weekly Report, 55*(RR-11). Retrieved September 30, 2008, from http://www.cdc.gov/STD/treatment/2006/sexual-assault.htm

Waibel-Duncan, M. K. (2004). Identifying competence in the context of the pediatric angenital exam. *Journal of Child and Adolescent Psychiatric Nursing, 17*(1), 21–28.

Yeager, J. C., & Fogel, J. (2006). Male disclosure of sexual abuse and rape. *Topics in Advanced Practice Nursing eJournal, 6*(1), 1–10. Retrieved April 22, 2006, from http://www.medscap.com/viewarticle/528821_print

Intimate Partner Violence

27

SUE GABRIEL

I. Definition of Intimate Partner Violence (IPV)
   A. The Family Violence Fund (2004) defines IPV as "a pattern of assaultive and coercive behaviors that may include physical injury, psychological abuse, sexual abuse, progressive isolation, stalking, deprivation and threats. These behaviors may be precipitated by someone who is, who was, or wishes to be in an intimate or dating relationship with an adult or adolescent, and are aimed at establishing control by one partner over the other." (Family Violence Fund, 2004, p. 2; Family Violence Council, 2006, p. 1)
   B. IPV has no boundaries regarding gender, sexual orientation, ethnicity, age, religion, or socioeconomic status.

II. IPV as a Cause of Death
   A. IPV is the seventh leading cause of early death in U.S. women.
   B. It is the leading cause of death (COD) in African American women aged 15–45 years.
   C. Of U.S. women murdered, 40–50% die at the hands of
      1. Husbands/ex-husbands
      2. Lovers/ex-lovers
      3. Boyfriends/ex-boyfriends

III. Femicide (Killing of Women)
   A. Frequently occurs in IPV relationships
   B. 60–70% experience a form of physical abuse prior to their murder

IV. IPV in the Military
   A. As of 2001, there had been 10,000 *reported* cases of IPV.
      1. Over 1,000 reports have been received since 2003.
      2. The numbers continue to grow.
   B. The numbers are inclusive of enlisted women and female spouses of military men.

C. IPV numbers continue to rise in military families, especially after husbands return from active duty from such as the Gulf War and the war in Iraq.
   1. This is important information for health care providers to acknowledge when doing health histories and intake assessment on patients.
   2. Maybe a question such as, "Has anyone in your immediate family recently returned from active duty?" should be added to IVP questionnaires.

V. IPV Victims
   A. Numbers are skyrocketing in epidemic proportions.
      1. Nationally
      2. Internationally
   B. Numbers of IPV victims continue to rise in all cultures, countries, and ethnic backgrounds. Globally, IPV appears to peak in those 16–24 years old.
   C. Violent relationships account for 30% of all female homicides.
   D. IPV reports affecting males have seen increasing numbers yearly. This may be due to a healthier comfort level in reporting among males.
   E. Women continue to remain at a six times greater risk for IPV than men.

VI. Rape and Physical Assault by Intimate Partners
   A. The number climbs yearly: 47:1,000 women per year.
   B. The number is 32:1,000 men per year.
   C. This accounts for over 2 million injuries per year.
   D. This accounts for 1,500 deaths per year (remember that these are just the reported cases).
   E. Women remain at a high risk for violence even during periods of
      1. Separation
      2. Divorce

VII. Emergency Department Visits and IPV
   A. Emergency department (ED) visits speak to the necessity of education of staff and adequate screening of patients of all ages and gender for IPV.
   B. Of women who experience IPV, 44% visit the ED twice before their death. Of these women, 93% have just one visit prior to their death from IPV.
   C. Of women seeking treatment in the ED, 22–33% are victims of violent relationships.
   D. Of injuries seen in women in the ED, 95% are the result of IPV.

E. Of women, including teenage women, 50–66% experience physical injuries from dating violence.

VIII. Stalking as Part of IPV
   A. There are 1.4 million victims of stalking per year.
   B. There are over 200,000 serial stalkers in the United States.
   C. Close to 400,000 men are stalked yearly by intimate partners. These numbers are representative of same-sex partners and heterosexual partners.

IX. Violent Relationships
   A. In the United States, 4–6 million women are in violent relationships yearly.
   B. Every year, 3 million children witness violence in their homes. Children often become inadvertent casualties as the result of physical violence in the home.
      1. 45% of incarcerated children who have committed a homocide killed their parent's batterer.
      2. And many children who witness violence in the home become victims or batterers themselves.
   C. Of victims, 44% suffer a lifetime of IPV.
   D. Of pregnant women, 20–29% are victims of IPV.
      1. Screening each month with prenatal visits should be conducted to indicate a status change in the home situation.
      2. Violent relationships are either initiated or escalate with pregnancy.
         a. Because of the woman becoming more focused on her personal health status and attention toward the growing fetus
         b. As a result of jealousy over affection shown by the partner toward the infant and less toward the abuser
         c. Increased financial burden of the pregnancy and infant
      3. Women are being sent home in weakened conditions after normal childbirth or cesarean birth to violent living conditions.
      4. Postnatally, infants can become secondary causalities of abusive relationships present in the home as they become recipients of the abuser's anger toward his or her partner.

X. Physical Abuse Associated With IPV
   A. Restraining
      1. Stopping the victim from leaving
         a. Unwanted holding, hugging
         b. Pointing a finger and poking
         c. Choking/strangulation

           d. Kicking
           e. Punching
           f. Slapping
      2. Any unwanted physical contact
   B. This can include abuse of children as punishment for the adult victim

XI. Sexual Abuse Associated with IPV
   A. Threats of harming the victim's reputation
   B. Verbal put-downs by the abuser, belittling the victim in private or in public
   C. Refusal of the abuser to have sex with his or her partner (used as a form of punishment)
   D. Being treated as a sex object by the abuser
   E. Forcing the victim to look at pornography
   F. Forcing the victim to have sex
   G. Forcing the victim to engage in rough sex
   H. Forced/unwanted positions during sex
   I. Forcing unwanted sex (rape)
   J. The abuser may use child sexual abuse as punishment directed at his or her partner

XII. Social Abuse
   A. Verbal put-downs in public by the abuser
   B. Ignoring the victim in public
   C. Not letting the victim see friends or family and/or restricting visitation
   D. Being mean to the victim's friends or family
   E. Making scenes in public when out with the victim
   F. A change of personality seen in the abuser when out in public compared to what is seen in the home (a Dr. Jekyll and Mr. Hyde personality)
   G. Refusing to take responsibility for children
   H. Embarrassing the victim in public or in front of the children
   I. Using the children as threats against the partner
   J. Using the children as weapons against the partner

XIII. Emotional, Verbal, or Psychological Abuse
   A. Intimidation of the victim
   B. Making victim fearful
   C. Playing mind games with the victim (saying one thing, doing another)
   D. Name calling of the victim or of the children done in front of the victim

E. Threats against the victim
F. Sarcastic, belittling, degrading of victim or the victim's friends or family
G. Abuser chooses his or her family over the victim
H. Laughing in the victim's face
I. Brainwashing tactics used on the victim to make him or her feel incapable, inferior, stupid, or useless as a human being
J. Inappropriate expressions of jealously such as physical abuse, shouting, threatening to do harm to whoever the abuser is jealous of, destruction of the victim's property, harming the victim's pet
K. Lying about the victim to family, friends, or the children
L. Making false accusations about the victim
M. Excluding the victim from a conversation as if he or she is nonexistent
N. Abuser is unfaithful or accusing the victim of being unfaithful
O. Treating the victim as a child
P. Finding and verbalizing all of the victim's faults
Q. Making degrading remarks about the physical appearance of the victim or comparing the victim in a negative way to other women
R. Having a double standard (rules for the victim and rules for the abuser)
S. Telling the victim women- or men-bashing jokes
T. Expressing threats of harming victim's friends, family, children, or pets to terrorize the victim

XIV. Financial Abuse
A. Withholding funds to buy food and clothing and then punishing the victim for having nothing to eat in the house
B. Diverting funds for the abuser's personal pleasure and punishing the victim for not being able to manage finances
C. Embezzling funds from work or home and blaming the victim
D. Controlling family funds for medical care, clothing, food, utilities, or fuel
E. Not letting the victim buy necessities for daily living but buying anything and everything for self. This has a multifaceted effect on the victim. The victim has no brush, soap, makeup, or appropriate clothing, and without these necessities of daily living the victim is unable to leave the house, causing added isolation and control over the victim and adding more fuel for the abuser to criticize the victim's appearance.

XV. Learned Hopefulness Theory
- A. The victim is conditioned to believe she or he is at fault for provoking the incident.
- B. The victim begins to think the situation will get better if:
  1. I try harder
  2. I am a better partner
  3. I do what the abuser says/wants
  4. I never question
  5. Then life will get better

XVI. The Cycle of Violence
- A. The victim walks on eggshells trying to be perfect and trying harder, entrenched in "learned hopefulness."
- B. Tension builds.
- C. Explosion and confrontation occur.
- D. The cool down period or apologies for the abuse (honeymoon phase) occurs.
  1. "This will never happen again."
  2. "I love you."
- E. Excuses used by the abuser during the honeymoon phase include: "This happened because I was stressed, drinking too much; you didn't follow my directions; if you would only do as I say this wouldn't have to happen," and so on.
- F. The cycle starts all over; with each additional cycle of abuse, the violent acts last longer and the honeymoon phase becomes shorter, until either the victim is a fatality or the honeymoon phase is completely gone and the violence escalates to the point that it never ends. Violence becomes a daily and many times a minute-by-minute occurrence until the victim either surrenders life or will to the abuser.

XVII. Pregnancy and IPV
- A. There are two desperate times in the lives of women:
  1. Being abused in an intimate partner relationship
  2. Being pregnant and abused in an intimate partner relationship
- B. Having children can
  1. Initiate abusive relationships: a partner becomes jealous because of the attention the mother gets during pregnancy and because of the relationship the mother has with the newborn
  2. Escalate an already-abusive relationship because of added stress, responsibility, and attention
- C. Regarding attempted or completed homicides (femicide) in women:

1. These are three times greater during pregnancy.
2. Blunt force trauma is the most common cause of nonobstetrical-related deaths during pregnancy.
3. Of *all* pregnant women, 20–29% are abused.

D. Pregnant women stay in violent relationships while pregnant because of the following:
1. They form a bond with the fetus.
2. They believe in the creation of a family.
3. Pregnancy and family bind the victim's commitment to stay.
4. Leaving an abusive relationship during pregnancy is extremely rare.

E. Abused women have low birth weight babies.
F. Abused women have a higher percentage of perinatal deaths.
G. Physicians and nurses do not like to do IPV screening on pregnant women because this should be a "happy" time and not a time of "gloom and doom."

XVIII. Teen Dating Violence
A. Of the 4 million victims of dating violence, 25% are teens.
B. In high school students, 18% are involved in abusive relationships.
C. Teens and Young adults ages 15 to 20 years old:
1. Have been involved in one act of violence during dating.
2. 24% of teens have experienced extreme dating violence in the form of
   a. Rape
   b. Threats with a weapon (gun, knife, etc.)
D. In teen mothers aged 12–18 years:
1. One in 8 experiences a violent act by the baby's father.
2. Forty percent experience a violent act by a family member or relative.
E. When there is teen violence, 25% of the time there is violence in the home.

XIX. Adult Dating Violence
A. Occurs 22% of the time
B. Combined teen and dating violence broaches approximately 40–66%.

XX. Ethnicity, Age, and IPV
A. For every one Caucasian female who dies from IPV
B. Five African American young women aged 15 to 19 years will die from IPV.

XXI. Physical Signs of an Abusive Relationship
  A. Scratches
  B. Bruises
  C. Welts
  D. Knife wounds: Defensive wounds to palmar side of hands and forearms
  E. Broken bones
  F. Blunt force trauma
    1. Skull
    2. Neck
    3. Chest (fractured ribs, pneumothorax)
    4. Face
    5. Abdomen (lacerated and contused liver, spleen, kidneys)
  G. Lacerations and abrasions from
    1. Fingernails
    2. Ropes or other restraints
  H. Patterned injuries left from the devices used to inflict the injury
    1. Cigarette burns
    2. Burns from heated weapons
    3. Welts left from the weapon used
      a. Belt buckles
      b. Electrical cords
      c. Sticks, baseball bats
  I. Petechial hemorrhages in the conjunctiva and periorbital region
    1. Choking
    2. Strangulation
    3. Restraining
    4. Striking with hands or other implements
  J. Bite marks
    1. On breasts
    2. On buttocks
    3. On genitalia
    4. Or any other part of the body
  K. Genital injuries
    1. Rectal/vaginal bleeding from coerced sexual intercourse
    2. Other genital tears requiring surgical repair: Does the story fit the description of what happened to cause the injury?
  L. Low birth weight babies
  M. Perinatal death
  N. Pelvic pain
  O. PTSD (post-traumatic stress disorder)
  P. Sleeping or eating disorders
  Q. Detachment

R. Clothing may appear inappropriate for the season
  1. Long-sleeved, high-neck clothing in the summer is used to cover up visible injuries on the victim.
  2. Clothing may also be drab in color to draw less attention.

XXII. Nonphysical Signs of an Abusive Relationship
  A. Large overlap between IPV and child abuse
    1. With IPV, look for child abuse if there are children in the home
    2. With child abuse suspicions, look for IPV in the home
  B. Depression
  C. Anxiety
  D. Antisocial behaviors
  E. Fear of intimacy
  F. Very low self-esteem
    1. Victim cannot make decisions.
    2. Victim has poor eye contact with others.
    3. Victim will not do anything without abuser's permission, even something as simple as being given a prescription for antibiotics to treat an illness.
  G. Social behaviors
    1. Victims experience restricted access to health care and other supportive services; when visiting with a known or unknown victim, do not criticize her for not seeking medical attention as she may not be allowed or able to do so.
    2. Strained relationships may exist with the employer and health care providers. Employers want a "quick fix" so the victims will not be absent so much or be unable to work because of a physical injury.
  H. Health behaviors seen in victims of IPV
    1. Substance abuse: Self-medicating to erase the abuse from their memory
    2. Alcohol abuse: Another self-medicating act often used to erase the abuse or deal with it
    3. Eating disorders: under- or overeating
    4. Suicide attempts
    5. Unprotected sex: a self-destructive act used by the victim
    6. Multiple sex partners: a self-destructive act used by the victim

XXIII. Economic Costs of IPV to Society
  A. Over $8 billion in direct patient care yearly is spent on victims of IPV.

B. A loss of 8 million days of work, equivalent to 32,00 full-time jobs
C. A loss of over 5 million days of household productivity yearly

XXIV. Groups at Risk for Violent Relationships
A. Native American men and women
B. Alaskan men and women
C. African American women
D. Hispanic women
E. *Any* young woman
F. Women living below the poverty level
G. Women who were abused sexually or physically as children
H. Children who live in homes with violence

XXV. How to Help
A. Do an abuse assessment on each patient in the ED, clinics, obstetrical and gynecological offices, and community-based health care facilities.
   1. Most assessments are three to five questions in length and can be answered with yes or no replies or check marks.
   2. The assessment tool should only be completed when the nurse and patient are the *only* ones in the room.
B. Do regular IPV assessments with *each* trimester or *each* monthly appointment in pregnant females.
C. Do assessments with *each* visit to primary care providers: Check for a status change in the patient.
D. *Do not* complete the IPV assessment with *anyone* else in the room; that person could be the abuser.
E. Do not give handouts and expect the victim to take them.
   1. Abusers will search the victim's belongings for indications of seeking help or trying to leave the relationship; this often puts the victim at a greater risk for a more dangerous situation.
   2. Give the victim one number to call and tell the victim to memorize it.
   3. Ask if the victim has a safety plan for self and children.
F. Even though the victim may not appear to be listening, *every* bit of information is filed away in the safety of the victim's memory.
   1. Failure to take pamphlets offered or acting disinterested does not indicate that you have failed to help.
   2. Victims are voraciously taking in every bit of information.
   3. They can only memorize so many things.
   4. Visit with them about a safety plan for themselves and their children; if they do not have one, help them devise one.

G. Let them know you are there to help, not to punish them for choosing to live under these circumstances.
   1. It may be the safest thing for them right now.
   2. Health care providers must trust that in cases of IPV, often the patient does know what is best for him or her at the present time.
   3. Leave the door open to the victim for when he or she does need to take the next step.
H. Know that leaving or trying to leave a violent relationship puts the victim and children at a higher risk for becoming homicide victims; trust what your victim chooses to do. They often do know what is safest for them at the moment.
I. Be aware that the average number of attempts it takes a victim to completely sever a violent relationship is *seven*.
J. In many instances, abusers return to their victims within 10 years to finish what was started.

XXVI. Why Women Remain in Violent Relationships
A. Many women state that the violence began while dating and escalated during marriage.
B. Staying is safer than trying to leave.
C. Financially, leaving is not feasible, or so they have been brainwashed into believing this.
D. They hope that their abuser will change if only *they* try harder (learned hopefulness theory).
E. Many victims continue to love their abusers and have emotional attachments to them.
F. The victim may carry the disgrace of culpability for inciting the wrath of the partner.
G. Many times, family and friends, health care providers, and even law enforcement view the victim as weak or enjoying the masochistic situation and blame he or she receives for remaining in a violent relationship.

XXVII. Why Women Leave a Violent Relationship
A. The victim reaches a point at which she no longer thinks about changing the behavior of the abuser because she or he realizes there is little hope.
B. They need to provide for the safety of the children.
C. Victims become smarter and wiser.
D. Violence becomes more intense.
E. Violence never gets better.
F. Injuries escalate in frequency and severity.

G. Leaving may be seen by the victim as the only way to regain his or her life.

H. Seemingly helpful friends, family, health care providers, and law enforcement individuals who encourage a victim to leave a violent relationship need to be aware of the following:
   1. Leaving increases the risk of femicide 45%.
   2. Of female homicide victims, 75% are those who are attempting to leave or those who have left violent relationships.

XXVIII. Phases of Leaving
A. Precontemplation Phase
   1. Victims do not realize the abuse in which they are living.
   2. Victims believe it is normal for a relationship to operate in this fashion.
   3. Victims have no thoughts for change.
   4. Friends, family, or coworkers may notice or suspect that a problem exists.
   5. The victim may minimize the problem.
   6. The victim may defend the abuser.
   7. The victim will make excuses for visible injuries.
      a. "I am so clumsy."
      b. "I fell down the stairs."
      c. "I ran into the door jam, broke my glasses, and got this black eye."
   8. The victim tends to remember the "good times" prior to the abuse; this prevents change from taking place.
   9. By traumatic bonding to the abuser, victims
      a. Remain loyal
      b. Have dependence on the abuser
      c. Have emotional connectedness
   10. Social isolation makes the victim numb to what is really happening.
   11. Victims begin to believe the stories they repeatedly tell others to cover their personal pain and agony.
   12. Victims have a hopelessness, powerlessness, and dependent attitude regarding their abuser.
   13. It is in this stage that health care providers can place the seed of doubt that this behavior is normal.
      a. This nagging doubt can turn into a sliver of hope for many victims.
      b. Victims begin the journey of assessing if their relationship and the changing process begins even before the victim realizes what is occurring.

B. Contemplation Phase
   1. This phase can last for many years.
   2. The victim begins to view the abuse as "not normal."
   3. Victims begin to recognize the brutalities that have occurred over time.
   4. Victims begin to weigh the advantages and disadvantages of change and disclosing their abuse to others.
   5. Ambivalence escalates the victim's anxiety of what to do or not do.
   6. Old memories of love and a seemingly caring relationship tend to invalidate the need for change.
   7. Escalation of abuse or increased danger to children is often the jolt of insight that causes the victim to realize change is necessary.
C. Prepreparation phase
   1. Active plan for changes
   2. Motivation to carry out the changes
   3. Victims begin disclosing their abuse to family and friends
   4. Call hotlines, look for safe havens
   5. Seek counseling and legal and financial help
   6. They transform into committed victims
D. Disclosure phase
   1. Victims may disclose to health care professionals.
   2. What victims want from providers during this phase is
      a. Affirmation that abuse did occur
      b. Information on available resources
      c. Education on the short- and long-term effects that abuse has on adults and children
      d. Accurate documentation of injuries and disclosure by providers
      e. Help in leaving abusive relationships from family, friends, and clergy. Many are counseled to remain in the relationship for religious reasons during this phase.
E. Action phase
   1. All plans are in place.
   2. This is a very anxiety-causing time for victims.
   3. Self-affirmation in victims helps with the "forward motion;" this often occurs with a final act of battering.
   4. At this point, victims have no doubt that they need to leave; there is no hesitation or second guessing their decision.
F. Maintenance phase
   1. Victims continue down the uncertain path of a "new life."
   2. They learn what "normal" is really like.

3. Victims need to practice what normalcy really is, such as
    a. Making decisions
    b. Buying certain foods, wearing certain clothing
    c. Letting someone open the door for them and being able to walk through first
    d. Choosing a selection from a menu
    e. Enjoying practices that many people take for granted
4. Victims are tempted to return to the old relationship when memories of happy times occur; utilization of inner strength and support groups is helpful at this time.
5. Successful victims who complete their journey from darkness into light find
    a. New strength they did not know existed
    b. Uncertainty of what the future may bring
    c. A great relief
    d. Freedom of physical and mental anguish
    e. A beginning look toward future goals
    f. Most have some continued feeling of being "on guard" when out by themselves.

XXIX. Who Are the Abusers in IPV?
    A. Offenders are often products of abusive families and abusive relationships. They can be either male or female, with the majority being male.
    B. There is intergenerational abuse.
        1. Abusers are not taught how to deal with frustrations of life.
        2. They only know how to lash out at intended victims.
    C. There is mental illness or chemical dependency; when "under the influence," abuse will escalate.
    D. Most abusers seem nice outside of marriage.
    E. Most abusive relationships are perceived as happy by friends and relatives.
    F. Most victims of IPV refer to their partners as having Dr. Jekyll and Mr. Hyde personalities.
    G. Abusers like power and control over victims. This makes them feel "powerful."
    H. Abuse in families often centers on punishment for the victim for spending too much time with childrearing. Fatherhood is seen as an annoyance rather than a joy and privilege.
    I. The personality of the abuser is often seen as
        1. Deceptive
        2. Evasive
        3. Controlling

    4. Vindictive
    5. Aggressive
    6. Manipulating
    7. Arrogant
    8. Selfish
    9. Self-centered
J. To others, the abuser can be seen as
    1. Charming
    2. Articulate
    3. Highly verbal
    4. Superficial
    5. Emotionally immature
    6. Not trustworthy
    7. Sexually immature
    8. Incapable of intimacy
    9. Prejudiced
    10. Compulsive
    11. Attention seeking
    12. Highly defensive
    13. Having oscillating moods
    14. Having behavior that can be described as unpredictable

XXX. Lived Abuse and Severing Model. This model depicts the abuse experience and how ties are severed. This model speaks to the male batterer; however, it could also apply to the female batterer.

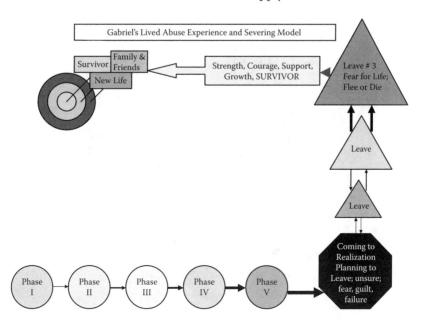

Gabriel's Lived Abuse Experience and Severing Model

Survivor | Family & Friends

New Life

Strength, Courage, Support, Growth, SURVIVOR

Leave # 3 Fear for Life; Flee or Die

Leave

Leave

Coming to Realization Planning to Leave; unsure; fear, guilt, failure

Phase I   Phase II   Phase III   Phase IV   Phase V

A. Phase I depicts the potential victim surrounded by family, friends, and future goals and self-worth.

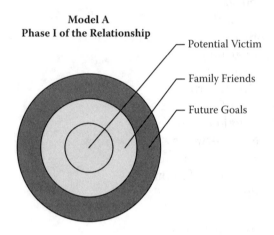

Model A
Phase I of the Relationship

— Potential Victim

— Family Friends

— Future Goals

B. Phase II depicts how surreptitiously the offender appears, often bearing gifts, and stations himself between the family and goals and self-worth of the intended victim. The offender begins initiating subtle control.

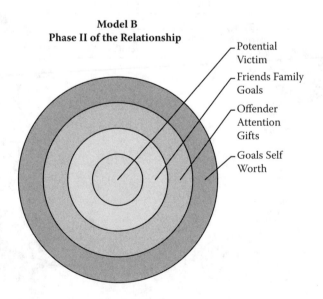

Model B
Phase II of the Relationship

— Potential Victim

— Friends Family Goals

— Offender Attention Gifts

— Goals Self Worth

C. Phase III depicts the offender beginning to put distance between the victim and family and friends, causing diminishing self-worth and future goals to the victim. In this phase, the offender is stationed closer to the intended victim and has increased control, and violence makes an appearance.

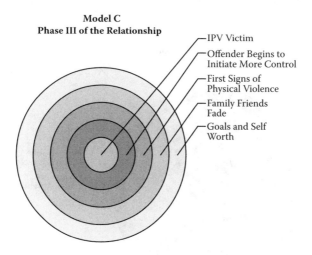

Model C
Phase III of the Relationship

— IPV Victim
— Offender Begins to Initiate More Control
— First Signs of Physical Violence
— Family Friends Fade
— Goals and Self Worth

D. In Phase IV, family and friends are pushed further away as the offender adds a layer of isolation around the victim. The isolation takes the victim further from her support system. During this phase, the abuse and control have escalated in frequency and intensity.

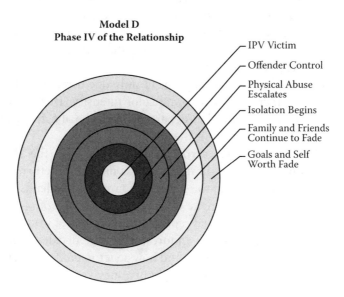

Model D
Phase IV of the Relationship

— IPV Victim
— Offender Control
— Physical Abuse Escalates
— Isolation Begins
— Family and Friends Continue to Fade
— Goals and Self Worth Fade

E. In Phase V, the intensity of abuse and control are at their peak. The victim fears for her life. The realization by the victim of what the future may hold if she remains is depicted by the hexagonal shape of a stop sign. The arrows between the phases become thicker and more intense, representative of the abuse and control inflicted.

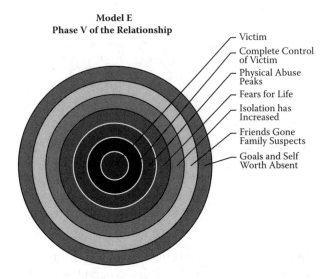

Model E
Phase V of the Relationship

Victim
Complete Control of Victim
Physical Abuse Peaks
Fears for Life
Isolation has Increased
Friends Gone Family Suspects
Goals and Self Worth Absent

F. The triangles represent attempted departures from the abuser, the arrows representing the vacillation of leaving and returning. The arrows begin as fine, uncertain lines, gaining momentum with each trial. Likewise, the triangles become larger, representing more self-assurance and confidence in making the right decision and knowing the impending danger of staying in the relationship.

G. Finally, the arrows point in only one direction; the triangle has increased in size and color intensity. This is the acme of the realization that departure from the abusive relationship must occur now or the victim will die.

H. The pale, thick arrow is representative of the elements of knowing the right decision was made, the returning of self-confidence, and the support of family and friends; future life goals begin to make their return to the life of a victim. This model is a pictorial representation of how a woman becomes a victim, what she endures, when she decides to leave, how this is accomplished, and how a victim comes full circle from an IPV relationship to that of a survivor.

Bibliography

American Bar Association. (n.d.-a). *Warning signs.* Retrieved July 14, 2004, from http://www.abanet.org/domviol/warning.html

American Bar Association. (n.d.-b). *What if you are the friend of a victim?* Retrieved July 14, 2004, from http://www.abanet.org/domviol/friendofvictim.htm

American Bar Association. (n.d.-c). *What is teen dating violence?* Retrieved July 14, 2004, from http://www.abanet.org/domviol/teendatingviolence.html

American Bar Association. (n.d.-d). *Why is it so prevalent?* Retrieved July 14, 2004, from http://www.abanet.org/domviol/prevalent.html

Barclay, L., & Lie, D. (2006, March 8). Audiotape may be better than written questionnaire for intimate partner violence screening. *Medscape,* pp. 1–5. Retrieved March 30, 2006, from http://www.medscape.com/viewarticle525124

Barkley Burnett, L., & Adler, J. (2006, January 17). Domestic violence. *eMedicine.* Retrieved November 26, 2006, from http://www.emedicine.com/emerg/topic153.htm

Bellig, L. L. (2006). Domestic violence in pregnancy. *The International Journal of Childbirth Education, 21*(2), 18–20.

Bensley, L., MacDonald, S., Van Eenwyk, J., & Wynkoop Ruggles, K. (2000). Prevalence of intimate partner violence and injuries: Washington, 1999. *MMWR Morbidity and Mortality Weekly Report, 49*(26), 589–592. Retrieved April 6, 2006, from http://www.cdc.gov/mmwr/preview/mmwrhtml/mm4926a2.htm

Black, M. C., Noonan, R., Legg, M., Eaton, D., & Breiding, M. J. (2006). Physical dating violence among high school students: United States, 2003. *MMWR Morbidity and Mortality Weekly Report, 55*(19), 532–535. Retrieved May 18, 2006, from http://www.cdc.gov/mmwr/preveiw/mmwrhtml/mm5519a3.htm

Blair, M., & Wallace, C. (2002). Violence in society: Nursing faculty respond to a health care epidemic. *Journal of Nursing Education, 4*(8), 360–362.

Bryant, S. A., & Spencer, G. A. (2002). Domestic violence: What do nurse practitioners think? *Journal of the American Academy of Nurse Practitioners, 14*(9), 421–427.

Burgess, A. W., Burgess, A. G., Koehler, S. A., Dominick, J., & Wecht, C. H. (2005). Age-based factors in femicide. *Journal of Forensic Nursing, 1*(4), 151–157.

Campbell, J. C., Webster, D., Koziol-McLain, J., Block, C., Campbell, D., & Curry, M. A. (2003, July). Risk factors of femicide in abusive relationships: Results from a multisite control study. *American Journal of Public Health, 93*(7), 1089–1097.

Chamberlain, L. (2005, January). The USPSTF recommendation on intimate partner violence: What we can learn from it and what can we do about it. *Family Violence Prevention and Health Practice, 1,* 1–24.

Coben, J. H., & Fisher, E. J. (2005, June). Evaluating the implementation of hospital based domestic violence programs. *Family Violence Prevention and Health Practice, 1*(2), 1–11.

Creswell, J. W. (1998). *Qualitative inquiry and research design: Choosing among the five traditions.* Thousand Oaks, CA: Sage.

Donohoe, M. (2005). Violence against women in the military. *Medscape OB/GYN and Women's Health, 10*(2). Retrieved September 23, 2005, from http://www.medscap.com/viewarticle/528821_print

Durborrow, N. (2005, June). Commentary on evaluating the implementation of hospital based domestic violence programs. *Family Violence Prevention and Health Practice, 1*(2), 1–8.

Durose, M. R., Wolf Harlow, C., Langan, P. A., Motivans, M., Rantala, R. R., & Smith, E. L. (2005, June). *Family violence statistics.* (Bureau of Justice Statistics NCJ 207846). Washington, DC: United States Department of Justice, Bureau of Justice Statistics, pp. 1–72. (Original work published n.d.)

Elliot, B. A., Haller, I. V., & Peterson, J. M. (2005, June). Targeted IPV education: Sustained change in rural and mid-sized medical settings. *Family Violence Prevention and Health Practice, 1*(2), 1–6.

Family Violence Council. (2006). Identification, assessment, treatment, and referral. In *Healthcare Provider Guide to Intimate Partner Violence* (pp. 1–24). Omaha, NE: Healthcare Provider Guide of the Domestic Violence Coordinating Council.

Family Violence Prevention Fund. (n.d.-a). *The facts on domestic violence.* San Francisco: Author.

Family Violence Prevention Fund. (n.d.-b). *The facts on international gender-based violence.* San Francisco: Author.

Gabriel, L. S. (2008, May). *Intimate partner violence: The lived experience of an individual's perception of the holistic severing of one's self from an intimate partner violence.* Unpublished Doctoral Dissertation, College of Saint Mary.

Garcia-Moreno, C., Jansen, H. A. F. M., Ellsberg, M., Heise, L., & Watts, C. (2005). *WHO multi-country study on women's health and domestic violence against women: Initial results on prevalence, health outcomes and women's responses.* Zurich: World Health Organization, pp. 1–198.

Gelles, R. J. (2004). Domestic violence [Electronic version]. *Encarta Premium.* Retrieved July 14, 2004, from http://encarta.msn.com/encyclopedia_762529482/domestic_violence.html

Grossman, N. B. (2004). Blunt trauma in pregnancy. *American Family Physician, 70*(7), 1303–1310.

Hastings, D. P., & Kaufman Kantor, G. (2003). Women's victimization history and surgical intervention. *American Operating Room Nurses, 77*(1), 163–180.

Haywood, K. S., & Weber, L. M. (2003). A community partnership to prepare nursing students to respond to domestic violence. *Nursing Forum, 38*(3), 5–10.

Heinzer, M. M., & Krimm, J. R. (2002). Barriers to screening for domestic violence in an emergency department. *Holistic Nursing Practice, 16*(3), 24–33.

Herzig, K., Huynh, D., Gilbert, P., Danley, D., Jackson, R., & Gerbert, B. (2006). Comparing prenatal providers' approaches to four different risks: Alcohol, tobacco, drugs, and domestic violence. *Women and Health, 43*(3), 83–101.

Hornor, G. (2005). Domestic violence and children. *Journal of Pediatric Health Care,* 206–212. Retrieved September 4, 2005, from www.medscape.com/viewarticle508291

Jackson, N. A. (Ed.) (2007). *Encyclopedia of domestic violence.* New York: Routledge.

Johnston, B. (2007). Intimate partner violence screening and treatment: The importance of nursing care behaviors. *Journal of Forensic Nursing, 2*(4), 184–187.

Klaus, P. L., & Rennison, C. M. (with BJS Statisticians). (2002, February). *Age patterns in violent victimization, 1976–2000.* (Crime Data Brief, NCJ 190104, pp. 1–3). Washington, DC: United States Department of Justice. (Original work published n.d.)

Kolstee, R., Miller, J., & Knapp, S. (2004). Routine screening for abuse: Opening Pandora's box? *Journal of Manipulative and Physiological Therapeutics, 27*(1), 63–65.

Leal, C., & Brackley, M. (2004). There's more to a battered woman's experience than her partner and the abuse. *Journal of Multicultural Nursing and Health, 10*(2), 57–61.

Lee, D., James, L., Sawires, P., Falkenberg, N., & Stout, S. (with Bass and Howes). (1999, October). Clinical guidelines on routine screening. *Preventing Domestic Violence.* San Francisco: Conrad N. Hilton Foundation and the United States Department of Health and Human Services. (Original work published n.d.)

Lipsky, S., Holt, V., Easterling, T., & Critchlow, C. (2004). Police-reported intimate partner violence during pregnancy and the risk of antenatal hospitalization. *Maternal and Child Health Journal, 8*(2), 55–63.

Locsin, R. C., & Purnell, M. J. (2002, April). Intimate partner violence: Culture-centrism and nursing. *Holistic Nursing Practice, 16*(3), 1–4.

Lutenbacher, M., Cohen, A., & Mitzel, J. (2003). Do we really help? Perspectives of abused women. *Public Health Nursing, 20*(1), 56–64.

Lutz, K. F. (2005). Abused pregnant women's interactions with health care providers during the childbearing year. *Journal of Obstetric, Gynecologic and Neonatal Nursing, 34*(2), 151–162.

McAlister Groves, B., Augustyn, M., & Lee, D. (2004, August). Consensus recommendation for child and adolescent health. In *Identifying and Responding to Domestic Violence* (pp. 1–75). San Francisco: Family Violence Prevention Fund. (Original work published September 2002)

McCook, A. (2004, July). Brief screening spots domestic violence. *Medline Plus,* pp. 1–2. (Original work published June 2004)

McFarlane, J., Campbell, J. C., Sharps, P., & Watson, K. (2002). Abuse during pregnancy and femicide: Urgent implications for women's health. *Obstetrics and Gynecology, 100,* 27–36.

McNutt, L. A., Waltermaurer, E., McCauley, J., Campbell, J., & Ford, D. E. (2005, December). Rationale for and development of the computerized intimate partner violence screen for primary care. *Family Violence Prevention and Health Practice, 3,* 1–13.

Moore, K. (2003). *Lesbian, gay, bisexual, and transgender domestic violence: 2003 supplement.* New York: National Coalition of Anti-Violence Programs, pp. 1–35.

National Center for Injury Prevention and Control. (2004, June 28). Intimate partner violence. In *Fact Sheet: Intimate Partner Violence* (pp. 1–4). Atlanta, GA: United States Centers for Disease Control. (Original work published n.d.)

National Center for Injury Prevention and Control. (2006, September 7). Intimate partner violence. In *Fact Sheet: Intimate Partner Violence* (pp. 1–13). Atlanta, GA: National Center for Injury Prevention and Control. (Original work published n.d.)

National Women's Health Information Center. (2003, November). Violence prevention for men. *4Women.gov.* Washington, DC: United States Department of Health and Human Services, pp. 1–4. (Original work published n.d.)

Nemours Foundation (with TeenHealth). (2004). *Abusive relationships.* (Original work published n.d.). Retrieved July 14, 2004, from http://kidshealth.org/teen/your_mind/relationsips/abuse.htm.

Pence, E., & Paymar, M. (1993). *Domestic violence information manual.* Retrieved November 29, 2006, from http://www.eurowrc.org/05.education/education_en/12.edu_en.htm

Physical dating violence among high school students; United States, 2003. (2006, May 19). *MMWR Morbidity and Mortality Weekly Report, 55*(19), 532–535.

Power, C. (2004). Domestic violence: What can nurses do? *Australian Nursing Journal, 12*(5), 1–4.

Reichenheim, M., & Moraes, C. (2004). Comparison between the abuse assessment screen and the revised conflict tactics scales for measuring physical violence during pregnancy. *Journal of Epidemiology Community Health, 58*(6), 523–527.

Rennison, C. M., & Welchans, S. (2002, January 31). *Intimate partner violence* (Bureau of Justice Statistics: Special Report). Washington, DC: United States Department of Justice, pp. 1–11. (Original work published May 2000)

Rhodes, K. V. (2005, December). The promise and problems with using information technology to achieve routine screening for intimate partner violence. *Family Violence Prevention and Health Practice, 3*, 1–14.

Rogers, C. S., Lang, A. J., Twamley, E. W., & Stein, M. B. (2003). Sexual trauma and pregnancy: A conceptual framework. *Journal of Women's Health, 12*(10), 961–970.

SafeNetwork (with Minnesota Center Against Violence and Abuse). (1999). *Herstory of domestic violence: A timeline of the battered women's movement.* SafeNetwork. Retrieved July 20, 2007, from http://www.mincava.umn.edu/documents/herstory/herstory.html

Scrandis, D. A., Fauchald, S. K., & Radsma, J. (2004). Global gendercide: Interwoven threats to women's health and nursing obligations. *Journal of Multicultural Nursing and Health, 10*(1), 7–14.

Sheehan Berlinger, J. (2004). Taking an intimate look at domestic violence. *Nursing2004, 34*(10), 42–46.

Stinson, C. K., & Robinson, R. (2006). Intimate partner violence: Continuing education for registered nurses. *The Journal of Continuing Education in Nursing, 37*(2), 58–62.

Swisher, K., & Wekesser, C. (1994). *Violence against women.* San Diego, CA: Greenhaven Press.

Syllabus for JUS 300. (2004, January 6). Justice Department. [Intimate violence]. Retrieved May 7, 2005, from http://faculty.ncwc.edu/toconnor/300/3001ect05.htm

Tan, L., & Quinlivan, J. (2006). Domestic violence, single parenthood, and fathers in the setting of teenage pregnancy. *The Journal of Adolescent Health, 38*(3), 201–207.

Tilley, D., & Brackley, M. (2004). Violent lives of women: Critical points for intervention-phase I focus groups. *Perspectives in Psychiatric Care, 40*(4), 157–166.

Tjaden, P., & Thoennes, N. (1998a, April). *Stalking in America: Findings from the national violence against women survey.* (National Institute of Justice: Centers of Disease Control and Prevention: Research Brief, NCJ 169592, pp. 1–20). Washington, DC: United States Department of Justice: Office of Justice Programs. (Original work published n.d.)

Tjaden, P., & Thoennes, N. (1998b, November). *Prevalence, incidence, and consequences of violence against women: Findings from the national violence against women survey.* (National Institute of Justice: Centers of Disease Control and Prevention: Research Brief, NCJ 172837, pp. 1–16). Washington, DC: United States Department of Justice: Office of Justice Programs. (Original work published n.d.)

Torres, S., & Han, H. R. (2003). Women's perceptions of their male batterers' characteristics and level of violence. *Issues in Mental Health Nursing, 24*, 667–669.

Tubman Family Alliance. (n.d.). *Domestic violence history.* Retrieved November 26, 2006, from http://stopfamilyviolence.com/want_info/philosphy/violence_history.html

Tucker, S., Cremer, T., Fraser, C., & Southworth, C. (2005, December). A high tech twist on abuse. *Family Violence Prevention and Health Practice, 3*, 1–5.

United Nations. (2006, November 25). UN: More countries confronting violence against women. Radio Free Europe radio library. Retrieved November 26, 2006, from http://www.rferl.org/featuresarticleprint/2006/11/69787fb9–4811–4alb-9b94–2039971206

United States Center for Disease Control and Prevention (with Department of Health and Human Services). (2006, May 19). Physical dating violence among high school students: United States, 2003. *Morbidity and Mortality Weekly Report, 55*(19), 532–535.

Valladares, E., Pena, R., Persson, L., & Hogberg, U. (2005). Violence against pregnant women: Prevalence and characteristics. A population-based study in Nicaragua. *An International Journal of Obstetrics and Gynaecology, 112*(9), 1243–1248.

Williams-Evans, S. A., & Myers, J. S. (2004, March/April). Adolescent dating violence. *American Black Faculty Journal,* pp. 35–37.

Williams-Evans, S. A., & Sheridan, D. J. (2004, March/April). Exploring barriers to leaving violent intimate partner relationships. *American Black Faculty Journal,* pp. 38–40.

Women's Health Care Physicians. (2004). *Interpersonal violence against women throughout the life span.* Violence Against Women Fact Sheet. American College of Obstetricians and Gynecologists. (Original work published n.d.)

World Health Organization. (1997, July). Violence against women: A priority health issue. In *Women's Health and Development* (pp. 1–34). Geneva: Author.

World Health Organization (with Family Violence Prevention Fund). (2007, August 14). *WHO says world must step up violence prevention.* Retrieved September 30, 2007, from http://www.endabuse.org/newsflash/index.php3?Search=Article&NewsFlashID=897

Yost, N. P., Bloom, S. L., McIntire, D. D., & Leveno, K. J. (2005). A prospective observational study of domestic violence during pregnancy. *Obstetrics and Gynecology, 106*(1), 61–65.

Zero tolerance for domestic violence. (2005, January 8). *The Lancet, 365*, 1556.

Zoucha, R. (2007). Considering culture in understanding interpersonal violence. *Journal of Forensic Nursing, 2*(4), 195–196.

Cyberspace Crimes against Children

28

SUE GABRIEL

I. Introduction
   A. Cyberspace crimes against children are defined as records "of sexual activity involving a prepubescent person. Pornography records include still photos, videos, audio recordings."
   B. History of cyberspace crimes
      1. Children have always been treated as sexual objects
      2. History has recorded erotic drawings and literature involving children.
      3. In modern times, child erotica escalated with the invention of the camera; almost instantly, sexually provocative images of children were produced, traded, and collected around the world.
      4. 1960s
         a. There was a relaxation of censorship.
         b. There was an increase in availability of child pornographic photos.
      5. 1977: There were over 250 child porn magazines in circulation in the United States and Europe.
      6. 1980s
         a. The Internet was introduced.
         b. The Internet changed the scale and nature of child pornography as it was once known.

II. Offshoots of Child Cyberpornography That Link to Other Cruel Crimes against Children
   A. Violence and fatalities
   B. Neglect and abuse
   C. Abandonment
   D. Hazardous material exposure (clandestine drug labs)
   E. Trafficking of children and sexual exploitation
   F. Illegal adoption agencies
   G. Runaway juveniles

H. Internet related
    1. Stalking
    2. Monetary theft
    3. Coercion and blackmail
    4. Harassment
    5. Defamation of character
I. Sexual solicitation of children
J. Identity theft
K. Computer hacking
L. Photo cropping images to depict children in sexual poses
M. All or one of these crimes perhaps resulted in childhood suicides

III. Legislation History
A. In the 1880s in the United States, the age of legal consent was 10 years.
B. By 1977, only two states had legislation forbidding use of children in obscene or indecent materials.
C. By 1978, the first federal law referring to computers and child porn was introduced and passed, the Sexual Exploitation of Children Act.
D. In 1988, the Child Protection and Obscenity Act passed.
E. In 1996, the Child Pornography Protection Act addressed pornographic virtual images of children on the Internet and virtual pornographic images appearing to be minors on the Internet.
F. In 1998, the Child Protection and Sexual Predator Punishment Act mandated Internet providers are to report any knowledge of child porn appearing on the Internet.
G. In 2002, in *Ashcroft v. Free Speech Coalition*, virtual images were ruled not to be pornography, and the statement of "appearing to be a minor" was stricken from the law because it was felt that the statement was too broad.
H. Laws today
    1. A child under the age of 18 years is a minor.
    2. Child porn can include
        a. Obscene behavior
        b. Suggestive or sexually explicit content or images involving children
        c. Production or possession of child porn; images on the Internet just have to be accessed (not saved) to be an offense
    3. Laws vary among states.

IV. Children and the Internet
    A. Children comprise the fastest-growing group of users.
    B. Every second, six new people sign on to the Internet.
    C. Over 30 million children are users of the Internet yearly.
    D. One in five children in the age group 10 to 17 years have had unwanted sexually explicit solicitation within the last year.
    E. One in 33 children received aggressive sexual solicitation.
    F. The following is the time children spend daily on the Internet:
        1. 66% spend 1–5 hours working or surfing the Web.
        2. 79% spend 1–5 hours e-mailing or doing work.
        3. 75% spend 1–5 hours doing homework.
    G. Regarding today's teens,
        1. They hold Internet users in high social esteem.
        2. Those teens using or not using the internet view other Internet users as
            a. Cool
            b. Clever
            c. Friendly
            d. Trendy

  V. The Internet and Children as Easy Targets

The Internet makes children of all ages easy targets for the following:

    A. Theft
    B. Stalking
    C. Sexual molestation
    D. Gathering information about potential victims
    E. Being lured from their home for meetings that advance to sexual activities

VI. Pornography via the Internet
    A. Is used to
        1. Break sexual inhibitions of teens and children
        2. Validate that sexual encounters between adults and children are normal
        3. Gives an offender power over the victim
    B. Depicts sexual assault of a child
    C. Used by offenders to
        1. Recruit
        2. Seduce
        3. Control

VII. The Internet
   A. Is a rich pool of unsupervised victims and a marketplace for offenders
   B. Allows children to become susceptible to manipulation by predators
   C. Capitalizes on the natural curiosity of children
   D. Allows predators to surf chat rooms of children to look for the most vulnerable

VIII. When a Sexual Encounter Becomes Boring to Perpetrator

Once a sexual encounter (either via the Internet or in person) becomes boring to the perpetrator, the following may occur:

   A. Pictures are used as blackmail: "Don't tell or else I will … ."
   B. Posting of pictures on the Internet becomes
      1. Enduring memories to the child of what took place
      2. An irretrievable record of the account
      3. Shameful for the victim
   C. The cycle begins anew to
      1. Create demand for new material
      2. Create demand for new victims
      3. Cause voyeurs to live out fantasies

IX. How Cyberspace Crimes against Children Occur
   A. Solicitors are creative.
   B. Solicitors advertise Web sites with "Disney" or "Barbie" names.
      1. Names familiar to children are used.
      2. Children will think the sites are okay.
   C. Of kids, 75% are willing to provide personal information to anyone on the Internet to receive free goods and services: "Answer the following questions and receive a month's supply of [free candy, tickets to a movie, designer clothing, etc.]."

X. How Children Are Enticed into "Offline" or Face-to-Face Meetings
   A. Online
      1. No physical behaviors of the perpetrator are visible to alert children, such as
         a. Shifting eyes
         b. Tense posture
         c. Strange demeanor
      2. No nonverbal cues are apparent for children.

  B. Meetings in online chat rooms soon progress to
   1. E-mails
   2. Gradually initiated sexual conversations and conversations about desires
   3. Phone calls
   4. Actual face-to-face meetings

XI. Red Flags and Education for Parents and Guardians Regarding the Internet and Children
  A. Know what your child is doing on the internet
  B. Be wary if
   1. You notice secretive behavior of the child.
   2. There are numerous e-mail accounts set up by the child.
   3. You find questionable e-mails received or sent.
   4. You find unusual Web sites have been visited.
   5. You find photos of your child with someone you do not know.
  C. Remember: Computers are a part of children's lives today. They are accessible at
   1. Home
   2. School
   3. Public libraries
   4. A friend's house
   5. The teen's place of work if employed
  D. Use software to restrict the Internet usage of children.
  E. View Web ratings and sites being used by children and teens.
  F. Use child-oriented search engines.
  G. Station the computer in the center of a room commonly used by other family members.

XII. The Internet If Used Improperly by Children
  A. Can be a threat to their health and safety
  B. Can cause child porn and endangerment to increase
  C. Does increase the activity of predators
  D. Can be used to access vast quantities of child porn globally
  E. Gives instant access anywhere and to anyone, at any time
  F. Access used as a private and anonymous way of luring children and teens to dangerous places
  G. Directs sharing among users for both good and dangerous uses
  H. Is inexpensive
  I. Offers a variety of formats
  J. Permits access to "morphing" of images
  K. Provides high-quality images

L. Provides easy storage of materials
M. Allows networking among child predators
N. Seeks out and grooms child and teen victims
O. Is used in cyberstalking
P. Promotes sexual tourism
Q. Is used in the trafficking of children for sexual exploitation

XIII. Internet Productions of Children's Photos and Child Pornography
    A. These are collections that are bought and sold by child predators.
    B. Predators use the following means to display child pornography:
        1. Web cams
        2. Videos
        3. Digital cameras
        4. YouTube
    C. Mobile phones (multimedia messaging) can be used for Internet productions.
        1. Clandestine photography of children in public places is an increasing problem.
        2. Cell phones are being used to distribute pornographic photos to teens and children.
    D. Children's and teens' photos and information can be sent
        1. To Web pages
        2. To Web sites
        3. To E-mail
        4. To Web cams
        5. To E-groups
        6. To newsgroups
        7. To bulletin board systems
        8. To chat rooms
        9. Peer to peer

XIV. Passing Child Pornography to Others via Downloading to Chat Rooms and Newsgroups
    A. Closed sites
    B. One must pay to enter
    C. Password needed

XV. Extent of the Child Pornography Problem
    A. Currently, there are greater than 1 million Internet images of child pornography on the Internet.
    B. Greater than 200 new images are posted daily.
    C. Offenders may possess over 500,000 images in their personal collection.

    D. Child porn sites get 1 million hits per month.

    E. It is estimated that 50,000–100,000 pedophiles are involved in organized child porn rings in the world; one third are located in the United States.

XVI. "Type" of Person Who Engages in Cyberspace Crimes against Children

    A. A person who engages in cyberspace crimes against children may be someone who is not necessarily engaged in child abuse.

    B. The individuals come from all walks of life.
1. Are employed
2. Are in a relationship
3. Have average to above-average IQ
4. Are college educated
5. Have no criminal record
6. Are white, male, 26–40 years old
7. Are heavy Internet users
8. Are everyday people, such as, but not limited to
    a. Judges
    b. Law enforcement individuals
    c. Teachers
    d. Those in academia
    e. Rock stars
    f. Soldiers
    g. Physicians
    h. Dentists
    i. Clergy
    j. Public officials

XVII. Cyberspace Offender Styles

    A. Browsers
1. Accidentally find child porn
2. Knowingly save it

    B. Trawlers: Seek out child porn

    C. Fantasizers
1. Seek to satisfy personal desires
2. Will morph images into child porn

    D. Nonsecure collectors: Frequent chat rooms with high-level collectors

    E. Secure collectors or closed groups
1. High-level collectors who buy and sell child porn
2. Often have to pay or use secure password to enter

F. Groomers
   1. Develop online relationships with children to groom them for "hands on" meetings
   2. Directly abuse children
   3. Send children pornographic materials to lower their inhibitions and depict child-adult sexual acts as normal
G. Physical abuser
   1. Sexually abuses children with porn secondary to pedophilic interests
   2. Will record the abuse for their own pleasure
H. Producers: Record sexual abuse of children with intention of giving it or selling it to others
I. Distributors
   1. Disseminate images to others
   2. May distribute only for profit
   3. May buy and sell child porn to satisfy desire or just likes it

XVIII. Most Children Participating in Cyberspace Crimes
   A. Are not abducted or forced into participation
   B. They know perpetrator most of the time

XIX. Effects of Cyberspace Crimes on Children
   A. Children are victimized once when crime happens.
   B. Children are victimized each time pornography is accessed by viewers.
   C. Crimes have devastating physical, emotional, social, and psychological affects on children.
   D. A child often will not disclose the perpetrator due to
      1. Threats made by the perpetrator to harm the child, the child's family, a pet
      2. Knowledge of the perpetrator as a family friend or relative, teacher, clergy, doctor, and so on
   E. Children bear loyalty to the offender.
   F. Children feel shame for their behavior.
   G. Feelings intensify over the years, causing deep despair, depression, and physical and emotional problems.

XX. Relationship between Pornography and Child Abuse
   A. Porn usage is an expression of existing sexual interests.
      1. Physical and sexual abuse with the addition of pornography is the seeking of sexual gratification.
      2. The offender's sexual interest causes the use of porn.

B. Pornography primes the person to offend, such as an individual who purposefully views child porn prior to offending and finds this stimulating prior to offending.

C. Pornography has a corrosive effect.

  1. As a person's interest increases in child porn, there is an increase in the severity of the pornography viewed, which in turn desensitizes the offender to the harm victims feel.

  2. Long-term porn usage increases the chance of actual child sexual abuse.

D. Pornography may be used as a catharsis.

  1. Viewing child porn is a sole outlet for the person's sexual attraction to children.

  2. It can be a substitute for helping the offender to resist in engaging in actual "hands on" encounters with a child.

E. Pornography may be a by-product of pedophilia:

  1. Created in the process of sexual abuse

  2. Used to groom future victims for abuse

XXI. Reporting

A. Suspected cyberspace crimes can be reported to the CyberTipline: *www.missingkids.com/cybertip/* or 1-800-843-5678 (1-800-THE-LOST).

Bibliography

Burgess, A. W., Mahoney, M., Visk, J., & Morganbesser, L. (2008). Cyber child sexual exploitation. *Journal of Psychological Nursing 46* (9), 38–45.

Hall, E. (2008, April 9). Cell phone porn could bring criminal charges. ABC News. Retrieved December 28, 2008 from http://www.abc3340.com/news/stories/0408/510227.html

Hernandez, A. E. (2006, September 26). *Sexual exploitation of children over the internet: The face of a child predator and other issues.* United States Department of Justice.

Interpol (2008). *Crimes against children.*

Medaris, M., & Girouard, C. (2002, January). *Protecting children in cyberspace: The ICAC task force program* (NCJ191213). Washington, DC: United States Department of Justice, Office of Justice Programs, Office of Justice and Delinquency Prevention.

Motivans, M., & Kyckelhahn, T. (2007, December). *Federal prosecution of child sex exploitation offenders, 2006* (NCJ19412). Washington, DC: Bureau of Justice Statistics, United States Department of Justice, Office of Justice Programs.

National Institute of Justice. (2007, December). *Special report: Commercial exploitation of children: What do we know and what do we do about it?* (NCJ215733). Washington, DC: United States Department of Justice, Office of Justice Programs.

National Law Enforcement and Corrections Technology Center. (2002). *Child Internet safety.*

Sheffield, R., & Luciew, J. (2008, January 11). Sex video could bring child porn charges. Patriot News. Retrieved December 28, 2008 from http://www.pennlive.com/midstate/index.ssf/2008/01/sex_video_could_bring_child_po.html

Strauss, G. (2005, December). Cell phone technology rings in pornography in USA. *USA Today.* Retrieved December 28, 2008 from http://www.USAtoday.com/tech/products/services/2005-12-2-pornography-cellphones-x.htm

Wortley, R., & Smallbone, S. (2006, May). *Child pornography on the Internet* (No. 41). Washington, DC: United States Department of Justice, Office of Community Oriented Policing Services.

Human Trafficking

29

SUE GABRIEL

I. Introduction
  A. The United Nations defines *human trafficking* or *trafficking in* as "the recruitment, transportation, transfer, harboring or receipt of persons by means of threat or use of force or other forms of coercion, of abduction, of fraud, of deception, of the abuse of power or of a position of vulnerability or of the giving or receiving of payments or benefits to achieve the consent of a person having over another person, for the purpose of exploitation. Exploitation shall include, at a minimum, the exploitation of the prostitution exploitation, forced labor or services, slavery or practices similar to slavery, servitude or the removal of organs." (United Nations Economic and Social Commission for Asia and the Pacific, 2009, p. 1; UNODC, IPU, 2009, p. 12)
  B. Human trafficking is also referred to as *trafficking in*.
  C. It is a human rights violation.
  D. No country is immune.
  E. There are 600,000–800,000 men, women, and children trafficked in yearly across international borders.
    1. Many believe this is a conservative number.
    2. The number is rapidly increasing.
    3. This is 21st century slave trade.
  F. Over 300,000 children are trafficked yearly.
  G. The following pertains to victims of trafficking:
    1. They are bought or sold into prostitution rings.
    2. They are sweatshop workers.
    3. They work as domestic help.
    4. They are involved in involuntary servitude.
    5. They perform manual labor.
  H. Over 50% are trafficked for sexual exploitation.
  I. Over 1 million are trafficked within their home country.

II. Why Does This Happen?
   A. Most trafficking involves criminal acts.
   B. Some is the result of poor economics in underdeveloped countries.
      1. Parents believe they are sending their children to a better life.
      2. Parents sell their children for food and money to survive.
   C. Trafficking is the result of corrupt governments.
   D. Trafficking is the result of social disruption.
   E. Trafficking is the result of natural disasters.
   F. Trafficking is the result of armed conflicts.
   G. Trafficking is the result of political unrest.

III. Trafficking Is a Profitable Business
   A. Trafficking is one of the top three highest revenue incomes in organized crime.
   B. It is third behind narcotics and arms deals.

IV. Children Are Sold and Trafficked for the Sole Purpose of Sexual Exploitation
   A. These children suffer physical and social damage from
      1. Premature sexual activity
      2. Forced substance abuse
      3. Exposure to a variety of sexually transmitted infections, such as
         a. Human immunodeficiency virus (HIV)
         b. Hepatitis B
         c. Gonorrhea
         d. Chlamydia
         e. Human papilloma virus (HPV)
         f. Many other infectious diseases
      4. This can cause permanent damage to reproductive organs due to disease or injury
   B. Women and children are often trafficked to areas where they do not speak the language, making it almost impossible for them to seek help.

V. Laws Concerning Human Trafficking
   A. 2003 Trafficking Victims Protection Reauthorization Act
      1. This act addresses countries that have not yet made plans to initiate laws to halt human trafficking.
      2. This law puts these countries on a "watch list."
      3. The act allows persons from other countries apprehended in the United States to be prosecuted and sentenced.

    B. Protection Act of 2003
       1. This act allows the United States to prosecute
          a. Americans who specifically cross borders for sexual exploitation of minors
          b. Increases punishment for "sexual tourism"
          c. Helps protect children from sexual predators
          d. Has no statute of limitations for children who have been sexually abused
       2. Child sexual offenses were the fastest growing federal criminal caseload from 1994 to 2006, and this continues to grow.

VI. Transnational Trafficking of Children to the United States
    A. There are large networks composed mainly of prostitution rings.
    B. Many networks are family owned:
       1. They bring the child or children in for individual buyers who have requested a certain culture, size, age, hair color, country, and so on.
       2. They traffic for the buyers' personal use.
    C. Some traffickers smuggle illegal children for sales in
       1. The labor force
       2. Prostitution networks

VII. Child and Adult Victims
    A. These victims are recruited to fill a demand according to
       1. Age
       2. Appearance
       3. Race
       4. Language spoken
       5. Country of origin
    B. Countries with high supply and demand requests are
       1. Mexico
       2. Honduras
       3. Vietnam
       4. China
       5. India

VIII. Trafficking Children for Prostitution, Pornography, and Sexual Exploitation
    A. Traffickers have many ways of luring young children and teens away from the safety of home and parents.
       1. They use children of the same age to befriend the unsuspecting child or teen.
       2. They offer friendship, jobs, modeling opportunities, photography classes.

3. These children and teens are drugged, threatened, beaten into submission, and end up as a piece of human flesh bought and sold for the sexual pleasures of others.
4. Children who end up as victims of human trafficking:
    a. Are thought to be "runaways" who will eventually return, so not much effort is made to find them.
    b. Many law enforcement agencies may not believe that such networks exist.
    c. Victims of trafficking think they are going to a better life.
    d. Many think they have struck it big in the modeling or acting scene.
    e. There are any number of stories used by traffickers to entice potential victims.
B. During trafficking, children are moved from country to country, state to state, and city to city.
    1. For example, girls were brought to the Midwest and disbursed to 24 states and Canada for prostitution.
    2. This was a family-owned business.

IX. The Internet Makes Trafficking Easier
    A. The Internet is used for recruitment.
    B. The Internet advertises the victims to potential buyers and sex offenders.
    C. Traffickers establish Web sites that advertise "companions."
    D. Children are stalked in chat rooms.
    E. Offenders may meet with a child, sexually abuse the child, then sell the child to another trafficker.
    F. There is a large market for child pornography in the United States.

X. When a Child Victim Is Brought to a Location

Many things happen to the unsuspecting victim. These victims are subjected to

    A. Brutal beatings
    B. Repeated acts of rape
    C. Severe mental abuse
    D. Torture
    E. Starvation
    F. Death threats to the victims or their families back home
    G. The withholding of their international papers. The victims can "earn" their papers back by subjecting themselves to acts of prostitution.

H. When victims are nearing the total dollars to "buy" their freedom, they are resold. They must then pay the debt off again, by restarting at a "zero" balance.

I. The victims are sold by a trafficker who makes 5–20 times what was paid for each victim.

XI. Why Human Trafficking Goes Undetected

A. Victims are isolated on arriving from another country, state, or city.

B. Traffickers prevent victims from disclosing what is happening to them. Victims are

1. Drugged
2. Threatened
3. Beaten

C. Public service providers have not been aware until now of the extent of human trafficking.

XII. Scope of the Problem

A. This is not just a third-world country problem; it is happening to children every day in the United States.

B. Yearly, the industry garners $7 billion.

C. It is low risk compared to drugs and arms deals.

D. There is a supply and demand.

E. It is a secretive business.

F. It is a dangerous business.

G. Not many agencies are able to count the number of victims.

H. "Trafficking" has many definitions between countries and agencies.

I. How many of our "missing children" are really victims of human trafficking?

XIII. Big Supplies of Human Trafficking Victims

A. Historically, victims always have been from Asia.

B. After the collapse of the former Soviet Union, a whole new pool from which to draw was created.

C. Major suppliers for the sex industry now are

1. Belarus
2. Moldova
3. Ukraine*
4. Latvia
5. Russia*

(*The largest suppliers today)

XIV. Popular Destination Countries for Victims of Trafficking
　　　A. Canada
　　　B. Czech Republic
　　　C. Germany
　　　D. Greece
　　　E. Hungary
　　　F. Turkey
　　　G. Netherlands
　　　H. United Arab Emirates Republic
　　　I. United States
　　　J. Yugoslavia
　　　K. Korea (has a large number of Ukraine women for prostitution at military bases)
　　　L. Israel and Turkey have such a large population of Russian women, they are referred to as "Natashas," meaning prostitutes.

XV. Recruitment Methods
　　　A. False advertising lures 20% to
　　　　　1. Work as models
　　　　　2. Acting careers
　　　　　3. High-paying jobs as maids, domestics, retail salespeople
　　　B. Marriage agencies (mail order brides) may be used.
　　　C. The most common way of recruiting is through a friend or an acquaintance.
　　　D. The "second wave" of recruiting sometimes occurs when the victim moves out of bondage and becomes a perpetrator.
　　　E. Traffickers are becoming more creative and aggressive with how they recruit. They place other teen prostitutes at malls and even in middle and high schools to befriend other teens and unsuspectingly abduct them and turn them into victims of trafficking.

XVI. Commercial Sexual Exploitation of Child Victims
　　　A. Half the traffickers operate at a local level.
　　　B. 25% belong to citywide crime rings.
　　　C. 15% belong to regional or national networks.
　　　D. 10% belong to international sex crime networks.
　　　E. Some traffickers are also part of drug networks that use children to move drugs into and across the United States.

XVII. What Can Be Done
　　　A. Parents, schools, and law enforcement agencies need to partner in educating children and parents about the "Achilles' heel" of technology.

B. We must educate parents
1. About children who would be at risk for trafficking
2. About who would reply to advertising or Internet scams
3. About who would want to give their children a "better life" (especially true in third-world countries)
C. We must educate the public about trafficking
1. Teachers and school officials
2. Mall owners
3. Those who own recreational spots where teens spend time
D. Stress the importance of Internet supervision.
E. Promote a positive role for women and children in society; many children are still viewed as "replaceable commodities" and property by some people.

XVIII. Who to Call If You Suspect Human Trafficking
A. Human Trafficking Resource Center, 1-888-373-7888
B. Local resources in your community
C. National Center for Missing and Exploited Children (NCMEC), 1-800-THE-LOST
D. Department of Justice Human Trafficking Office, 1-888-428-7581
E. National Hotline (English), 1-866-US-TIPLINE (1-866-878-4754)
F. Korean Hotline, 1-888-976-5274
G. Spanish Hotline, 1-888-80-AYUDA (1-888-802-9832)
H. E-mail: Report@PolarisProject.org

Bibliography

Albanese, J. (2007, December). *Commercial sexual exploitation of children: What do we know and what do we do about it?* Washington, D.C. United States Department of Justice, Office of Justice Programs (NCJ 215733) pp. 1–14.

Bales, K. & Lize, S. (2005, November). *Trafficking in persons in the United States.* Washington, D.C., United States Department of Justice: A report to the National Institute of Justice (NCJ 211980) pp. 1–160.

Clawson, H. J., Lang, M., & Small, K. (2006, December). *Estimating human trafficking into the United States: Development of a methodology.* Washington D.C., United States Department of Justice, Office of Justice Programs, National Institute of Justice (NCJ 215475) pp. 1–50.

Ebbe, O. N. I., & Das, D. K. (Eds.). (2008). *Global trafficking in women and children.* Boca Raton, FL: CRC Press.

Flores, T. L. (2007). *The sacred bath: An American teen's story of modern day slavery.* New York: iUniverse.

Hodge, D. R. (2008, April). Sexual trafficking in the United States: A domestic problem with transnational dimensions. *Social Work: A Journal of the National Association of Social Workers, 53*(2), pp. 142–152.

Hughs, D. M. (2001, January). The "Natasha" trade: Transnational sex trafficking. *National Institute of Justice Journal,* (NCJ 186186) pp. 8–15.

Interpol. (n.d.). *Crimes against children.* Fact sheet. Retrieved September 1, 2008, from http://www.interpol.int/Public/Children/Default.asp

Interpol. (n.d.). *Trafficking in human beings.* Fact sheet. Retrieved September 1, 2008, from http://www.interpol.int/Public/THB/default.asp

Motivans, M. & Kyckelhahn, T. (2007, December). *Federal prosecution of child sex exploitation offenders, 2006.* Washington, D.C. United States of Department of Justice, Office of Justice Programs (NCJ 219412) pp. 1–8.

Moynihan, B. A. (2006). The high cost of human trafficking. *Journal of Forensic Nursing. 2*(2), 100–101.

National Crime Victims' Rights Week. (2005, April). *Human trafficking.* Retrieved November 8, 2007 from http://www.ojp.gov/ovc/ncvrw/2005/pg51.html

Newton, P. J., Mulcahy, T., & Martin, S. E. (2008, October). Finding victims of human trafficking. Washington, D.C. United States Department of Justice, Office of Justice Programs, National Institute of Justice (NCJ 224393) pp. 1–186.

Phinney, A. (2007). *Trafficking of women and children for sexual exploitation in the Americas: An introduction of trafficking in the Americas.* Retrieved March 12, 2008 from http://www.oas.org/CIM/english/PROJ.Traf.Alisonpaper.htm pp. 1–15.

United Nations Economic and Social Commission for Asia and the Pacific, (2009). *Gender and human trafficking.* Retrieved June 3, 2009 from http://www.unescap.org/esid/GAD/Issues/Trafficking/index.asp

United Nations Office on Drugs and Crime and Inter-Parliamentary Union (UNODC, IPU), (2009). *Combating trafficking in persons: A handbook for parliamentarians,* pp. 1–140. Vienna, United Nations Publications.

United States Department of Education. (2007). *Human trafficking of children in the United States: A fact sheet for schools.* Washington, DC: United States Department of Education, Office of Safe and Drug Free Schools. Retrieved November 5, 2008 from http://www.ed.gov/about/offices/list/osdfs/factsheet.html

United States Department of Justice. (n.d.). *Trafficking in persons: A guide for nongovernmental organizations.* Washington, DC: United States Department of Justice, Civil Rights Division.

United States Department of State. (2004, June). *Trafficking in persons report* (Publication 11150). Washington, DC: United States Department of State, Office of the Under Secretary for Global Affairs.

Mass Disasters

30

SUE GABRIEL

I. Types of Mass Disasters
  A. Natural
    1. Earthquakes
    2. Floods
    3. Hurricanes
    4. Tornados
    5. Tsunamis
  B. Human
    1. Pollution
    2. Bioterrorism. This is defined as "a terrorist action that uses either naturally occurring or potentially modified pathogens as bio-weapons to infect and cause illness in targeted populations" (Beaton & Murphy, 2002 p. 183). It includes biochemical warfare.
    3. Fires
    4. Toxins
    5. Civil unrest
    6. Terrorism. The definition by the Federal Bureau of Investigation (FBI) states terrorism to be "the unlawful use of force or violence committed . . . against persons or property to intimidate or coerce a government or the civilian sector . . . in furtherance of political or social objective" (Beaton & Murphy, 2002).

II. Disaster Management Application

Disaster management assists to

  A. Minimize risks for humans and the environment
  B. Reduce infections (foodborne)
  C. Reduce work-related homicides
  D. Reduce weapon carrying
  E. Federally, guarantee that state health departments establish training plans, protocols, and conduct multidisciplinary drills to prepare for disaster

III. Disaster Preparedness
 A. Disaster preparedness can include simple and realistic drills.
 B. Remember that there is no disaster plan that ever fits perfectly; adjustments may be needed with the nuances of each disaster.
 C. Disaster preparedness can be implemented even if all key players are not present.
 D. Key players in disasters are the following:
  1. Centers for Disease Control and Prevention (CDC)
  2. United States Department of Health and Human Services
 E. Since the attack on the home soil of the United States on September 11, 2001:
  1. Disaster preparedness for health care has been mandated by the Joint Commission on the Accreditation of Healthcare Organizations (JCAHO).
  2. All smaller communities must join with larger facilities and community partners to plan (August 30 citywide drill each year).
  3. Fines will be issued and enforced if community preparedness does not occur.

IV. Personal Preparedness
 A. Find out how to protect yourself during a disaster.
 B. Create a personal plan for yourself and your family.
 C. Make a checklist of things to do and what items will be needed to ensure a safe environment for yourself and family members.
 D. Practice personal drills with your family.
 E. Utilize your local and state agencies for available information, such as
  1. The American Red Cross
  2. Community emergency response team (CERT) training. This team is beneficial in the first 3 days following a disaster.
  3. Civil Air Patrol. Can aid in search and rescue
  4. Medical Reserve Corp. In your community this is an organization consisting of local nurses who can be of assistance in an emergency
  5. DMAT (Disaster Medical Assistance Team)
   a. A national response team of volunteer medical personnel and paraprofessionals
   b. Aids communities in the care of sick and injured following a mass disaster or other event
   c. Composed of physicians, nurses, and other health care ancillary personnel
   d. Under the jurisdiction of

        (1) National Disaster Medical System (NDMS)
        (2) Federal Emergency Management Agency (FEMA)
        (3) Department of Homeland Security (DHS)
    e. Check Web sites for more information: http://www.dmat.org/ and http://www.hhs.gov/aspr/opeo/ndms/teams/dmat.html
    f. DMAT volunteers were present for
        (1) September 11, 2001
        (2) Hurricane Katrina
        (3) Tsunami in Southeast Asia
    g. Focus on disaster medicine and humanitarian aid
  6. DMORT (Disaster Mortuary Operational Response Team)
    a. A national response team of volunteers who have expertise in care of the nonliving after a mass disaster or an event
    b. Functions under the National Response Framework (NRF) and utilizes the NDMS as part of the Department of Health and Human Services
    c. Assists with collection and identification of victims following a mass fatality incident, including
        (1) Temporary morgue facilities
        (2) Victim identification
        (3) Forensic dental pathology
        (4) Forensic anthropology methods
        (5) Processing
        (6) Preparation
        (7) Disposition of remains
    d. Identification accomplished by use of
        (1) DNA that is collected from victims at the site of a disaster or event
        (2) Dental impressions
        (3) Clothing identification
        (4) Medical history information
    e. The job of this team of professional and paraprofessionals is to make sure the deceased is identified and transported back to correct family members with dignity and respect.
    f. Online information available through the U.S. Department of Health and Human Services: http://www.hhs.gov/aspr/opeo/ndms/teams/dmort.html

V. Professional Preparedness
  A. Maintain a copy of your nursing license with you at all times
    1. This was a lesson learned during and after the attack of September 11, 2001

2. Response organizations had no way of checking professional licensure, which prevented these professionals from assisting during a time of need.
3. During this event, it was found that there was no way of checking professional licensure during a disaster or mass fatality event.

B. Remember there are differences in state licensure
C. Forms of official identification are
   1. Driver's license
   2. Passport
   3. Red Cross ID
D. Have copies of certification to present, such as certification for
   1. CPR (cardiopulmonary resuscitation)
   2. PALS (pediatric advanced life support)
   3. NRP (neonatal resuscitation program)
   4. ACLS (advanced cardiopulmonary life support)
   5. NP (nurse practitioner)
   6. APRN (advanced practice registered nurse)
   7. PA (physician's assistant)
   8. CRNA (certified registered nurse anesthetist)
   9. Disaster training verification of any level

VI. The International Nursing Coalition for Mass Casualty Education (INCMCE)
   A. Organized after September 11, 2002 with goals
      1. To develop some standardization of a response plan for mass disaster unique to health care professionals
      2. To develop a plan that could be used at any level of response
   B. Recognize that disasters are becoming more prominent
      1. They are not going away; they are only becoming more frequent.
      2. Disasters can be either natural or manmade.
   C. Findings of the coalition
      1. Less than 30% of all nursing schools have a class in disaster preparedness.
      2. There are no faculty to teach such classes.
      3. Faculty and students can lend a wealth of resources during disasters.
      4. Participation in disaster aid can be an active learning experience for students.
         a. They can get class credit.
         b. They can develop and participate in projects to aid the community after a disaster.

        c. This can give students a sense of community partnering, altruism, and the far-reaching effects nursing comprises.

VII. Community Preparedness
   A. Know how your community would respond to a disaster of any kind.
   B. Check with the Office of Emergency Management (OEM) to find out your community's plan and how you can be of help.
   C. Check with your county and state levels for a preparedness plan.
      1. Contact your county health department.
      2. If you work in a hospital, know your plan and your responsibility for disaster response.
   D. Learn your roles *prior* to a disaster
   E. *Cooperation* is the key word; know who would be in command
   F. Key players in the *medical* arena are
      1. Hospitals
      2. Mental health providers
      3. Pharmacies
      4. Doctors
      5. Nurses
      6. Medical examiner
      7. Respiratory therapists
      8. Laboratory personnel
      9. Emergency medical services (EMS) personnel
   G. Key *nonmedical* players
      1. Clergy
      2. Firefighters
      3. Law enforcement
      4. Mortuary personnel
      5. Media
      6. Government officials
         a. Local level
         b. State level
         c. Federal level
      7. National Guard
      8. Civilian volunteers (e.g., Civil Air Patrol, ham radio operators)

VIII. National Response Plan (NRP)
   A. Emergency support functions, includes 15 agencies
   B. If the president declares a disaster, the following respond
      1. Department of Public Health
      2. CDC
      3. Department of Health and Human Services (DHHS)

4. DHS
5. NDMS
    a. DMAT
       (1) Triage and medical care
       (2) Practice philosophy is "the greatest good for the greatest numbers"
       (3) Disaster medicine and humanitarian aid
       (4) National or international
    b. DMORT
       (1) Victim identification
       (2) National or international
       (3) Ten regional teams

IX. After a Disaster Response
  A. Survivor guilt
    1. Repeated thoughts of event
    2. Feelings of deep loss
    3. Fear
    4. Not always able to express feelings
  B. Community response to a disaster depends on
    1. Type, location, cause
    2. Magnitude
    3. Extent
    4. Warning (enough, little, or none)
  C. The #1 group called in for disaster response is nurses. Questions to ponder:
    1. Are nurses as a group given any education in crisis response?
    2. Does everyone react the same to disasters?
    3. Do nurses have education in how to deal with survivors?
    4. Do nurses have knowledge of groups that would need special provisions?
      a. Young
      b. Elderly
      c. Disabled
        (1) Cognitively impaired
        (2) Physically impaired
    5. Would nurses be able to make decisions under the motto "the greatest good for the greatest number"?
    6. What effect would disaster response have on nurses with little or no knowledge of disaster response?

X. Nurses' Roles and Questions to Ponder
  A. Triage
    1. What is normal triage?

2. Does it change in a disaster setting?
3. Are nurses prepared to look a friend or loved one in the eyes and know they will not be treated (according to "the greatest good for the greatest number")?
B. What was learned after the September 11 experience?
   1. Only minor injuries were seen.
   2. Triage stations were set up within the hour.
   3. Nurses finally figured out after waiting and waiting for victims that no one would be coming.
   4. Who helps the nurse deal with this realization?
   5. Regarding shelters for survivors,
      a. How should nurses be utilized efficiently?
      b. Who works in the shelters?
      c. How does the nursing shortage have an impact on disasters?
   6. Regarding international relief,
      a. How do you feel about this?
      b. Who is usually sent to other countries?
   7. Regarding relief workers,
      a. Who takes care of them?
      b. What kind of care may these volunteers need?
   8. Post-traumatic stress disorder (PTSD)
      a. Know the signs:
         (1) Depression
         (2) Fear
         (3) Physical ailments
         (4) Loss of workdays
         (5) Over- and undereating
         (6) Disturbed sleep behaviors
            (a) Sleeping too much
            (b) Not sleeping
         (7) May separate self from family and friends
      b. Know the people who have a higher propensity to suffer from PTSD:
         (1) Survivors
         (2) Health care workers
      c. Is on site or postdisaster help available for victims of PTSD? This is a key factor for disaster planning, especially for
         (1) Workers
         (2) Health care
         (3) Survivors
   9. Recovery after a disaster incorporates many agencies.

XI. Roles Student Nurses Could Play
   A. Participating in initial triage within their scope of practice and training at the time of the event.
      1. Taking vital signs
      2. Staying with patients
      3. Runners
      4. Upper level students could start IVs, give prescribed medications
      5. Do assessments
      6. Admit patients
      7. Take histories
   B. Giving vaccinations
   C. Helping families find the correct agency for help
   D. Joining public health teams for education and developing different postdisaster programs to help families
   E. Intaking family information to identify survivors or find family members who may have been separated from loved ones during or after the disaster
   F. Participating in recovery projects
   G. Creating health care projects for healing the community
   H. Follow up on the effectiveness of the established programs
   I. Researching what could be changed
   J. Utilizing disaster experiences as interactive classroom experiences
      1. Students feel useful.
      2. Students develop an understanding of all processes that must come together to have an effective response.
      3. Students put didactic information into action.
      4. Students do what primary workers often do not have time to do.
      5. Students may achieve college credit.
      6. Students develop a sense of community connectedness.

XII. Nursing Faculty and Colleges of Nursing Are a Gold Mine of Resources during a Disaster.
   A. They can help in a capacity within scope of practice.
   B. Communities need to tap into these resources and include them in disaster preparedness.
   C. Nurses working with agencies during a disaster
      1. Find a deep and fervent renewal of pride for their profession
      2. Realize a passion for humanity that they have never known or seen before in such immense proportions

Bibliography

American Association of Critical Care Nurses. (2005). When disaster struck, nurses responded. *American Association of Critical Care Nurses News, 22*(10), 2–3.

Badger, J. M. (2004). A nurse's perspective on a nightclub fire: Fostering resilience during a disaster response. *American Journal of Nursing, 104*(2), 72AA–72FF.

Baez, A. A., Sztajnkrycer, M. D., Smester, P., Giraldez, E., & Vargas, L. E. (2005). Effectiveness of a simple Internet-based disaster triage educational tool directed toward Latin-American EMS providers. *International EMS, 9*(2), 227–230.

Baldwin, K., LaMantia, J., & Proziak, L. (2005). Emergency preparedness and bioterrorism response: Development of an educational program for public health personnel. *Public Health Nursing, 22*(3), 248–253.

Barnes, J. (2006). Mobile medical teams: Do A & E nurses have the appropriate experience? *Emergency Nurse, 13*(9), 18–23.

Beaton, R., & Murphy, S. (2002). Psychological responses to biological and chemical terrorist threats and events. *Official Journal of the American Association of Occupational Health Nurses, 50*(4), 182–189.

Beeber, L. S., & Shandor Miles, M. (2001, July). Turning danger into opportunity: Teaching psychiatric nursing in the aftermath of a disaster. *Issues in Mental Health Nursing, 22*(5), 533–548.

Bond, E. F., & Beaton, R. (2005, September). Disaster nursing curriculum development based on vulnerability assessment in the Pacific Northwest. *Nursing Clinics of North America, 40*(3), 441–451.

Centers for Disease Control and Prevention. (2005). When disaster strikes. *The Nurse Practitioner, 30*(10), 6–8.

Chaffee, M., Conway-Welch, C., & Sabatler, K. (2001, July/August). Nursing leaders plan to educate nurses about response to mass casualty events. *The American Nurse,* p. 20.

Cole, F. L. (2005). The role of the nurse practitioner in disaster planning and response. *Nursing Clinics of North America, 40*(3), 511–521.

Cox, E., & Briggs, S. (2004). Disaster nursing: New frontiers for critical care. *Critical Care Nurse, 24*(3), 16–22.

Davidhizar, R., Eshleman, J., & Wolff, L. (2003). Living with stress since 9/11. *Caring Magazine, 22*(4), 26–30.

Davies, K. (2005). Disaster preparedness and response: More than major incident initiation. *British Journal of Nursing, 14*(16), 868–871.

Davies, K., & Higginson, R. (2005). Evolution and healthcare impact of a 21st century avian flu pandemic. *British Journal of Nursing, 14*(20), 1066–1068.

Davies, K., & Moran, L. (2005). Nurses need advanced skills in disaster health care. *British Journal of Nursing, 14*(4), 190.

Dickerson, S. S. (2002). Nursing at ground zero: Experiences during and after September 11 World Trade Center attack. *Journal of the New York State Nurses Association, 33*(1), 26–32.

DiMaggio, C., Markenson, D., Henning, K., Redlener, I., & Zimmerman, R. (2006). Partnership for preparedness: A model of academic public health. *Journal of Public Health Management and Practice, 12*(1), 22–27.

Eiland, J. E., Pritchard, D. A., & Stevens, D. A. (2004). Home study program: Emergency preparedness—is your OR ready? *American Operating Room Nurses, 79*(6), 1275–1288.

Emergency Nurses Association. (2005, July–September). Mass casualty incidents. *Topics in Emergency Medicine*, pp. 238–239.

Glick, D. F., Jerome-D'Emillia, B., Nolan, M. A., & Burke, P. (2004). Emergency preparedness: One community's response. *Family and Community Health, 27*(3), 266–273.

Hamid, A. Y. S. (2005). Indonesian nurses respond quickly to disaster. *Canadian Nurse, 131*(2), 33.

Hardin, E. (2002). Disaster planning and management. *Topics in Emergency Medicine, 24*(3), 71–76.

Hassell, C. (2005). Nursing students' perceptions about disaster nursing. *Disaster Management and Response, 3*(4), 97.

Hayward, M. (2004). Facing danger. *Nursing Standard, 19*(3), 20–21.

Heitkemper, M. M., & Bond, E. F. (2003). State of nursing science: On the edge. *Biological Research for Nursing, 4*(3), 151–164.

Hinton-Walker, P., Garmon, S. C., & Elberson, K. L. (2005). Research issues in preparedness for mass casualty events, disaster, war, and terrorism. *Nursing Clinics of North America, 40*(3), 551–564.

Ihlenfeld, J. T. (2003). A primer on triage and mass casualty events. *Dimensions of Critical Care Nursing, 22*(5), 204–207.

International Society for Traumatic Stress Studies. (2005). Indirect traumatization in professionals working with trauma survivors. Retrieved May 20, 2006, from http://www.istss.org/terrorism/indirect_trauma.htm

Jackson, B. (2005, October). Disaster preparedness: Students learn about the nurse's role. *LookSmart*, pp. 1–2.

Jani, A. A., Fierro, M., Kiser, S., Ayala-Simms, V., Darby, D. H., Juenker, S., et al. (2006). Hurricane Isabel-related mortality—Virginia, 2003. *Journal of Public Health Management and Practice, 12*(1), 97–102.

Jennings, Y. (2005, December). Lessons from a blizzard. *Nursing2005,* 32cc5.

Lee, P. (2002). Thinking the worst: Major incidents involving children. *Paediatric Nursing, 14*(3), 14–17.

Lipley, N. (2005). Preparing for the worst. *Emergency Nurse, 12*(10), 5.

Mitchell, A. M., Sakraida, T. J., & Zalice, K. K. (2005). Disaster care: Psychological considerations. *Nursing Clinics of North America, 40*(3), 535–550.

Orr, M. L. (2002). Ready or not, disasters happen. *Online Journal of Issues in Nursing, 7*(3), 1–10. Retrieved May 23, 2006 from http//ana.org/ojin/topic19/tpc19_2.htm7

Pestronk, R. M. (2005). Why just prepare for emergencies when full use is possible? *Journal of Public Health Management and Practice, 11*(4), 298–300.

Reed, M. (2001, July 30). Nurses meet disaster. *Nursing Spectrum,* 1–6. Retrieved May 23, 2006, from http://community.nursingspectrum.com/MagazineArticles/articles.cfm?AID=4567

Reineck, C. (2004). The readiness estimate and deployability index: A self-assessment tool for emergency center RNs in preparation for disaster care. *Topics in Emergency Medicine, 26*(4), 349–356.

Riba, S., & Reches, H. (2002). When terror is routine: How Israeli nurses cope with multicasualty terror. *Online Journal of Issues in Nursing, 7*(3), 1–13. Retrieved May 20, 2006, from http://ana.org/ojin/topic19/tpc19_5.htm

Saarikoski, T. (2005, November). Nurses' role in disaster work undervalued. *Mental Health Practice, 9*(3), 6.

Saladay, S. (n.d.). Natural disasters: Putting your life on the line. *Nursing 2006, 36*(2), 24.

Saliba, D., Buchanan, J., & Kington, R. (2004, August). Function and response of nursing facilities during community disaster. *American Journal of Public Health, 94*(8), 1436–1441.

Sebastian, S. V., Styron, S. I., Reize, S. N., Houston, S., Luquire, R., & Hickey, J. V. (2003). Resiliency of accomplished critical care nurses in a natural disaster. *Critical Care Nurse, 23*(5), 24–36.

Slepski, L. A. (2005). Emergency preparedness: Concept development for nursing practice. *Nursing Clinics of North America, 40*(3), 419–430.

Springgate, B., Boyte, W. R., Braner, D., Conlin, J., Leckman, S., & Chuang, G. T. (2006). Comfort stories. *Health Affairs, 25*(2), 481–488.

Stanley, J. (with INCMCE Committee). (2003, August). *Educational competencies for registered nurses responding to mass casualty incidents.* International Nursing Coalition for Mass Casualty Education, pp. 1–17.

Stanley, J. M. (2005). Disaster competency development and integration in nursing education. *Nursing Clinics of North America, 40*(3), 453–467.

Tseng, H. C., Chen, T. F., & Chou, S. M. (2005). SARS: Key factors in crisis management. *Journal of Nursing Research, 13*(1), 58–64.

Ulster students in "disaster" lesson. (2005). *Nursing Standard, 20*(6), 11.

Underwood, R. A. (2005, November). Survey survival: Don't fool with mother nature. *Nursing Homes: Long Term Care Management,* pp. 66–67.

Urbano, T. (2002, January/February). Nursing coalition for mass casualty education steps up initiatives. *The American Nurse,* p. 8.

Vere-Jones, E. (2006). Nurses reveal 7 July failures. *Nursing Times, 102*(3), 4.

Weiner, E., Irwin, M., Trangenstein, P., & Gordon, J. (2005). Emergency preparedness curriculum in nursing schools in the United States. *Nursing Education Perspectives, 26*(6), 334–339.

Wheaton, D. (2005). Katrina teaches hard lessons. *Journal of Trauma Nursing, 12*(3), 65–66.

White, J. H. (2002). The American psychiatric nurses association responds to the September 11 tragedy. *Online Journal of Issues in Nursing, 7*(3), 1–9. Retrieved May 23, 2006, from http://www.nursingworld.org/ojin/topic19/tpc19_3.htm

Additional Violence in Society

31

SUE GABRIEL

I. When Violence Occurs
   A. Nurses care for
      1. Victims
      2. Perpetrators
      3. Witnesses
      4. Families
   B. Violence is the 12th leading cause of death (COD) in the United States.
   C. Violence is the sixth leading cause of mortality in the United States.
   D. Youth violence is the greatest single crime problem in today's society.
   E. Targeted audiences for violence include
      1. Schools
      2. Workplaces
      3. Specific targeted audiences

II. Schools Today
   A. Are assuming more parenting roles
   B. Have larger classes
   C. See more behavior problems
   D. Deal with more anger issues (children often model how they see their parents deal with anger), which causes the cycle to continue
   E. Still use corporal punishment, which only reinforces students' need to strike out, as do parents who use this type of punishment
   F. Deal with bullying
      1. Bullying is a behavior intended to harm or disturb a victim.
      2. It is a contributor to youth violence.
      3. It is viewed as a public health problem.
      4. Every 7 minutes, a child is bullied.
      5. Children experience bullying daily.

6. Children in elementary and high schools can be either
   a. The bully
   b. The bullied
7. One in five children admits to being a bully in school.
8. 43% of students are afraid to use school restrooms for fear of being bullied.
9. 8% of students miss one day of school per month because of being bullied.
10. Bullying can assume many faces:
    a. Verbal
    b. Physical
    c. Psychological
    d. Teasing
    e. Hitting and attacking victims
    f. Name calling
    g. Making threats
    h. Spreading rumors (verbal, written, via Internet)
    i. Distributing provacative pictures (via cell phones, the Internet, or any other means)
    j. As a source of intimidation
11. Many children who bully at school or at home may be victims themselves in either of these environments.
    a. Children who bully are currently or have been victims of bullying themselves.
    b. For example, children who bully siblings may
       (1) Be victims at school
       (2) Bully others at school and are victims in the home or other places
G. School violence and shootings appear to be on the rise
   1. Statistics show shootings rank as only a small percentage compared to all other crimes committed in the schools:
      a. Theft
      b. Simple assaults (altercations with others)
   2. There are 100,000 students who carry guns to school.
   3. Of youth who carry a gun to school, 28% also witness violence in the home.
   4. Being a victim of abuse at home or a witness to others being abused at home can be correlated to violence in schools.
   5. School homicides
      a. Actually have decreased since the early 1990s
      b. Rank very low compared to those killed in motor vehicle accidents

H. Profiles of school shooters
1. None; still searching for crucial indicators
2. Behavioral
3. Environmental
4. No "check list" of behaviors
5. Trying to profile school shooters can be dangerous, shortsighted
6. Can mistakenly label nonviolent students
7. Extremely difficult to predict an individual who has never acted out in the past and who will do so in the future
8. Nearly impossible to predict school shooting
9. No identified traits to predict a school shooter
10. Knowledge from past experience shows
   a. Individuals do not just "snap."
   b. Individuals plan.
   c. Individuals acquire weapons.
   d. Individuals tell others what they are planning.
   e. Individuals usually plan over long periods of time.
   f. It is more important to ask about behavior over time.
   g. Individuals who are interested in violence.
   h. Individuals who initially may be "joiners," then lose interest or do not feel welcome.
   i. Attempts by individuals to fit in and socialize fail.
   j. Individuals are not necessarily loners.
I. Prevention of school violence
1. Every school should address
   a. Safety
   b. Educational practices
   c. Programs promoting and supporting needs of students' well-being
      (1) Social
      (2) Emotional
      (3) Behavioral
   d. Communication (imperative)
   e. Helping students feel connected to their school community
2. Children are shaped by
   a. Collective life experiences, both positive and negative
   b. Family
   c. Environment
   d. School
   e. Peers
   f. Community
   g. Culture

        h. Biases
        i. Prejudices
        j. Emotions
        k. Values
        l. Responses to
           (1) Stress
           (2) Authority
    3. The problem and solution belong to each
        a. School
        b. Family
        c. Community

III. Workplace Violence
    A. Workplace violence can be defined as offensive or threatening language, violent acts, physical assaults or threats of assaults directed at a person on duty at work.
    B. Everyone is at risk for this.
    C. Jobs are less secure today.
    D. There are stressful home and work environments.
    E. Employees often see themselves as overworked and underpaid.
    F. There is a very competitive workforce in today's society.
    G. The motto "do more with less" in turn leads to stress.
    H. An employee may have a certain job and
        1. Feels it is out of necessity
        2. Sees it as not desirable
        3. Feels trapped in a job he or she dislikes
        4. Resorts to violence to solve job dissatisfaction

IV. Health Care Violence
    A. Employees in health care are at a high risk for workplace violence.
    B. Of nonfatal injuries to employees, 48% occur in health care settings, which is almost five times greater than the general sector of employment settings. These settings include
        1. Hospitals
        2. Long-term care
        3. Residential care facilities
    C. Health care workers come into direct contact with violent patients or family members. Violence can occur
        1. With those under the influence of drugs or alcohol
        2. While working in understaffed areas, especially at mealtimes and visiting hours
        3. When transporting patients
        4. When treating minor injuries

 5. When treating major injuries
 6. When dealing with those who have had to wait for long periods before accessing treatment
 7. When dealing with those who experienced long periods of time in waiting rooms
 8. When dealing with those who have temporary or permanent physical disabilities
 9. When dealing with those who are experiencing psychological traumas
 10. When dealing with those who have dementia
 11. When dealing with those who are dealing with a mental illness
 12. When death occurs
 13. When dealing with those who have access to firearms
 14. When the employee works alone in an area of the hospital
 15. When in hospital areas that are poorly designed for viewing by other coworkers
 16. When in areas where there is unrestricted public access
 17. Where there is poor lighting in halls, rooms, parking lots, and parking garages
 18. Because of lack of education in how to deal with and deescalate volatile situations

D. Healthcare workers at high risk for coming in contact with workplace violence in order of highest to lowest are
 1. Nurses
 2. Nursing assistants and/or technicians
 3. Emergency response personnel
 4. Hospital security officers
 5. All other health care workers

E. The areas where the highest incidence of violence occurs in health care are
 1. Psychiatric settings
 2. Emergency departments
 3. Waiting rooms
 4. Geriatric units

F. All hospital workers should maintain caution and be alert to potential volatile situations when working with patients and visitors.
 1. When help is needed, workers should use known emergency alarms and signals.
 2. Metal detectors, cameras, and adequate lighting should be provided in high-risk areas
 3. Security escorts to parking lots and garages should be available.

    4. A security response system to signal a needed response to an area should be in place.
    5. Staffing patterns should be changed to eliminate lone workers.
    6. A system that restricts public access to high-risk areas should be in place.
    7. Be alert to visitors with weapons or potential weapons.
    8. Employees should be provided with useful training in workplace violence and helpful tips on deescalation of volatile situations.

V. Drugs and Alcohol in Teens
  A. National drugs of choice
    1. Alcohol
    2. Cigarettes
    3. Marijuana
    4. All used to self-medicate, relieving stress, tension, depression, anxiety, fears
  B. Cause addiction and addictive behaviors
  C. Easily accessible by any age child
  D. Children are using at an earlier age
  E. Drugs and alcohol escalate and amplify violent behavior

VI. Effect of Violence in the Media
  A. Violence in movies, television, and handheld electronic games is increasing; children and teens are becoming desensitized to violent acts.
  B. Often, children and teens act out violence through play or in real life; such as
    1. Murder
    2. Rape
    3. Robbery
    4. Beatings
    5. Fights
  C. Television and movies have a captive, impressionable audience. Watching violence can have a negative impact on children as well as adults.
    1. The message to children is that this behavior is okay.
    2. Violent behavior is a way to settle disputes.
    3. Violent behavior is a way to earn money.
    4. How to treat your fellow human beings is depicted through violent acts.
    5. Continued violent viewing makes watchers insensitive to violence and violent acts, which can teach impressionable people that this is how to treat others, how to solve disputes, etc.

6. By the age of 18 years, a child has witnessed over 1,800 murders on television alone along with countless other acts of violence.

VII. Organized Religions
   A. Give sense of belonging, values, worth
   B. Often provide positive role models
   C. Many organized religions are slow to recognize family violence
      1. Intimate partner violence (IPV)
      2. Abuse of any kind
      3. Women/children are consequently forced to remain in these relationships, which in turn teaches the child this is the way people in relationships are treated and are supposed to act.

VIII. Homicides in General
   A. Homicide is the number one leading COD for African American males and females 15–34 years old.
   B. Annually, 2,000 children are victims of homicides.
   C. A person's chance of being murdered is highest the day of birth than at any other time in life.
   D. Individuals in 40% of fatalities are less than 1 year of age.
   E. Individuals in 75% of fatalities are less than 5 years of age.
   F. Nearly half of juvenile homicides (47,000) from 1980 to 2002 were the result of firearms.
   G. Of children 6 years and younger, who are homicide victims, 48% are killed with hands and fists.

IX. Homicides within Families

Homicides within families are related to

   A. Abuse
   B. IPV
   C. Neglect
   D. Drugs and alcohol
   E. Dating violence
   F. Domestic abuse. 45% of incarcerated males ages 11–20 years old are responsible for killing their mother's batterer.

X. Gang Violence
   A. Gang violence occurs in 8 out of 10 cities with a population of 50,000 or more.
   B. Gang violence is more likely to be present in schools of 1,000 students.

C. Firearm possession and gang membership have a significantly close correlation.

D. Gang violence offers more opportunity to settle disputes with violence and rationalize the violence to be acceptable.

E. Gangs become families for many children who
   1. Have low self-esteem
   2. Come from poverty
   3. Are from single-parent homes
   4. Experience violence as a way of settling problems
   5. Are minority populations
   6. Are drug users or come from homes where drug use is prevalent
   7. Engage in precocious sexual experiences
   8. Have friends in gangs
   9. Have aggressive peers and use the safety of gangs to defend and protect themselves
   10. Have little or no community attachment
   11. Are low achievers
   12. Are labeled by teachers
   13. Feel a lack of safety at school and use gangs for protection or intimidation of others
   14. Have a high truancy rate

XI. Suicide as Defined by Gender and Age
   A. Males
      1. Suicide is the eighth leading COD for all U.S. men (Anderson and Smith, 2003).
      2. Males are four times more likely to die from suicide than females (Centers for Disease Control and Prevention [CDC], 2007).
      3. Suicide rates are highest among whites and second highest among American Indian and Native Alaskan men (CDC, 2007).
   B. Females: Women report attempting suicide during their lifetime about three times as often as men (Krug et al., 2002).
   C. Youth: Suicide is the third leading COD among young people aged 15 to 24 years.
   D. Elderly
      1. Suicide rates increase with age and are very high among those 65 years and older.
      2. Most elderly suicide victims are seen by their primary care provider a few weeks prior to their suicide attempt and are diagnosed with their first episode of mild to moderate depression (Department of Health and Human Services [DHHS], 1999).

3. Older adults who are suicidal are also more likely to be suffering from physical illnesses and be divorced or widowed (DHHS, 1999).

XII. Youth Learn from a Violent Society
    A. When there is violence in the home
    B. When they enter schools
    C. When they enter the workforce
    D. When they enter into relationships
    E. When they have families of their own
    F. Violence within a society is perpetuated to the next generation.

Bibliography

American Association of Critical Care Nurses. (2004, April 12). *Workplace violence prevention*. Aliso Viejo, CA: American Association of Critical Care Nurses, pp. 1–5.

American Association of Suicidology. (2004, December 1). *Elderly suicide fact sheet*.

Anderson, C. (2002). Workplace violence: Are some nurses more vulnerable? *Issues in Mental Health Nursing, 23*, 351–366.

Anderson, R. N., & Smith, B. L. (2003, November 7). *CDC National Vital Statistics Report, 52*(9). United States Department of Health and Human Services, Centers for Disease Control and Prevention.

Bon, S. C., Faircloth, S. C., & LeTendre, G. K. (2006). The school violence dilemma. *Journal of Disability Policies Studies, 17*(3), 148–157.

Borum, R., Fein, R., Vossekuil, B., & Berglund, J. (1999). Threat assessment: Defining an approach for evaluating risk of targeted violence. *Behavioral Sciences and the Law, 17*(3), 323–337.

Brunner, J., & Lewis, D. (2006). Telling a "red flag" from the real threat with students of today. *Education Digest, 72*(4), 33–36.

Bulach, C., Penland Fulbright, J., & Williams, R. (2003). Bully behavior: What is the potential for violence at your school? *Journal of Instructional Psychology, 30*(2), 156–164.

Bullying: What's being done and why schools aren't doing more. (2005). *Journal of Juvenile Law, 25*, 26–36.

Bureau of Justice Statistics. (2005, November 20). *School violence rate stable: Lowest level in a decade* (BJS06001, pp. 1–2). Washington, DC: United States Department of Justice, Office of Justice Programs.

Burgess, A. W. (2002). *Violence through a forensic lens*. King of Prussia, PA: Nursing Spectrum.

Burgess, A., & Dowdell, E. B. (2002). Forensic nursing and violent schoolchildren. In: *Violence: Through a forensic lens* (pp. 253–262). King of Prussia, PA: Nursing Spectrum. (Original work published 2000)

Centers for Disease Control and Prevention. (2002, April). *Violence: Occupational hazards in hospitals* (DHHS NIOSH 2002-101). Atlanta, GA: United States Department of Health and Human Services, Centers for Disease Control and Prevention, National Institute for Occupational Safety and Health.

Centers for Disease Control and Prevention. (2006). *Understanding suicide.* Fact Sheet. Atlanta, GA: National Center for Injury Prevention.

Centers for Disease Control and Prevention. (2007, Summer). *Suicide.* Facts at a Glance. Atlanta, GA: National Center for Injury and Prevention.

Centers for Disease Control and Prevention. (2008a, June 16). *National Institute for Occupational Safety and Health: Occupational violence.* Retrieved July 10, 2008, from http://www.cdc.gov/niosh/violence

Centers for Disease Control and Prevention (2008b, Summer). *Suicide.* Facts at a Glance. Atlanta, GA: National Center for Injury Prevention.

Chapin, J., de las Alas, S., & Coleman, G. (2005). Optimistic bias among potential perpetrators and victims of youth violence. *Adolescence, 40*(160), 749–760.

Cornell, D. G. (1999, May 13). Psychology of the school shootings. *Testimony at the House Judiciary Committee* (pp. 1–6). Charlottesville, VA: Virginia Youth Violence Project, Curry School of Education.

Courtroom Television Network. (n.d.-a). *Columbine.* CourtTV Crime Library. Retrieved February 11, 2007, from http://www.crimelibrary.com/serial_killers/weird/kids1/columbine_3.html

Courtroom Television Network. (n.d.-b). *Conduct disorders.* CourtTV Crime Library. Retrieved February 11, 2007, from http://www.crimelibrary.com/serial_killers/weird/kids2/disorders_4.html

Courtroom Television Network. (n.d.-c). *Copy cats.* CourtTV Crime Library. Retrieved February 11, 2007, from http://www.crimelibrary.com/serial_killers/weird/kids1/cats_4.html

Courtroom Television Network. (n.d.-d). *Dark ambitions: A born killer.* CourtTV Crime Library. Retrieved February 11, 2007, from http://www.crimelibrary.com/serial_killers/weird/kids2/9.html

Courtroom Television Network. (n.d.-e). *Does television have an effect?* CourtTV Crime Library. Retrieved February 11, 2007, from http://www.crimelibrary.com/serial_killers/weird/kids2/effect_5.html

Courtroom Television Network. (n.d.-f). *Kipland Kinkel.* CourtTV Crime Library. Retrieved February 11, 2007, from http://www.crimelibrary.com/serial_killers/weird/kids1/kinkle_2.html

Courtroom Television Network. (n.d.-g). *The list.* CourtTV Crime Library. Retrieved February 11, 2007, from http://www.crimelibrary.com/serial_killers/weird/kids1/index_1.htm.

Courtroom Television Network. (n.d.-h). *A party beyond recognition.* CourtTV Crime Library. Retrieved February 11, 2007, from http://www.crimelibrary.com/serial_killers/weird/kids2/party_8.html

Courtroom Television Network. (n.d.-i). *The rampage killer.* CourtTV Crime Library. Retrieved February 11, 2007, from http://www.crimelibrary.com/serial_killers/weird/kids1/killer_6.html

Courtroom Television Network. (n.d.-j). *School violence and the media.* CourtTV Crime Library. Retrieved February 11, 2007, from http://www.crimelibrary.com/serial_killers/weird/kids1/media_7.html

Courtroom Television Network. (n.d.-k). *Signs of danger.* CourtTV Crime Library. Retrieved February 11, 2007, from http://www.crimelibrary.com/serial_killers/weird/kids2/danger_7.html

Courtroom Television Network. (n.d.--l). *The unthinkable.* CourtTV Crime Library. Retrieved February 11, 2007, from http://www.crimelibrary.com/serial_killers/weird/kids2/index_1.html

Courtroom Television Network. (n.d.-m). *Thrill killing.* CourtTV Crime Library. Retrieved February 11, 2007, from http://www.crimelibrary.com/serial_killers/weird/kids2/killing_3.html

Courtroom Television Network. (2007-n). *Types of killers.* CourtTV Crime Library. Retrieved February 11, 2007, from http://www.crimelibrary.com/serial_killers/weird/kids2/killers_2.html

Courtroom Television Network. (n.d.-o). *Violence and the brain.* CourtTV Crime Library. Retrieved February 11, 2007, from http://www.crimelibrary.com/serial_killers/weird/kids2/brain_6.html

Courtroom Television Network. (n.d.-p). *What kids say.* CourtTV Crime Library. Retrieved February 11, 2007, from http://www.crimelibrary.com/serial_killers/weird/kids1/say_5.html

CSPV school violence fact sheets. (2004). Retrieved February 11, 2007, from http://www.colorado.edu/cspv/publications/factsheets/schoolviolence/FS-SV03.html

Department of Justice. (2008, May 29). *Workplace violence and victimization.* Washington, DC: United States Department of Justice.

DeVoe, J. F., Peter, K., Noonan, M., Snyder, T. D., & Baum, K. (2005, November). *Indicators of school crime and safety: 2005* (NCJ 210697, pp. 1–7). Washington, DC: United States Department of Justice, Bureau of Justice Statistics.

Disease Control Priorities Project. (2006, April). *Injuries and violence: Unintentional injuries and violence impose a tremendous but preventable health burden, especially in developing countries.*

Distasio, C. A. (2002). Violence in the workplace. *Nursing2002, 32*(6), 58–64.

Gardiner, S. (2004). School shootings: After the tragedy. *Buildings, 98*(3), 30.

Gedatus, G. (2000). *Violence at school.* Mankato, MN: LifeMatters, pp. 1–64.

Goss, R. M. (2001). Commentary: Carers deserve care too. *British Medical Journal, 323,* 1363–1364.

Gough, P. (2001). Could guidelines reduce number of incidents? *British Medical Journal, 323,* 1363.

Information Please. (2006). *A time line of recent worldwide school shootings.* Information Please Database Pearson Education. Retrieved February 11, 2007, from http://www.infoplease.com/ipa/AO777958.html

Krug, E. G., Dahlberg, L. L., Mercy, J. A., Zwi, A., & Lozano, R. (2002). *World Report on Violence and Health* (ch. 7, pp. 183–212). Geneva: World Health Organization.

Leiper, J. (2005). Nurse against nurse: How to stop horizontal violence. *Nursing2005, 35*(3), 44–45.

Lockwood, D. (1997, October). *Violence among middle school and high school students: Analysis and implications for prevention* (National Institute of Justice: Research in Brief, NCJ166363). Washington, DC: United States Department of Justice: Office of Justice Programs, pp. 1–9.

Loomis, D., Marshall, S. W., Wolf, S. H., Runyan, C. W., & Butts, J. D. (2002). Effectiveness of safety measures recommended for prevention of workplace homicide. *Journal of the American Medical Association, 287*(8), 1011–1055.

Love, C. C., & Morrison, E. (2003). American Academy of Nursing expert panel on violence policy recommendations on workplace violence. *Issues in Mental Health Nursing, 24,* 599–604.

Lubell, K. M., Kegler, S. R., Crosby, A. E. (2007, September 7). Suicide trends among youth and young adults 10–24 years in the U.S. 1990–2004. *MMWR Morbidity and Mortality Weekly Report.*

McAdams, K., Russell, H., & Walukewicz, C. (2004). Gangstas: Not in my hospital: Gang violence is a real and prominent threat in any healthcare environment: Can you recognize and manage the risks? *Nursing2004, 34*(9).

Minino, A. M., Heron, M. P., Murphy, S. L., & Kochanek, K. D. (2007, August 21). *Deaths: Final report for 2004* (National Vital Statistics Report). Washington, DC: United States Department of Health and Human Services, Centers for Disease Control and Prevention.

National Consortium of School Violence Prevention Researchers and Practitioners. (2006, November 2). *Fall 2006 school shootings position statement,* pp. 1–5. Retrieved from http://www.ncsvprp

National Institute of Health (with Kathy Knoll). (2001). *Bullying statistics.* Retrieved February 11, 2007, from http://www.atriumsoc.org/pages/bullingstatistics.html

National School Safety Center. (2003). *Serious violent crimes in schools.* Retrieved February 11, 2007, from http://youthviolence.edschool.virginia.edu/violence-in-schools/school-shootings.html

O'Hanlon, L. H. (2006). Hostile halls. *Current Health, 233*(2), 16–18.

O'Toole, M. E. (n.d.). *The school shooter: A threat assessment perspective.* Washington D.C.: United States Department of Justice: Federal Bureau of Investigation, pp. 1–46.

Pieri, L. (2004, June/July). Are nurses receiving enough education on workplace violence? *Association of Women's Health, Obstetric and Neonatal Nurses,* pp. 187–189.

Rugala, E. A. (Ed.) (2002, June 10). *Workplace violence: Issues in response.* Quantico, VA: Critical Incident Response Group, National Center for the Analysis of Violent Crime, FBI Academy, United States Department of Justice, Federal Bureau of Investigation, pp. 1–79.

School-based prevention of problem behavior: What's being done, where, and how well. (1999, October). *At-a-Glance: Recent research findings* (179065, pp. 26–28). Washington, DC: United States Department of Justice, Office of Justice Programs.

Serious and violent juvenile offenders. (1998, May). *Juvenile Justice Bulletin* (170027, pp. 1–8). Washington, DC: United States Department of Justice, Office of Justice Programs.

Sheley, J. F., & Wright, J. D. (1998, October). *High school youths, weapons, and violence: A national survey* (National Institute of Justice: Research in Brief, NCJ172857). Washington, DC: United States Department of Justice, Office of Justice Programs, National Institute of Justice, pp. 1–7.

Snyder, H. N., & Sickmund, M. (2006, March). Juvenile suicide. In: *Juvenile offenders and victims: 2006 National Report* (pp. 25–26). Washington, DC: United States Department of Justice, Office of Justice Programs.

Steinberg, L. (2000, April). Youth violence: Do parents and families make a difference? *National Institute of Justice Journal,* pp. 31–38.

Stover, D. (2006). Treating cyberbullying as a school violence issue. *The Education Digest, 72*(4), 40–42.

Suicide. (n.d.) Injury Prevention: Indian Health Services: Portland Area.

Twemlow, S. W. (2002). Premeditated mass shootings in schools: Threat assessment. *Journal of the American Academy of Child and Adolescent Psychiatry, 41*(4), 475–477.

United States Department of Health and Human Services. (1999). *At a glance: Suicide among the elderly.* Washington, DC: Office of the Surgeon General. Retrieved January 2007 from http://www.surgeongeneral.gov/library/calltoaction/fact2.htm

United States Department of Labor. (2002). *Workplace violence* (OSHA Fact Sheet). Washington, DC: United States Department of Labor and Occupational Safety and Health Administration.

United States Department of Labor. (2004). *Guidelines for preventing workplace violence for health care and social service workers.* Retrieved January 18, 2009, from http://www.osha.gov/Publications/OSHA3148/osha3148.html

United States Department of Justice. (2008, May 29). *Workplace violence and victimization.* Retrieved July 8, 2008, from http://www.ojp.gov/ovc/ncvrw/2005/pg5u.html

Violence hits hard. (2004, March). *Current Health, 230*(7), 6–12. Retrieved March 6, 2007, fromhttp://csmdbprox1.csm.edu:2152/hww/results/results_single_fulltext.jhtml. 32hn1–32hn4

Violence in the workplace. (2001, December 8). *British Medical Journal, 323,* 1362.

Vossekuil, B., Fein, R. A., Reddy, M., Borum, R., & Modzeleski, W. (2002, May). Implications for the prevention of school attacks in the United States. In: *Final report and findings of the safe school initiative* (pp. 1–49). Washington, DC: United States Secret Service and the United States Department of Education.

Weir, K. (2003). Drug problem. *Current Sciences, 89*(7), 8–9.

Whitaker, L. (2000). *Understanding and preventing violence: The psychology of human destructiveness.* Boca Raton, FL: CRC Press

Workplace violence and crime. (2008, May 29). Retrieved July 8, 2008, from http://www.ojp.gov/ovc/ncvrw/1998/html/workplace.htm

Emergency Department Dos and Don'ts

32

SUE GABRIEL

I. Potential Medicolegal Cases
  A. First and foremost treat the victim as indicated for any injury, whether minor or life threatening.
  B. Document names of who had contact with person during transportation to the emergency department (ED); document the type of medical treatment given.
  C. Whether the victim or, in many cases, the perpetrator presents to the ED either alive or deceased,
    1. View everything as evidence or potential evidence. Never throw any items away that came in with the victim or perpetrator or on the victim or perpetrator no matter how insignificant they may seem, for example,
       a. Chewing gum
       b. Clothing
       c. Insects on clothing
       d. Grasses
       e. Debris
       f. Dirt from shoes or clothing accumulated in the sheets
       g. Matchbook covers
       h. Drink containers
       i. Body piercing jewelry
    2. Document objectively not subjectively.
       a. This means to document *only* what you see or hear or what was said. (This should be charted in quotation marks, with the specific words used, even when the language seems offensive or "off color" to you. What is stated verbally needs to be charted *exactly* the way it was said by victim or perpetrator.)
       b. Use a narrative form.
       c. Use drawings or diagrams to indicate where injuries are located.

    d.   Measure the size and describe the shape and color of injuries.

    e.   Photograph if a permit is possible to obtain.

3. Document the location of injuries.

    a.   Use a point of reference,

    b.   Example 1: There is a 3 × 1 cm vertical laceration 12 cm distal up from the heel on the center of the left lower leg.

    c.   Example 2: There is a 5 × 2.5 cm horizontal purple contusion 15.25 cm down from the center crown of the head on the right mandible, extending along the angle of the jaw to the center of the chin.

4. Note colors and shapes of injuries.

    a.   This may tell which weapon was used to inflict the injury.

    b.   Note colors of contusions and abrasions.

    c.   Are the contusions clustered in one area?

    d.   Example: At 4 cm down from the center anticubital area on the lower anterior surface of the left forearm, there is a cluster of multiple contusions, ranging in size from 2.5 cm to 0.5 cm. Some are on top of others. They are circular in shape and range in color from reddish purple to tan.

5. Look for patterned injuries:

    a.   Bite marks

        (1) Are defined as a pattern made by the teeth in a medium (food, tissue, a substance that can be compressed when the pressure of biting occurs)

        (2) The most important part is to recognize them.

        (3) If bite marks go unrecognized, they are undocumented and become valuable "lost evidence."

        (4) Bite marks can yield identification of the perpetrator and are just like fingerprints.

        (5) bite marks are unique to each person or animal species.

        (6) Human bite marks have a circular or oval ring appearance formed by two opposing arches; each point of contact leaves the size and shape of individual teeth that make up the bite mark.

        (7) Animal bite marks vary among breeds.

            (a) Generally, canine bite marks appear as a long and narrow arch.

            (b) There are often deep punctures made by the "fangs" or incisors.

            (c) In canine bites, drag marks across the skin are seen with lacerations, made by the dog

hanging on and shaking, or are caused as the animal loses hold of the tissue as the person pulls away.
    (d) Claw marks can also accompany bites.
  b. Human bite marks.
    (1) Commonly occur in conjunction with
        (a) Domestic violence injuries
        (b) Child abuse
        (c) Elder abuse
        (d) Crimes of passion/torture
        (e) Sexual abuse
    (2) On any part of the body, commonly
        (a) Breasts
        (b) Arms
        (c) Legs/thighs
        (d) Head
        (e) Neck
        (f) Genitalia
        (g) Buttocks
        (h) Abdomen
        (i) Face
        (j) Back
    (3) When you see one bite, look for others.
    (4) Bites contain DNA from the offender, so they should be swabbed, measured, photographed, and documented with the location of where they appear on the body. A forensic odontologist is able to reconstruct impressions from victims' bite marks and match them to impressions obtained from a suspected perpetrator.
  c. The weapon shape. Patterns on skin should be measured, described/photographed, and documented. Examples of specific weapons that leave patterns:
    (1) The human hand, as in slap marks
    (2) Chains
    (3) Cords
    (4) Loops of cords
    (5) Flyswatters
    (6) Wooden spoons
    (7) Hilt of a knife
    (8) Boards
    (9) Sticks
    (10) Poles

              (11) Hammers

              (12) Screwdrivers

              (13) Soles of shoes

      d. It make take several hours to days before a patterned injury appears, so check your victim daily for new bruising. Some implements leave immediate patterns; this is often dependent on the location of the injury and the force applied to inflict the injury.

   6. Note and document any odors detected.

      a. Example 1: "The victim's shirt smelled of gasoline."

      b. Example 2: "When the victim arrived, there was a slight almond-like odor detected."

      c. Example 3: "The odor of alcohol was detected around the victim's mouth and nose and on his clothing."

   7. Document what the victim may say (put the victim's words in quotation marks).

      a. "My wife took a knife to my arm."

      b. "He tried to kill me."

 D. Clothing with injury marks on it, such as a shirt with evidence of a penetrating wound from a

   1. Stab wound

   2. Incised wound

   3. Gunshot

      a. *Never* cut through the penetration site in the clothing.

      b. Cut *around* the penetration site.

II. Cleansing a Patient Who May Be Considered a Medicolegal Case

 A. If possible, obtain photos prior to cleansing the victim. If photos are not possible, use a body diagram and narrative to describe what the injury/patient looks like.

 B. Gather evidence.

   1. General. Use sterile swabs to gather or collect evidence; if necessary, the swab tip can be moistened with sterile water or sterile saline.

   2. Technique. Use a rolling motion of the swab over the collection site. *Do not* "scrub" the swab. All sides of the swab should come in contact with the area being swabbed.

   3. Gunshot residue. Swab hands for gunshot residue; law enforcement has special swabs for this.

   4. Blood.

   5. Saliva.

   6. Semen.

7. Vomit. This may need to be collected in a container such as a sterile urine cup with a lid or a plastic suction canister, which can also be used for other body fluids.

8. Label. Make sure all evidence is labeled with date and time and sealed with the collector's name and initials date and time on the tape used to make the seal.

C. If clothing is removed:

1. Use paper bags to package clothing; air dry wet clothing if possible.

2. Keep bagged clothing in the room with you until you are able to hand it to law enforcement to maintain the chain of custody.

3. If bags are not available, put in a white sheet or wrap in white exam table paper.

4. Carefully fold the sheet on which the patient was lying, taking care not to lose debris and dried body fluids that may be contained on the sheet. Place this all in a paper bag.

5. Document what you collected, what you did with the items, and who you gave them to. Secure with available tape, label what is in the bag, indicate date and time of collection, your initials, and who it was given to.

6. *Never* package anything in plastic bags.
   a. This makes the contents airtight.
   b. This allows mold and bacteria to grow, ruining any evidence.

7. *Always* use paper or sheets; they breathe and prevent overgrowth of mold and bacteria.

D. If there is a ligature around the victim's neck,

1. Take a photo or draw the ligature's appearance.

2. *Never* untie the ligature knot.

3. *Never* cut through the knot itself.

4. If the patient is deceased, the ligature should remain intact on the patient until autopsy.

5. If the ligature needs to be removed,
   a. *Never untie* a ligature knot: *Cut* it away from the victim, allowing at least 6 inches from the knot.
   b. Specific types of knots may give information to the investigator.
   c. Document which side the knot is located on the victim.
   d. Place the removed ligature in an evidence bag and label as discussed; also document in a narrative form and use a body diagram.
   e. Maintain the chain of evidence
   f. Note skin colors seen on the victim and their location.

        g. Document what was used as the ligature, for example,
           (1) Rope
           (2) Nylon
           (3) Wire
           (4) Cord
     6. Document the appearance of the furrow on the victim's neck (size, width, depth, and color).
  E. If the patient received medical treatment via emergency medical services (EMS) at the scene,
     1. Document names of people who came in contact with the patient.
     2. Indicate what kind of treatment was performed.
     3. Indicate who was present in the ED.
     4. Did EMS remove any clothing? If so, where is it? What is it?
  F. Bag any belongings.
     1. Bag, label, date, time, and initial each item in a separate paper bag. This is to prevent transfer of evidence.
     2. Put one item of clothing in each bag, especially if blood is on clothing.
  G. Document in your notes the name of the officer and case number responding to the case.
  H. Document who you gave the evidence to, along with the date and time of each item of evidence. Example: "Bags 1–13 given to Officer Smith on 1/11/09 at 1600"; then, sign your name.

III. Trauma: Time Is of the Essence
  A. During the times that traumas are brought into the ED, time is of the essence, and all should be considered to be medicolegal cases.
  B. Each case has needed evidence that should be collected.
  C. Lay a white sheet on a spare table or even in the corner of the room.
     1. As clothing is removed, expediently it can be tossed onto the white sheet to dry and be packaged later.
     2. This evidence can also be watched by one person in the room.
  D. When there is time to package and label the evidence, remember to include the white sheet as evidence.
     1. Keep all debris that is on the sheet there (on the sheet).
        a. Soil
        b. Leaves
        c. Sticks
        d. Insects
        e. Any debris
     2. Fold the sheet and package it in a paper bag, sealing as described.

    E. If insects are present,
      1. Collect and place them in a rubbing alcohol solution using a sterile urine container.
      2. Collect in a white envelope.
      3. Date and label as described.
      4. Call your local forensic entomologist for pick up or give the insects to law enforcement and document this in your narrative.
      5. Maintain your chain of custody.
    F. If the victim is deceased and you are waiting for the medical examiner to assume custody of the body, place paper bags over each foot and hand and secure them to the victim. This prevents the evidence from being lost and provides a container for any evidence that may drop from the victim's hands.

IV. Simple Rules
    A. Always put treatment of the patient first.
    B. Never throw away anything that is or could be evidence.
    C. Never cut through or untie ligature knots.
    D. Never let the victim or perpetrator wash his or her hands; they may contain gunshot residue, blood, saliva, semen, or any other form of evidence,
    E. Always document what you see, hear, and smell.
    F. Photograph evidence when possible.
    G. Draw diagrams.
    H. Measure.
    I. Document thoroughly.

Bibliography

Di Maio, V. J. M., & Dana, S. E. (1998). *Handbook of forensic pathology*. Austin, TX: M. D. Press, pp. 5–8.

Dorion, R. B. J. (Ed.). (2005). *Bitemark evidence*. New York: Dekker, pp. 31–41, 59–80.

Dudley, M. H. (Ed.). (2002). *Forensic medical investigation: Forensic protocols*. Albuquerque, NM: Dudley, pp. A-1–U-1.

Geberth, V. J. (2006). *Practical homicide investigation: Tactics, procedures, and forensic techniques* (4th ed.). Boca Raton, FL: CRC Press, Taylor Francis Group, pp. 47–61, 116–117.

Lynch, V. A. (with Duval, J. B.). (2006). *Forensic nursing*. St. Louis, MO: Elsevier Mosby. pp. 559–577.

Bridging the Gap between the Living and the Nonliving

33

SUE GABRIEL

I. What Can Nurses Do?
   A. For living victims, families, and perpetrators:
      1. Assess for injuries
      2. Treat all with respect and maintain their dignity
      3. Treat all with a team approach
      4. Forensic nurses can assist victims and families directly and indirectly
         a. With physical healing
            (1) Nutritionally
            (2) Medically
         b. With emotional healing
         c. By meeting their psychosocial needs
         d. By meeting their mental health needs
         e. By expressing empathy and sympathy
         f. By expressing an understanding of what victims and families are saying
         g. By identifying family disharmony and offering resources to help
         h. By asking victims and families what they see as needed resources, then helping victims and families get connected with those resources available to them
         i. By interpreting what has taken place, defining terms or other things that are not understood by victims, families, and even the perpetrator, such as those concerning
            (1) Medical conditions
            (2) Surgery
            (3) Medications
            (4) Activities suitable for their medical condition
            (5) Outcomes
            (6) Goals

        (7) Short- and long-range plans

        (8) Cause and effect of illness and injury or surgery and rehabilitation

        (9) The medicolegal system

      (10) Legal resources when necessary

B. For the nonliving victims, families, and perpetrators:

  1. Assess the situation

  2. Treat them all with respect and maintain their dignity

  3. Explain to survivors the terminology used in death and death investigation

  4. Assist survivors and their families directly and indirectly with

    a. Physical healing

      (1) Nutritionally

      (2) Medically

    b. Emotional healing

    c. Psychosocial needs

    d. Mental health needs

    e. Empathy and sympathy

    f. Understanding of grieving and mourning their loved ones

    g. Family issues resulting from a death

    h. Resources available for short- and long-term issues that are present

    i. Deciphering information and helping survivors understand it

      (1) As it applies to victim identification

      (2) As it includes laboratory testing to ensure a positive identification of the deceased by means of

        (a) DNA testing for a positive identification

        (b) Dental records

      (3) Regarding upsetting questions that help with identification or that are asked by strangers, such as law enforcement, health care personnel, insurance providers, mortuary personnel, and medical examiners, concerning such things as

        (a) Scars

        (b) Clothing

        (c) Birthmarks

        (d) Defining characteristics

    j. Explaining what an autopsy entails and why it may be necessary; assuring families that their loved one will be treated with dignity and respect

      k. Providing information and resources regarding organ donation decisions

      l. Explaining the death certificate and terminology used on it
        (1) Cause of death
        (2) Mechanism of death
        (3) Manner of death

      m. Discussing the outcomes and findings of
        (1) The medicolegal autopsy
        (2) The medical cause of death of their loved one

      n. Discussing the goals of the family or caregivers

      o. Discussing how a death investigation proceeds and a general time line of expected events

      p. Discussing long-range plans of the
        (1) Family
        (2) Medical examiner
        (3) Legal system

      q. Discussing the cause and effect of the illness or injury leading to the death of the loved one

      r. Offering families
        (1) A better understanding of the entirety of the situation in terms they can comprehend and deal with
        (2) A time to ask the questions they need to ask and clearing up misconceptions
        (3) A time for answering questions pertaining to the death of their loved one

II. Bridging the Gap and Providing Comprehension
    A. Forensic nurses offer help for families by bridging the gap between the living and nonliving and a comprehension of the entire story.
    B. Forensic nurses help families understand the impact that a traumatic injury or a death has on survivors.
    C. Forensic nurses give families permission to ask questions and receive needed answers.
    D. Forensic nurses answer questions for families on a level compatible with their understanding and cognitive processing.
    E. Forensic nurses show respect for the loved and the lost.
    F. Forensic nurses can be the "touchstones" or comforting links for families between what was once the life they knew and the new life they will begin to live.
    G. Forensic nurses are able to help families learn to grieve and mourn their loss so they can begin the healing process.

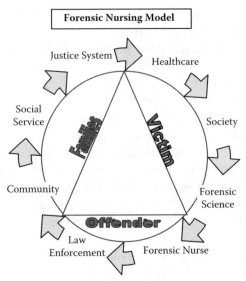

"A wound that goes unacknowledged and unwept is a wound that cannot heal." (Wolfelt, 2007, p. 105)

JOHN ELDREDGE

Bibliography

Burgess, A. W. (2002). *Violence through a forensic lens.* King of Prussia, PA: Nursing Spectrum, pp. 275–292.

Lynch, V. A. (with Duval, J. B.). (2006). *Forensic nursing.* St. Louis, MO: Elsevier Mosby, pp. 309–315.

Whitaker, L. (2000). *Understanding and preventing violence: The psychology of human destructiveness.* Boca Raton, FL: CRC Press, pp. 61–69.

Wolfelt, A. D. (2007). *Living in the shadow of the ghosts of grief: Step into the light.* Fort Collins, CO: Companion Press.

Profiling

34

GARY PLANK

Contents

Introduction

The goal of this chapter is to provide a greater understanding of the origins of profiling, what profiling is, what is needed for a profile, and how nurses will be able to assist in the profiling process by gathering behavioral information from victims of violent crimes.

History of Profiling

One of the first crime assessments (which has been called a profile by some authors) completed for law enforcement was provided for the Lindbergh kidnapping in 1932. Psychiatrist Dudley Shoenfeld reviewed case information and concluded that the victim was dead when the ransom note was written or shortly thereafter, and that the crime was perpetrated by a single male offender. This information proved to be correct and was considered to be a valuable part of the investigation (Tanay, 1983). It should be noted that this was more of a discourse analysis of the ransom note by Shoenfeld, who reviewed the note and among other things determined that the use of plural pronouns was simply for deceptive purposes.

A psychological assessment was used during World War II when the Office of Strategic Services (OSS) acquired the services of psychiatrist William Langer to prepare a profile on Adolph Hitler. The OSS wanted information

349

about Hitler's possible reactions to apprehension or defeat (Ault & Reese, 1980). This was done by studying all known aspects of Hitler's personality and personal history. In today's vernacular, this might be called a personality assessment, which is an examination of an individual to determine possible behaviors the person may exhibit in specific situations.

In a third situation, a criminal profile was also completed in the late 1950s by psychiatrist James A. Brussel. Law enforcement officials requested that Brussel profile the "Mad Bomber" of New York City. Over a 16-year period, the offender detonated 32 devices. After Brussel had examined the letters written by the bomber and studied the crime scene information, he compiled a profile of the bomber. Brussel theorized that the bomber was in his 40s or 50s and lived with an unmarried female relative. Brussel also surmised that the bomber hated his father but loved his mother. The psychiatrist diagnosed him as a paranoiac. (Paranoia's onset is around 35 years of age. Since the bombings had been going on for about 16 years, this helped to determine the subject's age.) The person was meticulous in his personal habits. When he was found, Brussel said, he would be wearing a double-breasted suit, buttoned. After determining the bomber was a Consolidated Edison employee due to his writings, a review of disgruntled employees was conducted, and George Matesky was determined to be a suspect in the case.

Law enforcement officials investigated the lead and interviewed Matesky at his home, where he confessed to the crimes. George Matesky was arrested for the bombings. At the time of his arrest, Matesky was living in Waterbury, Connecticut, with two maiden sisters. Matesky was a disgruntled ex-employee of the local utility company, Consolidated Edison (Porter, 1983). It should be noted that when Matesky was first contacted by police it was in the evening, and Matesky was wearing a housecoat. Yet, when Matesky was advised he was being arrested, he changed clothes and emerged from his room wearing a double-breasted suit—buttoned.

While this profile seemed to be extraordinarily accurate, there were many aspects of the profile that did not fit Matesky. Yet, the profile did provide investigative leads that helped to develop Matesky as a suspect and helped to explain some of the offender's behaviors and motivations.

While profiling is not always perfect, it has been useful to law enforcement in many cases. In the last several decades, law enforcement officers have seen a new era in criminal behavior dawn. They have recognized that a large percentage of crimes are perpetrated by serial offenders. The most troubling is the serial murderer, which may not be as new a phenomenon as we want to believe, but we are now better able to link these cases and detect these offenders. A serial murderer should not be confused with the mass murderer, who kills more than three people in a single event, or a spree killer, who kills three or more people over a relatively short period of time without a cooling off period between crimes. The serial murderer will kill time after time utilizing similar behaviors on each victim. The behaviors to obtain and kill the victims may vary, but the reason the victims were selected and the crime motives are the same.

The majority of homicides are committed by friends, relatives, or acquaintances of the victims. Solving crimes when the individuals are acquainted or have some type of connection is easier because a motive is often evident. More recently, there has been an increase in cases in which the offender is not acquainted with the victim, which makes investigating these cases more difficult. Until the late 1960s, 85–95% of all murders were solved; from the 1970s to the 1980s, that statistic changed to only 75–80% of all murders being solved (Kismet, 1984). Since 1980, it appears that more offenders are killing people with whom they are not acquainted. This type of offender has presented some special challenges to investigators, as exemplified by the conviction rate falling even further in the 1990s and 2000s. In 2001, the murder clearance rate was 62% according to the Federal Bureau of Investigation's (FBI's) *Crime in the United States* report. In the early 1970s, the FBI began to realize that there were trends in criminality that were not being effectively combated by traditional criminal investigation methods; therefore, they attempted to assist local agencies with criminal investigative analysis (CIA) (FBI, 2001).

In the 1970s, the FBI's Behavioral Sciences Unit (BSU) profiled cases on a limited basis. By 1978, the BSU members were profiling more than unsolved homicides; they were also profiling rape, arson, extortion, and other violent and nonviolent offenses (Ressler, Burgess, & Douglas, 1988, p. 104). The BSU has experienced several name changes over the years and is now called the Behavioral Analysis Unit (BAU). In 1981, U.S. Attorney General William French Smith established the Attorney General's Task Force on Violent Crime. For this task force, Smith assembled individuals from all disciplines who were experts in their fields. Smith also required all the agencies in the Department of Justice to develop plans and submit reports outlining what each agency could do to assist in the national effort to reduce violent crime (Ressler et al., 1988, p. 100).

The 98th Congress of the United States also showed great interest in specific violent crimes, such as "missing and murdered children," "sexual exploitation of children," "unidentified dead bodies," and "serial killers." On June 21, 1984, President Ronald Reagan announced the establishment of the National Center for the Analysis of Violent Crime (NCAVC). The primary mission of the NCAVC was to track and identify repeat offenders (Ressler et al., 1988, p. 101). The primary focus of the NCAVC has changed over the years and now has an emphasis on counterterrorism and crimes against children. The NCAVC was housed at the FBI Academy's BSU but is now at an off-site location not far from the academy.

The FBI's BAU began its CIA program in response to the national concern over violent crime. Currently, it is divided into four specialty areas:

counterterrorism and threat assessment (BAU 1); crimes against adults (BAU 2); crimes against children (BAU 3); and the Violent Criminal Apprehension Program (ViCAP), which is a database of violent crimes used in crime analysis and linkage. The BAU now consults with the military as well as federal, state, and local law enforcement agencies on unsolved cases on a much larger scale. Along with consultations, the BAU also developed training programs for law enforcement agencies and a violent crime research program. The NCAVC and the BAU represent a powerful weapon for law enforcement to use in combating violent crimes.

Introduction to Modern Profiling

The word *profiling* is defined and used in many different ways by different professions. Even within law enforcement, there are many different types of profiles and understandings of the meaning of that word. This chapter looks specifically at the way profiling is defined and used by law enforcement criminal investigative analysts (commonly referred to as *profilers*). Over the years, the term has evolved from psychological profiling to criminal personality profiling as well as other terms that have been used regionally, nationally, and internationally. The term *psychological profiling* was changed due to its original association with psychologists and their work. The term *profiling* was abandoned because of its many uses even within law enforcement and many other professions. The term *criminal investigative analysis* was selected and is still used because it best reflects the work product of those who provide that service (Hazelwood & Michaud, 2001). This term properly conveys the idea that the analysts have a criminal investigation background and use their knowledge of the behavioral sciences to assist in the analysis of the criminal behavior.

Profiling is actually a small part of the larger discipline that is criminal investigative analysis. Profiling is a concept that has been used, misused, misrepresented, and abused for many years. Television programs, movies, and the media have portrayed profiling as a sometimes supernatural phenomenon. Sometimes, the profiler has visions of the crime that are used to solve it and catch the offender. Other times, the profiler takes case information to convicted serial killers and asks the killer for a profile. Fortunately, real profilers do not have visions or take sensitive case data to incarcerated felons. Imagine explaining to a judge and jury while on the witness stand during a homicide trial or other court proceeding that your part of the casework came to you in a vision or that you took the case reports to the prison to have a convicted killer help you. The world of forensics is not ready for supernatural evidence or jailhouse detectives. Good criminal investigations are performed by law enforcement officers who build cases based on solid evidence gathered using sound principles for use in legal proceedings.

The media further perpetuates some myths about the field of CIA by the way they view the discipline. Many movies portray profilers as the only person with insight into the investigation and the offender's personality or motives. This image may also be seen in characters like Sherlock Holmes as he was portrayed by Sir Arthur Conan Doyle. While Holmes does exhibit one aspect of profiling that is deductive in nature, many of his determinations are simply the result of keen observation. Nevertheless, there are more than deductive reasoning and keen observations that go into the development of a criminal profile. Deductive reasoning is only one part of the work done by a profiler. What is not often explained is the hands-on experience in the investigation of violent offenses and the knowledge of or research conducted by these individuals that looks into many offenses and offenders to better understand the crime, the offender, and the victims of these offenses. The truth is that profilers do not "solve" cases; detectives and investigators are the backbone of any investigation, and it is through their hard work that cases are solved. The most difficult cases are solved by law enforcement officers who meticulously investigate every lead and viable suspect in a case using their training, experience, and powers of observation as well as all other investigative tools available.

Cases that are most appropriate for profiling are unsolved violent crimes for which all investigative leads have been exhausted (Hazelwood & Michaud, 2001). It is also important to understand that even if a profile is not appropriate, there are ways that a criminal investigative analyst can be helpful in certain cases. Some of the services provided could include proactive investigative techniques (which may include working with the media to release certain information that will in turn bring about observable behaviors to assist in apprehension of the offender), interview strategies (based on the personality of the individual), personality assessments (to determine if this is the type of person who would commit this type of crime), and investigative suggestions. Other services that a criminal investigative analyst may provide are equivocal death analysis (to determine the most probable manner of death: accident, suicide, homicide, or natural), threat assessment (which can be used in stalking, workplace violence, school violence, extortion, kidnapping/ransom cases, inappropriate communications, threats, or other related incidents), and other behaviorally oriented services.

It is important to understand that not every case is amenable to the discipline of profiling. For example, it would be difficult to profile cases for which there is no known cause of death, an unidentified victim, or little behavior has been exhibited between the offender and the victim. The last is especially essential because a central profiling premise is that behavior reflects personality. Behavior that occurs between the offender and the victim must be observed and recorded before it can be analyzed.

For those cases that are amenable to profiling, new insights or leads in a case may be produced when all previous leads have been exhausted. It is also important to note that when extensive psychopathology (behavioral indicators of mental disorders) is present, it may be beneficial to bring a criminal investigative analyst into the case in the early stages for assistance in understanding the motivation of the offender and the dynamics of the crime.

Profiling is a concept that should be examined in the same manner as banks use to train tellers to detect counterfeit currency. When banks train tellers to detect counterfeit currency, they do so by explaining the intricacies of authentic currency and having the trainees only handle legitimate currency to get the "feel" of the real thing. The result is a greater understanding of the intricacies of genuine currency and in turn a keen ability to spot counterfeit currency. Because there are many variations and methods available to produce counterfeit currency, it would be extremely time intensive and counterproductive to study all of the counterfeiting methods. When a person has a solid working knowledge of the real thing, it is hard to fool that person with a fake. The same is true for profiling. This discipline has been misused in so many different ways it would be impossible to study each separately. The best method is to study what profiling is and how it can be applied; then, by knowing the real thing, counterfeits will become quickly evident.

Criminal Investigative Analysis

Criminal investigative analysis is a relatively new tool available to law enforcement. It is an investigative technique used to identify personality and behavioral characteristics exhibited by offenders based on the examination and analysis of the crime committed as well as the victimology (thorough examination of the victim's demographics, personality, habits, characteristics, and even special interests or hobbies). Although not all crimes lend themselves to profiling, crimes of violence for which the offender exhibits some form of psychopathology are suitable for profiling. Examples of psychopathology are offenses involving sadism, evisceration, postmortem activity with the victim, apparently motiveless arsons, lust murders, ritualistic crimes, and sexual offenses (Geberth, 1981).

Personality profiling cannot take the place of a thorough, well-planned investigation. Cases best suited for profiling are those that involve interpersonal violence and an unknown offender and must be cases for which all investigative leads have been exhausted (Hazelwood & Michaud, 2001). While almost any crime evidencing "mental, emotional, or personality aberration can be profiled, certain crimes are particularly appropriate for the process" (Hazelwood & Burgess, 1987, p. 139). These crimes include serial rapes, lust murder (mutilation or removal of the sexual organs), serial murders, child molesting, other ritualistic crimes, and serial arson (Hazelwood & Burgess, 1987). Profiling has also been useful in identifying authors of anonymous communications and persons who make written or spoken threats of violence (Douglas, Ressler, Burgess, & Hartman, 1986). This technique of identifying authors is called *authorial attribution* (usually performed by a forensic linguist). An assessment may also be completed regarding the threat to determine the seriousness of the threat or if a threat is real (de Becker, 1997). This procedure is called *threat assessment* and is a specialty area in the FBI's BAU and an area of expertise for many profilers and other trained professionals.

Components of a Profile

The criminal personality profile is only as accurate as the investigation and subsequent information submitted for the analysis.

ITEMS NEEDED FOR A CASE ANALYSIS AND PERSONALITY PROFILE CONSTRUCTION

I. Crime scene investigation as listed in Ressler et al., 1988, pp. 136, 137
   A. Physical evidence
   B. Patterns of evidence
   C. Body positions
   D. Type of weapon
   E. Description of the crime scene
   F. Weather conditions
   G. Crime scene sketches indicating distance, directions, and scale
   H. Maps of area (commercially produced maps are preferred due to the details of main routes of travel, industrial areas, schools, hospitals, and other important information included and should include the significant crime locations)
   I. Preliminary police reports
   J. Police observations
   K. Time of crime
   L. Synopsis of crime
   M. Victim's statement (if applicable) (Hazelwood & Burgess, 1987, pp. 139, 140)

II. Background information as listed in Ressler et al., 1988, pp. 136, 137
   A. Neighborhood socioeconomic status
   B. Crime rate
   C. Political and social environment

III. Victimology as listed in Ressler et al., 1988, pp. 136, 137
   A. Background
   B. Habits
   C. Family structure and relationships
   D. Location and when last seen
   E. Age
   F. Occupation
   G. Reputation
   H. Fears
   I. Physical condition
   J. Personality
   K. Criminal history
   L. Social behaviors
   M. Race
   N. Education level (Hazelwood & Burgess, 1987, pp. 139, 140)
   O. Hobbies and interests (Douglas et al., 1986)

IV. Medical and scientific information listed in Ressler et al., 1988, pp. 136, 137
   A. Cause of death
   B. Wounds: sequence
   C. Pre-/postmortem sexual acts
   D. Autopsy report: medical examiner's determinations
   E. Laboratory reports: toxicology/serology
   F. Impressions on estimated time of death

V. Photographs as listed in Ressler et al., 1988, p. 137
   A. Aerial photographs of crime scene and surrounding area
   B. Crime scene photographs
   C. Victim photographs
   D. Autopsy photographs; include photos of cleansed wounds (Douglas et al., 1986).

It is important to identify as many of the crime scenes as possible. These may include scenes such as the abduction site, the assault site, the murder site, or the body disposal site. Often in the case of homicide, the only site available or known to law enforcement is the body dump site. Knowing as much as possible about the crime and the steps the offender took in committing the crime will assist greatly in determining the type of offender who would commit that type of crime. The sequence of events and criminal behavior are important keys to understanding the offense as well as the offender, which will assist in the subsequent construction of the profile.

Through the process of identifying the crime scenes and sequence of events, the investigator is gathering behavioral evidence needed to construct a profile of the unknown offender. One way to gather behavioral evidence is to photograph the crime scene extensively. The actions of an offender at the crime scene indicate the amount of time spent there and the offender's comfort level at the scene. This has great significance to the analyst. One example of a thorough investigation yielding important information for the profile may be a case in which feces were deposited at the crime scene by the offender. A thorough investigation may note that the feces were loose. This may have significance because loose feces may indicate the perpetrator was nervous, anxious, or fearful, and this offense may be a new experience for the offender. If the feces were solid, however, that could indicate that the offender was comfortable in the commission of the crime and with the location of the crime scene and may indicate that this offender has committed similar offenses (Hazelwood, 1984).

Profiles can provide investigators with a variety of information that could help them focus their investigation.

PROFILE INFORMATION MAY INCLUDE

1. Race
2. Sex
3. Age range
4. Marital status
5. General employment
6. Reaction to questioning by police
7. Degree of sexual maturity
8. Likelihood that the individual will strike again
9. The possibility that he or she committed similar offenses
10. Possible police records (items 1–10 from Ault & Reese, 1980)
11. Mode of transportation
12. Social abilities
13. Residence in relation to the scene
14. Degree of planning
15. Other behavioral indicators

Take, for example, a case for which the analyst responded by stating that the offender may have an extensive pornography collection. For example, an offender who attempts to re-create scenes that are typical in the pornographic media may script the victim. This means that the offender will tell the victim what the offender wants to hear, like, "Tell me I am the greatest lover you have ever had." There is much controversy in the area of pornography's role in violent crime. For example, pornography may have played a part in the violent crime ideation of Ted Bundy, which was related in his interview with James Dobson, Ph.D., days prior to Bundy's execution in Florida. During that interview, Bundy stated that he was attracted to violent pornography as a young man, and it may have helped to form his interests in sexual violence (Stiles, 1989).

DOES PORNOGRAPHY CAUSE VIOLENT BEHAVIOR?

Even though there may appear to be a link between use of pornography and violent crime, we must be careful to understand that there is no causal link between viewing of pornography and committing violent crime. It should be noted that pornography use is prevalent among many males who do not commit violent crimes. Research has determined that sight is the primary sexual sense for males; therefore, the use of pornography among males may be high. These purveyors of pornography are also known to be attracted to different types of pornography depending on their own sexual interests or paraphilias (psychosexual disorder), such as a sexual desire for children, the elderly, or an object. It should also be noted that research of violent offenders such as serial murderers, sexual sadists, and others has revealed that as many as 80% of these serious offenders are purveyors of pornography.

Uses of Profiling

Homicide offenders are often categorized as organized, disorganized, or mixed by the FBI's BAU. For example, if an offender with a disorganized personality has a psychopathic or an antisocial personality, he or she may exhibit the following traits: (a) unable to develop warm relationships; (b) disregards accepted norms or standards of behavior; (c) exhibits a lack of guilt feelings; (d) fails to learn from discipline or punishment; (e) desires immediate personal satisfaction; (f) displays continual sexual experimentation (generally with a nonresponsive victim); (g) has an undue dependence on others; and (h) generally remains close to home. The organized offender also displays a lack of concern for the victim but on the other hand has a much greater sense of independence and a desire to travel a great distance for anonymity and to seek new victim populations.

There are so many different uses of the word *profiling* that it may be necessary to explain the difference between two of the more commonly referred to types of profiling. Retired FBI Special Agent Roy Hazelwood explained the types of profiling as prospective and retrospective. *Prospective profiling* is the type commonly used for drug couriers and terrorists. Prospective profiling uses statistical data from past offenses to determine commonalities in offenders and their offenses. The common traits are then used to observe individuals in similar situations to determine if they are possibly in the process of committing a crime. These individuals are observed, and an attempt is made to detect, identify, and intervene in those situations before the crime is completed. Prospective profiling is being proactive in law enforcement to prevent the crime from being completed.

Prospective profiling is often confused with the CIA type of profiling. These are two very different types of profiling that require different skills, training, education, experience, and research backgrounds. CIA is sometimes referred to as *retrospective profiling*. This is because we are looking back at the crime after it has been committed. This further makes the distinction between the two types greater in that prospective deals with the person who may be committing the crime and retrospective does not as there is no information about the offender except that gained through the examinations of behaviors exhibited at the crime scene. As Gilbert (2007) stated, mental health officials work from the individual (through a self-report) to the concerning behavior, whereas a profiler works from the criminal behavior (observed behavior) to the type of individual. Retrospective profiling therefore tries to paint a word picture of the personality characteristics of the type of person (not the exact person) who would commit this type of crime. While prospective profiling deals with the person being considered, retrospective profiling deals with the crime scene behavior to determine the type of people or person who might commit that type of crime (Hazelwood, 1998). Hazelwood has also explained that to the criminal investigative analyst a profile is a listing of characteristics and traits of an unidentified offender (Hazelwood & Michaud, 2001).

Profile Inputs

It is important to understand what profiling is about before one can know how investigative information can be gathered and how to gather case information regarding offender behavior that can assist should a profile be required. This can be done throughout all aspects of the investigation, which includes the crime scene investigation through the interviews to the evidence analysis. It is essential to find out all of the behaviors the offender engaged in during the crime. That would include answering questions like: When did the offender decide to commit the crime? How did the offender get to the scene? How did the offender select and gain access to the victim? How did the offender take control of the victim? What were the offender's exact words (if possible), exactly what did the offender do to the victim, and in what sequence did the offender do those acts? It is also important to know how the offender responded to the victim's actions or reactions physically and verbally.

To assist in gathering this type of information, we need to learn to ask victims and witnesses questions that will elicit information regarding offender behaviors. While it is always right to gather the traditional descriptions of vehicles, dress, and physique of the offender, we should also gather information about how the offender responded to unexpected situations during the incident. This behavior can be broken down into three main types: verbal, physical, and sexual behaviors (Hazelwood & Burgess, 1987). When questioning a victim, one should ask questions such as, "What did he first say to you?" "How did you respond?" and continue with, "What exactly did he say to that?" It is important to record the verbal interactions word for word.

Physical behavior can be gathered in similar fashion by asking questions like, "What was the offender doing when you first noticed him?" "How did he first contact you?" and "Did he have or display a weapon?" All physical behaviors should be explored and recorded in chronological sequence. Having a victim or witness methodically and chronologically recount the events of a serious matter may also assist the individual in recalling more details about the crime and offender.

The final area of questioning should be regarding the exact sexual behaviors demanded and perpetrated by the offender. These behaviors should also be reviewed chronologically with the victim. The order of sexual acts can reveal a great deal regarding the offender's experience, attitude toward women, and the fantasy that the offender is attempting to fulfill through the violent crime.

These sexual behaviors may also become important when reviewing a series of offenses to determine if an offender is becoming more violent. Samenow (2004) noted that criminal sexuality may become violent as the individual becomes bored with the same type of criminal acts as they are continually repeated. Some offenders discover a greater excitement when the level of violence and victim domination is increased (Samenow, 2004). This type of behavior differentiation and questioning for offender behavior should make the original investigation more complete and further assist with crime analysis and other behavioral assessments.

Other information to gather that will assist in crime analysis concerns the location selected by the offender for the crime and other crime environment factors. These factors can include time of day, vehicle and pedestrian congestion, number of crime locations (e.g., abduction site, assault site, and dump site), which can assist in determining the level of risk the offender was willing to engage in to commit the crime (Douglas, Burgess, Burgess, & Ressler, 1992). This type of information can be helpful to gain insight into the offender's planning, victim selection, level of impulsivity, criminal sophistication, motivation, and other important personal characteristics.

Conclusion

These types of behavioral investigative approaches should enhance conventional investigative methods and further improve the quality of information gained through the investigative process. It is important to keep in mind that the CIA process or need for a profile will not be necessary in all cases. For those cases that do require investigative assistance for further ideas regarding the offender type, personality, and motivation factors, profiling is just one more tool law enforcement is able to utilize. It is hoped a better understanding of the CIA discipline will lead to less confusion regarding the uses of profiling as well as the ways that profiling should not be applied in certain cases that lack behavioral evidence. Profiling can be an extremely useful tool when used appropriately and when applied by a qualified practitioner.

References

Ault, R., & Reese, J. (1980). A psychological assessment of crime: Profiling. *FBI Law Enforcement Bulletin, 49*(4), 24.

de Becker, G. (1997). *The gift of fear*. Boston: Little Brown and Company.

Douglas, J., Burgess, A., Burgess, A., & Ressler, R. (1992). *Crime classification manual*. New York: Lexington Books.

Douglas, J., Ressler, R., Burgess, A., & Hartman, C. (1986). Criminal profiling from crime scene analysis. *Behavioral Sciences and the Law, 4*, 401–426.

Federal Bureau of Investigation. (2001). *Crime in the United States*. FBI Uniform Crime Report Retrieved July 28, 2008 from www.fbi.gov/ucr.htm

Geberth, V. (1981). Psychological profiling. *Law and Order, 9*, 46–52.

Gilbert, J. (2007). *Criminal investigation* (7th ed.). Upper Saddle River, NJ: Pearson Prentice Hall.

Hazelwood, R. (1984, October). Douglas County (Nebraska) Homicide Conference. Criminal profiling lecture by FBI supervisory special agent. Omaha, NE.

Hazelwood, R. (1998, September). Texas Association of Sex Crimes Investigators Annual Conference. Lecture by FBI supervisory special agent. Fort Worth, TX.

Hazelwood, R., & Burgess, A. (Eds.). (1987). *Practical aspects of rape investigation: A multidisciplinary approach*. New York: Elsevier.

Hazelwood, R., & Michaud, S. (2001). *Dark dreams*. New York: St. Martin's Press.

Kismet, P. (1984, December). U.S. Attorney Law Enforcement Training Program. Criminal profiling lecture by FBI special agent. Omaha, NE.

Porter, B. (1983, April). Mind hunters: Tracking down killers with the FBI's psychological profiling team. *Psychology Today,* pp. 2–5.

Ressler, R., Burgess, A., & Douglas, J. (1988). *Sexual homicide patterns and motives*. Lexington: Lexington, pp. 100–104.

Samenow, S. (2004). *Inside the criminal mind*. New York: Crown.

Stiles, S. (Producer/Director). (1989). *Fatal addiction* [Film]. Pomona, CA: Focus on the Family Films.

Tanay, E. (1983, October). The Lindbergh kidnapping—A psychiatric view. *Journal of Forensic Sciences, 28*(3), 1076–1082.

From Crime Scene to Morgue

The Field of Forensic Anthropology

35

ERIN H. KIMMERLE

Contents

Introduction

Anthropology is the scientific study of the origin and behavior of humans, including their biological and cultural development. Forensic anthropology is a rapidly growing and changing subfield that is based in biological anthropology but also draws on archeology, cultural anthropology, law, biology, environmental sciences, medicine, chemistry, and geology. *Forensic anthropology* has been defined as the application of biological anthropology to legal and social problems. Therefore, forensic anthropologists are broadly trained within the four fields of anthropology: cultural studies, biology and evolutionary theory, archeology, and linguistics. There are a number of recent textbooks that focus on this subject (e.g., Brickley & Ferllini, 2007; Byers, 2008; Dupras, Schultz, Wheeler, & Williams, 2006; Kimmerle & Baraybar, 2008; Komar & Buikstra, 2008).

Forensic anthropologists are often employed at universities, in medical examiner's offices, and in other governmental and nongovernmental agencies and provide consultation as a scientific expert witness. Typically, to serve as an expert witness, a doctoral degree is required, as well as an extensive publishing record and casework experience. Forensic anthropologists are called by medical examiners, coroners, law enforcement, and lawyers to provide a scientific expert opinion on locating and excavating clandestine graves, human identification, or trauma analysis. Anthropologists are able to serve as technical and scientific expert witnesses because the methodology is grounded in scientific principles that have been demonstrated through scientific rigor. Yet, increasingly anthropological methods presented in court are being challenged in the adversarial system, prompting research that addresses the accuracy, repeatability, and reliability of methods. Scientific advances in bone chemistry, DNA analysis, and human rights investigations are also rapidly changing the field.

The cases in which anthropologists consult are diverse. Most typically, human remains that are skeletonized or decomposing are found in a public space. The medical examiner or law enforcement may call an anthropologist to assist in the field with recovery or may request the anthropologist's presence in the morgue at autopsy. The advantage of assisting in the field is that an inventory of skeletal elements may be completed to determine if every bone was properly recovered. Another advantage of using anthropologists in the field is that they employ archeological excavation techniques that recover all evidence, even as small as hair or fibers. In addition, they will collect soil, insect, and botany samples. Used in combination, these environmental variables provide a strong estimation for the time since death. Although most casework falls within this traditional purview, anthropologists may also be called on to provide an opinion on a wide range of topics. For example, they may be asked to provide an age estimate for a living individual from radiographs when a person's identity is in question; to create a facial reconstruction for decomposing or skeletonized remains; to review radiographs for trauma diagnosis; or to search property for a clandestine burial.

Who Are the Missing?

There are an estimated 4,400 cases of unidentified remains in the United States annually (Bureau of Justice Statistics, 2007). The majority of these cases are quickly resolved with a positive identification by visual recognition from someone who knew the victim, fingerprints, or DNA. Of these cases, there are approximately 1,000 cold cases unsolved annually. So, who are the missing? In the United States, many represent groups that are already at a higher risk for violence or criminal victimization, such as runaways, drifters or transients, the homeless, and abused women. In foreign countries, the missing are referred to as "the disappeared," and more commonly go missing for political reasons (Burns, 2007). Identification of these victims is critical for families who are searching for answers and for society when a crime has been committed. Investigators will not know who committed the crime until they know the identity of the victim and who last saw him or her alive and where.

Establishing the Forensic Context

Many skeletal cases that come through the office of forensic anthropologists turn out to be animal (faunal) remains. Concerned citizens may bring forth remains they found or call authorities, who then need to verify whether they are in fact human bones. The fact that humans are uniquely bipedal means that throughout the skeleton the bony structure is unique for humans compared to other mammals. There are a number of criteria to consider in distinguishing animal from human remains:

- The bony architecture or morphological structure of bone (i.e., the placement of the foramen magnum at the base of the skull, rather than on the posterior surface)
- Whether the remains are juvenile or adult
- Associated evidence (i.e., clothing) and context

Artifactual evidence such as clothing or orthopedic hardware is not enough to make the determination whether a bone is human as domestic animals may have had orthopedic implants. There have even been cases of faunal remains found wearing clothing, though the source of the hoax remains a mystery.

In some cases, human skeletal remains may be found in someone's possession, but it is unclear whether it represents a modern crime. It is not uncommon for skulls, archeological materials, or anatomic specimens to be in private possession. There are many cases when an elderly person dies, and the family, on clearing out the attic and basement, finds skeletal material. Determining whether skeletal remains have a recent origin rather than a historic or archeological origin can be challenging (Figure 35.1).

Establishing that the bones are human, the number of individuals, and the time since death creates the context. When the remains are more than 75 years old, they are referred to as *historic*. When remains are Native American and are much older, they may be classified as *archeological*. In historic or archeological cases, there is no medicolegal significance. However, there may be other legal issues that arise, such as disturbance to burials or archeological sites, illegal trafficking of human remains, grave robbing, or the illegal

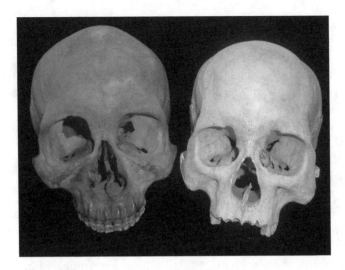

Figure 35.1 Frontal view of two archeological crania. The difference in color reflects soil staining from burial (left) and sun bleaching from surface exposure (right).

sale of museum specimens. Burials are protected under various state laws. In such cases, the state archeologist must be informed and may play a role in ultimately determining the final interment of the remains.

The best indicators to establish the context are on the remains themselves. Taphonomic features on the remains and human modification to teeth and bones during life provide insight into the relative timing and provenance of the remains (Table 35.1). The presence of some traits is clearly indicative of nonmodern remains, such as severe dental attrition, intentional cranial modification, or evidence of burial customs or body preparation for intentional burials (Figures 35.2 and 35.3). In contrast, dental modifications such as amalgams are indicative of a recent origin. It cannot always be assumed,

Table 35.1 Bone Taphonomy

Characteristics	Factors
Bone preservation	Good with outer cortex intact to poor with exfoliation of outer bone surface
Discoloration	Staining caused by soil, vegetation, the presence of metals or other chemicals
Adherent materials	Plant roots, soil, lichens, barnacles
Animal scavenging	Gnawing or carnivore tooth marks, dismemberment
Human modification	Trauma, burial modification, evidence of orthopedic hardware

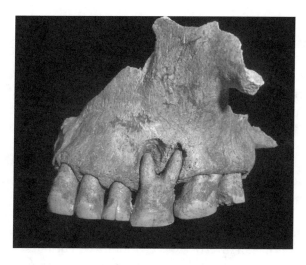

Figure 35.2 Archeological teeth remains exhibit severe attrition, tooth fractures (antemortem), and a large abscess.

however, that a lack of dental or medical intervention means the remains are historic. Some populations in the United States and globally do not have adequate dental and medical care. Therefore, such health disparities may be seen in the skeletal or dental remains.

While it is assumed that soft tissues decompose, bones will remain greasy or "wet" for years following death. In dry climates, soft tissues may become mummified and be preserved for thousands of years. In wet environments, fatty tissues in the body may turn into adipocere (grave wax) and may remain intact for hundreds of years. Therefore, the presence of desiccated soft tissues, such as mummified tissue or *adipocere*, cannot always contribute to establishing a timeline.

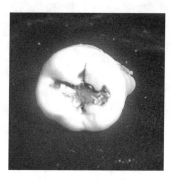

Figure 35.3 A modern tooth exhibits a contemporary amalgam, indicative of dental care, and very little tooth wear.

Archeological Methods for Locating, Recovering, and Documenting Evidence

Increasingly, archeological methods (sometimes referred to as *forensic archeology*) are being adopted for crime scene processing, whether or not human remains are present. Scientific approaches to process a crime scene are similar to those for an archeological site in that the very act of collecting evidence means investigators are destroying the scene. Therefore, meticulous steps need to be taken to ensure that all evidence is properly documented, collected, and stored. *Chain of custody*, the paper trail that accounts for what evidence is present and the timeline for when evidence was handled and by whom, must be maintained so that it is admissible in court. When this process is violated, investigators risk the chance that evidence will be deemed inadmissible or that an investigator's credibility will be questioned in court.

Archeological methods include prospection or survey work, excavation, mapping, and recovery. In some cases, investigators have reason to believe a grave exists on a particular property; however, information on the exact location may be lacking. Therefore, a systematic search of the property will ensure that either the burial is located or the area can be ruled out altogether (exclusion) (Figure 35.4). This is a very important point because in cases where a methodical, scientific approach is not used, the search may not yield a burial, yet investigators are left wondering if there was something else they could have done.

Figure 35.4 A mock crime scene is searched. All evidence, bones, or suspected burials are marked with pin flags. Possible clandestine graves are "ground-truthed" through probing, shovel testing, or evacuation.

Table 35.2   Examples of Field Methods for Locating Clandestine Graves

Field	Method	Factors Indicative of a Disturbance
Archeological	Line search	Flag any potential evidence
	Landscape topography	Sunken depression
	Probe	Changes in soil density
	Shovel testing	Changes in soil stratigraphy
	Soil chemistry	Changes in pH level or phosphates
	Heavy equipment	Changes in soil stratigraphy
Environmental	Vegetation	More or less vegetation (depending on age of grave)
	Entomology	Increased insect activity
	Soil	Staining from body fluids
Geophysical	Ground-penetrating radar	Underground disturbance in soil
	Metal detector	Near-surface metal object
	Electromagnetics	Shallow burial/metal objects
Aerial	Arial photography	Changes to the landscape
	Satellite images	Modifications to land use

There are number of methods available to aid in locating clandestine graves. As with any tool kit, it is important that investigators know the potential value and limitations of each method or tool (Table 35.2). Not all methods work in all situations. Forensic anthropologists are able to provide guidance to law enforcement on which tools will best serve their needs given the age of the burial, the particular type of vegetation and terrain present, and the soil matrix and amount of prior disturbance to the site from previous human activities. It is also important to know that some methods are destructive; therefore, it is a matter of choosing not only the right methods to get the job done but also the right sequence of methods, employing the least-destructive methods first.

Many of the archeological methods are based on an assessment of *stratigraphy* (the subsurface layers of soil and sediments) or soil chemistry (i.e., changes in pH levels). Before any search, a scene assessment consisting of background research is completed for the site. This initial assessment consists of compiling a history of land use, locating satellite images or aerial photographs, and soil maps (Figures 35.5 and 35.6). By putting together this information, it becomes clear how the landscape may have changed over time and what the "normal" or undisturbed ground should look like. Establishing a "normal baseline" becomes the measure against which possible burials may be compared. Through probing, shovel testing, or heavy equipment for larger areas, disturbed areas are evident by analyzing subsurface disruptions in the stratigraphy. Such disturbances may be indicative of a burial. Ultimately, *groundtruthing*, which is to excavate an area, is the only way to determine whether a disturbance is the result of a burial or some other cause.

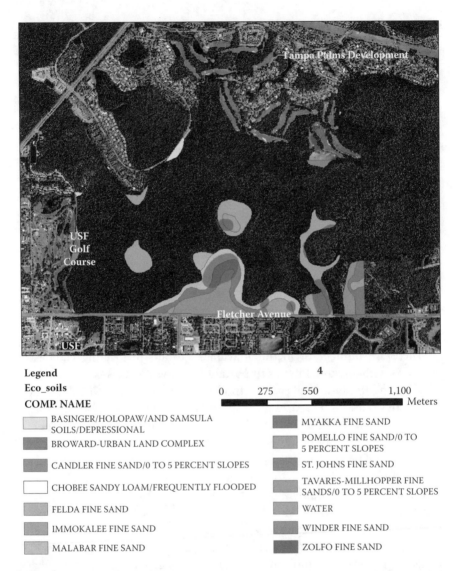

Figure 35.5 Soil map of University of South Florida (USF) Forensic Anthropology Research Area. Map illustrates soil matrix. This is the type of map generated for prospection of possible crime scenes prior to field work. (Map created by Rich Estabrook.)

Scenario 1

Authorities are looking into the death of an unidentified individual found in a wooded area. Human remains were found near a hiking trail by a jogger. This is not the first time a body has been found in these woods. No information has been released regarding the age or sex of the body part or any missing persons from the area. The Medical Examiner's Office calls an anthropologist to locate and recover the rest of the skeleton and associated evidence.

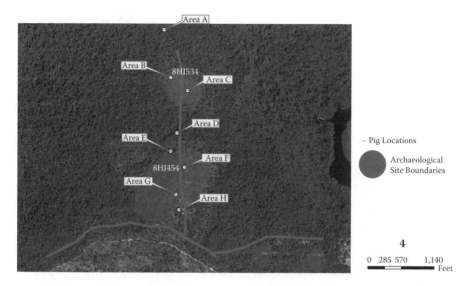

Figure 35.6 Map of the same USF research area, with burials plotted using GPS. Map is overlaid with known archeological sites of the area, representing continued land use over time. (Created by Rich Estabrook.)

RECOMMENDED SEARCH STRATEGY

Conduct background research for the area, including soil profiles, aerial maps, and prior land use. Search the area, flag remains and evidence, photograph the site, map evidence, create a scene sketch, and keep detailed notes and record logs. To map the site, units 1 meter square can be set up in a grid over the body and area in close proximity. This works well when remains are clustered in a small area. Recover and collect all evidence, including soil, insect, and vegetation samples. Inventory remains in the field to assess completeness of the search and complete site forms. Maintain chain of custody . . . or all of this hard work may be thrown out of court.

Scenario 2

A known drug dealer was shot and killed in his home. He was shot by a man who worked for him selling drugs. Since his death, authorities have been receiving anonymous calls that he once killed a man who also worked for him and buried him in the woods behind his house. Agents walked the grounds but were not sure if there was a burial there. Investigators called an anthropologist to provide assistance and develop a search strategy to look for a possible clandestine grave.

RECOMMENDED SEARCH STRATEGY

Conduct background research for area, including soil profiles, aerial maps, and prior land use. Create a systematic grid to search the area and flag any area that appears to have topographic or environmental changes. Decisions should be made about additional search tools to be used, depending on the appropriateness of each tool for the landscape and size of search area. These may include geophysical techniques, heavy equipment, or soil sampling for chemical analyses.

These areas can later be ground-truthed through probing, shovel testing, or excavation. Once a grave is uncovered, the site becomes a crime scene. Photograph the site, map evidence, create a scene sketch, and keep detailed notes and record logs. Recover and collect all evidence, including soil, insect, and vegetation samples. Inventory remains in the field to assess the completeness of the search and complete site forms. Maintain chain of custody. If no grave is recovered, the area may be confidently excluded.

Once a burial is located, careful excavation ensures that the site is well documented and all evidence is recovered. Documentation of the site requires photographing, mapping, sketching, and note taking. The site is photographed, including general views of the overall scene and close-up views of the body and other associated evidence (Figure 35.7). Mapping may be done using a compass and protractor or with more sophisticated mapping technology such as a *total station*, which is a surveying tool that calculates angles and distances to map objects using three-dimensional coordinates. Total stations may also use *global positioning systems* (GPSs), which transmit signals to satellites to calculate the position of the site. There are a number of current resources that address both tested methods and experimental research in forensic archeology (Connor, 2007; Dupras et al., 2006; Haglund & Sorg, 2001; Killam, 2004; Morse, Duncan, & Stoutamire, 1983; Tibbett & Carter, 2008).

Burials located on the surface or subsurface are excavated following traditional archeological methods, although depending on the context and location, sometimes these methods are adapted to the situation. Generally, a 1-meter unit is set up over the remains (Figure 35.8). Multiple units may be set up in a grid to cover a larger area. The top layer of soil is removed

Figure 35.7 Mock crime scene with surface burial. Bones scattered among leaves from animal scavenging. Site marked with flagging.

Figure 35.8 A clandestine grave was located through probing. A 1-meter unit is set up over the burial to guide excavation and provide measurements for mapping.

(Figure 35.9). Once the remains are evident, careful excavation is done with hand trowels. Soil is removed away from the body, and investigators work inward toward the remains. Evidence is logged and photographed *in situ*. Once the remains are fully exposed, they are photographed and removed (Figure 35.10).

Figure 35.9 Excavation of the unit begins by removing the top layer of soil. Note that only flat-nosed shovels are used so remains are not damaged. They also serve as an easy tool for keeping the edges of the unit straight and controlled.

Figure 35.10 Body is exposed and photographed prior to removal from the grave.

Estimating the Postmortem Interval

The immediate and critical questions that surface when unknown, unidentified human remains are recovered have to do with the identity of the victim and how long the victim has been deceased. Whether the human remains recovered have been decomposing for 6 weeks or 16 years has a dramatic effect on the nature of the investigation. Authorities begin their investigation in possible homicides by interviewing people who last saw the victim alive. Depending on that timeline, authorities have to adjust who they can interview and how to locate potential witnesses.

Understanding the decompositional process and quantifying the timeline associated with these variables has been a growing area of interest in forensic anthropological research (Bass, 1997; Galloway, Birkby, Jones, Henry, & Parks, 1989; Haglund & Sorg, 2001; Mann, Bass, & Jantz, 1990; Micozzi, 1986; Perper, 1997; Rodriguez & Bass, 1983, 1985; Vass, Bass, Wolt, Foss, & Ammons, 1992). Estimation of the *time since death* or *postmortem interval* (PMI) is constructed from a variety of techniques that are used in combination, including decompositional changes evident on the body, entomology, soil chemistry, botany, and the preservation of fibers or other evidence present with the body such as clothing or money (refer to Table 35.3). Many factors affect the rate of decomposition; therefore, the PMI is highly variable given many conditions, such as

- Temperature
- Amount of moisture or humidity
- Access to the body by insects

Table 35.3 Methods for Estimating the Postmortem Interval

Method	Characteristics	General Time Frame
Decomposition	Livor, rigor, and algor mortis	<36 hours
	Discoloration	Days
	Bloating	Weeks
	Skeletonization	Months–years
Entomology	Successional wave of insects	1 month–1 year
	Life cycle of species	<1 month
Botany	Root growth through remains	>1 year
Soil chemistry	Increased elevations of or changes in soil pH, phosphates, volatile fatty acids	Months–years
Preservation of material evidence	Paper	Weeks to months
	Natural fibers	Months–year
	Synthetic fibers	Months (preserves longer than natural fibers)
Animal scavenging	Birds, rodents, carnivores	Days–years

- Modification to the body, such as dismemberment or burning
- The location of body deposition (i.e., buried, on the surface, or in water)
- Use of container (i.e., body wrapped in blanket, put into trunk or dumpster)
- Age and weight of the decedent
- Presence of trauma at time of death

Given the number of variables and range of factors that influence the PMI, the estimation usually ranges from several days to several months or years (Figures 35.11, 35.12, and 35.13). Bass (1997) defined several stages of decomposition:

- Fresh
  - Generally within the first 24 hours.
  - Egg masses start to form; *algor mortis*, *rigor mortis*, and *livor mortis* occur.
  - Some discoloration of body tissues due to *putrefaction*.

- Early decomposition/bloat
  - Body tissues bloat and increase dramatically in size.
  - Skin slippage begins to occur.
  - Marbling of the vascular system is very pronounced.
  - Body fluids purge from the mouth, nose, and eyes.
  - Purging of body fluids will kill nearby vegetation and stain the soil a dark color.

Figure 35.11 Within minutes of carrying a pig corpse to the woods, flies land on the body. Entomology is a very useful tool for estimating PMI, particularly in the first month following death.

Figure 35.12 This individual shows few signs of decomposition 2 days after death.

Figure 35.13 The same individual as pictured in Figure 35.12 exhibits advanced decomposition, including bloating, marbling, skin slippage, and discoloration 5 days after death.

- Advanced decomposition
  - Facial bones become skeletonized.
  - Body is no longer bloated.
  - Soft tissues continue to break down.
  - Adipocere forms in wet environments, either in water or wet graves.

- Mummification or skeletonization
  - Soft tissues are completely desiccated and dry or absent, leaving only skeletonized remains.
  - Remains may be disarticulated due to animal and bird scavenging.
  - Over time, cortex of bone begins to show cracking and flaking.
  - Bones may become stained from sun bleaching, decaying vegetation, or the soil.

The two primary processes in which the body decomposes are autolysis and putrefaction. *Autolysis* is the chemical breakdown of body tissues caused by intracellular enzymes. *Putrefaction* is the chemical breakdown of body tissues caused by the bacterial flora in the gastrointestinal tract that permeate the vascular system, producing a *marbling* appearance of the vascular system (Spitz, 2006).

Given the significant influence of climate and environmental factors in the rate of decomposition, research is needed for a range of different ecological areas. Rather than discuss time since death in terms of days or months, investigators are standardizing this timeline using *degree days* (DD). *Accumulated degree days* (ADD) are calculated by adding the average daily temperature over a given period of time. Since temperature is one of the most influential factors in the rate of decomposition, using ADD provides a standard scale that can be applied to any place on Earth. For example, for a body to decompose to the point at which bloating occurs may take an average of 285 DD. In Alaska, where average temperatures are 65°F, this may equal 4.4 days, whereas in Florida, with average temperatures of 95°F, it may take only 3 days. In this example, the time since death may vary by as much as 1.5 days, depending on the temperature and geographical location.

Human Osteology and the Biological Profile

Human osteology is the cornerstone of forensic anthropology. The methods and techniques available to estimate individual characteristics about a person from skeletal remains set forensic anthropology apart from forensic pathology. Pathologists are trained to study soft tissues, whereas forensic anthropologists are trained in hard tissues—bones and teeth. The fundamental osteological protocol (refer to Table 35.4) asks a series of questions that lead to the identity of the decedent, the circumstances surrounding the death, and reconstructs injuries that may have contributed to the individual's death.

Table 35.4   Osteological Protocol

Category	Criteria
Establish the context	Historic, archeological, forensic
Biological profile	Age, sex, ancestry, stature
Human identification	Unique characteristics, facial reconstructions, photo superimpositions of faces or boney architecture
Health history	Disease, healed trauma, evidence of history of abuse
Trauma analysis	Injuries at the time death that may have contributed to the death, manner of death, reconstruct circumstances around death

Biological Profile

The initial parameters for establishing an individual's identity are the individual's age, sex, height, weight, ancestry, and facial shape and form. Individual traits that are unique to each person include health history, the presence of disease or past healed trauma, congenital anomalies, and the unique bony architecture and morphology. The first methods used to estimate biological profiles were developed by human anatomist Thomas Dwight (i.e., in 1878 and 1894). Today, method development is at the forefront of research in forensic anthropology. Methods are based on either metric analysis of bony structures or morphological characteristics that capture both the shape and size of a trait. As many methods as possible are typically applied for identification so that a comprehensive assessment may be accomplished.

Anthropological methods include a series of qualitative descriptive methods based on shape and texture or what is referred to as *morphology.* Methods also include highly sophisticated quantitative techniques based on metric analysis. There is a variety of instruments used to measure various bones, including three-dimensional digitizing tools that enable coordinate data in the *x, y,* and *z* planes to analyze shape and size. For an overview of methods used for biological profiling, there are a number of useful texts (e.g., Bass, 1991; Buikstra & Ubelaker, 1994; Byers, 2008; Krogman & Iscan, 1989; Kimmerle & Baraybar, 2008; Komar & Buikstra, 2008; Ubelaker, 1989).

Sex estimation among adults may be based on morphological features of the skull and pelvis that are highly dimorphic (Figures 35.14 and 35.15). Due to secondary sex traits, these bones are readily discernible as female or male. Adult age and ancestry estimation has to take into account differences among males and females. Therefore, the other methods for biological profiling are often dependent on first establishing a reliable estimation of sex. Tables 35.5 and 35.6 provide lists of morphological traits unique to each sex and simple sectioning points for several long bone measurements, respectively. Discriminant function analysis is also a tool used for sex estimation based on a series of bone measurements. Metric analysis has been shown to be even more accurate for estimation

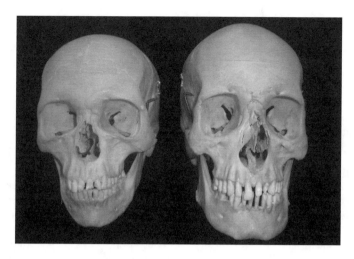

Figure 35.14 Frontal view of female (left) and male (right) crania showing marked sexual dimorphism.

than morphological methods alone. Further, different populations vary in the degree to which they are sexually dimorphic (Kimmerle, Ross, & Slice, 2008). Therefore, applying one standard to different populations can be precarious. Biological parameters for individual estimation should take population and human variation into account (Kimmerle & Jantz, 2008; Kimmerle, Jantz, Konigsberg, & Baraybar, 2008; Kimmerle, Konigsberg, Jantz, & Baraybar, 2008; Kimmerle, Prince, & Berg, 2008; Prince, Kimmerle, & Konigsberg, 2008).

Several methods for estimating sex among juvenile remains have also been developed (Saunders, 2008). The reliability of these methods vary due to the fact that children who have not undergone puberty are less sexually

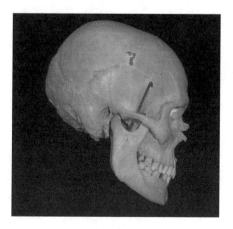
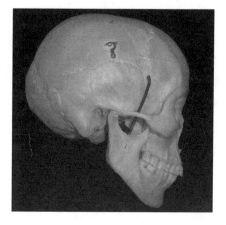

Figure 35.15 Left lateral view of female (right) and male (left) crania showing marked sexual dimorphism.

Table 35.5 Morphological Criteria for Sex Estimation

	Female	Male
Cranial traits		
Shape of forehead	Vertical	Retreating
Temporal lines	Absent/slight	Developed
Nuchal lines	Absent/slight	Developed
Suprameatal crest	Absent/slight	Developed
Gonial angle	>125°	Close to 90°
Pelvic traits		
Ventral arch	Present	Absent
Subpubic concavity	Present	Absent
Ischiopubic ridge	Ridge present	Broad/flat
Greater sciatic notch	Wide	Narrow
Preauricular sulcus	Wide	Narrow
Auricular surface	Raised	Flat
Superior inlet	Oval shaped	Heart shaped
Pubic bone	Rectangular present	Triangular
Scars of parturition		Absent
Sacral traits		
Body shape	Straight	Curved
Body-to-ala ratio	Body = ala	Body > ala
Auricular surface	1–2 segments	1–3 segments

dimorphic. With only a 60–70% accuracy rate, most forensic anthropologists will provide age estimates for both juvenile males and juvenile females. Since the goal in creating a biological profile is to limit the potential pool of matches without falsely excluding a missing child, sex estimation among juveniles is typically left open-ended.

Table 35.6 Metric Criteria for Sex Estimation (Bass, 2005)

	Female	Male
	Humerus	
Maximum head diameter	<43.0 mm	>47.0 mm
Biepicondylar width	<56.0 mm	>63.0 mm
Septal aperture	Present	Absent
	Femur	
Maximum head diameter	<42.5 mm	>47.5 mm
Bicondylar width	<72.0 mm	>78.0 mm
Midshaft circumference	<86.0 mm	>86.0 mm
Head-neck angle	~90°	>120°
	Tibia	
Midshaft circumference	<90.0 mm	>90.0 mm

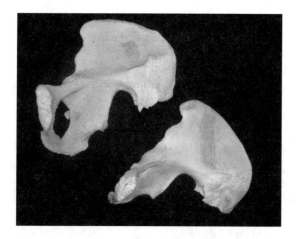

Figure 35.16 Right os coxae of male (top) and female (bottom) showing sexual differences of the pelvis. The pubic symphysis and auricular surface are also used to estimate adult ages at death.

There are many methods and techniques available to estimate age at death among both juveniles and adults. Methods for juvenile age estimation are based on bone development and growth. Because the skeleton is undergoing so much change throughout childhood, many different bones and teeth can be used to estimate age. Among juveniles, the age ranges tend to be narrow and highly accurate. Age estimates are based on

- Bone ossification
- Bone fusion
- Long-bone length
- Tooth formation
- Dental eruption

Differentiating between juveniles and adults based on dental and skeletal remains is generally guided by the eruption and root development of the third molars, fusion of the vertebral body to the epiphyseal rings, fusion of the first and second sacral bodies, and fusion of the medial clavicle to its epiphyseal ring. Aging methods for young adults are based partly on the development of key anatomical features, whereas methods are focused on degenerative changes of key anatomical features for middle and older-aged adults. As individuals age, the estimates become wider. Research into forensic anthropology aging methods is focused on testing the accuracy, reliability, and repeatability of methods (i.e., Kimmerle, Prince, & Berg, 2008) as well as developing new techniques (i.e., DiGanzi, Bethard, Kimmerle, & Konigsberg, 2008). For individual age estimates, numerous skeletal and dental traits can and should be used in combination for each case (Figure 35.16), including:

- Cranial suture closure
  - Sutures are open and fuse with age.

- Lamdenin tooth metrics
  - With age, tooth height becomes less but alveolar resorption increases.

- First rib
  - The costal face and tubercle facet change throughout life. The margins of the costal face initially are narrow with a shallow cavity, and become irregular with a filled in cavity as one ages. The tubercle facet is relatively smooth in young adults and morphs into an irregularly shaped facet with micro or macroporosity and lipped margins later in life.

- Fourth sternal rib end
  - Young adults exhibit a flat, billowed surface.
  - With age, the surface becomes deep, irregular, and pitted with porosity, and overall the bone exhibits a loss of bone density and osteophyte formation around the surface.

- Auricular surface of the ilium
  - The surface in young adults is evenly billowed and regular in shape.
  - Older-aged adults exhibit irregular shape and pitting with either micro- or macroporosity. Also, osteophytic growth forms around the rim.

- Pubic symphysis of the pubic bone
  - Young adults exhibit evenly spaced billowing. The rim eventually fills in, and the surface becomes smooth. With advanced age, the rim will become irregular and pitted. The bone will lose density. Macroporosity will be evident on the surface.

- Vertebral bodies
  - The rim fuses to the vertebral body in late adolescence. With advancing age, small spicules form on the anterior rim and eventually around the rim. The bodies become depressed in age and irregular in texture. Porosity forms along with osteophytes.

- Articular surfaces of joints
  - With age, joints exhibit degenerative processes, including a raised or elevated rim, osteophyte formation, and micro- and macroporosity. In regions where the cartilage becomes destroyed, the two articulating bones may be in direct contact and result in a greater amount of porosity and eburnation.

- Bone density
- Overall, with age there is a loss of bone density. This may be evident throughout the skeleton and will be particularly noticeable in areas with a large amount of trabecular bone.

Human Identification

Facial reconstructions are used to estimate what a person looked like in life with the hope that someone who knew the decedent will recognize the image that will lead to identification. Reconstructions are based on the biological profile of the individual and the individual's unique facial structure. Standard tissue depths are used, and a face is "built" over the skull. There are many options for facial reconstructions today, including traditional clay sculpture, three-dimensional virtual methods, and photographic composites. Reconstructions are never used to make a positive identification but rather are used to trigger the memory of someone who knew the victim, thereby creating a presumptive identification. Biological profiles contribute to three forms of identification (Kimmerle, 2007):

- *Presumptive identification:* Postmortem variables match antemortem criteria but are based on factors that could change or be true for more than one person, such as sex and age or clothing.
- *Positive identification:* Postmortem variables match antemortem criteria and are based on factors that do not change, such as DNA, fingerprints, trabecular bone patterns, or dental morphology.
- *Collective identification:* Group characteristics such as sex, age, religion, or ancestral affiliation place individuals into a particular group. This form of demographic or group identification has been critical to investigations into genocide, by which people are targeted because of these factors.

Photographic and radiological superimpositions are used to determine a positive identification, including not only faces but also any bony structure for which there is a preexisting antemortem radiograph with which to compare the postmortem radiograph. The underlying assumption is that antemortem dental and medical records exist and can be located for comparison.

Skeletal Pathology

Many conditions, syndromes, diseases, and afflictions are evident skeletally. Although a precise diagnosis from bone alone can at times be elusive, more often the general disease category can be determined. Evidence of skeletal pathology has several important functions in forensic anthropology, including understanding the contributing factors to the cause of death, identifying unique features about a decedent for human identification, or documenting evidence of chronic abuse or neglect.

Diagnosing skeletal pathology begins with a clinical approach and uses a method of differential diagnosis and deduction. The cultural context, exposure of the population to various pathogens, the life cycles of parasites, the age and sex of the individuals affected, and individual susceptibility are factors to be considered. Lesions, whether they are lytic or proliferative, are described for each bone affected. The distribution of lesions throughout the skeleton informs regarding the particular disease or condition (Figure 35.17). While

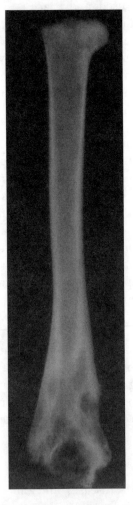

Figure 35.17 Radiograph of right juvenile humerus with healed fracture and severe osteomyelitis. Note that the proximal and distal epiphyses are unfused. Epiphyseal union and long-bone length indicate the age at death was 9–12 years.

skeletal tissue has a limited number of responses, proliferation or resorption, the type of bony response, distribution of affected areas, and age and sex of the individual are used in combination to formulate a diagnosis. For example, evidence of nutritional deficiencies in juveniles, such as vitamin deficiencies, in combination with shortened stature, Harris lines, or enamel hypoplasias may indicate chronic neglect. Particular vitamin deficiencies such as scurvy, rickets, or iron deficiencies leave characteristic bony lesions that are clearly discernible on examination of skeletal tissues.

Trauma Analysis

The reconstruction of skeletal fractures is critical evidence for determining the circumstances, cause, and manner of death. The morphology of skeletal trauma is shaped by internal factors (i.e., the particular bone affected), extrinsic factors (i.e., the type of weapon), and epidemiological factors (i.e., whether it resulted from act of volition) (Kimmerle & Baraybar, 2008). From skeletal trauma, information is learned about the type of weapon, the number of injuries, and the sequence of injuries (Figures 35.18–35.21). A critical first step is to differentiate perimortem trauma from postmortem or taphonomic artifacts. In other words, fractures that result at the time of death and may have contributed to the death have to be differentiated from animal scavenging, warping due to ground pressure for buried remains, or excavation damage (Figure 35.22). Once trauma is delineated,

Figure 35.18 Anterior surface of cervical vertebrae with several small, uniform cut marks. Sharp force trauma inflicted by a knife. (From Kimmerle and Baraybar, 2008. Reprinted with permission.)

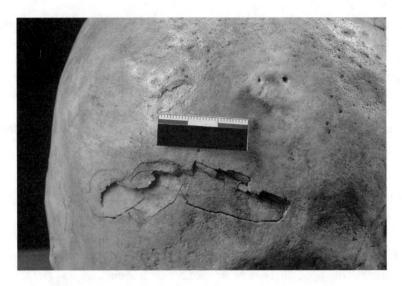

Figure 35.19 Blunt force trauma to the posterior surface of the cranium. There is a patterned depressed defect with associated fractures. Other complete fractures indicate multiple blows. The weapon was the leg of a chair. (From Kimmerle and Baraybar, 2008. Reprinted with permission.)

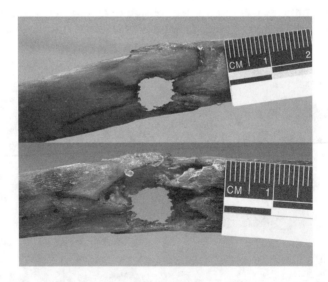

Figure 35.20 Anterior and posterior surface of the body of a rib with a single gunshot wound. Characteristics of these defects are indicative of the direction of fire, back to front. (From Kimmerle and Baraybar, 2008. Reprinted with permission.)

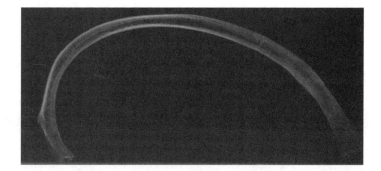

Figure 35.21 Radiograph of rib with a healed fracture along the medial third of the shaft. Healed trauma can be useful for identification when antemortem medical records are available. In some cases, it can also be indicative of prior or chronic abuse, particularly among children and the elderly.

the morphology of wounds, defects, and fractures provides information on the mechanism of injury (Kimmerle & Baraybar, 2008):

- Blunt trauma
  - An object crushes tissue. The object may strike the individual, or the decedent may have been expelled toward an object.
  - Example objects include fist, baseball bat, hammer, dashboard, floor.

- Sharp trauma
  - A penetrating object cuts tissues and bone.
  - This may be associated with blunt trauma, particularly with hacking types of weapons such as machetes or axes.
  - Example objects include knife, axe, hatchet, machete, glass.

- Gunfire
  - Injuries characterized by handgun, rifle, or shotgun.
  - Class of weapon, distance of shot, number and sequence of injuries can be determined from skeletal injuries.

- Blast injuries
  - These create thermal, blunt, sharp, and penetrating trauma.
  - Shrapnel creates irregular-shaped penetrating defects in skeletal tissue and may become embedded in bone.
  - Largely affected by extrinsic factors such as the type of explosive, location of the incident (i.e., in an enclosed space), and the type of surrounding materials.

- Burning injuries
  - These cause discoloration, fractures, bone shrinkage, and dismemberment.
  - Trauma inflicted prior to burning is still evident even after severe burning.
  - Burning may result from an incident at time of death, such as an automobile accident or explosion. Burning may also be used postmortem in an attempt to hide or destroy evidence.

- Chronic abuse
  - Multiple fractures in various stages of healing, nutritional deficiencies, malnutrition or starvation, untreated medical conditions, or insufficient dental care are evidence of chronic abuse.

The Global Context: International Trends in Forensic Anthropology

The use of forensic anthropology globally as a tool for human rights enforcement is growing (Kimmerle, 2007; Okoye, Kimmerle, & Baraybar, 2006). Nations that are transitioning to peace following war or civil conflict are increasingly confronting the past through truth commissions, domestic courts, civil action, international tribunals, or military tribunals. Furthermore, investigations into torture in prisons and extrajudicial executions are bringing forensics and anthropology into the human rights arena. Demonstrating that torture occurred from skeletal remains is similar to documenting other forms of chronic abuse, such as child or elder abuse. The use of forensic science and forensic anthropology in particular is critical as anthropologists are able to offer a range of services from grave excavation to human identification. Depending on the circumstances, the objective in an international context may be simply to document that atrocities did in fact occur. Since these investigations tend to be conducted many years after the fact, reconstructing injuries to assess the cause and manner of death rests on the ability of an investigator to analyze skeletal remains.

Whether in a domestic homicide or foreign civil war, families of the missing are searching for more than remains. They are searching for truth and justice. Holding persons accountable through criminal prosecution and establishing a historical record is imperative for families and communities. The search for the Missing in the United States is being redefined as a human rights issue. With increased federal funding and training for Cold Cases, the attention of the public and law enforcement is being directed toward solving the problem of missing persons.

Acknowledgment

I would like to thank Sue Gabriel and Donna Bader for inviting me to write this chapter and for working as pioneers among nurses in the forensic sciences to bring education and truth forward. I would also like to thank Ruth Estabrook for creating the maps used in these figures.

References

Bass, W. M. (1997). Outdoor decomposition rates in Tennessee. In W. D. Haglund & M. H. Sorg (Eds.), *Forensic taphonomy*. New York: CRC Press.

Bass, W. M. (2005). *Human osteology: A laboratory and field manual*. Special Publication 2; 5th edition. Missouri Archaeological Socity.

Brickley, M. B., & Ferllini, R. (Eds.). (2007). *Forensic anthropology: Case studies from Europe*. Springfield, IL: Thomas.

Buikstra, J. E., & Ubelaker, D. H. (Eds.). (1994). *Standards for data collection from human skeletal remains: Proceedings of a seminar at the Field Museum of Natural History*. Fayetteville, AR: Arkansas Archeological Report Research Series.

Bureau of Justice Statistics. (2007).

Burns, K. R. (2007). *Forensic anthropology training manual* (2nd ed.). Upper Saddle River, NJ: Pearson Prentice Hall.

Byers, S. N. (2008). *Introduction to forensic anthropology* (3rd ed.). Boston: Allyn & Bacon.

Connor, M. A. (2007). *Forensic methods: Excavation for the archaeologist and investigator*. Lanham, MD: AltaMira Press.

DiGanzi, E. A., Bethard, J. D., Kimmerle, E. H., & Konigsberg, L. W. (2009). A new method for estimating age-at-death from the first rib. *American Journal of Physical Anthropology, 138*, 164–176.

Dupras, T. L., Schultz, J. J., Wheeler, S. M., & Williams, L. J. (2006). *Forensic recovery of human remains*. Boca Raton, FL: CRC Press, Taylor and Francis Group.

Dwight, T. (1878). *The identification of the human skeleton. A medicolegal study*. Prize essay, Massachusetts Medical Society, Boston.

Dwight T. (1894). The range and variations in the human skeleton. *Boston Medical and Surgical Journal, 131*(4), 73–76, 97–101.

Galloway, A., Birkby, H. W., Jones, A. M., Henry, T. E., & Parks, B. O. (1989). Decay rates of human remains in an arid environment. *Journal of Forensic Sciences, 34*, 607–616.

Haglund, W. D., & Sorg, M. H. (Eds.). (2001). Method and theory of forensic taphonomy research. In W. D. Haglund & M. H. Sorg (Eds.), *Forensic taphonomy*. New York: CRC Press.

Jantz, R. L., Kimmerle, E. H., & Baraybar, J. P. (2008). Sexing and stature estimation criteria for Balkan populations. *Journal of Forensic Sciences, 53*(3), 601–605.

Killam, E. W. (2004). *The detection of human remains*. Springfield, IL: Thomas.

Kimmerle, E. H. (2007). Current trends in the forensic investigations of human rights abuse: Human identification of victims of mass graves. In M. Okoye & C. H. Wecht (Eds.), *Forensic investigation and management of mass disasters* (pp. 221–240). Tucson, AZ: Lawyers and Judges.

Kimmerle, E. H., & Baraybar, J. P. (2008). *Skeletal trauma: Identification of injuries resulting from human rights abuse and armed conflict.* Boca Raton, FL: CRC Press, p. 493.

Kimmerle, E. H., & Jantz, R. L. (2008). Variation as evidence: Introduction to a symposium on international human identification. *Journal of Forensic Sciences,* 53(3), 521–523.

Kimmerle, E. H., & Jantz, R. L., Konigsberg, L. W., & Baraybar, J. P. (2008). Skeletal estimation and identification in American and East European populations. *Journal of Forensic Sciences,* 53(3), 524–532.

Kimmerle, E. H., Konigsberg, L. W., Jantz, R. L., & Baraybar, J. P. (2008). Analysis of age-at-death estimation through the use of pubic symphyseal data. *Journal of Forensic Sciences,* 53(3), 558–568.

Kimmerle, E. H., Prince, D. A., & Berg, G. (2008). Inter-observer variation in various aging methodologies including the pubic symphysis, sternal rib, and teeth. *Journal of Forensic Sciences,* 53(3), 594–600.

Kimmerle, E. H., Ross, A. H., & Slice, D. (2008). Sexual dimorphism in America: Geometric morphometric analysis of what matters most? *Journal of Forensic Sciences,* 53(1), 54–57.

Komar, D. A., & Buikstra, J. E. (2008). *Forensic anthropology: Contemporary theory and practice.* Oxford, U.K.: Oxford University Press.

Krogman, W., & Iscan, I. (1986). *Human skeleton in forensic medicine* (2nd ed.). Springfield, IL: Thomas.

Mann, R. W., Bass, W. M., & Jantz, L. M. (1990). Time since death and decomposition of the human body: Variables and observation in case and experimental field studies. *Journal of Forensic Sciences,* 35, 103–111.

Morse, D., Duncan, J., & Stoutamire, J. (1983). *Handbook of forensic archaeology and anthropology.* Tallahassee, FL: Rose.

Okoye, M. I., Kimmerle, E. H., Baraybar, J. P. (2006). Forensic investigations of human rights violations, abuse, mass graves, and war crimes. In C. H. Wecht (Ed.), *Forensic sciences* (Vol. 2). New York: LexisNexis Bender.

Perper, J. (1997). Time of death and changes after death. Anatomical considerations. In W. Spitz and D. Spitz (Eds.), *Spitz and Fisher's medicolegal investigation of death* (pp. 87–127). Springfield, IL: Thomas.

Prince, D. A., Kimmerle, E. H., & Konigsberg, L. W. (2008). A Bayesian approach to estimate skeletal age-at-death utilizing dental wear. *Journal of Forensic Sciences,* 53(3), 588–593.

Rodriguez, W., & Bass, W. (1983). Insect activity and its relationship to decay rates of human cadavers in east Tennessee. *Journal of Forensic Sciences,* 28(2), 423–432.

Rodriguez, W., & Bass, W. (1985). Decomposition of buried bodies and methods that may aid in their location. *Journal of Forensic Sciences,* 30(3), 836–852.

Saunders, S. R. (2008). Juvenile skeletons and grow-related studies. In M. A. Katzenberg & S. R. Saunders (Eds.), *Biological anthropology of the human skeleton* (2nd ed., pp. 117–148). Hoboken, NJ: Wiley-Liss.

Spitz, W. (Ed.). (2006). *Spitz and Fisher's medicolegal investigation of death* (4th ed.). Springfield, IL: Thomas.

Tibbett, M., & Carter, D. O. (2008). *Soil analysis in forensic taphonomy*. Boca Raton, FL: CRC Press.

Ubelaker, D. H. (1989). *Human skeletal remains: Excavation, analysis, interpretation* (2nd ed.). Washington, DC: Taraxacom.

Vass, A., Bass, W., Wolt, J., Foss, J., & Ammons, J. (1992). Time since death determinations of human cadavers using soil solution. *Journal of Forensic Sciences, 37*(5), 1236–1253.

Appendix: Medicolegal Death Scene Investigation
Guidelines for the Forensic Nurse Death Investigator (FNDI)

DONNA GARBACZ BADER

Contents

Part I: Investigative Tools and Equipment

A. Investigative Tools

1. Gloves
2. Writing tools
3. Body bags
4. Communication equipment
5. Flashlight
6. Body identification tags
7. Camera
8. Investigative notebook
9. Measurement instruments

Adapted from National Institute of Justice, 1999.

10. Official individual identification
11. Watch
12. Paper bags
13. Specimen containers
14. Disinfectant
15. Departmental scene forms
16. Blood collection tubes, syringes, and needles
17. Inventory lists
18. Paper envelopes
19. Clean white linen sheet (stored in plastic bag)
20. Evidence tape
21. Business cards
22. Foul weather gear
23. Medical equipment kit (scissors, forceps, tweezers, exposure suit, scalpel handle, blades, disposable syringe, large-gauge needles)
24. Phone listing of local county, state, and federal law enforcement agencies; area hospitals; social service personnel and agencies; medical examiner or coroner; spiritual and psychological resources.
25. Tape and rubber bands
26. Disposable paper jumpsuits, hair covers, face shield
27. Evidence seals
28. Pocketknife
29. Shoe covers
30. Trace evidence kit
31. Hand sanitizer
32. Thermometer
33. Crime scene tape
34. First aid kit
35. Latent print kit
36. Local maps
37. Plastic trash bags
38. Gunshot residue analysis kits
39. Photo placards
40. Boots
41. Hand lens
42. Portable electric area lighting
43. Barrier sheeting
44. Purification masks
45. Reflective vest
46. Tape recorder
47. Basic hand tools
48. Body bag locks

49. Video camera
50. Personal comfort supplies (insect spray, sunscreen, hat)
51. Presumptive blood test kit

Part II: Arriving at the Scene

A. Arriving at the Scene

Principle

Allow the forensic nurse death investigator (FNDI) to establish formal contact with other official agency representatives. The FNDI must identify the first responder to determine if any artifacts or scene contamination were introduced. Scene safety must be established prior to entering the investigative scene.

Authorization

Medical examiner or coroner official office policy manual; state or federal statutory authority.

Policy

The FNDI should identify essential personnel, establish rapport, and determine scene safety.

Procedure

On arrival at the scene and prior to entering the scene, the investigator should

1. Identify lead investigator and present identification.
2. Identify other essential officials at the scene and explain FNDI role in the investigation.
3. Identify and document the identity of the first essential officials to arrive to the scene to determine if any artifacts or contamination may have been introduced to the death scene.
4. Determine scene safety.

Summary

Introductions establish collaborative investigative effort, identification of all scene authority, and scene safety.

B. Exercise Scene Safety

Principle

Essential to the investigative process. Risk of environmental and physical injury must be removed prior to initiating a scene investigation. Risks may include hostile crowd, collapsing structure, and traffic, environmental, and chemical threats.

Authorization

Medical examiner/coroner official office policy manual; state or federal statutory authority.

Policy

FNDI needs to maintain a safe investigative environment to prevent injury or loss of life, including contacting appropriate agencies for assistance with other scene safety issues.

Procedure

On arriving at the scene and prior to entering the scene, the investigator should

1. Assess or establish physical boundaries.
2. Identify incident command.
3. Secure vehicle and park as safely as possible.
4. Use personal protective safety devices.
5. Arrange for removal of animals or secure.
6. Obtain clearance/authorization to enter scene from the individual responsible for scene safety.
7. Protect the integrity of the scene and evidence to the extent possible from contamination or loss by people, animals, and elements.

Note

As a result of potential scene hazards, the body may need to be removed prior to the continuation of the investigation.

Summary

Environmental and physical threats to the investigative team must be removed to conduct a safe scene investigation. Protective devices must be used to prevent investigative staff injury, and the investigator must attempt to maintain the integrity of the crime scene.

C.   Confirmation or Pronouncement of Death

Principle

Appropriate personnel must make a determination of death prior to the initiation of the death investigation. Confirmation or pronouncement of death determines jurisdictional responsibilities.

Authorization

Medical examiner/coroner official office policy manual; state or federal statutory authority.

Policy
The FNDI shall ensure that appropriate personnel have viewed the body and that death has been confirmed.

Procedure
On arriving at the scene, the investigator should

1. Locate and view the body.
2. Check for pulse, respiration, and reflexes as appropriate.
3. Identify and document the individual who made the official determination of death, including the time and date of determination.
4. Ensure death is pronounced as required.

Summary
Once death has been established, rescue and resuscitative measures cease, and medicolegal jurisdiction can be established. It is vital that this occur prior to the medical examiner or coroner assuming any responsibilities.

D.   Participate in Scene Briefing

Principle
Scene investigators must recognize the varying jurisdiction and statutory responsibilities that apply to individual agency representatives. This is essential in planning the scope and depth of each scene investigation and release of information to the public.

Authorization
Medical examiner/coroner official office policy manual; state or federal statutory authority.

Policy
The FNDI shall identify specific responsibilities, share appropriate preliminary information and establish investigative goals of each agency present at the scene.

Procedure
On participating in the scene briefing, the investigator should

1. Locate the staging area (entry point to scene, command post).
2. Document the scene location consistent with other agencies.
3. Determine nature and scope of investigation by obtaining preliminary investigative details.
4. Ensure the initial accounts of incident are obtained from the first witnesses.

Summary

Scene briefing allows for initial and factual information exchange. This includes scene location, time factors, initial witness information, agency responsibilities, and investigative strategy.

E. Conduct Scene Walk-Through

Principle

The scene "walk-through" provides the investigator with an overview of the entire scene and the first opportunity to locate and view the body, identify valuable or fragile evidence, and determine initial investigative procedures.

Authorization

Medical examiner/coroner official office policy manual; state or federal statutory authority.

Policy

The FNDI shall conduct a scene walk-through to establish pertinent scene parameters.

Procedure

On arriving at the scene, the investigator should

1. Reassess scene boundaries and adjust as appropriate.
2. Establish a path of entry and exit.
3. Identify visible physical and fragile evidence.
4. Document and photograph fragile evidence immediately and collect if appropriate.
5. Locate and view the decedent.

Summary

The scene walk-through is essential to minimize scene disturbance and to prevent the loss or contamination of physical or fragile evidence.

F. Establish Chain of Custody

Principle

The FNDI ensures the integrity of the evidence by establishing and maintaining a chain of custody that is vital to an investigation. This is a safeguard against subsequent allegations of tampering, theft, planting, and contamination of evidence.

Authorization

Medical examiner/coroner official office policy manual; state or federal statutory authority.

Policy

Prior to the removal of any evidence, the custodians of the evidence will be designated and will generate and maintain a chain of custody for all evidence collected.

Procedure

Throughout the investigation, those responsible for preserving and maintaining the chain of custody should

1. Document location of the scene and time of arrival of the death investigator at the scene.
2. Determine custodians of the evidence, determine which agencies are responsible for collection of specific types of evidence, and determine evidence collection priority for fragile or fleeting evidence.
3. Identify, secure, and preserve evidence with proper containers, labels, and preservatives.
4. Document the collection of evidence by recording its location at the scene, time of collection, and time and location of disposition.
5. Develop personnel lists, witness lists, and documentation of times of arrival and departure of personnel.

Summary

Maintaining a proper chain of custody for evidence is *essential*. Through proper documentation, collection, and preservation, the integrity of the evidence can be assured. This will also reduce the likelihood of a challenge to the integrity of the evidence

---

**Individual
Evidence Log**
Date:_____Time:_____
Collected by_____
Agency_____
Case Number_____Log Item Number_____
Description_____
_____
_____
Location_____
_____
_____
Container_____
_____
_____
Comments_____
_____
_____

Continued

Chain of Custody

Received from_____

Received by_____

Reason for Transfer_____

_____

Date_____Time_____

Received from_____

Received by_____

Date_____Time_____

Reason for Transfer_____

Received from _____

Received by_____

Date_____Time_____

Reason for Transfer_____

_____

_____

Initials: Name:

Initials: Name:

Initials: Name:

Created by Donna Garbacz Bader.

G. Follow Laws Related to the Collection of Evidence

Principle
The FNDI must follow local, state, and federal laws for the collection of evidence to ensure its admissibility. The investigator must work with the law enforcement and the legal authorities to determine laws regarding collection of evidence.

Authorization
Medical examiner/coroner official office policy manual; state or federal statutory authority

Policy
The FNDI working with other agencies must identify and work under appropriate legal authority. Modification of informal procedures may be necessary, but laws must be always followed.

Procedure
The investigator, prior to or on arrival at the death scene, should work with other agencies to

1. Determine the need for a search warrant.
2. Identify local, state, federal, and international laws.

3. Identify medical examiner/coroner statutes or office standard operating procedures.

Summary
Following the laws related to the collection of evidence will ensure a complete and proper investigation in compliance with state and local laws, admissibility in court, and adherence to office policies and protocols.

Part III: Documentation and Evaluation of the Scene

A.   Photograph Scene

Principle
Photographic documentation of the scene creates a permanent historical record of the scene. Photographs provide detailed collaborating evidence that constructs a system of redundancy should questions arise concerning the report, witness statement, or position of evidence at the scene

Authorization
Medical examiner/coroner official office policy manual; state or federal statutory authority.

Policy
The FNDI shall obtain detailed photographic documentation of the scene that provides both instant and permanent high-quality images.

Procedure
On arrival at the scene, and prior to moving the body or evidence, the investigator should

1. Remove all nonessential personnel from the scene.
2. Obtain an overall (wide-angle) view of the scene to spatially locate the specific scene to the surrounding area.
3. Photograph specific areas of the scene to provide more detailed views of specific areas within the larger scene.
4. Photograph the scene from different angles to provide various perspectives that may uncover additional evidence.
5. Obtain some photographs with scales to document specific evidence.
6. Obtain photographs even if the body or other evidence has been moved.

Note
If evidence has been moved prior to photography, it should be noted in the report. Do not reintroduce the body or other evidence once it has been removed or moved.

Summary

Photography allows for the best permanent documentation of the death scene, provides a permanent record of the event and the evidence, and should be obtained before releasing the scene.

Photograph/Video Log

Case Number _____

Item-Number	Time Military	Date: Spell Out	Content	Location	Initials

Initials:	Name/Title:
Initials:	Name/Title:
Initials:	Name/Title:

Log developed by Donna Garbacz Bader.

B.   Develop Descriptive Documentation of the Scene

Principle
Written documentation of the scene provides a permanent record that may be used to correlate with and enhance photographic documentation, refresh recollection, and record observations.

Authorization
Medical examiner/coroner official office policy manual; state or federal statutory authority.

Policy
The FNDI shall provide written scene documentation.

Procedure
After photographic documentation of the scene and prior to removal of the body and other evidence, the investigator should

1. Diagram/describe in writing items of evidence and their relationship to the body with necessary measurements.
2. Describe and document, with necessary measurements, blood and body fluid evidence, including volume, patterns, spatters, and other characteristics.
3. Describe scene environments, including odors, lights, temperature, and other fragile evidence.

Note
If evidence has been moved prior to the written documentation, it should be noted in the report.

Summary
Written scene documentation is essential to correlate with photographic evidence and to re-create the scene for police, forensic scientists, and judicial and civil agencies with a legitimate interest.

C.   Establish Probable Location of Injury or Illness

Principle
The location where the decedent is found may not necessarily be the actual location where the injury or illness that contributed to the death occurred. It is imperative that the investigator attempt to determine the location of any and all injuries or illnesses that may have contributed to the death. Physical evidence at any and all locations may be pertinent in establishing the cause, manner, and mechanism of death.

Authorization

Medical examiner/coroner official office policy manual; state or federal statutory authority.

Policy

The FNDI shall obtain detailed information regarding any and all probable locations associated with the individual's death.

Procedure

1. Document location where death was confirmed.
2. Determine location from which the decedent was transported and how the body was transported to the scene.

Establish Probable Location of Injury or Illness

1. Identify and record discrepancies in rigor mortis, livor mortis, and body temperature.
2. Check body, clothing, and scene for consistency or inconsistency of trace evidence and indicate location where artifacts are found.
3. Check for drag marks on the body and ground.
4. Establish postinjury activity.
5. Obtain dispatch records.
6. Interview family members and associates as needed.

Summary

Personal property and evidence are important items at a death investigation. Evidence must be safeguarded to ensure its availability if needed for future evaluation and litigation. Personal property must be safeguarded to ensure its eventual distribution to appropriate agencies or individuals and to reduce the likelihood that the investigator will be accused of stealing property.

Death Scene Investigation Evidence Log

Case Number _____

Date: Spell Out	Military Time	Evidence/Container	Location	Initials

Continued

Date: Spell Out	Military Time	Evidence/Container	Location	Initials

Initials:	Name/Title:
Initials:	Name/Title:
Initials:	Name/Title:

D. Collect, Inventory, and Safeguard Property and Evidence

Principle

The decedent's valuables or property must be safeguarded to ensure legal processing and eventually to be released to next of kin.

Authorization

Medical examiner/coroner official office policy manual; state or federal statutory authority.

Policy

The FNDI shall ensure that all property and evidence are collected, inventoried, safeguarded, and released as required by law.

Procedure

On completion of identification of property and evidence at the scene, the FNDI, with a witness, should

1. Inventory, collect, and safeguard any and all illicit drugs and drug paraphernalia at the scene or office.
2. Inventory, collect, and safeguard any and all prescription medications at the scene or office.
3. Inventory, collect, and safeguard any and all over-the-counter medications at the scene or office.
4. Inventory, collect, and safeguard any and all personal valuables and property at the scene or office.
5. Inventory, collect, and safeguard at the scene or office any and all personal valuables, monetary items such as coins or paper money, or any items that are identified as customarily used as a medium of exchange and measure of value.

Summary

Personal property and any and all evidence are major items of importance in a death investigation. Evidence must be documented and safeguarded to ensure its availability for future evaluation and litigation, if necessary. Personal property must be safeguarded and documented to ensure distribution to any and all appropriate agencies or individuals and to reduce or eliminate the possibility of any accusation of theft by the investigator or investigative team.

E. Interview Witnesses at the Scene

Principle

The documented comments of witnesses at the scene allow the investigator to obtain primary source data regarding discovery of body, witness corroboration, and terminal history. The documented interview provides essential information for the investigative process.

Authorization

Medical examiner/coroner official office policy manual; state or federal statutory authority.

Policy

The FNDI report shall include the source of information, including specific statements and information provided by any witness.

Procedure

1. Collect all available identifying data on witnesses.
2. Establish relationship/association of witness to the deceased.
3. Establish the basis of witness' knowledge.
4. Obtain information from each witness.
5. Note discrepancies from the scene briefing.
6. Tape statements if such equipment is available and retain them.

Summary

The final report must document witnesses' identity and must include a summary of witness statements, corroboration with other witnesses, and the circumstances of discovery of the death. This documentation must exist as a permanent record to establish a chain of events.

Part IV: Documentation and Evaluation of the Body

A. Photograph the Body

Principle

The photographic documentation of the body at the scene creates a permanent record that preserves essential details of the body position, appearance, identity, and final movements. Photographs allow sharing of information with other agencies investigating the death.

Authorization

Medical examiner/coroner official office policy manual; state or federal statutory authority.

Policy

The FNDI shall obtain detailed photographic documentation of the body that provides both instant and permanent high-quality images.

Procedure

On arrival at the scene and prior to moving the body or evidence, the investigator should

1. Photograph the body and immediate scene, including the decedent as initially found.
2. Photograph the decedent's face.
3. Take additional photographs after removal of objects or items that interfere with the photographic documentation of the decedent or after removal from a car.

4. Photograph the decedent with and without measurements as appropriate.
5. Photograph the surface beneath the body after the body has been removed.

Note
Never clean the decedent's face; do not change condition. Take multiple photographs if possible.

Summary
The photographic documentation of the body at the scene provides documentation of the body position, identity, and appearance. The details of the body at the scene provide investigators with pertinent information of the terminal events.

B. Conduct External Body Examination (Superficial)

Principle
Conducting the external body examination provides the FNDI with objective data regarding the single most important piece of evidence at the scene: the body. This documentation provides detailed information regarding the decedent's physical attributes, his or her relationship to the scene, and possible cause, manner, and mechanism of death.

Authorization
Medical examiner/coroner official office policy manual; state or federal statutory authority.

Policy
The FNDI shall obtain detailed photographs and written documentation of the decedent at the scene.

Procedure
After arrival at the scene and prior to moving the decedent, the investigator should, without removing decedent's clothing,

1. Photograph the scene, including the decedent as initially found and the surface beneath the body after the body has been removed.
2. If necessary, additional photographs should be taken after removal of objects or items that interfere with photographic documentation of the decedent.
3. Photograph the decedent with and without measurements, including a photograph of the decedent's face.

4. Document decedent's position with and without measurements.
5. Document the decedent's physical characteristics.
6. Document the presence or absence of clothing and personal effects.
7. Document the presence or absence of injury or trauma, petechiae, and other evidence as necessary.
8. Document the presence of treatment or resuscitative efforts.
9. Based on the findings, determine the need for further evaluation or assistance of forensic specialist, pathologist, odontologist, anthropologist.

Summary
Thorough evaluation and documentation of the deceased at the scene is essential to determine the depth and direction the investigation will take.

C. Preserve Evidence: On the Body

Principle
Photographic and written documentation of evidence on the body allows the investigator to obtain a permanent historical record of that evidence. To maintain chain of custody, evidence must be collected, preserved, and transported properly. Blood and other body fluids present must be photographed and documented prior to collection and transport. Fragile evidence must also be collected or preserved to maintain chain of custody and to assist in determination of cause, manner, and mechanism of death.

Authorization
Medical examiner/coroner official office policy manual; state or federal statutory authority.

Policy
With photographic and written documentation, the FNDI will provide a permanent record of evidence that is on the body.

Procedure
Once evidence on the body is recognized, the FNDI should

1. Photograph the evidence.
2. Document body fluids or blood on the body, location, and pattern *before* transporting.
3. Place decedent's hands or feet in unused paper bags and tape the bags.
4. Collect trace evidence before transporting the body.

5. Arrange for collection and transport of evidence at the scene.
6. Ensure the proper collection of blood and body fluids for subsequent analysis.

Summary
It is essential that evidence be collected, preserved, transported, and documented in an orderly and proper fashion to ensure the chain of custody and admissibility in a legal action. Preservation and documentation of the evidence on the body must be initiated by the investigator at the scene to prevent alterations or contamination

D. Establish Decedent Identification

Principle
Establishment or confirmation of the decedent's identity is paramount to the death investigation. Proper identification allows notification of next of kin, settlement of estates, resolution of criminal and civil litigation, and the proper completion of the death certificate.

Authorization
Medical examiner/coroner official office policy manual; state or federal statutory authority.

Policy
The FNDI shall engage in a diligent effort to establish/confirm the decedent's identity.

Procedure
To establish identity, the FNDI should document use of the following methods:

1. Direct visual or photographic identification of the decedent if visually recognizable.
2. Scientific methods such as fingerprints, dental, radiographic, and DNA comparisons.
3. Circumstantial methods such as personal effects, circumstances, physical characteristics, tattoos, and anthropologic data.

Summary
Numerous methods are available that can be used to properly identify the deceased person. This is essential for investigative, judicial, family, and vital records issues.

E. Document Postmortem Changes

Principle

The documenting of postmortem changes to the body assists the investigator in explaining body appearance in the interval following death. Inconsistencies between postmortem changes and body location may indicate movement of the body and validate or invalidate witness statements. Postmortem changes to the body, when correlated with circumstantial information, can assist the investigators in estimating the approximate time of death.

Authorization

Medical examiner/coroner official office policy manual; state or federal statutory authority.

Policy

The FNDI shall document all postmortem changes relative to the decedent and the environment.

Procedure

On arrival at the scene and prior to moving the body, the investigator should note the presence of each of the following in the report:

1. Livor consistent or inconsistent with body position (color, location, blanchability, Tardieu spots).
2. Rigor (stage/intensity, location on the body, broken, inconsistent with scene).
3. Degree of decomposition (putrefaction, adipocere, mummification, skeletonization).
4. Insect and animal activity.
5. Scene temperature (document method used and time estimated).
6. Description of body temperature (warm, cold, frozen) or measurement of body temperature (document method used and time of measurement).

Summary

Documentation of postmortem changes in every report is essential to determine an accurate cause and manner of death, provide information regarding the time of death, corroborate witness statements, and indicate that the body may have been moved after death.

F. Participate in Scene Debriefing

Principle

The scene debriefing assists the investigators from all participating agencies to establish postscene responsibilities by sharing data regarding particular scene finding. This activity also provides each agency the opportunity for input regarding special requests for assistance, additional information, special examinations, and other requests requiring interagency communication, cooperation, and education.

Authorization

Medical examiner/coroner official office policy manual; state or federal statutory authority.

Policy

The FNDI shall participate in or initiate interagency scene debriefing to verify specific postscene responsibilities.

Procedure

When participating in scene debriefing, the investigator should:

1. Determine postscene responsibilities (identification, notification, press relations, and evidence transportation).
2. Determine or identify need for a specialist.
3. Communicate with the pathologist about responding to the scene or to the autopsy.
4. Share investigative data.
5. Communicate special requests to appropriate agencies, being mindful of the need for confidentiality.

Summary

Scene debriefing is the best opportunity for investigative participants to communicate special requests and confirm all current and additional scene responsibilities. This also allows participants the opportunity to establish clear lines of responsibility for a successful investigation.

G. Determine Notification Procedures

Principle

Every reasonable effort should be made to notify the next of kin as soon as possible. The action initiates closure for the family and disposition of remains and facilitates the collection of additional information significant to the case.

Authorization

Medical examiner/coroner official office policy manual; state or federal statutory authority.

Policy

The FNDI shall ensure that the next of kin is notified of the death and that all successful and unsuccessful attempts at notification are documented.

Procedure

When determining notification procedures, the investigator should

1. Identify next of kin.
2. Locate next of kin.
3. Notify next of kin and record time of notification or, if delegated to another agency, gain confirmation when notification is made.
4. Notify appropriate agencies of notification status.

Summary

The FNDI is responsible for ensuring that the next of kin is identified, located, and notified in a timely manner. The individual assigned to notify the next of kin, the time and method of notification, the name and relationship of the person notified, and the response should be documented. Failure to locate next of kin and all efforts to do so should be documented. Documentation ensures that every reasonable effort has been made to contact the family.

H. Ensure Security of Remains

Principle

Ensuring security of the body requires the investigator to supervise the labeling, packaging, and removal of the remains. An appropriate identification tag is placed on the body to preclude misidentification on receipt at the examining agency. This function also includes safeguarding all potential physical evidence or property and clothing that remain on the body.

Authorization

Medical examiner/coroner official office policy manual; state or federal statutory authority.

Policy

The FNDI shall supervise and ensure the proper identification, inventory, and security of evidence or property and its packaging and removal from the scene.

Procedure

Prior to leaving the scene, the investigator should

1. Ensure that the body is protected from further trauma or contamination and unauthorized removal of therapeutic and resuscitative equipment.
2. Inventory and secure property, clothing, and personal effects that are on the body; removal is to be conducted in a controlled environment with witness present.

3. Identify property and clothing to be maintained as evidence in a controlled environment.
4. Recover blood or vitreous samples prior to release of remains (based on established authorizations or policies).
5. Place identification on the body and the body bag.
6. Ensure or supervise the placement of the body into the body bag.
7. Ensure or supervise the removal of the body from the scene.
8. Secure transportation.
9. *Document all procedures conducted.*

Summary

The security of the remains facilitates proper identification of the remains, maintains a proper chain of custody, and safeguards property and evidence.

Part V: Establishing and Recording Decedent Profile Information

A.   Document the Discovery History

Principle

Establishing a decedent profile includes documentation of a discovery history and the circumstances surrounding the discovery. The basic profile will determine the subsequent levels of investigation, jurisdiction, and authority. This information will also determine the necessity of further investigation.

Authorization

Medical examiner/coroner official office policy manual; state or federal statutory authority.

Policy

The FNDI shall document the discovery history, available witnesses, and the apparent circumstances leading to the death.

Procedure

To correctly document the discovery history, the investigator should

1. Establish and record person who discovered the body and the time, date, and location.
2. Document the circumstances surrounding the discovery: *who, what, when, where, how.*

Summary

The investigator must produce clear, concise documentation concerning who discovered the body, what the discovery circumstances were, where the discovery occurred, when the discovery was made, and how the discovery was made.

B. Determine Terminal Episode History

Principle
Preterminal circumstances are significant in determining cause and manner of death. Documentation of medical intervention or procurement of antemortem specimens help to establish the decedent's condition prior to death.

Authorization
Medical examiner/coroner official office policy manual; state or federal statutory authority.

Policy
The FNDI shall document any known circumstances and medical intervention prior to death.

Procedure
For the investigator to determine terminal episode history, the FNDI should

1. Document *when, where, how,* and by whom the decedent was last known to be alive.
2. Document incidents prior to the death.
3. Document any complaints or symptoms prior to death.
4. Document and review *all* complete emergency medical service (EMS) records.
5. Obtain copies of all relevant medical records.
6. Obtain relevant antemortem specimens.

Summary
Obtaining records of preterminal circumstances and medical history differentiates medical treatment from trauma. Such history and relevant antemortem specimens assist the medical examiner or corner in determining cause and manner of death.

C. Document Decedent's Medical History

Principle
Establishing the decedent's medical history assists in focusing the investigation. Documenting the decedent's medical signs or symptoms prior to death determines the need for additional examination or investigation. The

relationship between disease and injury may contribute to the cause, manner, and mechanism of death.

Authorization

Medical examiner/coroner official office policy manual; state or federal statutory authority.

Policy

The FNDI shall obtain the decedent's past and present medical history.

Procedure

Through interviews and review of the medical records, the investigator should

1. Document medical history to include
   a. Medications
   b. Alcohol and drug use
   c. Family medical history

2. Document information from treating physicians or health care facility to confirm history and treatment.
3. Document physical characteristics and traits.

Summary

A thorough medical history focuses the investigation and aids in the disposition of the case. It also assists in the determination of the need for a postmortem examination or additional laboratory tests or studies.

D.　Document Decedent's Mental Health History

Principle

The decedent's mental health history can provide insight into the behavior or state of mind of the individual. This may produce clues that may aid in establishing the cause, manner, and circumstances surrounding the death.

Authorization

Medical examiner/coroner official office policy manual; state or federal statutory authority.

Policy

The FNDI shall obtain information from sources familiar with the decedent pertaining to the decedent's mental health history.

Procedure

The investigator should

1. Document the decedent's mental health history to include hospital-ization and medication.
2. Document any history of suicidal ideations, gestures, or suicidal attempts.
3. Document mental health professionals who may have treated the decedent.
4. Document family mental health history.

Summary

Knowledge of mental health history allows for evaluation of the decedent's state of mind prior to death and contributes to the determination of cause, manner, and circumstances of death.

E. Document Social History

Principle

Social history includes marital, family, sexual, educational, employment, and financial information, daily routines, habits, activities, friends, and associ-ates. This provides a profile of the decedent and will aid in establishing the cause, manner, and circumstances of death.

Authorization

Medical examiner/coroner official office policy manual; state or federal statu-tory authority.

Policy

The FNDI shall obtain social history information from sources familiar with the decedent.

Procedure

When collecting relevant social history, the investigator should

1. Document marital/domestic history.
2. Document family history.
3. Document sexual history.
4. Document employment history.
5. Document financial history.
6. Document daily routines, habits, and activities.
7. Document relationships, friends, and associates.
8. Document religious, ethnicity, or any additional pertinent information.

9. Document education background.
10. Document criminal history.

Summary

Information from sources familiar with the decedent pertaining to social history will assist in the determination of cause, manner, and circumstances of the death.

Part VI: Completing the Scene Investigation

A. Maintain Jurisdiction Over the Body

Principle

Maintaining jurisdiction over the body allows the investigator to protect the chain of custody as the body is transported from the scene for autopsy, specimen collection, or storage.

Authorization

Medical examiner/coroner official office policy manual; state or federal statutory authority.

Policy

The FNDI shall maintain jurisdiction of the body by arranging for the body to be transported for autopsy, specimen collection, or secure storage.

Procedure

When maintaining jurisdiction over the body, the investigator should

1. Arrange for and document the secure transportation of the body to a medical or autopsy facility for further examination or storage.
2. Coordinate and document any procedures to be performed when the body is received at the facility.

Summary

By documenting the secure transportation of the body from the scene to an authorized receiving facility, the investigator maintains jurisdiction and protects the chain of custody of the body.

B. Release Jurisdiction of the Body

Principle

Prior to the release of the body, it is necessary to determine the person responsible for the certification of death. Information for the completion of the death certificate includes demographic information, date, time, and location of death.

Authorization
Medical examiner/coroner official office policy manual; state or federal statutory authority.

Policy
The FNDI shall obtain sufficient data to enable completion of the death certificate and release of jurisdiction over the body.

Procedure
When releasing jurisdiction over the body, the investigator should

1. Determine who will sign the death certificate.
2. Confirm the date, time, and location of death.
3. Collect blood, vitreous fluid (as authorized), and other evidence prior to the release of the body from the scene.
4. Document and arrange with the authorized receiving agent to reconcile all death certificate information.
5. Release the body to a funeral director or other authorized receiving agent.

Summary
The investigator releases jurisdiction only after determining who will sign the death certificate; documenting the date, time, and location of death; collecting specimens; and releasing the body to the appropriate agent.

C.   Conduct Exit Procedures

Principle
Closure of the scene investigation ensures that important evidence has been collected, and the scene has been processed. Also, a systematic review of the scene ensures that artifacts or equipment are not left behind, and any dangerous materials or conditions remaining at the scene have been reported

Authorization
Medical examiner/coroner official office policy manual; state or federal statutory authority.

Policy
At the conclusion of the scene investigation, the FNDI shall conduct a post-investigative walk-through to ensure the scene investigation is complete.

Procedure
When performing exit procedures, the investigator should

1. Identify, inventory, and remove all evidence collected at the scene.
2. Remove all personal equipment and materials from the scene.
3. Report and document any dangerous materials or conditions remaining.

Summary
A scene walk-through on exiting ensures that all evidence has been collected, that materials are not inadvertently left behind, and that any dangerous materials or conditions have been reported to the proper entities.

D. Assist the Family

Principle
The investigator provides the family with a timetable so they may arrange for final disposition and provides information on available community and professional resources that may assist the family.

Authorization
Medical examiner/coroner official office policy manual; state or federal statutory authority.

Policy
The FNDI shall offer the decedent's family information regarding available community and professional resources.

Procedure
When the investigator is assisting the family, it is important to

1. Inform the family if an autopsy is required.
2. Inform the family of available support services.
3. Inform the family of appropriate agencies to contact with questions.
4. Ensure that the family is not left alone with the body.
5. Inform the family of an approximate timetable for the release of the body.
6. Inform the family of the availability of the autopsy report, including cost if any is necessary.
7. Inform the family of any autopsy and/or autopsy report costs based on established policy.

Summary
Interaction with the family allows the investigator to assist and direct family members to appropriate resources. It is essential that families receive a timetable of the investigative events to make necessary arrangements.

References

Di Maio, V. J., & Dana, S. E. (2007). *Handbook of forensic pathology* (2nd ed.). Austin, TX: M. D. Press.

Dudley, M. H. (2003). *Forensic nursing.* Wichita, KS: Dudley.

Hammer, R. M., Moynihan, B., & Pagliaro, E. M. (2006). *Forensic nursing: A Handbook for Practice.* Sudbury, MA: Jones and Bartlett.

Lynch, V. A. (2006). *Forensic nursing.* St. Louis, MO: Elsevier Mosby.

National Institute of Justice. (1999, November). *Death investigation: A guide for the scene investigator.* Washington, DC: U.S. Department of Justice, Office of Justice Programs.

Index

A

Abrasions, 214
Abuse, 177
    identifying victims, xiii
    postmortem evidence, 388
    victim care, 7
Accidental death, 51
    in nursing homes, 186
Accumulated degree days (ADD), 377
ACLS certification, 314
Adipocere formation, 93–94, 367, 377
Administrative rule development, 129
Adrenoceptors, role in EDS, 203, 204
Age estimation
    bone and dental criteria, 381–383
    at death, 381
Alcohol
    abuse in IPV, 277
    use among teens, 328
    and victimization, 175
Algor mortis, 375
American Academy of Forensic Sciences
    (AAFS), 11, 12, 35
American Association of Critical Care
    Nurses (AACN), 21
American Association of Legal Nurse
    Consultants (AALNC), 12K
    certification and credentialing, 13
American Board of Medicolegal Death
    Investigators (ABDMI), 13–14
American Civil Liberties Union, 153
American College of Forensic Examiners
    Institute (ACFEI), 12
    certification and credentialing, 13
American Hospital Association Patient Bill
    of Rights, 131, 137
American Nurses Association (ANA), 8, 21
Ancient Greece, forensics in, 36
Animal remains, 365
Animals, postmortem effects, 92
Anthropology, 363. *See also* Forensic
    anthropology

Antisocial personality disorder, 159
Anxiety
    in IPV, 277
    in PTSD, 180
Appellate courts, 138
APRN certification, 314
Archeological methods, for locating,
    recovering, and documenting
    evidence, 368–369
Archeological remains, 365
    frontal view, crania, 366
    teeth, 367
Area maps, for profile construction, 355
Armed Services Medical Examiner
    System, 44
Asphyxia, 235
    chemical, 239
    by choke holds, 239–240
    by choking, 236
    environmental lack of oxygen and, 235
    by homicide, 235
    mechanical, 236
    positional, 236
    by smothering, 235
    by strangulation, 27–29
    by suicide, 235–236
    types, 235
Assault, 137
Assessment skills, 27, 28–29
    case study, 123–124
    and ethical decisions, 167
    in forensic nursing process, 121
Authorial attribution, 355
Autoerotic hanging, 239
Autolysis, 93
    in decomposition, 377
Automated Fingerprint Identification
    System (AFIS), 40
Autonomy, ethical issues, 166
Autopsy
    clinical, 111–112
    definition, 111
    examination procedure, 112–115